Ancient Egyptian Tombs

Blackwell Ancient Religions

Ancient religious practice and belief are at once fascinating and alien for twenty-first century readers. There was no Bible, no creed, no fixed set of beliefs. Rather, ancient religion was characterized by extraordinary diversity in belief and ritual.

This distance means that modern readers need a guide to ancient religious experience. Written by experts, the books in this series provide accessible introductions to this central aspect of the ancient world.

Published

Ancient Greek Divination
Sarah Iles Johnston

Magic in the Ancient Greek World
Derek Collins

Religion in the Roman Empire
James B. Rives

Ancient Greek Religion, Second Edition
Jon D. Mikalson

Ancient Egyptian Tombs: The Culture of Life and Death
Steven Snape

Forthcoming

Religion of the Roman Republic
Lora Holland

Ancient Egyptian Tombs

The Culture of Life and Death

Steven Snape

WILEY-BLACKWELL

A John Wiley & Sons, Ltd., Publication

This edition first published 2011
© 2011 Steven Snape

Blackwell Publishing was acquired by John Wiley & Sons in February 2007.
Blackwell's publishing program has been merged with Wiley's global Scientific,
Technical, and Medical business to form Wiley-Blackwell.

Registered Office
John Wiley & Sons Ltd, The Atrium, Southern Gate, Chichester, West Sussex,
PO19 8SQ, United Kingdom

Editorial Offices
350 Main Street, Malden, MA 02148-5020, USA
9600 Garsington Road, Oxford, OX4 2DQ, UK
The Atrium, Southern Gate, Chichester, West Sussex, PO19 8SQ, UK

For details of our global editorial offices, for customer services, and for information
about how to apply for permission to reuse the copyright material in this book please
see our website at www.wiley.com/wiley-blackwell.

The right of Steven Snape to be identified as the author of this work has been
asserted in accordance with the UK Copyright, Designs and Patents Act 1988.

Wiley also publishes its books in a variety of electronic formats. Some content that
appears in print may not be available in electronic books.

Designations used by companies to distinguish their products are often claimed as
trademarks. All brand names and product names used in this book are trade names,
service marks, trademarks or registered trademarks of their respective owners. The
publisher is not associated with any product or vendor mentioned in this book. This
publication is designed to provide accurate and authoritative information in regard to
the subject matter covered. It is sold on the understanding that the publisher is not
engaged in rendering professional services. If professional advice or other expert
assistance is required, the services of a competent professional should be sought.

Library of Congress Cataloging-in-Publication Data

Snape, S. R. (Steven R.)
    Ancient Egyptian tombs : the culture of life and death / Steven Snape.
      p. cm. – (Blackwell ancient religions)
    Includes bibliographical references and index.
    ISBN 978-1-4051-2089-0 (hardcover : alk. paper) 1. Tombs–Egypt. 2. Funeral rites
and ceremonies–Egypt. 3. Egypt–Social conditions. 4. Egypt–Civilization–To 332 B.C. 5.
Egypt–Antiquities. I. Title.
    DT62.T6S56 2011
    932–dc22

                                                                          2010034207

A catalogue record for this book is available from the British Library.

Set in 9.75/12.5pt Utopia by Thomson Digital

01   2011

For Philippa and Jack

Contents

List of Figures		ix
Preface		xiii
Acknowledgements		xv
	Introduction	1
1	**Nameless Lives at Tarkhan and Saqqara** Early Tombs and the *Ka*	7
2	**Pits, Palaces and Pyramids** Royal Cemeteries of the Early Dynastic Period and Old Kingdom	24
3	**Non-Royal Cemeteries of Dynasty 4**	35
4	**Unas, Teti and Their Courts** The Late Old Kingdom at Saqqara	51
5	**The Tombs of Qar and Idu** Families and Funerals in the Late Old Kingdom	68
6	**A Growing Independence** Court and Regional Cemeteries in the Late Old Kingdom	86
7	**Ankhtify** A Time of Change	105
8	**Osiris, Lord of Abydos**	117

9   'Lords of Life'   136
    Coffins

10 **Strangers and Brothers**   148
    The Middle Kingdom in Middle Egypt

11 **North and South**   166
    Middle Kingdom Tombs at the Royal Residence

12 **Ineni, Senenmut and User-Amun**   176
    New Tombs for Old

13 **Rekhmire and the Tomb of the Well-Known Soldier**   190
    Foreigners and Funerals in the Age of Empire

14 **Huya and Horemheb**   207
    Amarna and After

15 **Samut and the Ramesside Private Tomb**   223

16 **Sennedjem**   233
    Building and Buying at Deir el-Medina

17 **Petosiris**   245
    A Dying Tradition

References   260
Further Reading   276
Index   281

Figures

0.1 Map of Egypt showing the location of sites mentioned
in the text   xvi
1.1 Tarkhan Tomb 1845: the burial   9
1.2 Tarkhan Tomb 1845: the Burial Chamber and Offering
Chapel   12
1.3 Saqqara *Mastabas* 3471 (plan), 3036 (plan) and 3507
(cross-section)   16
1.4 Saqqara *Mastaba* 3505   18
1.5 The underground rooms of the Saqqara 'house' tombs
S.2302 (left) and S.2337 (right)   22
2.1 Plan of the tomb of Den at Abydos   26
2.2 Plan of the Cemetery Area at Abydos   27
2.3 The Step-Pyramid of Djoser at Saqqara   29
2.4 Simplified plan and cross-section of Saqqara *Mastaba* 3038   30
3.1 Plan (above) and cross-section (below) of a 'standard'
Dynasty 4 *mastaba* at Giza   36
3.2 The *mastaba* of Niankhkhnum and Khnumhotep at Saqqara   38
3.3 The (unfinished) False Door of the Lady Wadjkawes from
her tomb in the Unas Causeway Cemetery at Saqqara   40
3.4 The Overseer of *ka*-priest(s) Qar makes an offering to the
official Khenu in the latter's tomb in the Unas Causeway
Cemetery at Saqqara   43
4.1 The pyramid of Unas at Saqqara, looking westwards from
the causeway   52
4.2 Plan of the Teti Pyramid Cemetery at Saqqara, showing the
pyramids of Teti, Iput I and Khuit, and selected private tombs
of the Old Kingdom–Ramesside Period   57

4.3 Plan of the *mastaba* of Nebkauhor in the Unas Causeway
     Cemetery at Saqqara   58
4.4 Plan of the tomb of Nefer at Saqqara   60
4.5   Statue of the Princess Nofret from Meidum   64
4.6 Scribal statue   65
5.1 Funeral procession in the tomb of Qar at Giza   76
5.2 Funeral scene in the tomb of Debehen at Giza   77
5.3 Funeral procession in the tomb of Pepiankh Heny
     'the Black' at Meir   79
6.1 Tombs at Qubbet el-Hawa   92
6.2 The tomb of Harkhuf at Qubbet el-Hawa   93
6.3 The tombs of Mekhu and Sabni at Qubbet el-Hawa   94
6.4 The tomb of Khentika in the Dakhleh Oasis   96
6.5 A sub-elite tomb at Abydos, excavated by John
     Garstang in 1909   102
7.1 The 'pyramid' of Kom Dara   109
7.2 The tomb of Ankhtify at Moalla   110
7.3 The tomb of Ankhtify at Moalla (interior)   110
7.4 Subsidiary tombs at Moalla   112
7.5 The tomb of Wahka I at Qau   113
8.1 Middle Kingdom *mahat* and stela at Abydos
     excavated by John Garstang in 1908   123
8.2 Middle Kingdom *mahat* of Iy at Abydos excavated
     by John Garstang in 1907   124
8.3 Stela of Iy from 321 A'07 excavated by John Garstang
     in 1907   127
8.4 Stela of Sobek-khu from Abydos   130
8.5 Abydos Tomb 941-949 A'09 excavated by John Garstang
     in 1909   135
9.1 The box coffin of Userhet from Beni Hasan   142
9.2 The head of the anthropoid coffin of Khnum-Nakht from Rifeh 145
9.3 The box coffin of Userhet, containing his anthropoid
     coffin, in his tomb at Beni Hasan   146
10.1 View of the Beni Hasan cemetery   152
10.2 Elite tombs at Beni Hasan   152
10.3 Tomb façade at Beni Hasan   153
10.4 Elite tombs at Rifeh   159
10.5 Coffins in a shaft tomb at Beni Hasan   161
10.6 Wooden models on a coffin inside a shaft tomb
     at Beni Hasan   162
10.7 Shaft tombs at Beni Hasan   163
10.8 'Soul-house' from a Middle Kingdom tomb at Abydos   164

11.1 The 'temple-tomb' of Nebhepetre Montuhotep II at
Deir el-Bahri 167
11.2 Dynasty 11 tombs at Deir el-Bahri 168
11.3 Plan of the tomb of Senebtisi at Lisht, and its
most significant contents 173
12.1 View of the Valley of the Kings 179
12.2 Plan of the West Bank cemeteries at Thebes 180
12.3 View of the cemetery of Sheikh abd el-Qurna at Thebes 186
12.4 Plans of three Dynasty 18 tombs: A – Ineni; B – Rekhmire,
C – Amenhotep-Huy 186
12.5 Representations of the superstructures of Theban tombs
in the tombs of (left) Nebamun and Ipuky – TT181; and (right)
Rai – TT159 187
13.1 Selected scenes of royal service from the tomb of Rekhmire 193
13.2 Selected scenes of funeral from the tomb of Rekhmire 195
13.3 The tomb of Nebqed, as illustrated in his Book of the Dead 199
13.4 The interior of the tomb of Pahery at el-Kab 201
13.5 The 'autobiography' of Ahmose son of Ibana at el-Kab 203
13.6 Plan of the Burial Chambers in the family tomb of
Neferkhewet and Rennefer at Thebes 205
14.1 Plan and selected scenes from the tomb of Huya at Amarna 210
14.2 Plan and selected scenes from the tomb of Apuia at Saqqara 218
14.3 Plan of the tomb of Horemheb at Saqqara 219
15.1 Plan of the superstructure and of the winding passage to
the Burial Chamber in the tomb of Samut at Thebes 227
16.1 The site of Deir el-Medina, with the hill of Qurnet Murai
immediately behind it 234
16.2 Cross-section of the tomb of Sennedjem at Deir el-Medina,
Thebes 236
17.1 Mourning woman on a wooden stela of the Third
Intermediate Period 249
17.2 The tomb-chapels of the God's Wives of Amen at Medinet
Habu 253
17.3 The tomb of Montuemhat (TT34) in the Asasif cemetery
at Thebes 254
17.4 The Burial Chamber of a Third Intermediate/Late Period
tomb 255
17.5 The tomb of Petosiris at Tuna el-Gebel 256

Preface

This book has been written with the intention of making available to the general reader primary evidence and secondary discussion of a range of material relating to the ways in which the ancient Egyptians saw the tomb and the diverse ways in which it represented aspects of life, and the afterlife, for them. I have tried to indicate to the reader where they might further explore different aspects of this, bearing in mind that most readers of this book will have a preference for works in English. However, such is the range of primary publications and recent scholarship (especially in German) that it is important to point out some key publications which are in other languages.

In addition I have tried, wherever possible, to let the Egyptians speak to us in their own words since tombs are both an important physical context for Egyptian texts and (along with matters to which they relate, from personal autobiographies to presentations of views of the afterlife) an important subject for such texts. Once again I have tried to use translations from a relatively small number of reliable and wide-ranging anthologies. These include Lichtheim's well-known three-volume collection of key texts ranging over the Dynastic Period, but also the anthologies in the 'Writings from the Ancient World' series produced by the Society of Biblical Literature; the volumes on the Old Kingdom by Nigel Strudwick, the Amarna Period by Bill Murnane, and the Ramesside Period by Liz Frood have been, as will be obvious from the relevant chapters, particularly important as collections of relevant texts.

This book does not pretend to be an even chronological overview of tombs and burial practices in Egypt during the Dynastic Period (and a little later) because the evidence does not allow it to be so. It will be clear to the reader that there are some periods in which the creation of elaborate, well decorated and (crucially for us!) informative tombs was very important to the elite, and these tombs can themselves tell us about the religious and social context in which they appear – tombs of the late Old Kingdom in the Memphite necropolis, the early Middle Kingdom in Middle Egypt and Dynasty 18 at Thebes are especially informative in this regard. If I have given particular prominence to elite tombs from the Old Kingdom it is partly because this period sees the first examples of trends in tomb building and decoration and, more importantly, underlying belief and practice, which affect the rest of Egyptian history. In the periods following the Old Kingdom, while following the evidence and trying not to miss out anything important, I have endeavoured to stress changes in tomb types and decoration which represent important developments (or continuity) in underlying belief systems about the afterlife.

Inevitably the tombs which are the most informative are those which are the largest and best decorated, equally inevitably built for those in society with wealth and status. As Assmann (2003: 46) notes, 'The construction of sacred space in tomb architecture is a rather elitist concern.' The owners of these tombs can be referred to in a number of ways, and it is common to read about 'tombs of the nobles' or 'tombs of the courtiers'. I have chosen to use the term 'elite' tombs because it makes no specific assumptions about the owners of the tombs – it does not differentiate whether they received their position and tombs through the gift of the king or whether they built them from their own resources, whether they were part of the royal court or regional leaders, whether they were from a long-established 'aristocratic' family or *arrivistes*. All of these factors are, of course, important in providing a broader social and cultural context for the role of tombs and the status of their owners at different times and places in ancient Egypt. But, as a term to cover all of these structures and, more particularly, their owners, 'elite' seems to be the most suitable.

Royal tombs are relevant to this story – often they influence, sometimes in indirect ways, developments in private tombs – but they are not the centre of this story as it is with private tombs that we are most concerned here. Royal tombs are often significantly different from non-royal tombs not just in scale and form, but also in underlying ideas of the available afterlife, although these, too, could, as we shall see, 'bleed' into private practice.

Acknowledgements

It would be seriously remiss of me not to acknowledge the people who have helped to bring this book into being. For the reader who wishes to identify these people the References would be a good start. More specifically I would like to thank teachers, colleagues and students at the University of Liverpool, past and present, who have provided inspiration and/or stimulating discussion regarding the topics covered in this book: Aly Abdalla, Violaine Chauvet, Mark Collier, Ashley Cooke, Judith Corbelli, Khaled Dawoud, Roland Enmarch, Liz Frood, Glenn Godenho, Gina Laycock, Campbell Price, Ian Shaw, Peter Shore and, especially, Chris Eyre.

I acknowledge the School of Archaeology, Classics and Egyptology at the University of Liverpool for the use of images from John Garstang's excavations at Abydos and Beni Hasan.

I would also like to thank Wiley-Blackwell's anonymous readers for their helpful comments, Karen Exell for her practical assistance, and Joyce Tyldesley for her forbearance and support during the over-long gestation period of this book.

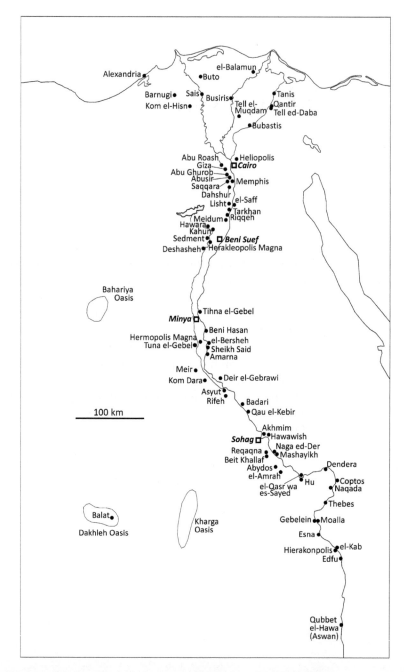

Figure 0.1 Map of Egypt showing the location of sites mentioned in the text

Introduction

ﾚﾚﾚﾚ

The Problem of the Dead

The death of a human being presents other human beings with a set of problems.

The first is the practical matter of the necessary disposal of the dead body. Despite imaginative solutions, such as 'sky burial', most humans, in most parts of the world, at most points in human history, have dealt with this issue in one of two ways: dig a hole and bury the body, or burn it until it becomes a more manageable collection of inert ashes and burnt bone (which themselves require disposal, albeit of a much less pressing and inconvenient kind than the body itself). For the ancient Egyptians, burial was the preferred option, although with added complications brought about by the particular ways in which the dead body was regarded as an active vehicle for the animated Dead. However, despite the 'active' nature of the dead body, access by the Living to the bodies of the Dead was strictly limited, and the burial chambers of the rich and the graves of the poor were normally very much off-limits.

The second problem is what to do about the property of the Dead. On the one hand, sometimes quite literally, are the items of personal jewellery which might be retained by the Living as a personal keepsake of the Dead, or which may be buried with the Dead, perhaps as a token of a personal relationship, such as a wedding ring. Such tokens are a rare exception to the general rule which applies to burials in the Jewish–Christian–Muslim tradition, and in the secular West, which is that of a minimal or non-existent deposition of objects with the body, in tombs and graves. This is, of course, diametrically opposite to the ancient Egyptian tradition, which is of significant deposition of objects with burials, for a variety of reasons. On a different level are other assets owned by the Dead such as land and other property of real economic value. These can no longer be enjoyed by the Dead, but are available to the Living. To what extent is the use to which the Living can put these assets limited by control by the Dead? Although one might argue that a will is a straightforward mechanism by which the Dead (while alive) can dictate the destination of their property once dead, the extent to which many lawcourts are willing to overturn the stated intentions of the now-Dead in favour of the complaining Living gives a clear sense of the weight given to the legal rights of the Living and the Dead; not only can the Dead not speak for themselves, this inarticulateness can be regarded as an aspect of the Dead being, effectively, non-persons. The ancient Egyptian situation, we shall see, is quite different; not only are the Dead very much regarded as 'persons', they are also seen as property holders, whose rights to that property need to be protected, because the Dead make active use of that property for their own benefit, in their status as a dead individual, for eternity.

The third problem is the most complex, although it is related to that of property. What is the relationship between the Living and the Dead? To what extent are the Living and the Dead part of one community? Is the nature of one's view of the Dead, and death itself, mediated through a wider belief system? Does the personality survive after death, and, if so, what form does it take, where does it reside, and can the Living communicate with it? The answers to these questions might be very varied. If we have a firm religious faith, we may have answers which are embedded within a divine plan for the universe. Otherwise our answers might be individual, disorganized or might simply tick the box 'don't know'. Once again the Egyptians developed clear answers to these problems, by following lines of reasoning based on a specific view (or, rather, views) about the nature of the human 'soul' and its specific nature both within and without this world.

Relationships with the Dead

A devoted son visits his mother's grave on Christmas Day every year, before returning to celebrate the season's festivities with his living family. Why? Does he expect some form of meaningful communication with her, in a cold village churchyard? Who can say – it is between him and her. What is very clear, though, is that this is an occasion of remembering, but, in some ways, a curious form of remembering. There is a paradox here in that the grave, with its headstone, on a cold hillside, is a very different locale from the places of the recollected landscape of the remembered past. This is a place of burial and a place of specific commemoration in the form of the headstone, but are the Dead really 'there'? Again this is a matter for individual belief, though in most cases the Living think of the happy Dead not as inhabiting cemeteries but as dwelling within 'a better place'. Yet the grave does have an important function: although the Dead may not 'be there', the function of providing a specific locale where a specific act of remembering is sanctioned is a means by which physical space is provided so that some form of relationship between the Living and the Dead can take place. The specifics of that relationship are dependent on individual attitudes to it, but it is essentially a one-sided relationship – one might 'talk' to a dead relation on such an occasion, but would probably regard any reply by the Dead as somewhat startling. The relationship being played out here is between a living individual and their memory of a dead person, not the dead person themselves, although this might well not be regarded as so by the individual concerned.

The headstone has another important function: the preservation of identity through the name and limited genealogy of the Dead. Dates also indicate when the person was a living being. The preservation of identity seems to be a fluctuating human need: 'Here lies one whose name was writ in water' is a sentiment which is paradoxically undercut by the very real materiality of the stone block into which the inscription was incised. Although the tomb is not the only place to do this, it is an obvious one given its connection to the remains of the physical body. So what is a tomb? A convenient place to dispose of a dead human body? A location where the Living can remember the Dead? An opportunity to display wealth and status? For the Egyptians the tomb was all of these things, but also very much more. Throughout the Dynastic Period the tomb took on a great number of roles and functions with, for the Egyptian elite, its importance often reflected in architectural and artistic elaboration. A whole range of factors came together to determine the nature of the tomb, some of which were determined by the expectations of the afterlife, which the tomb was intended to satisfy or facilitate, and the relationship of the Dead with the Living. As Godenho (2007: 7) notes, one function of Egyptian tombs was to 'embody social order by monumentalizing social relations'.

Egyptian Tombs and Egyptian Archaeology

Why are we, as archaeologists, so interested in ancient Egyptian tombs and their contents? The most obvious answer to this question is that the tombs which the ancient Egyptians built, decorated and equipped for themselves are one of the largest, richest and most informative classes of archaeological material anywhere in the world and from any period of human history. Funerary remains are the most obvious and remarkable physical remnants from ancient Egypt. Whether pyramids, mummies or Tutankhamen, it is tombs and the things which come out of them which provide the most instantly recognizable and (for most people) defining examples of ancient Egyptian-ness. These are funerary artefacts which are not just strange or opulent but also distinctive – no other civilization did things quite like the ancient Egyptians, especially in the provisioning of their tombs. They did this for a whole range of different, related reasons, which we shall be exploring in this book, but an important starting point is to note the very obvious physicality of the Egyptian response to the problem of death and what comes after. Ensuring a happy afterlife is often to do with having the right sort of tomb, the right equipment within the tomb, and the right hieroglyphic texts on the equipment. Eternity could be assured by having the proper kit. This is, of course, a simplification, but a simplification with a good deal of truth in it. The tombs and the objects within them are part of a more complex context of ways of imagining the nature of the human personality after death, the relationship between the Living and the Dead, and the relationship between humans and the divine, but these are, nevertheless, issues which are partly resolved by physical objects which provide the context and tools with which these problems can, to a significant extent, be solved.

A significant factor is that of preservation. Egypt is a land of very marked contrasts when it comes to the preservation of archaeological material. The damp soil and the annual flooding of the Nile in the floodplain of the Nile Valley and Delta were extremely prejudicial to the survival of all but the hardiest of materials. The Egyptian desert, with its dry, desiccating sands, is capable of preserving in remarkable condition even the most delicate of materials – textiles, flora, the human body. It was, naturally enough, the desert edges which were chosen as the locations of cemeteries when local conditions allowed it. The Nile Delta provides a more problematic environment, but for most of the Nile Valley the desert is never very far away and, in some places, comes close to the Nile itself, so that local cemeteries overlook both the local town and the river, providing a landscape in which the Living and the Dead are equally present. The desert edge was chosen for very practical reasons – putting cemeteries on productive agricultural land would be a waste and, more importantly, while the Living could move away from the rising waters of the often-unpredictable Nile inundation, the Dead could not. Towns, villages and houses could be, and were, easily rebuilt using mudbrick, the ubiquitous building material of living Egypt, but the flooding of tombs would be catastrophic. In fact the effects of preservation, viewed by the Egyptians, gave an impetus to preservation as a goal. When they saw the naturally preserved bodies of the Dead, desiccated by the sands of the desert, the Egyptians, who were well aware of the speed of decomposition of meat in a hot climate, seem to have given a special quality to this preservation. Preservation of the tomb, the grave goods, and especially the body became seen as the vehicles by which the afterlife could be achieved. But this stress on the material provision of tombs and tomb contents, allied to their high level of preservation, had another effect. It made cemeteries particular targets of early explorers and archaeologists. The knowledge that digging in a cemetery would yield a rich harvest of finds, certainly when compared to the slim pickings from settlement sites, made sure that the early history of Egyptology was characterized by the excavation of a high proportion of cemetery sites.

Two other factors encouraged this concentration. One was a general interest in religious beliefs and practices of 'primitive' humans which came out of the developing subject of comparative anthropology, best exemplified in the English-speaking world by James Frazer's *The Golden Bough* (1930). Egyptian myths, transmitted through Classical literature, could be seen as part of a wider set of comparable beliefs in the afterlife, and the discoveries made by early archaeologists in Egypt seemed to fit well within this scheme, especially with regard to ideas regarding the Egyptian version of the 'Dying God', Osiris. The second factor was the way in which early fieldwork in Egypt was conducted. Excavations organized by the major museums of the world which wished to develop a profile within Egyptology would, not surprisingly, have as one of their aims the acquisition of objects which would expand their collections and, in a more basic way, justify the expense of such archaeological work. This may have been only a minor concern in scholarly terms of the excavator, but a practical one. Some of the great collections of the world have grown directly as a result of such work. Sometimes the relationship between object discovery and support for the excavation was more overt. A particularly good example is John Garstang, Professor of Methods and Practice of Archaeology at the University of Liverpool and active excavator in Egypt from 1899 to 1909. His excavations were funded by a committee of patrons who, in return for their financial support, would receive a 'dividend' on their investment in the form of a proportion of the objects which Garstang excavated and which was granted by the Egyptian authorities as his 50 per cent share of all the objects he recovered. While many of Garstang's backers were motivated by philanthropic and scientific concerns, the pressure to produce a good 'yield' from each year's excavations was one (albeit only one) of the reasons Garstang chose to concentrate on cemetery sites, including some of the most important in Egypt such as Abydos and Beni Hasan. Even Flinders Petrie, the doyen of scientific archaeology in Egypt, recognized the importance of high-quality objects as important tools for the development of the subject when he wrote: 'Perfect and pretty things are no doubt very useful to serve as lures for attracting the public to the education prepared for them' (Petrie 1888: vi), while his development of important techniques such as seriation (which he called sequence-dating) was dependent on the analysis of a substantial number of complete groups of archaeological material from closed contexts (Petrie 1901). Only tombs were guaranteed to provide both 'pretty things' and the closed context groups. The reason that the study of ancient Egyptian tombs and their contents is so important is that they provide a wealth of primary evidence which can be used in different ways by archaeologists with very different research agendas. Whether these are the anthropological interest in the 'dying god', the arguments over diffusionism, the economic motives for human actions or a concern with the nature of self-constructed identity, the tombs of the ancient Egyptians continue to offer a multi-faceted range of material which can be used to try to understand the lives and afterlives of the ancient Egyptians.

It is probably worth issuing a word of caution at this point. In looking at tombs and what they have to tell us, it is all too easy to fall into generalizations which do not do justice to the complexity of the material, perhaps especially in ascribing monolithic belief systems and common, shared responses to those beliefs; the archaeological material and human responses to the problem of death are much more complex than that (Eyre 2009). Nevertheless, inevitably, a study with such a, perhaps unwisely, broad chronological scope is by its nature bound to focus on general trends and seek for a norm to describe. However, we must always be aware of the sometimes surprising results of looking at the ways the Egyptians did regard their tombs, sometimes with all too recognizable human ambivalence. Discussing the slow rate of progress on Amarna private tombs, and the lack of urgency in that project compared to house building at the site, Owen and Kemp (1994: 128) have remarked that it is possible that 'in the minds of some owners acquiescence in a slow rate of progress encouraged fate to be generous with their lifespan'.

CHAPTER 1

Nameless Lives at Tarkhan and Saqqara

Early Tombs and the Ka

リコリコ

Burials and Beliefs in Predynastic Cemeteries

One of the most regularly repeated refrains within Egyptian archaeology is the extent to which the subject is relatively blessed with the survival of ancient tombs and cemeteries when compared to settlement sites. Indeed many ancient towns and cities can only be located because of the survival of their cemeteries while the dwellings of the Living have disappeared beneath the floodplain of the Nile. This is especially true for the Predynastic – the period before the unification of Egypt at *c.*3050 BC. While shifts in the course of the Nile over the past six thousand years mean that a few Predynastic towns are now on the desert rather than submerged beneath the damp Nile silt of the cultivation, it is still the desert-edge cemeteries, deliberately placed there, which provide the best corpus of evidence for Egypt before the pharaohs (Wengrow 2006; Wilkinson 1999).

The evidence from the excavation of hundreds of Predynastic graves (Castillos 1982), especially from the cemeteries of southern Egypt, makes it possible to describe, in broad terms, typical burials of the Predynastic Period and its sub-divisions, although it should also be noted that, as later, no two graves of the Predynastic are identical in their form or contents. Typical burials of the Badarian (*c.*4500–3800 BC) consist of oval pits containing contracted burials, lying on their left side, head to the south, facing west, lying on a mat and wrapped/covered by a mat or gazelle skin. Grave goods

---

Ancient Egyptian Tombs: The Culture of Life and Death   By Steven Snape
© 2011 Steven Snape

include distinctive handmade pottery, long-toothed bone/ivory combs, slate palettes and personal jewellery (Midant-Reynes 2000: 153–8). Graves of Naqada I (*c.*3800–3500 BC) are essentially similar to those of the Badarian, but with some degree of differentiation based on the size of the grave and the number and quality of its contents, especially at the major centre of Hierakonpolis (Adams 1987; Midant-Reynes 2000: 170). This differentiation became more marked in Naqada II (*c.*3500–3300 BC). Other innovations of Naqada II included much less consistency in the orientation of the body and the replacement of animal skin coverings with matting and linen; in richer graves they were superseded by the introduction of coffins made of basketwork and, ultimately, wood. (Midant-Reynes 2000: 187; see Chapter 9 below). The move towards a clear differentiation between small numbers of large and well-provisioned tombs and a majority of much less impressive graves, probably indicating social status within larger, politically sophisticated communities, is seen most starkly during Naqada III (*c.*3300–3100 BC; Midant-Reynes 2000: 235ff.). However, the most remarkable tomb of the Predynastic – the so-called 'Painted Tomb' at Hierakonpolis – probably dates to Naqada II (Midant-Reynes 2000: 207ff.); in any case this tomb belongs to an owner who can certainly be regarded as elite, and probably quasi-royal, and a precursor to the definitely royal tombs of Dynasty 1 (see Chapter 2).

We can be reasonably confident about the reconstruction of these Predynastic graves and their contents owing to the exceptionally high levels of preservation of objects placed within the grave, which was filled with the dry, desiccating sand of the desert. These high levels of preservation extended to the body itself, which had effectively, but in all probability accidentally, been provided with ideal conditions for natural mummification as the dry desert sand acted as a natural absorbent for the potentially destructive decompositional fluids. This natural preservation of the body would have far-reaching consequences for Egyptians' attitudes to the body in their view of the afterlife and, consequently, tomb design itself. However, although these Predynastic graves and their contents are often extremely well preserved, we have little idea as to how, if at all, the position of the graves was marked since no substantial superstructures have survived until relatively late in the period. It is possible that a simple mound of sand/gravel was the most usual covering of these graves. In addition, we do not know how the graves of the Dead were regarded by the Living. In fact we have no real idea about what the Predynastic Egyptians actually believed would happen to them after death. The evidence of the graves themselves is ambiguous and capable of radically different interpretations.

A good case in point is a burial excavated by Petrie in 1912–13 at the late Predynastic cemetery of Tarkhan, which is 60 km south of Cairo on the West

Bank of the Nile. The interment in question was numbered 1845 by Petrie (1914) and was particularly important as it seems to have been the only one of the burials he excavated that season which had not been robbed, and therefore the only one where the placement of the objects within the grave could be confidently said to be a deliberate arrangement at the time of burial. On the basis of the pottery found within it, the grave was assigned Sequence Date (SD) 77, which places it just before the unification of Egypt; it might therefore be seen as sitting on the cusp between the somewhat enigmatic graves of the Predynastic Period and the explanation-rich tombs of the Dynastic Period. An alabaster bowl, with a slate palette placed over it, had been positioned in front of the face of the contracted body, lying on its left side with head to the south facing west, while other pottery storage jars had also been put into the grave (Figure 1.1).

Faced with this evidence, it is possible to produce a range of hypotheses which explain the observed phenomena. One might draw the conclusion that the grave and its contents represent a belief (or, rather, possible sets of beliefs) in the afterlife – the body buried in the foetal position might reflect the cycle of birth and death; the body facing west towards the setting sun and the land of the afterlife beyond the horizon; the objects within the tomb might have been placed there for the use of the Dead in the afterlife, or for their journey there. Predynastic graves might therefore display a developed spirituality in respect of the afterlife which can be directly traced into those belief-systems which are very clearly expressed in the Dynastic Period.

However, one might also look at the evidence of Tarkhan 1845 and decide that it represents a very different state of affairs in that the body buried in

Figure 1.1   Tarkhan Tomb 1845: the burial (after Petrie 1914: Pl. 12)

the crouched position within a shallow grave minimizes the effort needed to dispose of a dead human body by burial and that the objects placed within the grave represent a fairly minimal set of comparatively low-value objects which were personally associated with the dead individual and, for superstitious reasons, would not be wanted by a living member of the community. Predynastic graves might therefore represent a minimal effort to dispose of the inconvenient dead and no belief in the afterlife need be assumed.

Both these explanations represent extreme cases of trying either to find or to deny a belief in an afterlife in every feature associated with these burials, and the 'truth' is unrecoverable since we cannot reconstruct the mental states of those individuals who lived and died in Predynastic Egypt. In fact the interpretation of beliefs in an afterlife based on the fact of burial and the presence of grave goods is fraught with difficulties, and any ethnographic survey of burial practices and the social and belief-systems which gave rise to them presents us with a surprising kaleidoscope of possibilities; such a survey was carried out by Ucko (1969), from whose work the following examples are drawn. Burial itself does not necessarily imply any specific belief in an afterlife, nor may it be socially important to the society which carries it out – it may simply be the necessary disposal of waste in the form of an inconveniently large dead human body. For the Nuer of the Sudan, burial involved the disposal of the body, with little in the way of funeral ceremonies, in an unmarked grave. This raises the interest-ing issue that the treatment of the body after death does not necessarily correlate with ideas regarding an afterlife for the non-corporeal person; Dynastic Egyptians, as we shall see, were unusually concerned with the dead body as a vehicle for eternal well-being.

The objects placed within the grave might be interpreted as things which were needed by the Dead, but this is also not necessarily the case. For the Lugbara of Uganda, grave goods do not reflect a belief in an afterlife but rather the social personality of the tomb owner, with specific objects reflecting specific elements of the person – a quiver for a hunter/warrior, a stool for an elder, firestones for a wife, grinding stones for a mother. The issue of 'person-ness' connected to the tomb was a fundamental one for the Dynastic Egyptians and, at particular periods, the selection of material placed within a burial reflects this concern. It may also be the case that the disposal of objects within the grave represents not the needs of the Dead but those of the Living, who, at the time of burial of a loved one, 'simply wished to dispose of objects which had particular emotional connotations' (Ucko 1969: 265). It is also the case that the specific positioning of the body within the grave, although it hints at a special treatment of the body with a specific aim in mind, is also capable of varied interpretations. Is an eastwards-facing body always looking towards the rising sun, or one looking westwards towards the setting sun? Is the east or the west a place where the Dead face because that is where the Dead go? Are there specific local or more distant (e.g. Mecca for Muslims or Jerusalem for mediaeval Christians?) points of orientation which are more significant than cosmological factors?

The ambiguity of Tarkhan 1845 seems, as an example of Predynastic burials, to stand in marked contrast to the high-quality, understandable material from the elite tombs of Dynastic Egypt, and the interplay and different levels of explanation provided by that material – architecture in its localized context; extensive visual depictions and explanatory texts on the walls of those tombs; contents including specialized mortuary 'kit', among which is the body itself, elements of which are also often inscribed with explanatory text – which provide a very solid platform to understand the afterlife beliefs of the ancient Egyptians.

However, Tarkhan 1845, like other late Predynastic tombs from this site, and unlike most earlier Predynastic burials, had a carefully constructed superstructure which, although modest in size and made from simple mudbrick, indicates a significant development in tomb design which itself reflected the development of a major idea in the role of the tomb as a vehicle for the well-being of the Dead.

The Emergence of the Bipartite Tomb

Tomb 1845 at Tarkhan contains, as we have seen, an interment consisting of a shallow oval grave within which was buried a contracted body and a modest selection of grave goods which may, or may not, tell us something about the afterlife beliefs of the society which produced it. However, the wider context of the burial is rather more informative since the grave is only one part of a larger and more complex tomb. The grave was marked by being surrounded by a mudbrick rectangle which, if filled after burial, could form a rubble-filled, solid 'box' now more than a metre high. The position of the burial was therefore clearly marked, but equally clearly no-one was intended to enter this part of the tomb. Attached to the outside wall of this *mastaba* (the name derives from the low mudbrick benches found outside some village houses in Egypt) was an addition – a tiny room just big enough for a human to enter (Figure 1.2). Petrie found that this room, and the area outside the tomb near it, was filled with large pottery storage jars and food containers. This evidence need not in itself imply any particular beliefs in the afterlife since it might simply be the remains of a funeral feast by the living at the time of inhumation, but there is one further relevant detail: the

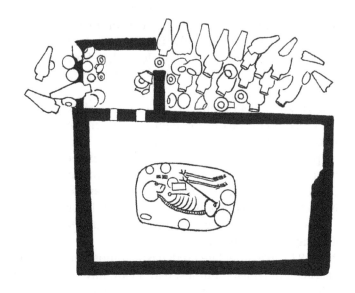

Figure 1.2   Tarkhan Tomb 1845: the Burial Chamber and Offering Chapel (after Petrie 1914: Pls 12 and 14)

body within the grave was orientated so that it faced the wall shared by the grave enclosure and the external room, and that wall was pierced by 'two slits in the brickwork of the *mastaba* wall, for the offerings to reach the deceased' (Petrie 1914: 2). This architectural feature was not unique to Tomb 1845, but shared by other similar tombs at Tarkhan. Although it would be dangerous on the basis of this evidence alone to draw wider conclusions about the beliefs behind the development of this tomb-type, two things seem reasonably clear: the importance of food to the Dead and the possibility of some connection between the Dead buried underneath the *mastaba* and the food brought by the Living and placed in the liminal zone of the attached room. In fact it is almost certain that these Tarkhan tombs represent an early version of what would become a fundamental feature in the way that the form of Egyptian tombs reflected their function – the tomb was essentially bipartite in nature, consisting of two distinct elements which were linked together through overall function, but significantly different in practical use. It is probably accurate at this stage to regard the external rooms at Tarkhan as Offering Chapels and the burials underneath the *mastaba*s as Burial Chambers.

However, the Tarkhan tombs only represent one solution to what seems to be a major issue in the afterlife beliefs and burial practices of late Predynastic/early Dynastic: the problem of providing food for the Dead. This problem seems to be the main determinant in the Tarkhan tomb with its separate, accessible Offering Chapel, but other approaches to the problem were experimented with at other sites, especially the among the elite non-royal tomb owners of Dynasty 1.

Elite Mastabas at Saqqara: The Tomb as a Storeroom

The unification of Egypt had a number of important effects on the way the Egyptians expressed the way they understood the afterlife through their tombs. One aspect of this was the apparently unique position of the king and, initially at least, the very separate nature of his burial at the exclusive Umm el-Qa'ab cemetery at Abydos (see next chapter). This royal exclusivity meant that emerging court elites – the high officials who acted for the king in the government of what had become the largest and potentially most powerful country in the early Bronze Age of the Near East – had to look elsewhere for a suitable place to be buried. This suitable place was, essentially, self-selecting. The unification of the Delta in the north and the Valley in the south required a new administrative centre from which both halves of the new country could be governed. The location chosen was Memphis, close to modern Cairo, which was (with a few breaks) the most significant administrative, economic and population centre of Egypt until the foundation of Alexandria in 332 BC. Partly because of the movement of the Nile in this part of its floodplain, the actual location of the city of Memphis shifted over the next 2,500 years, gradually moving eastwards to follow the river. Comparatively little of pre-New Kingdom Memphis remains to be seen today and the location of Old Kingdom Memphis is still unknown. However, although the houses, streets and districts of the ancient city now seem to be lost, the tombs of its cemeteries have survived to a very much greater degree since they were built on top of the desert escarpment immediately to the west of the ancient city.

The desert edge to the west of Memphis which was used as the cemetery for this ancient metropolis stretches a huge distance – *c*.30 km from Abu Roash in the north to Dahshur in the south, and even further if the southern outlier of Meidum is included – the result of rapid development during the Early Dynastic Period and Old Kingdom. As far as significant tomb building is concerned, the earliest part is North Saqqara, where the court officials of Dynasties 1 and 2 were buried in huge *mastaba*-tombs, probably overlooking the city in which they lived and worked (Emery 1938, 1949, 1954, 1958).

These *mastaba*s are so large, particularly when compared with what might appear to be relatively modest royal tombs at Abydos, that their excavator, Bryan Emery, came to believe that the Saqqara *mastaba*s of Dynasty 1 were in fact the real royal tombs of that period, with the Abydos structures merely being dummies or cenotaphs. The presence of royal names in these Saqqara tombs seemed to support this identification. However, when the 'funerary enclosures' at Abydos are brought into consideration, it is clear that the total amount of funerary provision made for the king at Abydos is greater than any of the Saqqara *mastaba*s. In addition, the presence of objects naming court officials found within the Saqqara tombs points the way to their real owners, members of the royal court based at Memphis and buried there.

There are a number of features shared by the elite Saqqara tombs throughout Dynasty 1. They were all designed to be strikingly impressive, with a superstructure consisting of a huge *mastaba* made of mudbrick, whose external appearance was embellished by decorative brickwork producing a series of plastered vertical niches of varying depth which, because of its supposed connection with early palace architecture, is often referred to as 'palace façade' decoration. In contrast to the large and deliberately visible superstructure, the burial apartments under these *mastaba*s were comparatively modest, essentially designed to house the body and those grave goods which were of especial connection to the deceased, or of significant value. The bulk of the objects which accompanied the deceased were housed not within the burial apartments under the *mastaba*, but within the body of the *mastaba* itself, which, initially at least, was not solid but composed of a series of closed 'cells', each one of which was effectively a sealed storeroom for the grave goods which were placed within them.

Perhaps the most famous example is the tomb of Hemaka (numbered 3035; Emery 1938), a high official who lived during the reign of King Den. His tomb is a typical large *mastaba*-tomb, made of mudbrick and with an external surface with elaborate palace façade decoration. The underground burial chamber was relatively modest in size but the *mastaba* itself was enormous, measuring over 65×25 m. The massive proportions of the superstructure made an impressive statement about the status of their owner, but there was an important functional element too since the interior of the *mastaba* was divided into a series of 45 individual cells which were intended to serve as closed storage rooms or magazines. Although robbed, Hemaka's *mastaba* still contained some of its original contents when it was excavated, which included ox-bones and, in a series of four connected rooms, over 700 large storage jars. Other objects from Hemaka's *mastaba* represent extremely high levels of craftsmanship in the creation of luxurious items, such as ivory gaming pieces and thin stone bowls of elaborate shape, but the vast majority of the objects discovered by Emery in Hemaka's tomb were ordinary storage jars for food and drink. Hemaka's *mastaba*, like those of his contemporaries, was, in effect, a huge larder. Whatever the uncertain specifics of the ideas about an afterlife represented by this tomb and its contents, it seems to have a concern with the provision of food which is not very different in essence to that of Tarkhan 1845. The difference seems to be, at least in the case of the tomb of Hemaka and some similar Dynasty 1 *mastaba*s, that the wealth of the owners meant that they were able to fill their tombs with the food they would need. The potential flaw in this system is that if the stored food is 'consumed' by the tomb owner, eventually any amount of stored food will run out and other systems need to be put in place to ensure a continued flow for eternity. Some of these changing ideas seem to have influenced the development of elite *mastaba*-tombs at Saqqara during Dynasty 1, which, despite their similarities, reveals a distinct evolution of the form. For the excavation reports of the *mastaba*-tombs described here see: 3035 (Emery 1938); 3471 (Emery 1949: 13–70, pl. 2); 3036 (Emery 1949: 71–81, pl. 14); 3507 (Emery 1958: 73–97, pl. 85); and 3505 (Emery 1958: 5–36, pl. 2).

Saqqara *Mastaba* 3471 (Figure 1.3) probably dates, on the evidence of jar sealings found within it, to the reign of King Djer, early in Dynasty 1. Its substructure consists of a series of seven rooms cut into the bedrock, and roofed with timber, the central, deepest room being the Burial Chamber

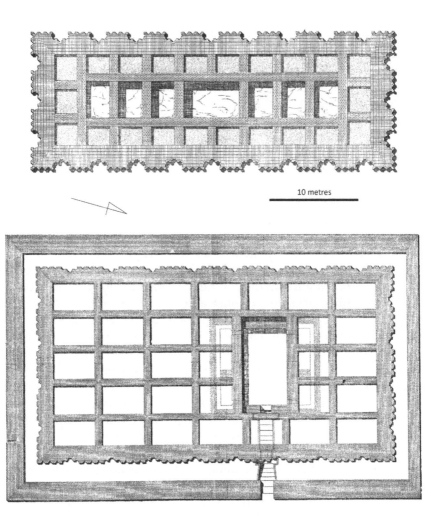

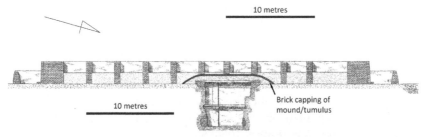

10 metres

10 metres

10 metres

Brick capping of mound/tumulus

Figure 1.3 Saqqara *Mastaba*s 3471 (plan, top), 3036 (plan, middle) and 3507 (cross-section, foot) (adapted from Emery 1949: Pls 2 and 4; 1958: Pl. 85)

itself. The superstructure is a rectangular mudbrick *mastaba,* just over 41 m long and 15 m wide, with palace façade niches, with its interior divided into 29/30 cells, turning the *mastaba* into a large storeroom. The superstructure rooms were largely empty, but the substructure rooms contained a range of grave goods, especially hundreds of copper vessels and implements.

Saqqara *Mastaba* 3036 (also Figure 1.3) probably belonged to Ankhka, who served under King Den. The superstructure of the tomb – a honeycomb of storerooms – is essentially the same as that of 3471, but there are a number of significant differences, particularly the depth of the burial pit and the ease of access to the Burial Chamber by the innovation of a stairway running down to it from the eastern side of the *mastaba.* Hemaka's tomb, from this reign, is also a 'stairway tomb'.

Saqqara *Mastaba* 3507 also dates to the reign of Den (Emery believed it to be the tomb of Queen Her-neith, mother of Den). It has much in common with 3471 and 3036. It may be earlier than 3036 (pre-stepped phase). But although the superstructure is dominated by the rectangular, niched *mastaba,* the superstructure has embedded within it a further feature: the burial chamber itself is covered by a mound or tumulus of sand and rubble, but given a casing of mudbrick to regularize this loose pile into a definite feature 10.5 m long × 9.2 m wide and just over 1 m high (Figure 1.3). It is possible that this is an artificial re-creation of the tumuli piled on top of earlier tombs; if so, this may represent a compromise between a 'mound' tradition of tomb superstructure and the development of the new rectangular niched 'palace façade' *mastaba*/enclosure, which some scholars argue comes to a full flowering in King Djoser's step-pyramid complex in Dynasty 3.

Saqqara *Mastaba* 3505 (Figure 1.4) is dated to the reign of King Ka'a, last ruler of Dynasty 1, and therefore the latest in this group. It represents a distinct break with the earlier *mastaba*s in a number of important respects. Superficially it looks the same, a large niched mudbrick *mastaba,* but the interior of the *mastaba* is not filled with storerooms but is solid. The underground burial apartments are accessed via a stairway on the east side of the *mastaba,* but the *mastaba* is within an enclosure, marked by a surrounding mudbrick wall. A remarkable object was found close to the southern end of the eastern wall of the *mastaba,* a limestone stela 1.73 m tall naming and depicting a high official called Merika. There has been much debate over this object (Bestock 2007: 102): Emery thought it belonged to a nearby subsidiary burial and that the *mastaba* was the tomb of King Ka'a himself, while other later scholars, led by Kemp (1967; this view is not universally shared – see Morris 2007b: 171), believe it to name the owner of the *mastaba* himself and that the stela originally occupied one of the nearby niches, in a position which would become standard in later

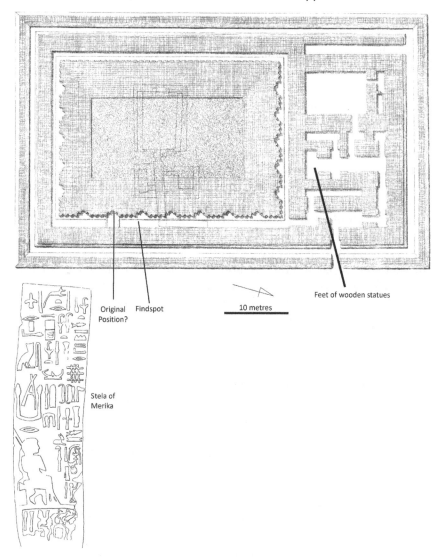

Figure 1.4 Saqqara *Mastaba* 3505 (adapted from Emery 1958: Pl. 2)

mastaba-tombs. But the tomb complex of *Mastaba* 3505 also housed another important structure, a multi-roomed mudbrick building built immediately to the north of the *mastaba* which it is tempting, based on parallels with later structures, to think of as a funerary temple/offering chapel, particularly as one of the rooms within this building contained the feet of a pair of standing wooden statues which, in later *mastaba*s, one would expect to be figures of the tomb owner, provided as a focus for offerings. It may be that *Mastaba* 3505 provided the prototype for later elite tombs of the Early Dynastic and Old Kingdom, not just in the early emergence of specific architectural features and stelae/statues but, much more fundamentally, in the abandonment of the idea of the tomb as being self-sufficient in stored food; instead it was to provide an appropriate reception point for the Living to bring food for the Dead.

This might be regarded as a triumph of the design model of Tarkhan 1845. It is certainly the case that the bipartite tomb – Burial Chamber and Offering Chapel – despite sometimes radically different local variants, and the over-layering of other requirements, became the model for almost all Egyptian tombs which followed for the next 3,000 years. In essence, the Burial Chamber is the place where the body, once interred, is intended to be left in peace. The Offering Chapel, in marked contrast, is designed to be a busy place, where the Living came to leave offerings – particularly food offerings – for the Dead. These two factors – a secure Burial Chamber and an accessible Offering Chapel – are the essential elements of tomb design. But underlying all of these architectural developments is a set of basic questions which still need to be answered. What happens to an individual after death? What is the relationship between the Dead and the Divine? What is the relationship between the Dead and the Living?

The Human Spirit (1): The Ka

The Egyptians have left us with a mass of evidence which relates to their answers to these three questions. Unfortunately their answers are not necessarily simple or consistent. This is perhaps to be expected since we are talking about the evolution of religious beliefs over 3,000 years, but the Egyptians' attitude to the afterlife, and indeed to the spiritual nature of humans in general, is also confusingly sophisticated.

The first point to note is that the Egyptians did not have a unitary view of the spiritual component of a human being. That is to say, they did not believe that a human being had a single 'soul' or 'spirit', but a cluster of spiritual entities, each with a different nature and different potential. Death caused the disaggregation of this bundle of spiritual entities, releasing them to their own specific afterlives. The unitary concept of the soul is one which is perhaps taken for granted by most people in the West and the debate regarding the afterlife centres on what happens to this single spiritual form. Is it reincarnated? Does it go to a much better (or much worse) place? Does it roam the world in an incorporeal state? Does it exist at all? For the Egyptians the multiple possibilities provided by the multiplicity of personal spiritual forms were a source of varied opportunities for a beneficial afterlife, but also multiple potential problems.

Another factor which needs to be taken into consideration is the ways in which expectations of an afterlife changed over time. Although there was no fundamental revolution in the ways the Egyptians viewed the afterlife, there was a gradual agglomeration of possibilities – new possibilities were added to older ones without necessarily replacing them. In particular, ideas which began as solely royal prerogatives filtered down to the population at large. By the New Kingdom a private individual could look forward to a kaleidoscopic existence after death compared to the more restricted range of opportunities available to his or her Old Kingdom predecessor. This evolution of possibilities is one of the drivers behind changes to the form of the tomb itself, its decoration and its contents.

The starting point for an examination of the spiritual entities which were released on death is the *k3* (*ka*), a word which is incorporated within the names of three of the individuals who owned elite Dynasty 1 Saqqara *mastaba*s: Hemaka, Ankhka and Merika. The *ka* as a spiritual entity remained of fundamental importance throughout Egyptian history, even when other expectations of the afterlife had developed (Bolshakov 1997). It was the entity which, in essence, determined the basic nature of the bipartite tomb as a place for the protection of the body and for interaction with the Living. It is often difficult to directly render into a simple word or phrase the religious or cultural concepts of different cultures. The *ka* is just such a concept. It might be defined as the 'life force' or 'spiritual essence' of a person, their 'spiritual double'. The word *ka* was usually written using a sign of two upraised arms, perhaps a sign of a person being embraced or protected by their *ka*, and the term is related to words for 'food' and is connected to the idea of sexual potency (Bolshakov 1997: 159–63). This indicates that the *ka* was rooted not in an ethereal existence beyond the limits of physical existence, but very much in the real world of the human body and its needs. It can best be summoned up by the idea of 'vital energy'; as such, a superhuman individual such as a god or a king could have more than one *ka*. The *ka*-force of the king was sometimes shown as a separate entity, and often identified with the god Horus. An important New Kingdom ceremony which was concerned with the rejuvenation of the king – the Opet Festival – saw the merging of the god Amen-Re with the *ka* of the king at Luxor Temple (Bell 1985). The origin of the *ka* seems to have been as a person's inner force, yet was also connected to their essential personality or even their destiny. But the Egyptians were skilled in taking spiritual entities and personifying them. A good example of this process is the concept of *maat*, the idea of rightness, justice, the antithesis of chaos – very much an intangible concept but one which was coalesced into the figure of the goddess Maat, a woman with an ostrich feather as her emblem. Other divine concepts were given personifications, but so too were human spiritual attributes, most importantly the *ka*. The 'inner *ka*' was personified as the 'external *ka*', a spiritual entity which, on death, became a quasi-independent entity separate from, yet connected to, the human body which it had inhabited.

But, although a spiritual entity, the *ka* was intimately connected to the body, not just in life, but also after death, when the direct link created at birth between the physical and spiritual had been broken. Crucially, the Egyptians chose to view the external *ka* as having a range of possibilities and limitations which it had shared with its living being/host: a body as a physical host, the sustenance of food and drink, a home in which to live. These limitations meant that the *ka* did not leave the physical world, but dwelt within it: although a spiritual form, it continued to need a physical host, ideally the body; although a spiritual form, it required sustenance in the form of food and drink. Other requirements, or desires, for a beneficial afterlife would follow, but the core need of the *ka* as a spiritual entity requiring physical necessities was one of the major factors which dictated the attitude of the Egyptians towards the Dead, including the form and use of the tomb as the place where the necessary ongoing relationship between the Living and the Dead was crystallized. This is obvious from the way in which the tomb developed during the Old Kingdom; it is also obvious from the term used by Egyptians of the Old Kingdom to refer to the tomb – *pr k3* – 'house of the *ka*'. Arguably, the tomb owner who is depicted on the walls of a non-royal tomb is not the living person but their *ka*. In this context it is important to note the stress which was also placed on the survival of the name, the *rn* (*rn*), as a vital component of the self. A tomb which was heavily labelled with the name(s) and titles of its owner provided an important means by which this could be achieved, and the labelled depiction of the tomb owner on its walls provided 'equipollent' attestations of the *ka* and the *rn* in image and text (Bolshakov 1997: 155). This combination was to become particularly important in the case of statuary within the tomb.

The Tomb as a House for the Ka

Therefore the Archaic Period and Early Old Kingdom saw the experimentation with the form of the tomb as a place of interaction between the Living and the Dead, driven by the nature of the *ka*, and centred on the Offering Chapel. However, it also saw a similar, if less extensive, period of experimentation with the form of the inner parts of the tomb – the Burial

Chamber(s) – in order to try to answer an important question: if the tomb was the house of the *ka*, how house-like should it be? This question was to have slightly different answers at different times, mostly revolving round the idea of a superficially house-like appearance to the tomb in which the Burial Chambers were small and simple and the Offering Chapel comparatively large and complex, but in Dynasties 2–3 attempts were made to create underground suites of rooms for tombs with the intention to re-create a multi-roomed house-like environment (Scharff 1947) which was isolated from access by the Living by one, and sometimes more, massive stone portcullis(es). This form of tomb was, by its nature, created

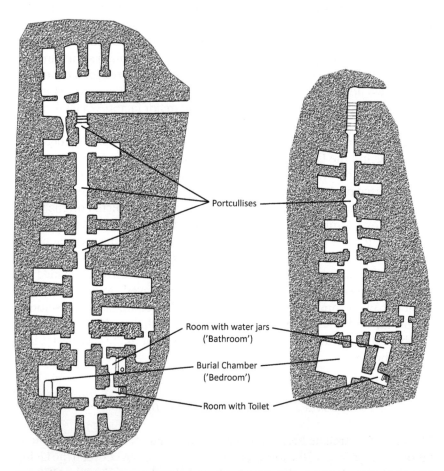

Portcullises

Room with water jars
('Bathroom')

Burial Chamber
('Bedroom')

Room with Toilet

Figure 1.5   The underground rooms of the Saqqara 'house' tombs S.2302 (left) and S.2337 (right) (adapted from Quibell 1923: Pl. 30 – no scale on the original plans, but S.2302 is approximately 60 m long)

for a small elite who owned both large multi-roomed houses and the tombs which replicated them, and this form of tomb was a relatively limited phenomenon found at Saqqara (for a provincial exception at Reqaqna see Garstang 1904), mostly excavated by Quibell in 1912–14 (Quibell 1923). Attempts to attribute specific functions to specific rooms in these tombs (Figure 1.5) are problematic (Bolshakov 1997, 29–30; Quibell 1923; Scharff 1947), although the identification of the smallest room in the *mastaba*, containing a lavatory, is unmistakable.

CHAPTER 2

Pits, Palaces and Pyramids

Royal Cemeteries of the Early Dynastic Period and Old Kingdom

ᒧᒧᒧᒧ

Royal Tombs of Dynasty 1

In the period between 4000 and 3000 BC the archaeology of Egypt, especially southern Egypt, provides evidence for a number of important developments which ultimately led to the emergence of a politically unified state around 3100 BC (Wengrow 2006; Wilkinson 1999). These developments include an increasing development of an agricultural economy, the growth of urban centres, increasing social stratification and the display of that social stratification by the emergent elites, including quasi-royal figures at what seem to be the capital cities of emerging mini-kingdoms, such as Naqada, Hierakonpolis and Abydos.

This royal display can be seen in the massive use of mudbrick architecture in these royal centres and also in the creation and deposition of high-value objects which, at their best, can be seen as works of art created by skilled craftsmen, sometimes using exotic materials. Some of these depositions took place in temple structures, and can be regarded as part of the emerging ideology of kingship, and the graphic display of that ideology: the famous Narmer Palette, which was found in the temple area at Hierakonpolis, showing Narmer wearing the regalia of a king of Upper and Lower Egypt smiting a defeated enemy before a god or gods, was a motif which would have been instantly recognizable to an Egyptian 2,000 years later. But although these early temple sites are important in providing evidence of the late Predynastic and Early Dynastic periods, the main archaeological sources for this period are cemeteries.

Ancient Egyptian Tombs: The Culture of Life and Death   By Steven Snape
© 2011 Steven Snape

The identification of important regional centres from this period has been made by archaeologists on the basis of the survival of prestige buildings, usually the result of the use of mudbrick on a monumental scale. Some of these buildings consist of massive enclosure walls to sacred areas or defended urban centres such as the 'fort' at Hierakonpolis. Another monumental use of mudbrick was in the creation of massive, low, rectangular superstructures for tombs with underground burial chambers, the *mastaba* form which was later used for elite Dynasty 1 tombs at Saqqara. The identity of the owners of these tombs at Predynastic sites such as Naqada is still much debated, but whether these were built for emerging royal individuals or not, they clearly mark a trend for the deployment of very significant resources into the creation of large tombs and equipping them with expensive and exotic goods.

By the end of the Predynastic Period there was a fundamental bifurcation between the nature and status of the king and that of the rest of the population of Egypt. Kingship was seen as a divine office, the king uniquely qualified to interact with the gods for the benefit of Egypt, and a being whose power was made manifest through royal buildings, including his tomb. What this meant in terms of the expectations of an afterlife for a Dynasty 1 king is difficult to say in any detail, but there is enough evidence to suggest that the differences between a royal and a non-royal afterlife, which are very evident in the Old Kingdom, began here. It is also possible that the development of royal tombs after the unification of Egypt was partly connected to the idea of appropriate displays of divine kingship in a mortuary setting, and that in the royal necropolis 'new features were successively added to the substructure, heightening the theatrical quality of the tomb as a setting for ritual action' (Wengrow 2006: 232).

One obvious manifestation of the difference between royal and non-royal burial is in the location of the royal cemetery. While most of the upper ruling class of Dynasty 1 Egypt were buried close to the new capital at Memphis, for kings of Dynasty 1, and some of Dynasty 2, the prime location for burial was at the southern site of Abydos. More specifically, the low desert mound of the Umm el-Qa'ab ('mother of pots' – so-called because of the scattered pottery sherds from the Dynasty 1 tombs and later offering pottery deposited at the site) was the desired location, possibly because it had already, by the beginning of Dynasty 1, achieved the status of an ancestral burial ground for kings with a southern origin. The royal tombs of Dynasty 1 at Abydos, although badly plundered (and possibly deliberately burnt) in antiquity, display the use of valuable and exotic raw materials both for architectural elements – granite from Aswan, cedar wood from Lebanon – and in the grave goods accompanying the burial – gold and semi-precious stone from the Eastern Desert, Palestinian wine. Perhaps the

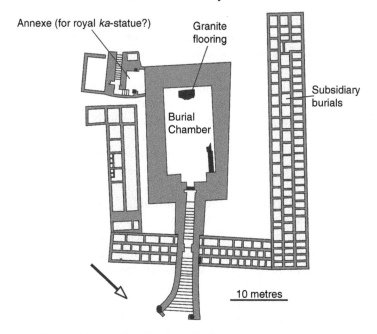

Figure 2.1   Plan of the tomb of Den at Abydos

most impressive of these tombs is that of Den (Figure 2.1), which was provided with an entrance stairway (unlike earlier 'pit' tombs), a granite floor to the burial chamber and, unique at the Umm el-Qa'ab, a separate annexe which may have been used for a *ka*-statue of the king similar to the later *serdab* in the Djoser complex at Saqqara.

However the tombs themselves, within the physical constraints of the Umm el-Qa'ab cemetery, are comparatively small, particularly in comparison with contemporary non-royal elite tombs at Saqqara, which, as we have noted, led Emery to his conclusion that the Saqqara tombs were the real burial places of the kings of Dynasty 1, with the Abydos structures being 'cenotaphs', or dummy tombs. It is also the case that the superstructures of the Umm el-Qa'ab tombs are very badly preserved, but are unlikely to have been significantly more substantial than a simple mound piled over the tomb, and therefore superficially unimpressive as monuments to royal power. However, the so-called 'North Cemetery' at Abydos (see Figure 2.2) also contains funerary monuments belonging to these early kings. The largest of these enormous mudbrick enclosures, still visible today, is the Shunet es-Zebib, which belongs to King Khasekhemwy of Dynasty 2, measuring 130×70 m and over 10 m in height. The function of these structures, although the subject of much scholarly speculation, remains

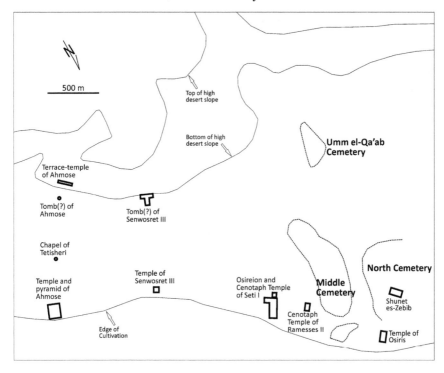

Figure 2.2 Plan of the Cemetery Area at Abydos

unknown, as do any ideas regarding the afterlife which the king was expected to enjoy. This is an important gap in our knowledge from a period when our understanding of non-royal afterlife beliefs is improving. It may be that these rectangular enclosures are intended to represent the royal palace within which the king was expected to exist for eternity, an idea which it is possible to see being developed in the Dynasty 3 step-pyramid complex of King Djoser. The discovery in 1990 (O'Connor 2009: 183–194) of a series of full-size boat burials arranged around the Shunet es-Zebib is also capable of a number of interpretations, from a royal fleet available for the king should he wish to leave his palace to a funerary flotilla to convey him to an afterlife beyond this world.

Certainly by the Old Kingdom it is clear that the royal afterlife was fundamentally different to that of everyone else, but the extent to which these ideas were already present in Dynasties 1 and 2 is obscure. One piece of evidence which might support the idea of royal differentness in the Early Dynastic Period is the retainer burials around the main royal tomb at the Umm el-Qa'ab, including that of Den, which some scholars have argued represent sacrificial burials of low-status servants, women and dogs to accompany the dead king (Morris 2007a). If this is the case, then the king is certainly different to everyone else, but it is also a short-lived phenomenon – retainer sacrifice was not practised in Dynastic Egypt, and wherever it was that a major Old Kingdom pyramid builder such as Snefru or Khufu went to from the starting point of his pyramid he went alone.

Stairway to Heaven? The Royal Step Pyramid

Dynasty 2 presents a confused picture in terms of the development of royal tombs. This is partly because Dynasty 2 is a little-understood period anyway, which may have included a period of civil war, and even the names and order of kings is far from clear. There seem to be a series of kings who were buried in tombs at Saqqara which had underground galleries, but no surviving superstructures (Wilkinson 1999: 240–43 and refs cit.). The end of the dynasty seems to see a return to Abydos, with the burial there of kings Peribsen and Khasekhemwy, the latter being the owner of the Shunet es-Zebib funerary enclosure. One intriguing piece of evidence comes in the form of a small granite statue of a kneeling priest named Hetepdief, now in the Cairo Museum, on whose shoulder are carved the names of three Dynasty 2 kings – Hetepsekhemwy, Nebra and Ninetjer – and it is likely that Hetepdief is an early example of a phenomenon which becomes very common during the Old Kingdom: a priest who serves the mortuary cult/cults of dead kings or private individuals.

The beginning of Dynasty 3 saw a decisive move to the Memphite necropolis, especially Saqqara, as the location for royal burial. Although this period has more than its fair share of unfinished and enigmatic potential royal tombs, it also has one of the great landmark (in every sense) buildings of the ancient world, the step-pyramid complex of King Djoser. Like many royal and private tombs, Djoser's pyramid is a combination of innovation and tradition. Many of its features can be seen in earlier buildings, including the rectangular, 'palace façade' enclosure-wall itself, which appears to be heavily influenced by mudbrick enclosures such as the Shunet es-Zebib at Abydos. The buildings within Djoser's enclosure are frustratingly lacking in explanatory texts, but a large open court to the south of the pyramid seems to be a *heb-sed*, or jubilee, court containing two pairs of symbolic cairns; the *heb-sed* was a festival which was connected to the rejuvenation of the king and the renewal of his kingship. To the east of the pyramid are a series of solid, dummy buildings which might represent important shrines in different parts of Egypt. Immediately to the north of the pyramid is a mortuary temple which could have been used for offerings to the dead king within the pyramid, and which included a small chamber, sealed apart from two eye-holes, which contained a life-size seated statue of Djoser. These different elements, and others within the complex, seem to hint at a variety of possibilities for the afterlife of the king, which might include the creation of a symbolic 'mini Egypt' over which the dead king might rule for eternity, and also locations where an offering cult to the dead king could be carried out by the living. It may be that none of this is very new, and that elements of this conception of an afterlife(s) can be seen in the tomb of Den at the Umm el-Qa'ab or in the Shunet es-Zebib, but the rendering of these ideas on such a scale (the complex measures 545 × 277 m) represents a startling development, as does the extensive use of stone to create what is, in essence, the first monumental stone building in the world. Djoser's complex, close enough to the edge of the escarpment at Saqqara to be visible for many miles, is also a statement of visible royal power. Like the later pyramid builders of Dynasty 4, Djoser's achievement was to create a structure which became part of the landscape.

But the most striking element of Djoser's complex is, of course, the pyramid itself (Figure 2.3). The technology of its construction shows a series of individual phases, moving from the familiar to the experimental. The first phase was the construction of a well-known form – a *mastaba* with a shaft running underground to a burial chamber and surrounding storage

Figure 2.3   The Step Pyramid of Djoser at Saqqara

galleries – but in a new building material, limestone. After the enlargement of the *mastaba*, the decision was taken to grow the tomb upwards by creating first a four- and then a six-stepped structure. Whether this had always been the intention or whether it was a sudden decision after the *mastaba* neared completion is not known; the Egyptians themselves credited this invention to Djoser's architect, Imhotep. The significance of the step-pyramid form is not immediately obvious, apart from its role as a horizon-dominating object over 60 m in height. It may be that its origins lie in the architectural formalization of the ancient tumulus seen in Saqqara *Mastaba* 3507 or, even more strikingly, in Saqqara *Mastaba* 3038 (Figure 2.4), which dates to the reign of Anedjib in Dynasty 1 and which is, in effect, a combination of two superstructures: a stepped 'mound' and a niched 'palace façade' enclosure. It may also be that with the step pyramid the cosmological significance of the ancient mound becomes clear or that it represents a new set of expectations of an afterlife away from the tomb. The latter explanation seems more likely given that the pyramid form is, during the Old Kingdom, a uniquely royal prerogative and that any wider expectations it represents are those of the king alone. This is not, however, a question which is capable of unambiguous resolution, and it is one which becomes complicated by the development of a new type of pyramid and, arguably more importantly, a new type of pyramid complex half a century later.

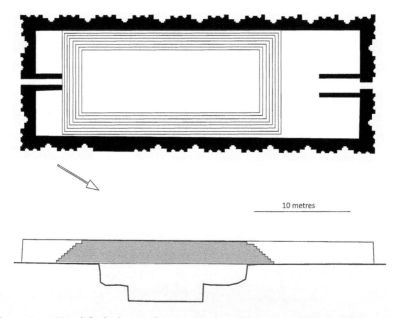

10 metres

Figure 2.4   Simplified plan and cross-section of Saqqara *Mastaba* 3038

The Rise of the True Pyramid

The building of Djoser's step-pyramid complex is an obvious indication that Egyptian kings were willing to embrace new materials and new technology in order to create impressively large and complex mortuary monuments. However, it is far from adequate warning that, after a series of short-lived kings with largely unfinished building projects, the end of Dynasty 3 and the beginning of Dynasty 4 would see, within the space of three or four generations of kings, the creation of five of the largest structures to be built before the twentieth century, including the iconic Great Pyramid of King Khufu at Giza. This period has many problems that are very specific (Why did Snefru build two pyramids at Dahshur? Is he or his (probable) father Huni largely responsible for the pyramid at Meidum?) or more general (What factors dictate the specific locations of Old Kingdom pyramids?), and which continue to baffle Egyptologists. Equally unanswerable is a very obvious question: why did they need to be so big? It is tempting to relate the size of a pyramid to its role as an expression of royal power and its legacy of landscape-altering permanence rather than a greater efficacy in its use in achieving a royal afterlife, but this is nothing more than a guess since Dynasty 4 pyramids are frustratingly mute regarding their function. This question might be approached from a different angle: if not the size, is there anything about the shape of the true, straight-sided pyramid which made it more desirable in Dynasty 4 than the step pyramid of Dynasty 3? This is a question best returned to when we have more supporting evidence, later in the Old Kingdom.

Another puzzling issue is that of the internal rooms within the pyramid. Among the five largest Dynasty 4 pyramids (assuming the Meidum pyramid is the work of Snefru and not his predecessor Huni), three (Meidum, Snefru's 'red pyramid' at Dahshur, Khaefre's pyramid at Giza) have very simple internal arrangements consisting of little more than an entrance corridor which makes its way from the north face of the pyramid to a modestly sized burial chamber which is cut into the bedrock underneath the pyramid, or at ground level. This is the format which is followed by most later Old Kingdom pyramids. However, Snefru's 'bent pyramid' at Dahshur and Khufu's pyramid at Giza have much more complicated internal arrangements consisting of multiple internal rooms and corridors and (in the case of the 'bent pyramid') multiple entrances. The reasons for these differences are not obvious, especially since there is no obvious chronological development and, in the case of Snefru, we have a king who has pyramids of both the simple and complicated internal form. It is conceivable, as noted by Stadelmann (1997), that there is an interplay between the relative simplicity or otherwise of the internal chambers of the pyramid and that of the mortuary temple attached to the pyramid, possibly as alternative venues for ritual connected with the burial of the king. Whatever the case, this theory points us in the direction of another important aspect of the evolution of the pyramid complex in Dynasty 4: the changes to the buildings adjacent to the pyramid as well as the pyramid itself.

In some ways the changes to the pyramid complex between Dynasties 3 and 4 are even more radical than those to the pyramid itself. The rectangular, self-contained enclosure of the step pyramid, with the royal tomb sitting in the middle of a series of surrounding structures, is abandoned in favour of a complex which is much less isolated and much more connected to the Egypt of the living. The 'true pyramid complex' consisted of a series of basic elements: the pyramid itself built on the desert escarpment, a mortuary temple built against the east side of the pyramid, a covered causeway running from the mortuary temples down from the escarpment to the edge of the Nile floodplain, and a valley building which acted as a reception area for the complex as a whole. The valley building and the causeway may have been specifically designed for the funeral of the king, but they also, like the mortuary temple, had an enduring role to play in the continued use of the complex. Variations to this basic format did occur, and other elements regularly appeared, including a smaller subsidiary pyramid (function unknown) and pits for the burial of full-sized boats, but the standard elements of the complex remained essentially unaltered until the demise of the pyramid as a royal tomb at the end of the Middle Kingdom.

Offerings for the King: Peopling the Pyramid Complex

Despite the problems associated with interpreting the pyramid as a royal vehicle for salvation in Dynasty 4, other ways by which the pyramid complex could serve the needs of the dead king become rather clearer. The afterlife of the king at or within the pyramid can be thought of in two distinct ways, the first being means by which the pyramid itself acted as a portal to a life beyond the tomb. The second was the perpetual existence of the king's multiple *ka*s within the pyramid in a manner very similar to that of the non-royal individuals we have already met at Tarkhan, since the king, like ordinary mortals, required the assistance of the living to ensure that his mortuary cult thrived in perpetuity, bringing the necessary food-offerings to the tomb.

The notion of a pyramid complex requiring a specific place for offering, which was outside the pyramid but as physically close to it as was possible, was present from the earliest examples. These might be small, simple locations such as that at Meidum pyramid or even that at the Khufu pyramid. However, most mortuary temples which came after that of Khaefre followed his example of providing a relatively large and multi-roomed structure. It might be argued that one of the general trends in pyramid building after the reign of Khufu was a diminution in the amount of resource which was invested in building the pyramid itself compared to an expansion of the effort put into building and, crucially, maintaining the mortuary temple. This is because pyramid complexes, like most Egyptian tombs, were not built to be forgotten, but were intended to be the scenes of intense activity centred on the interaction between the Living and the Dead for the benefit of the tomb-owner. The offerings required by the king were immense, and required the setting-up of extensive and complicated funerary estates. They also required the establishment of a system of organization for the numerous priestly staff who carried out the daily cult services at the pyramid complex.

The system used was one which was adopted from the terminology of ship's crews, perhaps especially the idea of that part of the crew that was on duty or 'watch' at any given time (Roth 1991). The total staff roster for the mortuary cult was divided into five, each sub-division being called a *sa* (*s3*), although the term more commonly used in Egyptology to refer to this group is the *phyle*, the Greek equivalent used in some bilingual Ptolemaic inscriptions referring to temple staffing. Our knowledge of how this system worked in practice comes from a number of administrative papyri discovered at Abusir which refer to the cultic operation of the Dynasty 5 pyramid complexes of kings Neferirkare and Neferefre (Posener-Kriéger 1976). In both cases the five *phyle* were each sub-divided into two, giving a total of 10 individual groups, of around 20 individuals, and each group served for one month at a time in a 10-month cycle. Therefore the *phyle* system was one of part-time employment, which is very much in keeping with the general ethos of the *ka*-priest. The duties of the *phyle*, as listed in the Abusir papyri, included daily processions around the pyramid, the servicing of the cult statues of the king within the mortuary temple, the guarding of the mortuary temple during the night, and, principally, the reception, storage and appropriate use of goods received from the pyramid's estates. This division of the staff of the pyramid complex into five or 10 groups is probably also reflected in the architecture of the mortuary temple itself. It is probably no coincidence that the mortuary temple which sets the basic standard in terms of design, layout and complexity for all subsequent Old Kingdom pyramids – that of Khaefre – includes a set of five storerooms. It is likely that each of these storerooms was used for the storage of the equipment used by each of the *phyle* to perform their duties. During the reign of Sahure the provision of ten storerooms became standard, the usual physical arrangement being in two groups of five facing each other across a central corridor or in parallel sets in different parts of the mortuary temple. This change from five to 10 storerooms suggests that the division of the five *phyle* to form 10 distinct units took place in the reign of Sahure.

There is one more way in which the pyramid complex was 'peopled'. An important aspect of the wider pyramid complex for kings such as Khufu and Khaefre was the 'town' composed of streets of *mastaba*-tombs arranged around the pyramid itself. These were the tombs of the courtiers who desired to be close to the king in death as in life and whose tombs incorporated design features which reflected the latest ideas about how a tomb could serve the needs of the tomb-owner in the Old Kingdom.

CHAPTER 3

Non-Royal Cemeteries of Dynasty 4

רJרJרJר

Dynasty 4 Mastabas at Giza

If royal tombs of Dynasty 4 have an enigmatic aspect to their specific purpose, non-royal tombs are much more informative. More specifically, those tombs which belonged to an admittedly very small proportion of the population – the literate elite who were able to afford tombs for themselves or have tombs provided for them – began to bear accompanying texts which explain how they were to be used. The places where these tombs are to be found are the royal cemeteries of the period, since the power of the kings of Dynasty 4, as demonstrated through their mortuary provision, was not limited to the pyramid complex itself but also extended to effectively making the tombs of their courtiers part of the design of the royal pyramid cemetery. It seems likely that *mastaba* cemeteries at Giza were initially planned as streets of broadly similar tombs which developed a more individual character only after they were distributed to specific members of the royal court (Der Manuelian 1998); although, as we shall see, there are several texts in which tomb-owners refer to the granting of a tomb as a more considered act of royal favour towards them. Unsurprisingly the largest pyramid – that of Khufu – is the best example of this, where rows and rows of essentially standardized, yet individually differentiated, *mastaba*-tombs were built around the royal tomb. *Mastaba* design had moved on since the end of Dynasty 1, but the basic conception of the tomb as reflected in its architecture was essentially the same as that of Saqqara *Mastaba* 3507, in that the basic form of the *mastaba*-tomb was an underground Burial Chamber with a solid rectangular block as the superstructure. Most

Ancient Egyptian Tombs: The Culture of Life and Death   By Steven Snape
© 2011 Steven Snape

attention was focused on the east side of the *mastaba* – the side facing the Living – with variations on the niches being elaborated into small chapels. At Meidum the elite tombs which accompanied the pyramid there, built for members of Snefru's family (particularly those of Rahotep and Nofret, and Nefermaat and Atet – Harpur 2001), show the niches being developed into small internal chapels of cruciform shape. But it is at Giza that the most significant developments took place during Dynasty 4, in tombs which are paradoxically very standardized and yet increasingly individual in character.

Although each tomb displays minor variations in form, it is possible to describe a 'standard design' Dynasty 4 *mastaba* at Giza based on the many examples excavated in the Khufu cemeteries by Junker (1929–55). This standardized *mastaba* (Figure 3.1) has a low solid superstructure, rectangular in plan, with slightly battened limestone walls casing a rubble core.

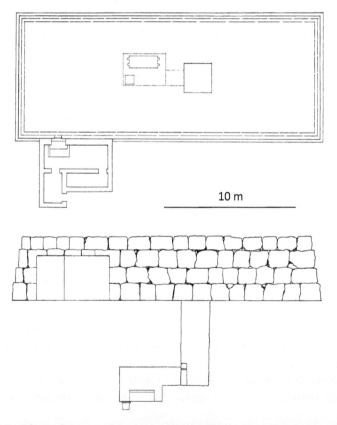

Figure 3.1 Plan (above) and cross-section (below) of a 'standard' Dynasty 4 *mastaba* at Giza (adapted from Junker 1929–55 (Vol. I): Figs 3–4)

A small external chapel of two/three rooms encloses a 'false door' or stela which is located at the southern end of the eastern external face of the *mastaba*. A single shaft runs vertically through the body of the *mastaba* into the bedrock below. At the base of this shaft is the entrance to the Burial Chamber, usually little bigger than the stone sarcophagus it is designed to contain, and in the floor is a niche for a canopic chest which contained the internal organs removed during mummification. The Burial Chamber is located on the southern side of the shaft, an orientation which puts the Burial Chamber as close as is reasonably possible to being directly underneath the small Offering Chapel. The fundamental nature of the tomb is therefore reflected in an architecture which conceptually connects the physically separate Burial Chamber and Offering Chapel. The intended inaccessibility of the Burial Chamber and the intended accessibility of the Offering Chapel are further stressed by elements which become more important within them, particularly the way in which the Offering Chapel is increasingly filled with texts, 2-D illustrations and statues which refine its functions, specifically as a house for the *ka*.

Tombs and Houses in Old Kingdom Egypt

In referring to the tomb as the 'House of the *Ka*', the Egyptians were making a natural equation. Just as the Living existed within specific physical limitations, so did the *ka*. In fact the *ka*'s limits were even greater than those of the Living, since it was effectively constrained within the tomb. Nevertheless the tomb could be a place of comfort, shelter and sustenance for the *ka*, just as the Living found those things in their homes. Clearly the tomb was not an ordinary type of house, nor could it be, given the special nature of its occupant, but the conceptualization of the tomb was firmly fixed within the realm of domestic comfort while, wherever possible, the physical nature of the house was replicated within the tomb, as we have seen in the underground rooms of some elite *mastaba*s of Dynasties 2 and 3. Even the most accessible part of the pyramid complex – the royal mortuary temple – is like a royal audience hall with restricted access. Private cemeteries were more like villages of houses with a similar bustle of activity around them; indeed the cemetery could be referred to by the most common word for town, *niwt*, as in a text on a block from the cemetery associated with the pyramid of Khufu at Giza, where the tomb-owner states, 'I have made this tomb in this town (*niwt*) of my Lord' (Strudwick 2005: 322).

It is difficult today to assess the extent to which a tomb, viewed from the outside, actually looked like an ordinary Egyptian house. The first problem is the lack of ordinary Egyptian houses with which to compare our rather magnificent data-set of surviving tombs. The second problem is a natural assumption that, given the appearance of these tombs, their close relationship to anything a living person might wish to live in seems improbable. However, one of the few places where Old Kingdom private housing survives to any significantly reconstructable degree is in the town attached to the tomb of Queen Khentkawes I at Giza. It is likely that these houses were occupied by priests involved in the funerary cult of the queen; if so, these are people who are not elite owners of major *mastabas*, but they are people of some status. These houses, as reconstructed by Felix Arnold (1998), consist of tightly packed rectangular rooms and courtyards, with differential roof height providing opportunities for limited clerestory lighting. These are houses which are designed primarily as refuges from the most severe aspect of Egyptian weather – the sometimes overwhelming heat and brightness of the sun. Their external appearance may well have been as geometrically 'blocky' as Arnold's reconstruction suggests, with white-washed walls. If so, they may not have appeared strikingly different from the appearance of some Old Kingdom *mastabas*, particularly those of the later part of the Old Kingdom such as that of Niankhkhnum and Khnum-hotep (Figure 3.2) with its 'blocky' appearance, portico entrance, inner courtyard and dark, cool interior rooms. However, even if this somewhat tenuous connection in external appearance between Old Kingdom houses

Figure 3.2 The *mastaba* of Niankhkhnum and Khnumhotep at Saqqara

and Old Kingdom tombs is ignored, it is clear that the conceptualization of the tomb as a functional space was based on that of the house. It had private apartments accessible only to the householder (i.e. bedrooms) or tomb-owner (Burial Chamber) and it had spaces for entertaining which were designed for social interaction around meals with invited guests. There is, however, one significant difference between the social interaction of dining in houses and tombs, which is that in the case of the tomb it is the guests who should provide the food, not the host.

False Doors and Real Offerings

Tomb Tarkhan 1845 provides us with an early example of an Offering Chapel – a place designed for the Living to bring offerings for the Dead, and with a physical connection to the Burial Chamber (two small slits in the brickwork) which only the Dead could use. Saqqara *Mastaba* 3507 provides an elaboration of that basic idea by using the exterior of the *mastaba* and the building to the north of it as places where specific objects could be located (a stela and statues) which could also serve as potential points of connection between the Living and the Dead as well as being important indicators of ownership of the tomb. Dynasty 4 *mastaba*s at Giza continued the development of this idea, particularly in the creation of a focal point within the Offering Chapel which could serve as an identifier of tomb ownership, a request for offerings, and a magical substitute should those offerings not appear. This focal point was a painted slab of limestone, a stela, bearing an image of the tomb-owner sitting in front of a table of offerings, with a text listing the food offerings which were required for the named (and appropriately titled) tomb-owner. This slab-stela developed into something more appropriate to the part of the tomb where the *ka* could enter the Offering Chapel from the underground Burial Chamber, a 'false door' stela (Strudwick 1985: 9–52; Wiebach 1981; Figure 3.3). The term 'false door' is something of a misnomer because although most false door stelae were set into the wall of the Offering Chapel behind which was nothing more than solid masonry or rubble fill, and were therefore unusable by the Living, they were, crucially, a viable portal for the *ka*. The false door stela is, in some ways, very indicative of how the Egyptians viewed the relationship between the Living and the Dead and the physical requirements of each. Even spiritual entities needed physical prompts which allowed them to interact with the living world, while the Living needed specific places at which such interaction would take place. Indeed, while the ubiquitous presence of name and titles of the stela-owner (and, in more elaborate examples, members of his family) appear to suggest a commemorative

Figure 3.3 The (unfinished) False Door of the Lady Wadjkawes from her tomb in the Unas Causeway Cemetery at Saqqara

aspect to the false door, and therefore make it seem like one of our contemporary funerary monuments, it is much more likely that the intention is simply to make it absolutely clear just who is to benefit from the functional aspects of the false door. These functional aspects are basically concerned with the main concern of the *ka*-spirit: to maintain a perpetual supply for food.

The problem of ensuring this perpetual supply of food is the most serious faced by the tomb-owner and one which was capable of a number of solutions, some more ideal than others. Hieroglyphic texts from false door stelae, and other parts of the tomb, are quite explicit about what they want to happen at the tomb. The ideal situation would be that real food and drink would be brought to the tomb by a living person, so that the *ka* could extract whatever nourishment it required from what was brought. The problem was how to ensure that this would be done, and done for eternity; since the *ka* was an everlasting spiritual entity with everlasting physical needs, it was essential that the systems set up to supply those needs were robust and self-perpetuating.

The first solution was to make the provision of offerings for the Dead a family and social responsibility. The idea of the son burying his father permeates the Egyptian view of the obligations the Living owed to the Dead. Providing food offerings for one's immediate and distant ancestors was regarded as a fundamental obligation. The perpetuation of this system was, of course, also in the interests of the Living if they too were ultimately to benefit from the beneficence of the Living when they too 'went to their *kas*'. This familial/social aspect of offering to the Dead, while presumably open to acts of personal piety towards the Dead, seems to have been given a broader social context around the idea of specific holidays and festivals during which it was seem as normal to spend time with the Dead, perhaps sharing food at the tomb. Lists of festivals at which the Dead would be expected to be fed sometimes form part of the list of requirements at the tomb itself. The tomb of Bia at Saqqara asks that offerings be made to him '[a]t the First of the Year-Festival, at the Opening of the Year-Festival, at the Festival of Thoth, at the *Wag*-Festival, at the Festival of Sokar, and at the Great Festival' (Strudwick 2005: 270).

There were, of course, a series of potential problems with this system based on family and social obligation. A descendant might not feel the obligation as keenly as one might wish; more fundamentally, the family line might die out with no suitable descendant to honour their ancestral dead. It was obviously necessary to set up additional systems for the eventuality that the social obligation system failed, and this gave rise to the institution of the *ka*-priest.

Priests, Temples and Cults

The normal way in which a god was served in a temple in ancient Egypt was through the operation of cult offerings. There is a very striking parallel here between the way in which a god was treated and the way in which the Dead were treated. The god was given a physical reality through their image – their statue – and was served by treating the statue as though it were the god's body – washed and dressed by appropriately qualified priests. But the god was also seen as needing offerings, including food and drink, and their provision was an important part of the cult. The standard cult-priest – *ḥm-nṯr* (*hem-netjer*), literally 'god's servant' – was, in essence, part of the domestic staff of the god's household, and the temple the house of the god. This was not a mere phrase, in the way one might refer to a church, synagogue or mosque as being a 'house of god', in that an Egyptian god was literally thought of as living within the temple and being provided with the physical necessities that he or she required. In this respect the temple was conceptualized in the same way as a tomb: a physical 'house' to contain a spiritual entity given physical form. There were, of course, significant differences – the god was not limited to the temple in the same way that the *ka* was to the tomb – but the common source of ideas about the ways in which spiritual entities were to be treated – the human experience of the real world – is striking.

In the Old Kingdom, priestly activity was, for the most part, a regular but short-term obligation imposed on members of the elite. It seems that serving for a given period in the temple of the local god was part of the normal portfolio of activity of provincial elites, and one with economic benefits. The offerings which were made to the god came primarily from resources owned by the god. At its simplest this might mean that a particular god would own a particular quantity of agricultural land, the produce of which (after deductions) would form the offerings in the temple. The deductions would include the portion of produce kept by the peasants who worked the land. In reality this land and its produce, the property of the god, would be part of the divine estate administered by the staff of the temple of the god. But there was one further critical factor. The Egyptians did not customarily practise the burning of offerings to release their essence for divine use. Instead it seems that the act of offering in specific designated places within the temple was enough for the god to extract whatever they needed. This would, of course, leave the food offerings superficially un-changed as far as human use was concerned and left them available for the 'Reversion of Offerings'. This system allowed the food to be 'consumed' by the god, but also passed on to the priests serving the god as their payment for making the offerings. In this way, as well as a being a religious duty, the operation of the cult of a god brought with it practical benefits for the priests concerned. This system was also used by kings to create a substantial real estate portfolio for their own mortuary cult: for instance, at Dahshur, King Snefru listed estates all over Egypt whose produce would flow to the pyramid complex in order to provide offerings for the dead king and to pay the priesthood which served the cult of that king.

Ka-*Priests and Funerary Estates*

The 'Reversion of Offerings' system which could serve the needs of temple gods and royal mortuary cults could also, albeit on a smaller scale, provide offerings for the tomb-owner without relying on the beneficence of future generations. A grant of land made to the tomb would provide both food offerings and payment for the priests who brought it to the tomb and offered it to the *ka*. The people who would do this – *ka*-priests – would derive a modest but worthwhile income from this office, which could be held at the same time as other administrative or priestly employment, or perhaps as one of a portfolio of *ka*-priesthoods for different tombs. This relationship was often emphasized by the depiction of specific, named *ka*-priests shown making offerings to the tomb-owner on the walls of the tomb where the offerings were intended to take place (Figure 3.4). The beauty of this system was that it did not rely on the charity of the Living towards the Dead, but was grounded in the self-interest of generations of *ka*-priests who found it worth their while to maintain the endowment for their own gain as well as that of the *ka*. The bequests to the tomb, and the duties of *ka*-priests in respect of these bequests, are sometimes specifically inscribed on the walls of the tomb as legal documents for all to see, for example in the Saqqara tomb of Niankhkhnum and Khnumhotep:

> As for these brothers and these *ka*-priests who deal with the offerings for us, and who act on our behalf in the necropolis; they shall not allow our children, our wives, or any people to have power over them. They are to deal with the offerings for us together with (those belonging to) our fathers and mothers who are in the necropolis. (Strudwick 2005: 194)

Figure 3.4 The Overseer of *ka*-priest(s) Qar makes an offering to the official Khenu in the latter's tomb in the Unas Causeway Cemetery at Saqqara

There was only one potential flaw in this system, which sensibly appealed to the self-interest of human nature. This was a fundamental reliance on the underlying stability provided by a system of law and property owner-ship which would prevent these estates from being detached from the tomb to which they had been bequeathed. The complicit self-interest of the Living (who would one day be dead) in the perpetuation of the system was one guarantee that this would be the case, but one thing that both kings and non-royals in the high Old Kingdom could not really anticipate was the utter collapse of established order in the First Intermediate Period, a time when, as we shall see, a fundamental revision in the attitude of non-royals to the afterlife was to take place.

Alternatives to the Ideal

Nonetheless, without anticipating the collapse of the complicated web of land-ownership at the end of the Old Kingdom, tombs of this period display a further level of pessimistic reality about what might or might not happen in the world of the Living to systems set up by the Dead. Alongside the ideal – the Living bringing real food to the tomb to feed the *ka* – other options were also created as failsafes if the ideal failed. The agency for these failsafes was magic.

For the Egyptians the written word itself was magic, having the power to create a reality by describing it. The spoken word was even more effective in creating what it described. The created realities need not be immediately visible. In fact, where interactions with the Dead were concerned, their effects were, by their very nature, invisible. While 'real' food was the ideal, food created by magical incantation was a good substitute. While a visitor to the tomb might not have brought food with them, the recitation of a spell to create food for the *ka* was a relatively simple thing. The first concern of the textual content of a tomb was the identification of its owner, closely followed by conventional texts which specified what was required for a visitor to the tomb to make a *prt ḫrw* (*peret kheru*), a 'Voice Offering', whose individual items were often listed. This list was largely conventional, particularly the food items 'bread and beer, flesh and fowl', but could be expanded to a wider range of wishes for a beneficial afterlife for the Dead. Sometimes the offering list was simply written as one of the texts inscribed on the false door stela, or other parts of the tomb, while on other occasions the potential reader is directly addressed, as in this example from the tomb of Khentika at Balat in the Dakhleh Oasis, where Khentika requests real offerings or, failing that, magical ones:

O you who live upon the earth and who shall pass by this tomb of mine. Those who love the king, especially any scribe, are those who will read out the writing on this stela and will give me bread and beer from that which you possess.

If you possess nothing then you shall make this pronouncement: 'A thousand loaves of bread and a thousand jars of beer for the boat captain and ruler of the oasis, Khentika'. (Strudwick 2005: 374)

As an encouragement to the passer-by, statements which portrayed the tomb-owner as a worthy individual who deserved such posthumous concern began to be added to the offering list, so Khentika goes on to say that he 'gave bread to the hungry, clothes to the naked and *merkhet*-oil to he who had none'. These brief statements were expanded in some tombs of the Late Old Kingdom into detailed autobiographies extolling the virtues of the tomb-owner, particularly the ways they served and gained the favour of the king.

A further level of security of food provision was provided by the depictions of food on the walls of the Offering Chapel which expanded beyond the central scene of the tomb-owner sitting at table to images of offering-bearers bringing choice cuts of meat, then to images of butchers preparing that meat. Ultimately this resulted in the depiction of extended scenes of landscapes where food was produced, landscapes which could also act as a 'virtual reality' parallel Egypt on the walls of the tomb to which the *ka* could have access. One of the major trends in tomb development during the Old Kingdom is the growth in size of the Offering Chapel, partly to provide the wall space required for this extended repertoire of tomb scenes in order to ensure the ultimate self-sufficiency of the *ka* within the tomb.

It might be asked at this point that, if images and lists of food could supply the Dead, why were the cumbersome and eminently fallible human-based systems continued? There are several answers to this question. One is that the models and images were back-up systems, but real food offerings were ideal. More fundamentally, the requirement of food offerings was the most obvious example of the way in which the Egyptians considered a continuing relationship between the Living and the Dead to be extremely important, and also the systems themselves provided important economic and social benefits to the Living who carried them out, as a source of redistributive income and an important social cement.

Acquiring a Tomb

Part of the social role of the tomb was as an indicator of status, particularly in relation to the king. The rows of *mastaba*-tombs at Giza suggest that these elite private tombs were, in addition to being individual vehicles for a pleasant afterlife, somehow connected to a wider royal project. It might be usefully asked at this point, how did an ancient Egyptian acquire a tomb? Here, we are once again primarily concerned with the tombs of the elite, since the acquisition of a tomb at village level was, we assume, a relatively straightforward matter involving the identification of an unused portion of the local cemetery and the marshalling of an adequate workforce to produce a simple tomb made of local materials. It is likely that this process did not take place until after the death of the tomb-owner, since their requirements could be met in a fairly limited timeframe, although it may be, for slightly more elaborate burials, that a pre-existing family tomb might be used. However, we need to remember once again that these guesses regarding tomb provision for the vast majority of the population of ancient Egypt are just that – guesses – since the archaeological record has not given us any significant evidence to reconstruct those processes with any degree of confidence.

In contrast, the elite of Old Kingdom Egypt, and especially those who lived and died around the king in the royal residence at Memphis – the participants in 'hieroglyphic culture' – had expectations of a provision for the afterlife far in excess of a peasant in the provinces. Those expectations were based on their position in society, which could, in a rather crude way, be thought of as reflecting their wealth – their personal control over economic assets – but also the degree to which they enjoyed the favour of the king. Royal favour was of paramount importance to the Memphite elite as a measure of status within the court hierarchy, which could be expressed as a statement of self-worth, presented on the walls of the tomb as a permanent memorialization of that favour. As Allen (2006: 13) puts it, '[T]he dominant sentiment of the Old Kingdom tomb biographies [is one] in which the individual's sense of personal identity and self-worth [is] measured in terms of his relationship to the king.' But there were also two practical elements to royal favour in the context of the tomb: the extent to which the king provided the tomb-owner with the tomb itself – or elements of it – was a practical marker of royal regard, as was the continued provisioning of the tomb. Statements of this type of royal favour appear within autobiographical texts in Memphite and provincial elite tombs of the Old Kingdom, although the evidence is too scattered and patchy to allow a completely coherent picture to emerge. The issue is discussed by Eyre (1987a) in an article which suggests some of the specific examples quoted in this chapter. The subject of royal versus private involvement in the building and provisioning of tombs is treated in detail by Chauvet (2004, 2007).

Perhaps the most interesting text from a tomb which describes the royal involvement in its creation is that belonging to Debehen at Giza (for a full translation of the texts from the tomb see Strudwick 2005: 271–2; it is also discussed by, *inter alia*, Alexanian 2006; Allen 2006; Chauvet 2004; Eyre 1987a).

> Concerning this tomb of mine, it was the King of Upper and Lower Egypt, Menkaure, who gave me its site, while he happened to be on the way to the pyramid plateau to inspect work being done on the pyramid of Menkaure.
>
> A royal decree was made for the overseer . . .. to make it, a tomb 100 cubits long by 50 cubits wide by 5 (or 8?) cubits [high].

The text, which is somewhat damaged, describes how the king arranged for various groups of workmen to come and build the tomb, even finding time to inspect the work himself. Among the specifically named elements of the tomb were 'a double false door and entrance doorway', 'a statue to receive offerings … it is finished on the desert with its statue-shrine', and 'two other statues which were authorized'.

This degree of apparent royal concern and involvement in providing a tomb for a courtier, or at least its detailed description, is unusual. Evidence of royal involvement in the basic construction of a tomb is hard to come by, with the possible exception of masonry marks on blocks from private tombs which mention royal work-gangs. In a discussion of this material, Eyre (1987a: 20) refers specifically to a Giza work-gang named after King Menkaure, but he also notes the reverse situation where masonry marks suggest work-gangs acting under the control of the tomb-owner or his subordinates, rather than the king. A more common situation is where the tomb-owner makes reference to the king providing particular parts of the tomb, especially elements which were made from types of stone which might be considered a royal monopoly. Perhaps the best example of this type of royal favour is described in the tomb of Weni at Abydos, who says;

> When I asked from the majesty of my Lord that a sarcophagus of white stone from [the limestone quarries at] Tura be provided for me, his majesty had the seal-bearer of the god and a boat crew under his command cross over [the river] and bring back this sarcophagus from Tura.
>
> He brought it himself in a great barge of the palace, together with its lid, a false door stela, an architrave, two jambs and an offering table.
>
> Never had the like been done for any servant. (Strudwick 2005: 353)

This sort of royal favour was important as an indicator of status in life, but it was also part of a wider provisioning of the tomb which would allow the tomb-owner to achieve a crucial state of being, that of an *imakhu*.

Being Imakhu

One of the most important desires of the tomb-owner, as stated in texts from Old Kingdom tombs, is to be an *imakhu* (*imȝḫw*). The late Dynasty 6 tomb of Bia, built close to the Unas Pyramid and that of Bia's employer the Vizier Mehu, although it now only survives as a group of fragmentary elements, makes several references to Bia being an *imakhu*:

> I am an excellent and true lector priest, and *imakhu* before his Lord...

> I am beloved by my father, favoured by my mother, an *imakhu* before his Lord every day. They used to say when they saw me coming in the door 'He is one who is truly *imakhu*'

> > The *imakhu* before Anubis ...
> > The *imakhu* before Osiris, lord of Busiris
> > The *imakhu* before the Great God, lord of the West;
> > The *imakhu* before Ptah-Sokar
> > > (Strudwick 2005: 270)

Bia also refers to himself as '[o]ne who has made the offerings and sought out the state of *imakhu*' and wishes to be 'among the *imakhu* who love the Great God'.

Older translations of the term *imakhu* refer to one who is 'revered', 'honoured' or 'venerable' – a heightened state of being, but one with no obvious context. However, it is clear from the examples cited above that the term is not always used in isolation, but in relation to a person whom one is *imakhu xr*, 'before' or 'in the sight of'. The meaning(s) of the term *imakhu* is discussed in important articles by Eyre (1987a) and Allen (2006).

It seems that the importance of being *imakhu* is in having a close association with another person or persons, who might be family, the king or various gods. That close association might be a relationship which implies a provision for the funerary estate for the one who is *imakhu*, such as the king providing elements of the tomb of a favoured courtier; Hetepherakhet, in his Dynasty 5 tomb from Saqqara, says: 'As a result of my state of *imakhu* before the king I made this tomb and a sarcophagus was made for me' (Strudwick 2005: 274), However, the general sense of being favourably close to other important persons – in his Dynasty 5 tomb at Giza, Kaikherptah refers to himself as 'doubly true *imakhu* before the god and before the king' (Strudwick 2005: 288) – seems to be more significant than any specific tangible benefits. In this context it is noticeable that in these *imakhu* texts we have our first occurrence of specific references to gods of the afterlife. These gods – Osiris, foremost of westerners; Anubis, patron of the necropolis; and Ptah-Sokar, localized patron of the Memphite necropolis – were gods within whose physical domain the tomb lay; their presence does not imply access to a divine afterlife beyond the tomb, but the tomb (and tomb-owner within) was part of a sacred landscape where the physical land of Egypt, in this case the desert-edge necropolis, was also the domain of specific deities. The idea of an afterlife in a landscape beyond that of Egypt itself was not one which was contemplated by non-royals before the end of the Old Kingdom. However, worthy of especial note are the frequent references to the 'Great God', whose identity is worth some consideration.

The 'Great God' and Osiris in the Old Kingdom

The most frequent references to a private person being *imakhu* are 'in association' with kings whom he served in his lifetime or the 'Great God'. From the late Old Kingdom, 'Great God' was an epithet of Osiris – the god who was a dead king – but this seems to have stemmed from an earlier royal god of the afterlife, probably best thought of as 'the figure who carried out the functions of king among and for the Dead, an amalgam of all dead kings continuing to function for their contemporaries' (Eyre 1987a: 22). As we shall see, one role of Osiris is to be a personification of deceased royalness (in contrast to the living Horus-king) suitable to be animated by myth but nonetheless a central part of the identity of the dead king and, increasingly, non-royals after the Old Kingdom who could be with and later become 'an Osiris'. This is yet another way in which the idea of reliance of the king for favour, even after death, was a fundamental aspect of the status of an elite non-royal during, and in several aspects after, the Old Kingdom.

The *ḥtp-di-nsw* formula

Perhaps the most long-lasting of these expressions of royal dependence – whatever the reality of the situation in terms of providing tombs and offerings – is the so-called 'Offering Formula'. One of the most commonly appearing texts on Egyptian funerary material – including tombs, coffins, statues – it begins with the phrase *ḥtp-di-nsw* (*hetep-di-nesu*), one of the most problematic phrases commonly encountered by the student of Egyptian language (Collier and Manley 1998: 35-9). Its meaning is probably: 'An offering that the king has given . . .', to serve as an introduction to a list of things which the tomb-owner needs and which were, seemingly, provided by the king. These things fall into two categories: the first is the gift of the tomb itself, or elements of the tomb, and the *ḥtp-di-nsw* formula does preface some such gifts (for examples, see Allen 2006: 14), but the overwhelming majority of texts refer to the regular offerings required by the tomb-owner. It might be questioned to what extent this *ḥtp-di-nsw* formula can be literally seen as representing a situation of royal resources channelled towards private tombs. Sometimes texts from tombs suggest that specific royal resources are in mind (cf. Eyre 1987a: 23), but it is clear that by the end of the Old Kingdom the phase had largely become a conventional trope introducing an equally conventional offering list.

It is notable that the king is not the only benefactor in the *ḥtp-di-nsw* lists; gods appear too. The precise direction in which the listed offerings flow has been the subject of much scholarly debate. Situations suggested by the *ḥtp-di-nsw* formula are that the king gives the listed offerings *to* the gods (via temple offerings?) so that the gods might allow the Dead to benefit from them. Another, possibly more likely imagined scenario, is that the king *and* the gods provide offerings for the Dead. Another level of ambiguity is provided by the most standard offering referred to: even when long lists of specific items are not provided, *ḥtp-di-nsw* lists regularly refer to requests for *prt-ḥrw* (*peret kheru*) 'Voice Offerings' of the type made by a visitor to the tomb who arrives without offerings but is willing to speak the offering list to make the items recited magically appear. The means and direction by which offerings might flow to the tomb-owner were, in magic as well as in practical reality, subject to much variation.

CHAPTER 4

Unas, Teti and Their Courts

The Late Old Kingdom at Saqqara

ᒋᒋᒋᒋ

Trends in Royal Tombs in the Late Old Kingdom

Before the development of private tombs in the Late Old Kingdom is considered, it is necessary to revisit the issue of royal tombs, specifically the nature of royal pyramids and the character of the court cemeteries associated with these pyramids. The three hundred year span of Dynasties 5 and 6 saw much less spectacular development in royal and private tombs than the three hundred which had preceded it. Royal pyramid complexes settled down to a regularity of form, size and location which contrasted markedly with the extraordinary changes in form (step pyramid to true pyramid, and the oddity of the monumental *mastaba* of Shepseskaf at Saqqara), size (no-one would build a bigger pyramid than Khufu, no-one would build more pyramid than Snefru) and specific location (Saqqara, Meidum, Dahshur, Giza and Abu Roash) which typified Dynasties 3 and 4.

The 14 pyramids belonging to kings of Dynasties 5 and 6, which were located in three neighbouring clusters at North Saqqara, South Saqqara and Abusir, do not show the extraordinary innovation or monumental ambition of their predecessors, but they do have a consistency which seems to indicate a settled contentment with what a pyramid was for, how it would serve the needs of the dead king, and what might be practically achievable. The latter factor was perhaps particularly applicable to those kings – such as Unas of Dynasty 5 (Figure 4.1) or Teti of Dynasty 6 (Figure 4.2) – who wished to plant their pyramids in the crowded and already ancient necropolis of North Saqqara. For Unas this meant the remodelling of the

---

Ancient Egyptian Tombs: The Culture of Life and Death   By Steven Snape
© 2011 Steven Snape

Figure 4.1 The pyramid of Unas at Saqqara, looking westwards from the causeway. The tombs of Wadjkawes (Fig. 3.3) and Khenu (Fig. 3.4) are immediately to the north of this upper section of the causeway

landscape in the area to the south of Djoser's pyramid enclosure in order to construct a suitably prominent monumental complex (Cooke 2005: 2).

Compared to the pyramids of Dynasty 4, those of Dynasties 5 and 6 appear unimpressive, although another important part of the complex, the mortuary temple, became larger and more elaborate. While it is difficult to be precise, owing to the poor condition of most Dynasty 4 mortuary temples, it is likely that, for example, the pyramid complex of King Sahure at Abusir had approximately four times the amount of wall space in its mortuary temple as that of any of the comparable structures belonging to Snefru and Khufu. There is a remarkable little variation in size among the late Old Kingdom pyramids. Khufu's pyramid has a base length of 230 m and a height of 146 m while, at 60 m high, nothing at Saqqara is taller than Djoser's step pyramid. The largest of the Dynasty 5/6 group, Neferirkare at Abusir, at 105 m has the same base length of the smallest of the Dynasty 4 pyramids, those of Menkaure at Giza and Radjedef at Abu Roash. Seven of this late group are essentially identical in size, with a base length of 78.5–79 m and a height of 47–52.5 m, including all of the four surviving pyramids of Dynasty 6: Teti, Pepi I, Merenre and Pepi II. The smallest of this group is that belonging to Unas, with a base length of 57.5 m and a height of 43 m, but this pyramid is one of the most innovatory of the Old Kingdom pyramids because it was the first to contain Pyramid Texts.

Pyramids – a user's manual?

The most important source of information regarding the expectations of the king's afterlife during the Old Kingdom is the body of religious literature commonly referred to as the Pyramid Texts. Faulkner (1969) and more recently Allen (2005) are convenient English translations of these texts. The term refers to the hieroglyphic texts which were inscribed on the walls of the corridors and inner chambers of pyramids and, in the cases of Teti and Ankhesenpepi II, on their sarcophagi. These texts have been found in the pyramids of Unas in Dynasty 5, Teti, Pepi I (and the satellite pyramid of Queen Ankhesenpepi II), Merenre, Pepi II (and the satellite pyramids of queens Neith, Iput II and Udjebten) in Dynasty 6, and Ibi in Dynasty 8. Each pyramid contains only a selection of individual sections, usually referred to as 'spells' or 'utterances', from what seems to be a much larger collection of religious literature, with the extensive originals presumably written on now-lost papyri (Allen 2005: 5). It has been noted that the grammar of most of the Pyramid Texts is considerably older than the pyramids in which they appear (Allen 2005: 4) but their specific antiquity is hard to judge. There are almost 1,000 known 'spells', with Unas having a modest selection of 236 and Pepi II the largest with 675.

The king's afterlife, as reflected in the Pyramid Texts, has three major aspects – solar, Osirian and stellar – which might be synthesized by saying of the king that 'as one of the gods, his spirit would join the sun and the stars in their daily journey across the sky, receiving each night the capability for this new life through union with Osiris' (Allen 2006: 9). It is difficult to know to what extent the Pyramid Texts represent the royal view of the afterlife before the end of Dynasty 5. It may be that the subterranean location of a pyramid's Burial Chamber, rather than being embedded in the body of the pyramid masonry, may reflect the idea of the king's body being that of Osiris in the *Duat*, the netherworld, awaiting the sun god on his night-time journey. If so, the early Dynasty 4 pyramids of Snefru and Khufu, with their internal chambers well above ground level, do not share in this vision and may reflect a stronger, earlier connection with a stellar afterlife which has its own architectural feature in the standard northern entrance to these and most later pyramids, in the form of a rising passageway leading to the exterior of the pyramid and the 'imperishable stars' of the northern sky beyond. The Pyramid Texts contain other ideas too, such as the 'Cannibal Hymn' (Eyre 2002), which describes the king devouring the gods to assume their powers. The descendants of the Pyramid Texts are the Coffin Texts of the Middle Kingdom and the *Amduat* of New Kingdom royal tombs, the latter of which also feature the night-time journey of Ra and the identification with Osiris, laid out on the walls of the royal tomb.

The placement of the Pyramid Texts within each pyramid was far from random, but part of a programme whereby specific texts were placed on specific walls within the pyramid in order that its inner rooms became a place of recurring ritual. The internal architecture of the pyramid was also intended to replicate a wider cosmos through which the king would travel to achieve an appropriate afterlife (Allen 1994). The region beneath the earth which was crossed every night by the barque of the sun-god Ra, and which was inhabited by the god Osiris, was known as the *Duat*. The area of the *Duat* closest to the eastern horizon where Ra would emerge every morning was known as the *Akhet*. Analysis by Allen (2005: 8-13) suggests that the Pyramid Texts describe the king, identified as Osiris, lying within his sarcophagus, which was itself identified as the goddess Nut. The king's *b3* (*ba* – for this spiritual form, see p. 202) left his body and entered the sarcophagus chamber, which was regarded as the *Duat*, through which it proceeded to the antechamber, which was regarded as the *Akhet*. Here the *ba* of the king would become an *3ḫ* (*akh* – for this spiritual form, see p. 70) by means of the set of spells referred to as *s3ḫw* (*sakhu*), 'akhifiers' (Allen 1994: 27). As an *akh*, the king would emerge from the *Akhet* into the day sky, which was identified with the rising corridor leading to the entrance to the pyramid.

But if the Pyramid Texts make it clear that the interior of the pyramid should be thought of as an architectural construction of a cosmic landscape, what about the exterior of the pyramid? It is likely that elements of the specialized nature of the royal afterlife may be reflected in royal funerary architecture, specifically the pyramid and its surrounding buildings which make up the pyramid complex.

The pyramid as solar symbol?

The pyramid itself is an intriguing structure which might be regarded in a number of ways. Clearly it is an expression of extraordinary royal power in the control of the resources of Egypt, human included, and an exceptional technical achievement. The final result, particularly in the case of the largest pyramids, built at the beginning of Dynasty 4, creates an obvious distinction in what is an appropriate monumental tomb for the king, and what is appropriate for everyone else. Beyond this obvious appreciation of the achievement of massing stone upon stone on a scale unprecedented and, arguably, unequalled in human history, the significance of much else connected with the pyramid is less clear, especially the significance of its shape. Was it simply chosen as a solid form which, despite its height, was essentially stable because of its broad supporting base? Was it a solar symbol like the pyramid-topped obelisks in the Dynasty 5 sun-temples at Abu Ghurob or (perhaps) the *benben*-stone in the temple of Ra at Heliopolis? Further to this latter idea, did it in fact represent the solidified rays of the sun which allowed the king to ascend to heaven? Was this a development of the step-pyramid form of Dynasty 3, which can itself be viewed in terms of both structure (a natural development from the *mastaba*-tomb in the creation of a 'stacked' structure using a new material – stone – on a massive scale) and symbolism (a stairway to heaven)? It is intriguing to note that when 'true' pyramids are in such a state of decay that they display a significant portion of their internal structure (such as the Dynasty 5 group at Abusir) they can be seen to be composed of an internal step pyramid which was converted into a straight-sided pyramid through the addition of stone packing and a smooth masonry casing.

Some of these questions might be answered if we knew how far back into the Old Kingdom (and earlier) the Pyramid Texts reflect royal afterlife expectations. It must be admitted that we cannot, with any real confidence, describe what the kings of Dynasties 1–3 thought would happen to them after death. Like much concerning the royal pyramids of ancient Egypt, there are real problems here and we should not ignore the fact that some of these problems are incapable of resolution. However, whatever the detail, the gulf in both deployment of resources and underlying expectations of the afterlife between, on one hand, the king and, on the other, everyone else in Egypt (including the highest elite) cannot be ignored.

Trends in Late Old Kingdom Private Tombs

As far as location is concerned, what was true for kings was also broadly true for their court – the royal cemeteries of the period are also the loci for the most important private tombs. However, there are a number of significant changes, especially if we expect to see contemporary tombs of superficially identical appearance, such as the *mastaba* cemeteries at Giza. Later Old Kingdom private tombs are not necessarily closely linked to the royal tomb of the period, nor are they very consistent in size and shape. In general, the tendency is for private tombs to become larger in the later part of the Old Kingdom, at a time when royal pyramids have become smaller, a phenomenon which has been linked to broader political and economic shifts. In the later part of the Old Kingdom there were a number of significant and related trends in tomb building (Janosi 1999). The most important of these seems to be a diminishing importance in being buried close to the king. Although

important court officials continued to be buried in the Memphite cemeteries during Dynasties 5 and 6, especially at Saqqara, the closeness of
relationship to the royal pyramid was diminished. In particular, the 'towns'
of tombs for court officials and members of the extended royal family,
which were such an important part of the pyramid complex in Dynasty 4,
were now a thing of the past.

The extent of this separation varied from reign to reign: that of Djedkare
Isesi shows a considerable detachment between the tomb of the king and
those of his court (Roth 1988), while that of Unas displays a return to a more
organized court cemetery close to the royal complex, including a 'zoning'
within that cemetery to give particular prominence to the *mastaba*s
belonging to royal women (Munro 1993: 1–8). However, unlike the *mastaba*-
cemetery of Khufu's pyramid at Giza, the tombs in the Unas Pyramid
Cemetery do not consist of rows of virtually identical structures. Some of
the larger *mastaba*s in the Unas cemetery form an orderly arrangement
parallel to the Unas causeway, but they are interspersed and flanked by
smaller, less well-ordered private tombs. Another good example of a private
cemetery developing close to the royal burial is the Teti Pyramid Cemetery
at Saqqara, which was a clearly designated area adjacent to the royal
pyramid and with its own enclosure wall, effectively forming a 'gated
community' of the elite dead (Kanawati 2003 and refs cit.; Quibell and
Hayter 1927). This cluster of tombs (Figure 4.2) is of particular relevance
since not only does it contain some of the largest and most important
mastaba-tombs of Dynasty 6, but it also includes tombs which are archetypal in form and decoration for the Middle and New Kingdoms, and so the
development of the Teti Pyramid Cemetery is of long-term interest for
tomb-types and tomb-use for a significant proportion of dynastic Egypt.

The trend during Dynasties 5 and 6 for royal pyramids which are
noticeably smaller than those of Dynasty 4 might indicate an inability or
unwillingness on the part of the king to deploy significant resources in the
construction of his tomb. By contrast, private tombs became larger and
better decorated. This is best exemplified in the Teti Pyramid Cemetery
itself. While Teti's pyramid is small, undistinguished and now in poor
condition, nearby private tombs, such as the *mastaba*s of Mereruka and
Kagemni, are magnificent in their multi-roomed architectural design and,
more obviously, in the carved and painted relief decoration which covers
the walls of their tombs with images of the life experiences, expectations
of the afterlife, and knowledge of Egypt of their owners (Harpur 1987). The
period of the reigns of kings Neferirkare and Niuserre seems especially
significant for changes in private tombs (Bárta 2005). Important innovations at this time include an increase in the provision of statues and *serdab*s
(see below – the tomb of Rawer at Giza contained 25 *serdab*s and 20 niches

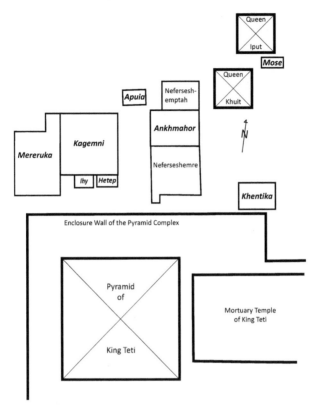

Figure 4.2 Plan of the Teti Pyramid Cemetery at Saqqara, showing the pyramids of Teti, Iput I and Khuit, and selected private tombs of the Old Kingdom–Ramesside Period (tombs mentioned in the text are named in bold italic)

to house over 100 statues; see Hassan 1932–60 (Vol. 1): 1–61), the decoration of Burial Chambers, the emergence of family tombs with shared Offering Chapels and multiple burial shafts, and the use of columned porticoes and open courts, leading to the emergence of the so-called multi-roomed *mastaba*.

Multi-roomed mastabas: *the tomb of Nebkauhor*

The cemeteries associated with the pyramids of Unas and Teti contain some of the largest and most complex *mastaba*-tombs of the Old Kingdom, their architecture and relief decoration providing clues as to the ways in which they were actually used as places for the performance of cultic activity for the benefit of the tomb-owner. An especially fine example of the individual architectural components of a multi-roomed *mastaba* is that of

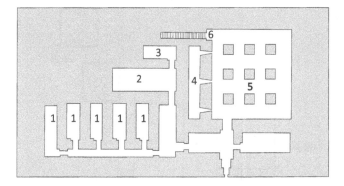

Figure 4.3   Plan of the *mastaba* of Nebkauhor in the Unas Causeway Cemetery at Saqqara

Nebkauhor in the Unas Pyramid Cemetery (Hassan 1975a). Nebkauhor lived at the end of Dynasty 6, and probably served Pepi II, but he was not the original owner of the tomb, that being Akhethotep of late Dynasty 5/early Dynasty 6, who was, because of the position of the *mastaba*, probably a high official under Unas. The *mastaba*, 34 × 18.6 m in floor plan, has a complex internal structure which is comparable to similar large multi-roomed *mastaba*s of the late Old Kingdom, including that of Niankhba (Hassan 1975b: 41–8), also from the Unas Pyramid Cemetery, and Merer-uka, Kagemni and Khentika from the Teti Pyramid Cemetery.

A number of distinct elements can be isolated within the Nebkauhor tomb (which can be compared to others in the group). The most striking of these are the use of non-local (Tura) fine white limestone for particularly important parts of the building, in addition to the locally obtained poorer quality limestone (Cooke 2005: 77–82), and a number of distinct architectural elements (see Figure 4.3):

1. A set of five undecorated storerooms, one for each *phyle* serving the *mastaba*, with integral shelving for the storage of cult equipment (Cooke 2005: Chapter 7). In the tomb of Nebkauhor these storerooms are grouped together in a row reminiscent of royal storerooms in, for instance, the mortuary temple of Niuserre at Abusir (Brinks 1979: pl. 15).
2. An Offering Room with false door and offering table.
3. A magazine/storeroom adjacent to the Offering Room. This differs from the five *phyle*-storerooms in that it is decorated with scenes of offering bearers. In the tomb of Nebkauhor some of the offering bearers depicted on the wall of the Offering Room are positioned

so that they make their way towards this magazine, not from it (Hassan 1975a: 53, pl. 41 B–C), as if they were on their way to fill this room with necessary stores, especially oil. It is likely that this room contained material used in the offering cult which was common to all the *phyle*, rather than the team equipment kept in the *phyle* storerooms.

4. A large *serdab*, with the space to accommodate a significant collection of statues.

5. A large, open courtyard (typical of Dynasty 5, e.g. Niankhkhnum and Khnumhotep) or columned hall (typical of Dynasty 6, e.g. Nebkauhor, Mereruka, Kagemni and Khentika). The most commonly suggested use for this court/hall is as a place where cattle were slaughtered for offering. The detail of this is contentious, with some authorities arguing that the leading of animals through the comparatively narrow entrance to the tomb and then manoeuvring potentially large beasts around the heavily columned court/hall is perhaps unlikely. However, comparative areas for slaughter have been recognized attached to the Dynasty 5 mortuary temples of kings Neferefre (Verner 1986) and Neferirkare (Posener-Kriéger 1968) at Abusir. Moreover, it is clear that one of the functions of tomb architecture was to provide appropriate space for actions performed there by the living and, as Eyre (2002: 187–8) notes, 'a place of slaughter is situated very close to the place of offerings and forms part of the ritual complex . . . cult at the tomb envisages sacrifice at the point of offering.' The presence of tethering stones within some of these tombs, including a particularly large, raised example in the tomb of Pepiankh at Meir (Ikram 1995: 100–2), seems to support this view.

6. A staircase, usually starting from the hall/court, running up to the roof of the *mastaba*. This may be associated with the slaughtering of cattle (the drying of meat? – see Eyre 2002: 182) or for ritual conducted on the roof of the tomb.

Nefer and his family: the tomb of the Singers

Although North Saqqara was a court cemetery in the Late Old Kingdom, not all its occupants were high state officials. Some were favoured members of the king's household; individuals from relatively humble backgrounds with a talent that took them close to the king. Such a person was Nefer, whose tomb was one of a group of Dynasty 5 tombs which were established in the area south of the Djoser pyramid enclosure before this part of the cemetery was selected by Unas for his pyramid complex. Unlike the

impressive *mastaba*s of the great officials of state like Nebkauhor, Nefer's
tomb (Moussa and Altenmüller 1971) was, unusually for Saqqara, rock-cut.
The enormous 'moat' which surrounded the step-pyramid complex of
King Djoser had gradually filled with sand during the Old Kingdom
while providing a neat vertical rock-face into which tombs could be cut.
Succeeding generations of tomb builders could cut their tombs into the
ever-higher opportunities of the moat. In the reign of King Niuserre the
rock-face was utilized once again to carve out a tomb chapel and burial
shafts which were used not just for the 'Overseer of Singers' Nefer, but also
for his extended family – people who could not have dreamt of elaborate
burial in the cemetery of kings but for the favour gained by their talented
relative. Other tombs in this group also belong to similar classes of
individual – not high-ranking officials but favoured members of the royal
households of Niuserre and Neferirkare.

The tomb excavated for Nefer and his family consists of an L-shaped
room cut into the face of the moat, only 8.45 m deep and 1.86 m wide
(Figure 4.4). The west wall of the tomb, as one might expect, essentially
consists of a row of false doors, each belonging to a member of Nefer's
family – one each for him, his wife, his father, his mother. But this was not
just a place of commemoration and offering; the floor of the tomb-chapel,
and the small courtyard in front of it, are filled with no fewer than 11 shafts,
each leading to a small chamber containing a body. This was, in all senses,
a family tomb, but one where the central figure was the *arriviste* Nefer,
making provision for his family, and proud to do so.

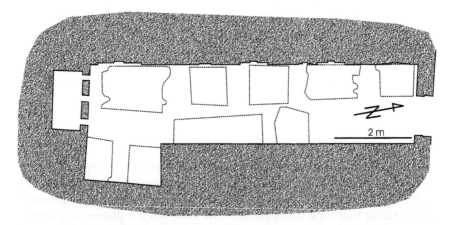

Figure 4.4 Plan of the tomb of Nefer at Saqqara. Note the nine burial shafts
inside the tomb, the series of false doors along the west wall and the *serdab*** at
the southern end of the tomb

The east wall of the tomb is covered by a series of horizontal registers which portray Nefer overseeing a range of busy individuals who seem to be going about their daily working lives. The impression given is that the tomb-owner, Nefer, is the owner of a great agricultural estate, and this aspect of his status and wealth is being depicted for the gaze of contemporaries and future visitors to the tomb. In the case of major state officials, for example the owners of the great tombs in the Teti Pyramid Cemetery, such as Mereruka or Kagemni, the ownership of country estates, and control of the wealth they produce, is very much a reality. The likelihood that the 'Overseer of Singers' Nefer was, in reality, a significant landowner, is slight. More telling, perhaps, are scenes showing trees being felled to provide the wood for coffin manufacture – something that would be used in the tomb itself. Indeed, as Eyre has noted, the purpose of these scenes of agriculture and production – especially food production – on the walls of Old Kingdom tombs is to 'in principle and over-simplified . . . depict the range of activities needed for the provision of the tomb and the continuation of life within it. They are not random depictions from the everyday life of the tomb-owner's household, although to a large extent coinciding with it' (Eyre 1987a: 27).

There is another feature of the tomb of Nefer which makes it remarkable. Two of the shafts within the tomb were found, on their excavation in 1966, to contain the bodies of their original occupants. One of these, that in shaft 8, was found to be in excellent condition; it is not certain whether this is the body of Nefer himself, although it has often been assumed to be so, and has been labelled 'the oldest mummy in the world'. However, there is rather more (or perhaps less) to this soubriquet than meets the eye. Although the 'mummy' of (let us assume) Nefer has a strikingly life-like appearance, that appearance is deceptive.

The Ideal Host

As far as the *ka* was concerned, the tomb served its two major requirements. The first of these was a continued supply of food and drink, and the tomb was the place where these were delivered. The design of the tomb was largely based on providing appropriate space for the reception of this delivery, but alternative systems were also developed to satisfy these requirements; the evolution of the false door into the more elaborate decorative schemes of elite Old Kingdom tombs amply demonstrates this. However, the *ka* had a second major need: an appropriate physical host. Ideally this would be the body, and the development of artificial means of preserving the body – or at least a body-like mass – was one way that this need could be served. The second part of the bipartite tomb – the Burial Chamber – was almost always much smaller than the Offering Chapel, largely because its purpose was relatively simple and straightforward: to house the body safely in a place where only the *ka* would have access to it.

By the end of the Old Kingdom, techniques to preserve the body as a viable host for the *ka* had progressed. However, that progression had not involved, to a significant degree, methods by which the body itself might defy decay. As early as the beginning of Dynasty 4, the removal of the internal organs of the abdomen as an essential first step in the separation of the soft tissues, with their potential for rapid putrification, had become part of the burial preparations of the hyper-elite. The earliest evidence for this is the presence of a four-sectioned alabaster 'canopic' chest in the burial equipment of Queen Hetepheres, mother of King Khufu.

However, despite the recognition that soft-tissue removal was necessary for genuine preservation of the body, the preparation of elite private bodies of the Old Kingdom (royal bodies are notable by their absence from the archaeological record) concentrated on external appearance. The package that was the wrapped body needed to appear to be lifelike to be an appropriate host for the *ka*, but it need not necessarily consist solely of the body. A surviving arm from the tomb of King Djer from the Dynasty 1 royal cemetery at Abydos, tightly wrapped with linen bandages, strongly suggests that tight wrappings, carefully moulded to the form of the body, might retain an appropriately lifelike appearance even when the body itself had decayed. By Dynasty 5 the technique had evolved to use not just linen bandages, but bandages soaked in resin or plaster which could easily be moulded to the appearance of the body within, but which would harden to form a lifelike shell encasing the skeleton and, perhaps, little else. This package, with its externally satisfactory appearance but internal decay, would be useful to the *ka* as an autoicon – something which was both the body and its substitute. With its carefully modelled face and applied ears, the mummy of the court singer Nefer (if it is indeed Nefer) is perhaps the finest surviving example of an Old Kingdom autoicon. It is perhaps ironic that while pyramids failed to preserve their royal contents intact, at least some modest tombs of the same period have been more successful. One might say (admittedly somewhat pretentiously) that it is, in a Shakespearean sense, fools, not kings, who have survived from the period of greatest royal power in ancient Egypt.

The body in stone: ka-*statues*

However, even with the protection of a coffin, an Old Kingdom mummy could hardly be called a well-preserved body. The best-looking examples (such as Nefer) were, as we have seen, essentially bundles of linen arranged to mimic the form of a human body, with an outer coating of painted plaster modelled on the features of the deceased. The original body was represented by the skeleton. The Old Kingdom mummy was therefore a confection with a human body at its centre but with an outer mantle of artificiality. But this did not matter – it could be recognized by the *ka* as the physical host to which it could return. In addition, as with the issue of providing food offerings, the Egyptians realized that an ideal situation was not always possible, and in attempting to preserve a human body they must have been aware that they were trying to preserve an object which was outstandingly prone to decay. The same principle of alternative arrangements when the ideal situation failed was put in place and, as far as the human body was concerned, there was an obvious candidate for an object which could both replicate the physical appearance of an individual in three dimensions, and be much more robust than that body – a statue.

The development of stone statuary in the Old Kingdom was largely predicated on providing an object within the tomb which could act as a *ka*-host, which was not only much more durable than a human body, but could also offer further possibilities. The collections of statues from Old Kingdom private tombs present an image of the elite Egyptians of that period as looking essentially similar. Most of the men are shown either as young, fit and physically healthy, or as older and with a social standing which might be displayed through the depiction of wealth as stored calories. This latter mode of depiction was clearly not considered suitable for statues of women, which seem to conform to stereotypes of a slim, youthful physical appearance. Although our interpretation of Egyptian conventions in sculpture is just that – interpretation – it is unarguable that the depiction of elite bodies in tomb statuary is driven by convention rather than naturalism. This can also be demonstrated by the conventional status-indicating skin tones of elite men and women, which might be explained as images of ruddy outdoors active men and pale indoors ladies (Figure 4.5), who, unlike peasant women, did not have to work in the sun. The conventional depictions of standing males with the left foot advanced and standing females with both feet together have also been explained as conveying aspects of gender roles within Egyptian elite society – active males and passive females – although whether such interpretations are erroneous modern deductions of ancient evidence is unclear. Similar attempts to interpret the pose and nature of other, more specialized, statue types include the possible explanation of statues of high-ranking royal officials in the role of young, junior scribes (Figure 4.6) as symbolizing the most important characteristic of such officials: their literacy in a state which was probably over 95 per cent illiterate. Family status might also be

Figure 4.5   Statue of the Princess Nofret from Meidum

detected in (usually) seated statues of the tomb-owner surrounded by diminutive figures of his wife and children around his feet. Another way of regarding this trend in private statuary in the Late Old Kingdom is to link it to contemporary developments in the way texts in tombs become more focused on presenting the tomb-owner in relation to a number of conventional roles and identities, something which has been described by Assmann (1996) in respect of both texts and statues as a 'self-thematization' (*selbstthematisierung*).

The most striking aspect of these statues to the modern viewer, apart from their static, stilted poses, is their similarity. Although some statues of the tomb-owner are described as being 'lifelike' (*twt r ꜥnḫ*), the general desire for iconographic perfection led to the creation of statues largely stripped of any physical differentiation as individuals. Exceptions are rare. The only significant deviation from the rule that Old Kingdom private statues are essentially devoid of a visually distinguishable identity are so-called 'Reserve Heads': a group of life-size limestone heads of strikingly individual

Figure 4.6   Scribal statue

appearance which are found in a limited number of elite Dynasty 4
tombs, particularly at Giza. The purpose of these heads, which seem to
have been placed at the bottom of the shafts leading to the
Burial Chamber or in the Burial Chamber itself, is still much debated
(Roehrig 1999).

Such similarity in appearance could potentially compromise the original
function of these statues as hosts for the *ka* as it was superficially difficult
for the *ka* to distinguish between 'his' statues and those of other similar
individuals. This problem was solved by use of a technique which the
Egyptians used in a number of different circumstances: not just expressing,
but also *giving* identity through labelling. The hieroglyphic text which
named the owner of the statue gave it his (or her) identity and therefore
made it a suitable host for the *ka*; 'In the Fifth Dynasty ... the inscription
tends to be regarded as a sufficient means of individuation and thus makes
physiognomic individuation dispensable' (Assmann 1996: 66). It may also

be that a properly labelled statue was regarded as an appropriate fusion of the *ka* with the *rn*.

Serdabs *and their contents*

There was, however, a practical problem: a statue which had lost its naming inscription could be re-inscribed to create a suitable host for the *ka* associated with the new name. This would not have been a significant issue if the *ka*-statue had been given the same security precautions as the body itself, by being placed within the Burial Chamber, but this was not usually the case since the *ka*-statue came to be regarded as an object with a dual function within the tomb. Not only was the statue a host for the *ka* in the sense of being a substitute for the body should the latter perish, but it was also realized that if it was placed within the Offering Chapel it could be approached by the living as an object which could be thought of as hosting the *ka* at the time that offerings were being made. Thus the statue could offer an alternative to the false door as a locus for the delivery of offerings. Indeed, in some cases a false door could include a figure of the tomb-owner with relief so high that it was effectively an engaged sculpture – the best example is in the tomb of Mereruka, where a sculpted figure of the tomb-owner is shown stepping over the threshold of his false door into the Offering Chapel having risen up from the burial chamber. However, such examples were rare and most statues were independent, freestanding figures in a variety of sizes, the ideal being the life-sized figure of the tomb-owner. Such statues were expensive and valued, but also potentially transportable and re-assignable by re-inscription – a process no more complicated than the changing of registration plates on a stolen car. This problem could be easily solved by abandoning the dual-function statue and placing it within the difficult-to-access Burial Chamber, but, as with a number of other aspects of mortuary provision (e.g. coffins), the Egyptians found other ways of dealing with problems of their own making. In this case the problem of the statue which could easily be stolen was solved by means of an architectural solution: the creation of a room within the tomb which had no door, but was provided with a slit or eye-holes through which the offering bearers could see, and offer to, the statue within, and the immured statue (or statues) could see out. This room, which is known as the *serdab* from the Arabic for 'cellar', was used as early as Dynasty 3 (in the step-pyramid complex of King Djoser) and became a common feature of large elite tombs in the later part of the Old Kingdom (Arnold 1999).

From the middle of Dynasty 5, *serdab*s regularly began to house statues which did not depict the tomb-owner but figures which might broadly be classified as 'servant statues'. These modestly sized figures are shown carrying out a variety of tasks, mostly concerned with the production of foodstuffs, presumably for the tomb-owner and as an adjunct to a wider set of scenes on the walls of the Offering Chapel. Roth (2002) believes that in many cases these figures can be identified as members of the tomb-owner's household – a few examples are named – who would have carried out similar tasks in life, and who would benefit from their presence in the tomb of their effective patron.

Not only do statues regularly appear in Old Kingdom tombs, so too does their depiction in scenes on the walls of those tombs. In the tomb of Niankhkhnum and Khnumhotep at Saqqara, for instance, a scene showing the transportation of standing statues is explained by the text, 'Accompanying the perfect statues, doubly in peace in the sight of the Great God. Accompanying the statues to the tomb of the necropolis, in peace. Accompanying the statues to the tomb' (Strudwick 2005: 408). This puts the statues within the realm of ritual, particularly the ritual of funeral. Moreover, the disappearance of *serdabs* from tombs at the end of the Old Kingdom, and their replacement by statues buried in the Burial Chamber, suggests shifts in the ritual use of these statues, particularly as part of the funeral itself (Roth 2002: 107).

CHAPTER 5

The Tombs of Qar and Idu

Families and Funerals in the Late Old Kingdom

⌐⌐⌐⌐

When compared to the great court *mastaba*s of Dynasty 4, the tombs built at Giza in the later part of the Old Kingdom were significantly less impressive in the scale of their superstructures. The main locations for elite tombs in Dynasties 5 and 6 were elsewhere, primarily Saqqara but also the royal pyramid cemetery of Abusir. However, although tombs of the Late Old Kingdom at Giza are neither the largest nor the best decorated, they are not necessarily the least informative of the concerns of tomb-owners of the period. The tombs of Qar and Idu, founded within the old G7000 cemetery at Giza (which was mainly associated with the pyramid of Khufu), are two such small gems.

The Tombs of Idu and Qar

It is probable that Idu and Qar were father and son or, possibly, the other way round – the filiations within the texts in the tomb are not specific enough. Both have titles mentioning Pepi I, so one can assume their adjacent tombs were part of a Dynasty 6 re-usage of the G7000 cemetery (Simpson 1976). By the time it came to be excavated by Reisner in 1924–5, the *mastaba* superstructure of Idu's tomb had virtually disappeared. However, the topography of this part of the cemetery meant that the tomb could be provided with a second element for the superstructure, an underground Offering Chapel which was accessed via a flight of stairs leading down from the *mastaba*. The Burial Chamber itself was lower still,

Ancient Egyptian Tombs: The Culture of Life and Death   By Steven Snape
© 2011 Steven Snape

accessed via a vertical shaft (one of seven which seem to be associated with this tomb) 8 m deep, with a chamber just large enough to contain a limestone sarcophagus. The Offering Chapel has an elaborate doorway over which two long texts summarize the main concerns and wishes for the afterlife of the tomb-owner. They express aspects of the relationships between the Living and the Dead, the Dead and the gods, and also something which was an increasing concern in texts in Late Old Kingdom tombs: the idea of proper behaviour in life having an impact on one's afterlife through the cultivation of the respect and approval of both the Living and the gods.

Recitation: I came forth from my town. I descended from my district.

I performed Maat for her lord. I satisfied the god with what pleased him. I spoke what was good and repeated what was good. I spoke truly and acted truly. I gave bread to the hungry and clothing to the naked. As far as I was able, I respected my father and was kind to my mother. I never spoke anything evil, unjust, or crooked against any people, because I desired that one be satisfied and unmolested and, that I might be *imakhu* before the god and before men forever.

An offering which the king gives and an offering which Anubis, foremost of the divine booth, he who is upon his hill, he who is in the *wt*, lord of the sacred land, lord of a goodly burial in the necropolis, gives.

An offering which Osiris gives, that he be buried well in his tomb which is in the west, that he travel upon the good ways, that he be accompanied by his *ka*s, that his document be received by the great god, that he be conducted upon the sacred roads on which the *imakhu* travel, that he be raised to the great god as an *imakhu*, whom the great god loves, lord of *imakhu*, possessor of a good burial in the necropolis.

May an invocation-offering come forth for him in the west in abundance. May he greatly be made an *akh* by lector-priests and *wt*-priests.

At the New Year's festival, at the Thoth festival, at first of the year festival, at the *Wag*-feast, at the festival of Sokar, at the great festival, at the fire-lighting festival, at the *Sadj* festival, at the coming forth of Min festival, at the half-month and month festivals, at the seasonal festivals, at the ten-day festivals, at all great festivals, throughout the course of every day.

A thousand oryxes thousand bulls, a thousand *ro*-geese, a thousand *tjerep*-geese, a thousand *set*-birds, a thousand *se*-birds, a thousand pigeons, a thousand of clothes, a thousand of linen, a thousand of bread, a thousand cakes, a thousand of beer, as pure (offerings) of the great god.

For the overseer of the allocation of divine offerings in the two houses, *imakhu* before the great god, the first under the king, staff of the *rekhyt*-people, pillar of *kenmet*, privy to the secrets of judgement, priest of Maat, royal letter scribe in the presence, overseer of scribes of the *meret*-serfs, *imakhu* before Anubis who is on his hill, who is in the *wt*, royal letter scribe in the presence, overseer of scribes of the *meret*-serfs, Idu. (Translation after Simpson 1976: 20-1; and Strudwick 2005: 277-9)

Within the Offering Chapel are two particularly interesting elements. The main focus of the west wall is, unsurprisingly a false door, painted red to imitate granite. However, only the upper part of the false door is shown and, instead of the lower half of the false door, there is a figure of Idu himself, modelled in high sculptural relief. Only the head and torso of the body of Idu is shown and the effect is to make it look as if he is rising up from the floor at the false door. His arms are stretched out in front of him, resting on the ground, palms up, in a posture to receive offerings from the offering table which is immediately in front of him. This figure of Idu is one of the most striking examples of the integration of architecture, sculpture and text, brought together in service of the *ka*.

The Human Spirit (2): the Akh

However, in addition to the *ka*, the text from the tomb of Idu refers to another spiritual form, the *akh* (*ȝḫ*). The name derives from the verb 'to be effective' and the *akh*, as an aspect of one's spiritual survival after death, was based on the idea of being an 'effective spirit' (Englund 1978). The *akh*-spirit also has connections to the quality of luminosity, and light generally, something which is more visible in the New Kingdom with the appearance of the *ȝḫ ikr n Rᶜ* (*akh iker n Ra*), although links between the solar deity Ra and the *akh* are referred to in the Pyramid and Coffin Texts. In Old Kingdom tombs the primary sense of the *akh* is a spirit with, perhaps, a less restricted range of movement than the *ka*, although the specific nature of its 'effectiveness' is not obvious. The prime medium by which one became an *akh* is ritual carried out at the time of the funeral, and, as we shall see, 'akhifier' spells (*sȝḫw*), which we have already met in the Pyramid Texts, are regularly referred to in the context of ceremonies conducted at the tomb by the specialist priests performing the energizing ritual of the funeral. According to Bolshakov (1997: 178), 'The akh seems to be regarded as the completion of the ideal form of the individual after death, one view of this being that "the *kȝ*, *rn* and *bȝ* are innate hypostases of man, the *ȝḫ* is what he turns to be after his death by means of the *sȝḫ* ritual."'

Funeral Ritual in the Old Kingdom

The entrance to the Offering Chapel in the tomb of Idu is in the middle of its north wall. Around that doorway, and covering the limited available space on that wall, are scenes which are remarkable and informative in that they are one of the few sets of scenes from Old Kingdom tombs which depict the funeral of the tomb-owner. The presence of these scenes is a hint to us that the multi-functional tomb had an important role on the occasion of the funeral itself. Not only is the tomb the destination of the funeral procession but it, and the wider mortuary landscape of the necropolis, has an important part to play as the physical venue for the performance of the rituals appropriate to this important time of transition. This is an aspect of funerary activity which we do not understand very well, since only the Theban tombs of Dynasty 18 provide us with any detailed level of information regarding the way in which the tomb and the mortuary landscape of the Theban West Bank are populated with ritual celebrants at the time of funeral, and the different rituals which took place within that landscape. For the Old Kingdom, even for the major necropolis at Memphis, we are much less well informed. At the level of royal provision, although we know that the royal pyramid complexes of Dynasties 4–6 are partly designed with funerals in mind – hence features such as the causeway along which the funeral cortège of the king could progress – the specific nature of the ceremonies that took place in specific parts of the complex, although hinted at within the Pyramid Texts, remains unclear. For private individuals, although the evidence is no means as extensive as that from the New Kingdom, we are reliant on a relatively small number of tombs: 16 from the Memphite necropolis and the provincial sites of Deir el-Gebrawi and Meir (Bolshakov 1991: 34–5). Only the tomb of Debehen dates to earlier than the reign of Niuserre as the depiction of funerals seems to be linked to a significant degree to the increased available wall-space made possible by the development of multi-room *mastaba*s in the Late Old Kingdom

The preparations before the funeral

The principal physical requirements for the preparation of the body, before it was taken to the tomb to be placed within its stone sarcophagus, were the oils for embalming, the bandages for wrapping the body, and the wooden coffin in which to place the prepared and wrapped body. From the site of Deir el-Gebrawi in Dynasty 6, Djau tells how he sought royal favour in preparing the body of his father – and namesake – for burial, and 'His Majesty had wood of Lebanon brought for the coffin, *setj*-oil, *sefetj*-oil, 200 bolts of *hatyw*-linen and *shemau*-linen for bandaging' (Strudwick 2005: 365). The period for embalming in the *wabet* or 'pure place' is indicated in a pair of complementary texts on the entrance to the tomb of Queen Meresankh III at Giza:

The King's Daughter Meresankh
Year of the first occasion, first month of shemu, day 21:
Her *ka* rested and she proceeded to the *wabet*.

The King's Wife Meresankh.
The year after the first occasion, second month of peret, day 18:
She went to her perfect tomb.

(Strudwick 2005: 380)

At a total of 273 days, this is somewhat longer than the 70 days suggested by Herodotus for the Late Period and the tomb of Djehuty at Thebes for Dynasty 18. It should be noted here that the term *wabet* (w^cbt), although often translated as 'place of embalming', and probably having the processing of dead bodies as its core activity, is perhaps better regarded as being a place where a variety of funerary equipment was manufactured

Depictions of funerals in Old Kingdom tombs

The fullest depiction of a funeral of the Old Kingdom comes from one of the Dynasty 6 tombs in the Teti Pyramid Cemetery at Saqqara, that of Mereruka. Similar scenes appear in the nearby tomb of Ankhmahor. The depiction of the funeral in Mereruka's tomb is presumably the most complete surviving version because of the size of that *mastaba* – one of the largest in the Memphite necropolis – which gave the available wall-space for an expansive expression of all the themes which Mereruka wished to be made available to him within his tomb. Together, the Dynasty 6 tombs of Mereruka and Ankhmahor at Saqqara, and those of Idu and Qar at Giza, contain the essential canon of Old Kingdom funeral scenes. The Dynasty 4 tomb of Debehen at Giza is an unusual exception to this generally late date for funeral scenes and will be discussed later. Unfortunately, the Mereruka scenes are not complete, having lost much of their upper portions, but enough survives, when supplemented by the evidence from the other surviving scenes, to construct a reasonably good overview of what the funeral of an elite individual at Memphis in the late Old Kingdom looked like (Bolshakov 1991; Simpson 1976; Wilson 1944).

Funeral scenes in the tomb of Mereruka

The location of the funeral scenes is significant: they are situated in the innermost parts of the Offering Chapel, on the wall facing the principal offering-niche/false door. The depiction of the action – the transportation of the coffin containing the body of Mereruka from his home to his tomb – is constructed as a 'continuous cinematic movement' (Wilson 1944: 201). Mereruka's journey begins in the *wabet*. Once the body had been prepared for burial, the funeral procession was formed up at the house of the deceased. The coffin, carried on poles by pallbearers, was accompanied by a group of distinctly identified individuals, specifically:

1. A woman or two women each identified as a *ḏryt* (*djeryt*) or 'kite'. Although only one *djeryt* is depicted in Mereruka's tomb, 'kites' regularly appeared as a pair, to play the role of chief female mourners at the funeral. The term 'kite' may derive from the screeching of those birds, which was associated with the keening of mourning women. These women became identified with the goddesses Isis and Nephthys following the 'Osirification' of funerary ritual after the Old Kingdom.
2. A man labelled 'Seal-Bearer of the god and chief *wt*'. Wilson (1944) regarded the importance of the title 'Seal-Bearer of the god (i.e. king)' in a funerary context as one who had the authority to organize official travel by river and was therefore connected with the canonical boat journey during the funeral. The term *wt* is problematic – it is usually translated as 'embalmer' but, just as the *wabet* had wider functions than simply being an embalming house, it may be that the function of the *wt* was to organize a broader range of activities connected with the funeral, including ritual at the tomb itself; roles which would later fall to the *sm*-priest and the lector-priest.
3. A man labelled '*wt* of Anubis'. This title also appears in connection with officials depicted on the causeway of the pyramid complex of King Unas and in the mortuary temple of King Pepi II.
4. A scroll-bearing man labelled 'Lector-Priest'.

It is noticeable that the class of priest which is vital to the ongoing operation of the tomb – the *ka*-priest – has no part to play in the funeral itself, although that would not prevent the *ka*-priest from taking on other roles more relevant to the funeral, especially in the case of individuals who could not apply the full panoply of state support to their funeral, as was the case with the Vizier Mereruka.

For the next stage of the process the coffin was loaded onto a barge for a water-journey. The necessity of such a journey is not immediately obvious if, as seems likely, a high official such as Mereruka would normally reside in an estate in the vicinity of the city of Memphis, on the West Bank of the Nile. Transport of funerary equipment via a canal system to the edge of the desert plateau at Saqqara is not unlikely, and was probably a common solution for the transportation of any bulky or heavy material in a country where land transport was much less developed than river/canal transport. It may also be that the idea of a water-crossing had a ritual significance which was equally significant as any practical necessity, if not more so, but this remains unexplained in the text which accompanies this scene in the tomb of Mereruka, 'Crossing in the Great Boat'. In other tombs two boats are shown, one bearing the coffin and the other an upright shrine, the latter probably containing a statue of the tomb-owner destined for the *serdab*. It might be appropriate to regard the paired transportation of body-in-coffin and statue-in-shrine as representing the two most important hosts for the *ka* within the different parts of the tomb: Burial Chamber and Offering Chapel. In fact, although scenes of the full funeral procession are comparatively unusual in Old Kingdom tombs, the abbreviated scene of the dragging of the statue to the tomb is not, and this should be regarded as part of the funeral ritual rather than simply the place-ment of a piece of equipment within the tomb.

The next major stage in the funeral was the disembarkation at the edge of the desert plateau. This is described in the tomb of Ptahhotep as: 'Going up onto the mountain of the necropolis, the grasping of his hand by his fathers and his *kas*' (Strudwick 2005: 213; Wilson 1944). But although the texts which describe the funeral seem to reflect real activity, the meta-phorical element is also very evident, since not only is Ptahhotep grasped by the hand by his ancestors and *kas* but, immediately before this text, he is said to be 'Crossing the firmament'. On arrival at the landing-stage of the necropolis the coffin was either carried or dragged on a sledge pulled by men and oxen to the tomb. Dragging on a sledge also seems to have been the standard way in which the shrine/statue was transported to the tomb.

Funeral scenes in the tombs of Qar and Idu

Although less extensive than those in the tomb of Mereruka, the tomb of Qar depicts the crucial elements of the funeral in two registers. The upper register (Figure 5.1) shows the procession of the coffin, borne on carrying-poles by 14 men led by a lector-priest (who reads from a papyrus scroll and is described as 'making *akh*'), followed by a *wt*-priest and a *djeryt*. This grouping of lector-priest, *wt*-priest and *djeryt* is repeated behind the coffin (not shown in Figure 5.1). The caption above the group states: 'Transporting in peace to the *ibw*-tent for purification by the followers of the *imakhu*.' To the right the *ibw*-tent itself is depicted, containing 'Requirements of the *ibw*-tent: a meal' and 'Requirements of the craft of the lector-priests', the latter presumably referring to the ritual equipment which would be required by the lector-priest. The lower scene shows the boat-journey of the coffin, presumably by canal rather than river as it is towed by two groups of men. Apart from the oarsmen and the coffin, the boat carries the lector-priest, the *wt*-priest and the two *djeryt*; their destination is the *wabet*.

The scenes within the tomb of Idu are not clearly structured, and there has been some debate as to the order of the individual stages of the funeral. It is likely that, unlike Mereruka, who had the luxury of extensive wall-space in a large tomb, the arrangement of the scenes in Idu are partly dictated by the location of the scenes, around a doorway facing the main offering niche/false door. This would account for the 'widest' scene – the depiction of the coffin on a sledge being dragged by men and oxen, and accompanied by the lector-priest – being placed above the doorway, with other 'shorter' episodes being placed in panels on either side of the doorway. To the east of the door are a series of groups of mourners, while to the west are four panels which depict:

1. Three men carrying the coffin on poles with the caption: 'Proceeding to the *wabet*, to the *wt*-priests'.
2. The depiction of the T-shaped *ibw*-tent with two doors and a causeway leading to a canal.
3. The transportation of the shrine by boat. The shrine is accompanied on the boat by a *wt* who is opening the shrine, and two *djeryt*, with the caption: 'Proceeding to the roof of the *Ibw*'.
4. Three men carrying the coffin, with the caption: 'Lo, behold the progress of the *imakhu*.'

Funeral scenes in the tomb of Debehen: the shrine on the roof?

One unique scene of a funeral appears in the Dynasty 4 tomb of Debehen at Giza (Bolshakov 1997: 101; Roth 2002: 107), the same tomb in which King Menkaure took such an interest. This scene shows rituals being conducted on the roof of a *mastaba*-tomb, the focus for these rituals being a shrine containing a standing statue of Debehen, and the rituals conducted by individuals who access the roof of the *mastaba* by means of a ramp (Figure 5.2). It is not clear whether this was standard

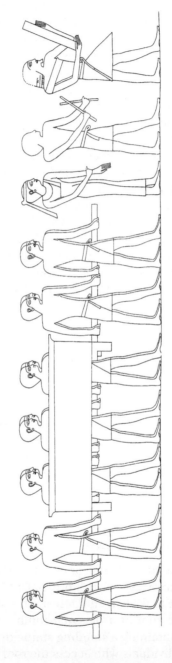

Figure 5.1   Funeral procession in the tomb of Qar at Giza (adapted from Simpson 1976: Fig. 24)

Figure 5.2   Funeral scene in the tomb of Debehen at Giza (adapted from Hassan 1932–60 (Vol. IV): Fig. 122)

procedure in Old Kingdom funerals at Giza, but only represented in the case of a small number of tombs – a ritual on the roof of the tomb is also described in the *mastaba* of Niankhkhnum and Khnumhotep (Moussa and Altenmüller 1977). This seems to make some sense since the flat top of a *mastaba*-tomb would be a satisfactorily public platform for the theatre of burial. It might also be noted at this point that the funeral rituals, described and depicted in a variety of Old Kingdom tombs, make no significant reference to the interment of the body in its coffin within the Burial Chamber, one rare exception being the texts on a group of Dynasty 6 sarcophagus lids from Teti Pyramid Cemetery at Saqqara which refer to the officials who were tasked with placing the lid upon the sarcophagus; the lid from the tomb of Khentika-called-Ikhekhi addresses the 'Lector Priests, men of the *wabet*, *wt*-priests, and 80 men of the necropolis who shall descend to this place (i.e. the burial chamber)', telling them to 'place this lid upon its base (lit. "mother") in the proper manner' (James 1953: 65–6; Strudwick 2005: 424). Since access to the roof of the *mastaba* – and the mouth of the shaft running down to the Burial Chamber – would be required for the committal of the body within the tomb, it may be that the roof of the *mastaba* was a very suitable place for the practicalities and ritual of the closing stages of the funeral. However, there is a difficulty with this interpretation in that the tomb of Debehen is not a *mastaba*-tomb; it is a rock-cut tomb within the 'Central Field' at Giza. It may be that the nature of the tomb meant that certain elements of it were constructed above the main Offering Chapel. Moreover, it has also been suggested – perhaps less persuasively – that the building depicted is the *wabet* rather than the tomb (Hassan 1932–60 (Vol. IV): 69–102, 175–9).

'Opening the Mouth' and rituals at the tomb

The ritual of 'Opening of the Mouth' (*wpt-r*) was one of the most fundamental and long-lasting ceremonies performed by the Egyptians (Fischer-
Elfert 1998; Otto 1960; Roth 1992). Its purpose was to take an inert object of
anthropoid form and make it usable and effective for a spiritual entity. The
principal objects on which the ceremony was performed were statues of
gods within temples and statues of tomb-owners within tombs, but it could
also be carried out on dead human bodies themselves. The idea of 'Opening
of the Mouth' was to allow the god or the *ka* within the statue to breathe, to
eat, to speak, in fact to make a unity of effective action between the spiritual
'guest' and the physical 'host'. As a ritual action the 'Opening of the Mouth'
seems to have consisted of the touching of the mouth of the statue by
appropriate ritual objects, including an adze. Although the extent of the
ritual might vary depending on circumstances, the 'Opening of the Mouth'
was fundamental to activating statuary within the tomb for the use of the
ka. Evidence from the New Kingdom suggests that, if not before, the
anthropoid coffin was now an appropriate substitute for the body itself
in 'Opening of the Mouth' ritual carried out in front of the tomb in the last
stages of the funeral. The statue on which these rituals were performed was,
presumably, the one which was regularly depicted as accompanying the
funeral procession (Bolshakov 1991: 46), which was probably already
thought of as an appropriate substitute for the body. Indeed there are
examples of statues being the subject of offering-cult even before the death
of their owner (Bolshakov 1997: 207).

Once the statue had become effective, further rituals could be performed. Chief among these was making the first of what were intended
to be many food offerings to the *ka*. Dancers are sometimes present – these
became more important in the New Kingdom – but the main activity
depicted is food offering, including the butchery of cattle and the presentation of choice cuts to the deceased. This, too, became a standard motif in
Old Kingdom and later tomb scenes which show the funerary meal and the
generality of ideal food offering.

Funerals in the provinces

Although most depictions of funerals in Old Kingdom tombs come from
the Memphite court cemeteries, there are provincial exceptions. The
most extensive comes from the tomb of Pepiankh Heny 'the Black' at
Meir (Blackman and Apted 1914–53 (Vol. V): 51–6, Pls 42–3). This large
and well-decorated tomb contains scenes of funeral which mirror
the sequence of events (*wabet*, procession, etc.) and participants of

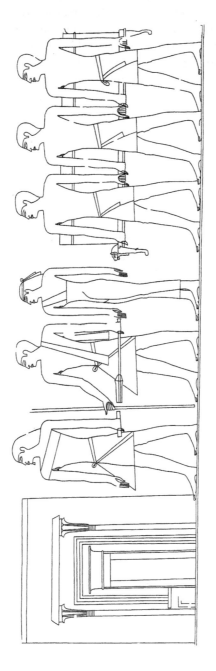

Figure 5.3 Funeral procession in the tomb of Pepiankh Heny 'the Black' at Meir (adapted from Blackman and Apted 1914–53 (Vol. V): Pl. 42)

the Memphite scenes, suggesting a common ritual. Here (Figure 5.3) the coffin, preceded as in the tomb of Qar by a lector-priest, a *wt*-priest and a *djeryt*, is carried in procession to a building labelled as the '*wabet* of the *wt*'. However, an interesting aspect of the Pepiankh Heny 'the Black' scenes is that, although the rest of the tomb is finished in painted relief, the funeral scenes are almost all only sketched in ink on the walls of an inner chamber of the tomb. This offers the tantalizing possibility that these scenes were quickly placed on the walls of the unfinished tomb in the period between death and burial, or possibly even after the funeral had taken place.

Protecting the Dead from the Living: Threats and Curses

The tomb was a very fragile organism. The well-being of the tomb-owner was dependent on the physical integrity of the structure of the tomb and its contents, and on the goodwill of the Living. Backup systems within the tomb could cope with the indifference of the Living, but not with an ignorant or active malfeasance. This could work on several levels, and commonly, from Dynasty 5 at Saqqara, and from Dynasty 6 at Giza and in the provincial cemeteries, texts within the tomb warned the Living against improper behaviour and, to further discourage such actions, made generalized or specific threats against the potential wrong-doer (Morschauser 1991; Plater 2001). These imprecations are generally re-ferred to as 'warnings' rather than 'curses'. The two primary concerns of the tomb-owner which are the subject of such warnings are best sum-marized on a loose block from a private tomb, found near the pyramid of Teti, which refers to 'any man who shall take stone from this tomb or who shall not enter in a pure state'. However, the tomb faced a series of threats, which might be categorized as the corruption of the tomb's purity, theft from the tomb, deliberate destruction in the tomb, and the usurpation of the tomb. All of these situations are referred to in various warning texts.

The corruption of the tomb's purity

We have already noted that the interior of the Offering Chapel was, in many ways, like a cult-temple. Therefore, as in a cult-temple, an appropriate level of physical purity was required of those entering it. A long festival-list over the doorway to the tomb of Merefnebef at Saqqara ends with the following imprecation:

As for any person who shall [enter] this tomb of mine of eternity in an impure state, having eaten an abomination which is abhorred by an *akh* who has gone to the necropolis, without removing the impurity in the manner in which they should be pure for the temple of a god ... they have acted in a most evil manner. (Strudwick 2005: 438–41)

The specific taboo foods are not mentioned, presumably because inscribing them on the walls of the tomb would itself be importing impurity.

A false door from the tomb of Pehenwikai at Saqqara particularly addresses 'any man who shall approach these statues in an impure state' (Strudwick 2005: 232), and notes that for anyone who does so 'I shall be judged with him in the place where judgement is.' In addition to impurity being caused by eating taboo foods, the other form of impurity is that of coming to the tomb fresh from sexual activity, hence the entrance to the tomb of Hezi from Saqqara prohibits access by 'any man who shall enter this tomb after he has eaten the abominations which an *akh* abominates or who has had sexual intercourse with a woman' (Strudwick 2005: 277).

Theft from the tomb

Given the extent to which kings were willing to remove significant portions of their predecessors' funerary monuments to use as building material, it is perhaps not surprising that the potential theft of high-quality stone from a private tomb was a concern to the tomb-owner. The façade of the tomb of Ankhi at Saqqara warns: 'Every workman, every stonemason, or every man who shall (do) evil things to the tomb of mine of eternity by tearing out bricks or stones from it, no voice shall be given to him in the sight of any god or any man' (Strudwick 2005: 217–18); likewise Nenki at South Saqqara, who says: 'As for any noble, any official, or any man who shall tear out any stone or any brick from this tomb of mine, I shall be judged with him by the Great God' (Strudwick 2005: 226).

Deliberate destruction in the tomb

The tomb of Inti at Deshasheh, which, perhaps not entirely coincidentally, is one of the earliest of the provincial tombs to show the scenes of conflict and warfare which would become more common in the First Intermediate Period and early Middle Kingdom, says:

As for any man who shall do damage to this (tomb), or who shall [erase] the writing therein, I shall be judged with them by the Great God, the lord of

judgement, in the place of judgement. As for any man who shall desire that he
be buried in his own tomb, and who will protect the property of one who has
passed away – he is an *imakhu* of the Great God. (Strudwick 2005: 371–3)

The different ways a tomb might be attacked were a special concern of
Ankhmeryremeryptah, a royal master-builder, who owned a tomb at Giza:

As for any man who shall enter therein in a hostile manner . . . I shall destroy
their descendants and their doorways on earth. . . . As for any man who shall
destroy anything in this tomb, I shall be judged with them by the Great God.
(Strudwick 2005: 268–9).

Usurpation of the tomb

The most profound problem which might be caused to the deceased is
that their tomb might be usurped in total or in part by later generations (for
a particularly striking example see Spencer 1982). This too was a concern of
Merefnebef who makes threats against anyone who might 'bury any (other)
person within this tomb of mine forever, whether his children, his siblings
or his *ka*-priests' (Strudwick 2005: 438–41).

Individual parts of a tomb might also be usurped; this was clearly the
concern of Idu Seneni, whose tomb at el-Qasr wa es-Sayed contained a burial
shaft for his wife Asenkai with an accompanying inscription which states:

As for this shaft which I have made (its) mouth measuring 6(+ x) cubits [and
with a depth of] 3(+ x) cubits, which I have given to my beloved wife Asenkai,
I shall prevail against any man who shall take it away from the aforementioned
Asenkai. I shall be judged with them by the Great God, the lord of heaven. I shall
seize their necks like a bird's. (Strudwick 2005: 188–9)

Less specific are imprecations such as that of Per-shenay from Abydos, who
warns 'any man who shall violently seize any of my (funerary) property, I
shall be judged with them by the Great God in the necropolis when I am in
the West, for they remember evil in the necropolis' (Strudwick 2005: 351–2).
It might be imagined here that 'property' might not simply refer to the tomb
and its contents, but also any land or other economic assets which were
vested in the funerary cult of the tomb-owner.

Retribution

So what happened to those who did not heed the tomb-owner's warnings? As in life, retribution could be a personal or a legal matter. A text in
the tomb of Ankhmahor in the Teti Pyramid Cemetery expresses the

concern that a person made impure by eating a taboo foodstuff might enter the tomb in an unclean state. For those who do so, Ankhmahor says that he will personally '[seize his neck] like a bird's and put fear in him so that the *akhu* and the living see and are fearful of an excellent *akh*', but also that he will testify against the offender who will be judged 'in that noble court of the Great God'. The idea of the Dead testifying against each other can be turned on its head so that they could also be supportive before the authorities, hence Ankhmahor goes on to say that for one who enters his tomb in a pure state to act in a beneficial way towards Ankhmahor, 'I shall be supportive of him in the necropolis and in the court of the Great God' (for Ankhmahor texts see Strudwick 2005: 264–5).

It is notable that the afterlife is imagined as a place where, as in life, judicial process can be invoked to judge between litigants and, just as the king is the ultimate judicial authority in life, it is not surprising that the 'Great God' has this role in the afterlife. However, the ability of the Dead to use supernatural forces against the Living is suggested in the so-called 'threat-formula', which implies that the Dead could direct elements of the natural world, as in the false door of Meni, which states: 'May the crocodile be in the water and the snake be on the land against him who shall do anything to this (tomb)' (Strudwick 2005: 253).

The fullest example of this threat-formula comes from the small tomb of Peteti at Giza, which bears a double threat:-

> (As for) any person . . . who shall enter this (tomb) and do something therein which is evil . . . it is the crocodile, the hippopotamus or the lion which shall consume them.
>
> (As for) any person who shall do anything evil to this (tomb) . . . the crocodile shall be against them in the water and the snake shall be against them on land, the hippopotamus shall be against them in the water and the scorpion shall be against them on land. (Strudwick 2005: 437)

Talking to the Dead

Although the curse-texts in tombs suggest reasons why the Dead might fear the Living, a more positive relationship was the hoped-for norm. One aspect of the relationship between the Living and the Dead – what the latter wanted from the former and how it was to be provided – has already been discussed in its different aspects. The other aspect of this contract is what the Dead might, in their turn, give to the Living. Whereas the Living have access to, and control over, things the Dead would ideally wish to have – principally food and the welfare of the bodies of the Dead – the dead have access to a parallel world made up of spirit forms which could, potentially, do ill to the Living.

This relationship is made clear in a class of text usually referred to as 'Letters to the Dead' (Gardiner and Sethe 1928; Plater 2001; Wente 1990, 211ff.). The name is slightly misleading in that the communications from the Living to the Dead are written on a range of media. Indeed it is easy to imagine that most communication between the Living and the Dead was verbal in nature, perhaps as an addendum to the recitation of the offering formula at the tomb. It may be that written versions of these requests were particularly urgent, or simply the result of the petitioner being unusually literate. Most of the surviving examples seem rather gnomic in character, as is often the case with an outsider looking at correspondence between individuals who are fully conversant with the subject matter of their exchange, but a few examples give a flavour of the chronological range and subject matter of these texts.

A cunning strategy was to inscribe the letters on objects which were, superficially, offerings to the tomb-owner. This was the case with a piece of linen from the tomb of Sankhenptah from Dynasty 6 at Saqqara on which the tomb-owner's son and wife ask him to intervene in a dispute involving family property. A similar example is a pottery bowl from the cemetery of Qau, dating to the Late Old Kingdom or First Intermediate Period, where, on the interior of the bowl, a man named Shepsi attempts to enlist his father's help in another dispute over property, while on the exterior of the bowl he addresses his mother. This latter text is particularly revealing in that Shepsi first reminds his mother how he has acted to perpetuate her mortuary cult (specifically, he had brought seven quails for her to eat, which she had requested), and that he now seeks her help against 'Sobe-khotep, whom I brought from another town to be buried in his town among his tomb-companions, having given him funerary clothing' (Strudwick 2005: 183). For some reason, Shepsi feels that Sobekhotep is acting against him, in an unspecified way, and he wishes his mother to intervene.

An example from the First Intermediate Period was written on the back of a tomb stela itself – another strategy to ensure that the dead relative would read the message and act on it:

> A message from Merirtifi to Nebitef: How are you? Is the West taking care (of you) [as you] desire? Look, I am your beloved on earth – fight for me, intercede for my name! I have not garbled a spell before you, while making your name to live upon the earth. Drive off the illness of my limbs! May you appear for me as a blessed one before me, that I may see you fighting for me in a dream. I shall lay down offerings for you when the sun's light as risen, and I shall establish an altar for you. (Parkinson 1991: 142)

The *quid pro quo* relationship between the living son and the dead mother could hardly be clearer.

The bowl as a medium for correspondence – presumably because the Dead would have seen the letter once they had consumed whatever foodstuff had been in the bowl – was also used in the Middle Kingdom. The most well-known example is the so-called 'Cairo Bowl' (Parkinson 1991: 143), on which Dedi writes to her (probable) husband, the priest Intef, urging him to fight against malevolent forces for the health of the ailing servant girl Imiu, who is clearly a crucial member of the household: 'Don't you know that it is this servant-maid who makes your house amongst men?'

CHAPTER 6

A Growing Independence

Court and Regional Cemeteries in the Late Old Kingdom

ᒧᒧᒧᒧ

Self-Presentation in Late Old Kingdom Tombs

In the *mastaba* cemeteries of Dynasty 4 the texts and illustrations within the tomb, insofar as they reflected the personal achievements of the deceased, stressed one thing above all others: royal approval. This could be conveyed in a simple way: strings of titles indicating a career at the highest levels of government – and therefore closeness to the king – had an obvious message. By Dynasty 5, a more personalized presentation of royal approval began to appear. One of the most significant tombs in the development of a personal narrative is that of Washptah, 'Overseer of Works of the King' in the reign of Neferirkare in mid-Dynasty 5. The texts on the façade and entrance doorway of Washptah's Saqqara tomb, although damaged, recount a specific instance of royal favour. It appears that Washptah was taken ill in the presence of the king, who then arranged his immediate treatment, praying to Ra, supplying him with alabaster vessels filled with palliatives, and providing him with a carrying chair. The reason for this special royal concern was, as Washptah tells us, because the king recognized the particular diligence that Washptah brought to his work for him. Moreover, the king did not just carry out these acts of favour; he also ordered that they be inscribed upon Washptah's tomb (Strudwick 2005: 318–20). Therefore the tomb of Washptah records not merely a generalized statement of royal favour, but a particular instance where that royal favour is made specifically manifest. The reference to the king

Ancient Egyptian Tombs: The Culture of Life and Death   By Steven Snape
© 2011 Steven Snape

ordering this event to be inscribed on the walls of the tomb links the royal favour explicitly to the tomb as a place of monumental memorialization of Washptah as a person rather than Washptah as an office-holder. This idea of a specific instance of royal concern for an individual courtier has already been noted in the unusual circumstances leading to the creation of the tomb of Debehen in the reign of Menkaure. The extent to which these texts represent genuine autobiography (a self-reflective text written by the subject) or were a 'commissioned' biography is open to some debate (Kloth 2002), but there is obviously a desire to express an individualized narrative specifying a particular act of royal favour, which is somehow linked to the presence of that narrative on the walls of the tomb.

Another key document in the development of this more individualized approach to royal approval can be found on the false door of the chief physician Niankhsekhmet, from his tomb at Saqqara (Strudwick 2005: 302–3). The text on the false door is extremely self-referential to the extent that it describes its own production as the result of a specific act of royal approval. The text describes how Niankhsekhmet asked King Sahure whether he would favour him by the gift of a stone false door for his tomb. In response:

> His Majesty had two false doors of Tura limestone brought for him. They were placed within the audience chamber which is called 'Sahure appears in the White Crown'. The Chief Controller of Craftsmen and a workshop of crafts-men were set to work on them in the presence of the king himself. The work was carried out every day, and the results were apparent every day in the court council. His Majesty arranged for pigment to be placed on them and they were decorated in blue/lapis-lazuli.

Within the confines of a decorum which made the king the ultimate giver of favour, a first-person voice is beginning to be heard. That voice would become louder and more sustained in the later part of Dynasty 5 and Dynasty 6, when texts appear on the walls of tombs which not only refer to royal favour, or even to episodes of particular royal favour, but consist of a narrative of the events which brought that favour. These are accounts which come closer to our understanding of (auto)biography in that they purport to recount actual events in which the subject of the narrative really participated. However, these narratives have an underlying purpose: all the events described reflect well on the narrator (i.e. the tomb-owner) and all have as their theme the sense that what one did attracted the admiration and reward of the king. This existed alongside, and complemented, another major theme in these self-presentations: that what one did in life was good in a wider, though vaguer, moral sense. This moral worthiness, expressed through specific action, would attract divine approval, and should also inspire the respect of future generations, with the practical result that they would wish to make an offering or say the offering prayer for the benefit of the deceased.

Old Kingdom tombs: the self-build option

While royal involvement in building one's tomb meant royal favour, paradoxically a tomb-owner could boast of the opposite situation where he constructed a tomb from his own resources (Godenho 2007: 116–28). This is part of a trend in the Late Old Kingdom, where self-reliance was made a virtue out of necessity given a declining level of royal support for the construction of private tombs and their maintenance. It is also noticeable that Dynasties 5 and 6, which saw an obvious decline in the royal ability and/or desire to build pyramid complexes on the same colossal scale as most of those from Dynasty 4, is the period which has produced some of the largest and most complex private tombs of the Old Kingdom (Cooke 2005). It is probably too simplistic to link the apparent decline in royal tombs with a growth in non-royal tombs as an index in the shift of control over resources in Late Old Kingdom Egypt. However, there are a number of general trends which seem to affect the nature of tombs and the identities of their owners in the Memphite court cemeteries, particularly the growing proportion of high officials who come from outside the royal family from the middle of Dynasty 5 (Eyre 1994: 107–8) and a loosening of the rule of general physical proximity between elite tombs and the contemporary royal pyramid, from about the same period.

Once again the tombs themselves provide evidence as to their manner of construction since the deployment of resources on the tomb can be seen as part of the tomb-owners' statement of their personal worth, in every sense. The stages of tomb construction can be traced through statements in these tombs. The official Akhetmehu tells us that he paid the workmen who constructed his Dynasty 6 tomb at Giza with 'bread and beer; every workman who worked on it thanked all the gods for me. I gave them clothing, oil, copper and grain in great quantity' (Strudwick 2005: 252). Part of the payment for work on the tomb might be to allow individuals to be represented within it, not just family members but workers, as seems to be the case in the Dynasty 4 tomb of Nebemakhet (son of King Khaefre), whose Giza tomb includes two figures of workmen entitled 'His *mehenek* [probably "royal loan-worker"] who inscribed this his tomb, the outline-draughtsman Semerka. His *mehenek* who made this his tomb as a work-project, Inikaf' (Strudwick 2005: 245), although the fact that this is one of the Dynasty 4 *mastaba*-tombs in the pyramid cemeteries at Giza makes this seem more like an individual favour than a form of payment. In a society without money, we should not be surprised to see elements of tombs being purchased using a variety of valuable goods An especially intriguing text comes from a Dynasty 6 tomb at Saqqara which was constructed for Iarti, but which also included a doorway bearing a text which suggests that it was bought for the tomb by Iarti's *ka*-priest. 'The guardian of the tomb', the *ka*-priest Khenemti, says: 'My lord [presumably Iarti] appointed me as assistant to the *ka*-priest. He arranged that I succeed him as *ka*-priest. This doorway was bought for a *daiu*-measure of cloth' (Strudwick 2005: 192). It is tempting to see this doorway to the tomb being built as a post-mortem addition by a grateful Khenemti on the occasion of his inheriting the full benefits of being *ka*-priest to the tomb of Iarti.

One aspect of this self-reliance is the extent to which an individual could provide a suitable burial not only for himself, but also for his dependants. There is significant evidence for the arrangements made by the Living for the burial of their dead relatives. One approach was to provide a burial place for a favoured relative within one's own tomb. This situation is attested archaeologically through rooms, burial shafts or false doors belonging to various family members within a tomb with an obvious main owner, as is the case within the tomb of Nefer. The Dynasty 5 tomb of Wepemnofret at Giza is remarkable in that it contains a text specifically stating the grant of part of the tomb to his son:

> I have granted forever to my son, the lector-priest Ihy, the northern burial place together with the northern tomb-chapel, together with the invocation-offerings which will be in my tomb of eternity of the necropolis, that he might be buried in it and that invocation-offerings might be made for him there. For he is *imakhu*. No brother, no woman, and no child shall have any rights to it, only my eldest son, the lector-priest Ihy, to whom I have granted it. (Strudwick 2005: 203)

Similarly, we have already seen a text describing the construction of a burial shaft for his wife Asenkai in the tomb of Idu Seneni (see Chapter 5, p. 82).

Outside the Memphite cemeteries, at the site of Deir el-Gebrawi, we have already seen the elaborate funeral preparations which Djau, 'Keeper of the Door of the South', made for his father (see Chapter 5, p. 71). Moreover, the younger Djau stresses his filial piety in that 'I saw to it that I was buried in one tomb together with this Djau, particularly through the desire to be with him in one place, and not because of the lack of means to build a second tomb' (Strudwick 2005: 365).

The Rise of the Regions: Local Autonomy and Self-Memorialization in the Late Old Kingdom

At the end of the Old Kingdom, and into the First Intermediate Period, there were three major trends in the building of elite private tombs. The first was the continuation of elite burial in long-established royal cemeteries, but in a less structured manner (see Chapter 5 above for Unas and Teti cemeteries at Saqqara). The second was the continued use of cemeteries which, for particular local reasons, had grown up in the Old Kingdom away from the royal centres – the Qubbet el-Hawa cemetery at Aswan is the best example here. The third, and perhaps most significant, was the development of new cemeteries in the provinces. This is not to say that people had not been buried in the provinces before, but the centralization of the Old Kingdom had meant that anyone who was anyone would wish a career in the Memphite court and a burial in the Memphite court cemeteries. The diminution of royal authority toward the end of the Old Kingdom saw the rise of provincial families who were able to develop their own cemeteries by using their own resources and, in their self-memorializations, celebrated their own achievements through presentations which, while paying lip-service to the presence and authority of the king in Memphis, had more to do with their own accomplishments in the region. This tendency would become stronger as royal authority evaporated in the First Intermediate Period, as provincial cemeteries became dominated by local elites, effec-tively regional dynasties, some of whom would become competitors in the struggle to gain political authority, and royal status. Away from Memphis, and without access to the skilled architects and artists of the Memphite royal atelier, provincial tombs developed in ways which both mirrored and diverged from those tombs which were built in the royal pyramid cemeter-ies. A common theme was that of personal resources as a major factor in tomb construction, and the extent to which those personal resources were influenced by political and economic change at the end of the Old Kingdom.

There has been much debate, and relatively little consensus, as to the factors which led to the gradual disintegration of royal authority at the end of the Old Kingdom. When we look at tombs we see the effects, not the causes, of change. But change is certainly apparent, and outside the Memphite area the way in which provincial cemeteries, and the tombs within them, develop gives a clear signal that economic and political power are moving away from the centre (the royal court at Memphis) to the rest of Egypt. It is perhaps not surprising that the most detailed and informative of these tomb-based self-presentations are away from Memphis itself, in the provinces. These were regions where possibilities for individual action were greater and one could more easily portray oneself as acting for the king in areas distant from him, especially in marginal regions. Therefore, at the end of the Old Kingdom, there was an increasing confidence among provincial administrators, who, theoretically appointed by and loyal to the king, were masters of their own regions – little hereditary dynasties with increasingly obvious control over resources in their regions, and the willingness to use those resources for their own self-promotion, manifest most obviously (at least as far as the surviving archaeological record is concerned) in tomb building. These are tombs which were constructed by provincial officials, in the provinces, using the materials and architectural forms which came to hand. In some cases an attempt to emulate Memphite *mastaba* construction can be seen, as with the peculiar rock-cut Dynasty 5 *mastaba* of the 'Overseer of New Towns' Nykaiankh, near the site of Tihna in Middle Egypt, which was later replaced by a second tomb (Fraser 1902; Strudwick 2005: 195–9). More successfully, local conditions were adapted to create a quite different form of elite burial: the rock-cut tomb of Upper Egypt. The masonry-built *mastaba*-tombs, while suitable for the plateau of the Memphite necropolis, were not well suited to most of Middle and Upper Egypt, although variants continued in suitable locations, including the important cemetery at Dendera (Fischer 1968; Petrie 1900). In many parts of the Nile Valley between Memphis and the first cataract of the Nile at Aswan, the river and its floodplain is overlooked not by a relatively low desert plateau, but by high, steep cliffs which often come very close to the river itself. These areas are not suitable for *mastaba* construction, but the local topography suggests a very different type of tomb, one which is cut into the face of the cliffs.

Living and dying on the edge: tombs at Aswan

One of the most important regional cemeteries of the Late Old Kingdom is that which is furthest from Memphis, on the southern border of Egypt at Aswan. Local officials based here, on the island of Elephantine, had the unique task of both protecting Egypt's southern border and leading trading and political missions into Nubia. In Dynasty 6 the importance of this role seems to have been reflected in the development of a series of large and obvious rock-cut tombs on the West Bank of the Nile in the cliffs at Qubbet el-Hawa (Edel 2008). These tombs are conventional and somewhat dull in their graphic content; scenes typical of contemporary tombs at Memphis – images of offering to the tomb-owner, fishing and fowling, etc. – dominate. However, the Qubbet el-Hawa tombs are notable for their striking presence high in the cliffs, visible for miles around (Figure 6.1), a landscape-dominating feature which was to become the

Figure 6.1   Tombs at Qubbet el-Hawa

most immediately obvious characteristic of First Intermediate Period and Middle Kingdom tombs at sites such as Beni Hasan. Some of the Qubbet el-Hawa tombs are approached by means of a steep ramp, direct from the river's edge, leading to the quarried façades of the larger tombs in this group. It was on these open façades, in contrast to the conventionality of the interior of these tombs, that hieroglyphic texts were carved which are extraordinary in the richness of detail they give in recounting the Nubian adventures of their owners. Two themes compete and merge in these texts: personal autonomy and royal reward. They set the scene for what will follow in the First Intermediate Period, where royal reward withers, but personal autonomy flourishes. Three of these tombs are worthy of particular attention: those of Harkhuf, Pepinakht/Hekaib and the shared tomb of Mekhu and Sabni.

The most important of these tombs, at least as far as the historical interest of its inscriptions is concerned, is that of Harkhuf, 'Overseer of Foreign Lands', who served under Merenre and Pepi II. His tomb has a wide open court cut into the side of the cliff, creating plenty of space on the façade of the tomb (Figure 6.2) for a detailed biographical text whose main subject matter is episodic: the four expeditions he led to Nubia (Strudwick 2005: 328–33). This text is significant in that it indicates the growing political integration of previously separate Nubian groups during the Late Old Kingdom. On a personal level, Harkhuf was especially pleased by a letter he received from the young king Pepi II at the conclusion of his fourth

Figure 6.2   The tomb of Harkhuf at Qubbet el-Hawa

expedition. Pepi had received a letter from Harkhuf announcing his safe return from Nubia and stating that he had brought back a 'dancing dwarf of the god from the land of spirits'. Pepi was thrilled by the prospect of seeing this dwarf and gave detailed instructions as to how Harkhuf should take good care of him. This seemingly trivial exchange was a specific instance of royal approval, and the letter from Pepi to Harkhuf was reproduced in full, occupying a substantial portion of the northern half of the façade of the tomb.

The tomb of Pepinakht (also known as Hekaib) also has (auto)biographical texts on its exterior, on either side of the doorway (Strudwick 2005: 333–5). As 'Overseer of Foreign Lands', Pepinakht undertook expeditions for Pepi II to subdue Nubia and to the land of the Aamu to recover the body of Ankhty, son of Kaaper, who had been killed by the 'sand-dwellers' while building a boat in order to travel to Punt. Pepinakht/Hekaib was also revered as a local saint, after a popular and long-lasting cult was established for him during the First Intermediate Period, focused on a chapel to him on the island of Elephantine (Habachi 1985).

One of the most remarkable of these tombs is the double tomb of Sabni and his father Mekhu (Figure 6.3). This tomb is approached by a double ramp leading to a broad, shared courtyard at the rear of which two doors each lead to a columned hall belonging to each man. Around the

Figure 6.3 The tombs of Mekhu and Sabni at Qubbet el-Hawa

door of Sabni's tomb is a biographical text which tells a remarkable story (Strudwick 2005: 335–9). The damaged narrative begins with Sabni being told of the death of his father Mekhu while on an expedition in Nubia. Assembling an expeditionary force including 100 asses, he set off to recover his father's body: 'I had him transported by the troop of my funerary estate. I made for him a coffin; I brought it together with its [lid] in order to bring him out of these foreign lands.' Apparently this filial act attracted the admiration of the king, who sent 'two embalmers, a senior lector-priest, one who is on annual duty, the inspector of the *wabet*, mourners and the whole of the equipment from the "House of Perfection"'. After burying his father 'in his tomb of the necropolis', Sabni went north to Memphis for the reward of the king in goods and promotion. There are 11 burial shafts associated with this tomb, presumably to cater for the families of Mekhu and Sabni, although there may have been a multi-generational aspect to this, as suggested by the inscription added by Mekhu (II), son of Sabni, on the façade of the tomb. In this text Mekhu II continues the theme of displaying filial piety and attracting royal approval through the burial of a father. He reports that on his return to Elephantine after a visit to the royal residence at Memphis he discovered that his father had died: 'I found him there in the *wabet* laid out in the manner of the dead in the *wabet*.' Returning to Memphis he informed the king, who then made sure that 'all the requirements of burial were provided from the places of the Residence (as would have been done for) a nobleman in the pyramid of Neferkare [i.e. Pepi II], for the one who is *imakhu* in the sight of the great god, Sabni'. By the 'pyramid of Neferkare' one should probably understand the provision of a tomb broadly associated with the pyramid complex of Pepi II at South Saqqara; the main thrust of this section, as it relates to the dead Sabni, is that royal favour and *imakhu* could apply to a servant of the king at this distant frontier just as it could for a member of the Memphite court. It is also notable that some of these individuals stationed on Old Kingdom Egypt's wildest frontier have titles which connect them to the court of the royal residence at Memphis: Pepinakht has titles which associate him with the priesthood of the pyramids of Pepi II and Merenre, while Sabni was connected to the administration of the pyramid of Pepi II.

Royal favour and self-reliance in the oases

Even more distant from the centre of Old Kingdom royal power was the oasis of Dakhleh in the western desert. This oasis had come under Egyptian control sometime in late Dynasty 5 / early Dynasty 6, with its administrative centre near the modern village of Balat. This site has two elements: a settlement at Ayn Asil and, 1.5 km away, the necropolis of Qila el-Dabba, which contains a series of tombs built for the 'Governors of the Oasis'. It is worth noting that the town of Ayn Asil contained a group of *ka*-chapels for the funerary cult of some of the governors who were buried in the Qila el-Dabba cemetery, a secondary yet important part of their funerary provision, and one which was, presumably, more convenient to use than the tombs themselves. The inspiration for the Qila el-Dabba tombs is the Old Kingdom *mastaba*, but with variations to fit local conditions, not least the amount of available space leading to the construction of expansive structures within mudbrick enclosure walls, containing a series of courts and chapels with niched 'palace-façade' decoration (Castel 2005). Perhaps the most impressive of these tombs is that built by Khentika, who, like most of the known tomb-owning governors, served under the long-lived Pepi II. This tomb was constructed by excavating a vast pit, at the bottom of which the chambers of the *mastaba* were assembled, after which the pit (apart from entrance corridors / shafts) was re-filled (Figure 6.4). The superstructures of the tomb of Khentika and his probable successor Khentikaupepi each contained a large stela which was the prime medium for conveying the texts found on the walls of Memphite *mastaba*s. That belonging to Khentika (Strudwick 2005: 374–5) is conventional in the way it expresses Khentika's wish to become an *akh* and to be *imakhu*. It also contains an extensive 'appeal to the Living' and notes that Khentika 'made this stela in the wish that my perfect name be

Figure 6.4   The tomb of Khentika in the Dakhleh Oasis

remembered by those who live upon the earth'. Khentikaupepi's stela
(Strudwick 2005: 375) tells 'you who live upon the earth' that 'I made this
tomb of mine in the West [in] three months, and I erected its enclosure wall
in ... months. I established it with servants of a funerary estate and I
established payment for them.' The general tenor of these stelae seems to
confirm what one might suspect from the tombs themselves: that they were
established far from royal involvement using the resources under the
control of these local governors. However, this likely self-reliance is tem-
pered on the stela of Khentikaupepi by the loyal statements that 'I am noble
in the sight of the king, and my name is better known by His Majesty than any
other rulers of the oases' and 'I have seen to it that these two obelisks of mine
are inscribed with details of what I have done for the Palace' (Strudwick 2005:
375). It is also the case that grave goods within these tombs include objects of
obvious favour, including alabaster vessels inscribed with royal names
(Minault-Gout 1992: 81–3; Valloggia 1986: 78–81) – a standard item of royal
gift-giving in Dynasty 6 (Arnold and Pischikova 1999).

New cemeteries: Meir and the Old Kingdom–Middle Kingdom transition

The Qila el-Dabba cemetery at Balat is a good example of new cemeteries
being founded during the Late Old Kingdom. The reason for this foundation

is understandable enough: an area coming under direct Egyptian control for the first time and the necessity of providing appropriate accommodation for the Living and the Dead of the new communities established there. But new necropolii could also be established in the Nile Valley itself, as a response to changing social and political conditions of Dynasties 5 and 6. A particularly good example of this is the site of Meir, cemetery of the ancient city of Cusae in Middle Egypt. An important regional centre from the Late Old Kingdom to the Middle Kingdom, Meir does not, unlike Moalla, Asyut or Thebes, seem to have been the cemetery of local dynasts who were major players in the competition for regional and, ultimately, national supremacy during the First Intermediate Period. Nevertheless, the necropolis of Meir displays a good deal of personal autonomy and dynastic solidarity in the tombs of its local elite. In the reign of Pepi II the nomarch Pepiankhheryib cut a tomb for himself in the cliffs of Meir, seemingly with the intention of founding a new necropolis for his family: '. . . in the area "Lord of Truth" (*Neb-Maat*), a pure and perfect place where there had been no (previous) activity, in which no other ancestor had done (anything). It was I who opened up this area, which shall function for me as a necropolis' (Strudwick 2005: 370). Pepiankhheryib's authority, as expressed in his biographical text, came from two sources. First was his political authority as the royally appointed administrator in the nome ('Vizier, Overseer of Royal Document-Scribes, Seal-Bearer of the King of Lower Egypt'), which gave him access to royal income which was deployed for royal purposes. Secondly, and possibly just as important, was his local economic authority, deriving from his position as 'Overseer of Priests of Hathor, Mistress of Cusae', which probably gave him control over the income from land held by the local temple. It may have been this income which allowed him to construct his large and well-decorated tomb. Thus his wealth and political autonomy gave him local power which could be expressed in tomb building.

Weni and the (Re-)Emergence of Abydos

Among the known regional tomb-owners of the Late Old Kingdom the most remarkable is Weni, who was buried at Abydos. This Upper Egyptian site was to have much wider importance from the Middle Kingdom as the burial place of Osiris, but, in the Late Old Kingdom, it seems to have been a politically sensitive area: the seat of the newly created Governorship of Upper Egypt and supplier of queens of kings Pepi I and Pepi II from the family of the powerful local dynast, Djau. The present overview of the way in which different parts of the Abydene cemeteries were used at different times takes as its starting point the end of the Old Kingdom. At the end of the Old Kingdom, Abydos seems to have been the seat of the Overseers of Upper Egypt, a higher echelon of administration designed to superintend the nomarchs of Upper Egypt (Fischer 1968: 201–2). Before the Middle Kingdom, no Thinite nomarchs were buried at Abydos, although several Overseers of Upper Egypt were (Fischer 1968: 202 n. 800).

The tomb of Weni at Abydos is notable for a number of reasons. One was the way in which it seems to have become the nucleus of a Late Old Kingdom necropolis which grew around this tomb of a local 'saint'. The second is the self-presentation which comes from the tomb, which, in its detail and extent, was unprecedented. Weni tells the reader how, during his long career in royal service, he served the king in a staggeringly varied number of ways (Strudwick 2005: 352–7; for a discussion of the career see Eyre 1994; Richards 2002). He notes that he began his career at court during the reign of Teti and was promoted under Pepi I, who he claims particularly favoured him, a favour which found concrete expression in royal provision for Weni's tomb:

> When I requested from the majesty of my lord that there be provided for me a sarcophagus of white stone of Tura His Majesty had the seal-bearer of the god and a boat-crew under his command cross over and bring back this sarcophagus from Tura.
>
> He brought it himself in a great barge of the Residence, together with its lid, a false door, an architrave, two jambs and an offering table.

As Eyre (1994: n. 32) notes, these architectural elements would have been intended for a tomb in the Memphite necropolis; whether they were stored and re-used at Abydos is unclear. Recently excavated inscribed parts of Weni's Abydos tomb were primarily inscribed with titles held by Weni late in his career, although Richards (2003: 405) suggests that some sections of decoration on the doorjambs of the Abydos Offering Chapel may have originated in a royal workshop.

Weni goes on to specify other instances of particular royal favour owing to his excellence, including responsibility for hearing a case within the royal harem against a queen, his leading of an army of 'many tens of thousands' in repeated expeditions to the Levant, and promotion by Merenre. Weni was also given the responsibility of procuring elements for Merenre's pyramid:

> His Majesty sent me to Ibhat in order to bring back the sarcophagus (which is called) 'Chest of the Living' and its lid, together with a costly and noble pyramidion for the pyramid of Merenre.
>
> His Majesty sent me to Elephantine in order to bring back a granite false door and its lintel, together with doors and associated elements of granite,

and in order to bring back a granite doorway and lintels for the upper chamber of the pyramid of Merenre.

His Majesty sent me to Hatnub in order to bring back a great offering-table of Hatnub alabaster, and I organized that this offering-table was brought down . . . despite there being no water on the sandbanks I moored successfully at the pyramid of Merenre.

His Majesty sent me to excavate five canals in Upper Egypt and to make three barges and four transport-ships. . . . I completed this task in the space of one year, including filling them with water and the loading of large amounts of granite for the pyramid of Merenre.

The great limestone slab bearing the autobiographical text of Weni, now in the Cairo Museum, was discovered by Mariette in 1860 as part of his poorly recorded excavations at Abydos, on a high part of the 'Middle Cemetery'. The size of the slab suggests that its original context was a significant funerary monument. That monument was discovered in 1999 by a team led by Janet Richards (Richards 2003). Excavating in the 'Middle Cemetery' (Figure 2.2), in an area known for its use in the Late Old Kingdom, Richards uncovered a massive mudbrick enclosure with walls 29 m long on each side, 3 m thick and at least 5.5 m tall. This enclosure, which contained a burial shaft, would have been filled and roofed after burial to create a huge *mastaba* on the highest part of the Middle Cemetery, the size and location of which would have made it strikingly visible. The exterior of the *mastaba* had a series of structures built against it, the niche for a false door and an Offering Chapel. The exterior of this chapel is the most likely original location for the autobiographical slab. The burial chamber of the tomb, accessed via a shaft within the *mastaba*, had suffered deliberate later burning, and an equally deliberate smashing of statues within Weni's *serdab* (Richards 2000). It is tempting to relate this destruction to the events mentioned in the *Instruction for Merikare* (see Chapter 7, p. 114), particularly as there seems to have been some attempt to restore this tomb, and indeed to respect this and other Late Old Kingdom tombs on the eastern part of the 'Middle Cemetery', especially during the intensive competition for space in the Abydos cemeteries during the Middle Kingdom.

Other elite burials in the Middle Cemetery included that of the Vizier Iww, father of Weni. His tomb, discovered by Lepsius but subsequently lost, had a substructure of a barrel-vaulted chamber, accessed by a square, vertical shaft and a superstructure of unknown form which contained at least one stela (Brovarski 1994b). The tomb of Nekhty/Idi, another Overseer of Upper Egypt, was close in both location and style to that of Weni. In addition, although there is relatively little in the way of indication of surface features, stelae of Late Old Kingdom date belonging to a range of elite individuals are known from Abydos suggesting a more general importance of the necropolis during Dynasty 6 (Brovarski 1994a, 1994b) as an 'eternal neighborhood of the wealthy and powerful' (Richards 2002: 77). Moreover, in a hint to the desirability that Abydos would achieve as a place for burial in the Middle Kingdom, texts within these tombs refer to their location for the burial (*krstt*) of Weni 'on the west of Abydos' (Richards 2002: 98) and for Iww 'in this his tomb of Abydos' (Brovarski 1994a: 105).

The extent to which Weni and his near contemporaries at Aswan acted under direct orders or on their own initiative is not always obvious. Weni seems to have been directed to carry out specific instructions by the king, but the Aswan texts are more ambiguous. The impression given is that these people have a general commission from the king to act within a set of expected parameters (e.g. to organize trading expeditions to Nubia, smite Asiatics, acquire stone), but that within those parameters their capacity for independent action was reasonably broad. This may not be true; trading expeditions of this kind may have been tightly controlled from the Memphite centre, although the specifics of what one might actually come across in Nubia was necessarily a matter of chance. The account of the dancing dwarf gives the impression of being a piece of serendipity rather than planning, and Sabni notes that his report to the king on the occasion of his father's death included a reference to a 'seven-cubit long lion-skin' which his father had acquired in Nubia. The impression given is of semi-independent individuals whose successful initiative attracted royal favour. The next level of personal initiative and action would be to become a fully independent individual whose actions attract not royal but divine favour. For this to happen the king needs to disappear, or at least to be sidelined, and this is the opportunity presented by the collapse of royal authority at the end of the Old Kingdom and the emergence of possibilities for individual advancement in the First Intermediate Period.

Sub-Elite Tombs in the Late Old Kingdom

The tombs of Weni and his relations at Abydos and of Harkhuf, Pepinakht, *et al.* at Aswan, are good examples of elite tombs of the Late Old Kingdom which, physically at least, do not exist within a subsidiary relationship to contemporary (or, indeed, non-contemporary) royal tombs, as was the common pattern in the Memphite necropolis. Indeed one might see the situation as being reversed in that these important provincial tombs, and others, were themselves the focus for the development of regional cemeteries whereby sub-elite tombs were built in deliberate relationship to them.

This idea of a focus on the tomb of an elite local individual as the nucleus for the growth of a regional cemetery was not new to the Late Old Kingdom; indeed there is an example at Abydos itself of a small Dynasty 3–4 cemetery near the North Cemetery/Kom es-Sultan ('Cemetery 'D' – Peet and Loat 1914: 8–22; Richards 2002: 85) which contains a few hundred small tombs built around two large *mastabas*. However, by Dynasty 6 the focus had shifted, with the tomb of Weni acting as the nucleus of a cemetery which, at least in part, grew up around this cluster of large, elite tombs on the highest part of the Middle Cemetery. It is unclear why this should have occurred, but the presence of hundreds of beer and offering jars of Dynasty 6 around the tomb of Weni (Richards 2002: 94) suggests that a level of provision of offerings was taking place which benefited both Weni and the poorer tombs clustered nearby. It may be that an extension of the principle of *imakhu* 'being provided for' included 'the duty of a more influential and richer person to take care of the poor and socially disadvantaged' (Malek 2000a: 113).

The sub-elite tombs consisted of simple shaft-and-chamber burials, with a limited range of grave goods and probably little in the way of visible superstructures, clustered on the so-called 'Eastern Ridge', a distinct hillock between the high hill of the Middle Cemetery and the cultivation. Several archaeologists dug on this ridge in the early decades of the twentieth century, especially John Garstang, who excavated 'several hundred tombs of the Vth and VIth Dynasties' on the Eastern Ridge (Garstang 1909: 127), followed by Ayrton and Loat (1909), Loat (1923), Peet (1914b) and Frankfort (1930). From the reports on their work it is possible to reconstruct a typical tomb of the Late Old Kingdom. The tombs had a square shaft between 1.5 and 3.5 m in depth; sometimes the top of the shaft was lined with mudbricks to prevent collapse from the loose surface gravel. A roughly cut single chamber at the bottom of the shaft, almost always on the south side and usually sealed with mudbricks, was just big enough for the coffin of a single interment. The body was placed in a small, plain wooden coffin. The body was almost always placed on its left side, the head to the north, extended with knees slightly bent. The arms were crossed on the chest or laid by the sides, occasionally with one hand on the pelvis, although Loat (1923: 162) maintained that there is no particular hand position. However, detailed studies of the position of the body may well be irrelevant; some bodies had clearly shifted to one end of the coffin, probably due to the tilting of the coffin to get it down the shaft of the tomb.

Grave goods were generally few in number. Ayrton identified female graves on the assumed basis that women were thought to have richer grave goods, so that any of the better graves were assumed to be those of women, although no examination of the skeletal material to determine the validity

Figure 6.5 A sub-elite tomb at Abydos, excavated by John Garstang in 1909
(© Garstang Museum of Archaeology, University of Liverpool)

of this hypothesis seems to have been carried out. 'Women's' tombs
typically contained a copper mirror and a wooden headrest. Alabaster
vessels were the most common find and were usually placed near the head,
but outside the coffin or on its lid. Pottery vessels were found, but in modest
numbers; some small fineware pottery vessels having their own wooden
box. Men's tombs typically contained a long wooden staff, sometimes with
a copper head, and a wooden headrest. Pottery vessels also occurred in
these tombs, as did, in a few exceptional cases, groups of copper objects.
Other objects found in these tombs which have not been traditionally
regarded as being gender-specific are the leg-bones of oxen placed on the
coffin-lid over the feet of the body (Figure 6.5). Ayrton and Loat's description of one of the more intact burials excavated by them, F.65, is probably
the most comprehensive we have of one of these 'Late Old Kingdom' tombs
at Abydos, and is worth quoting in full:

> Grave F.65 is a very good type of these burials. The skeleton (a woman) lay on
> the left side, with head to the north-west, arms at the sides, and knees slightly
> drawn up. Under the left temple were the remains of a wooden pillow. Before
> the face stood a large alabaster vase, behind the head was a flat red pottery
> vase with handles, and at the back of the neck a small red polished pottery
> vase. Before the breast lay a large copper mirror with a lotiform wooden
> handle, behind the knees was a large polished red pottery vase and a copper
> needle. Round the neck were two strings of green glazed steatite beads, one
> with a large carnelian bead in the centre, and the other supporting a steatite

button seal with the figure of a hornet cut on the face. On the lid of the coffin, over the knees, was placed a small red pottery vase, and against the outside of the coffin at the feet leant a large globular vase of rough pottery, over the mouth of which was placed an inverted polished red pottery bowl with a spout. (Ayrton and Loat 1909: 3)

There is very little evidence for superstructures associated with these tombs.

Reisner at Naga ed-Der, Brunton at Qau

However, despite the attention given to the Middle Cemetery at Abydos, the most thorough excavation and publication of a cemetery site of the 'Late Old Kingdom' before the Second World War is the work of George Reisner at Naga ed-Der (Reisner 1932). The proximity of Naga ed-Der to Abydos, c.33 km to the north, makes it a good data set with which to compare the cultural material from Abydos. In fact both the tombs and their contents are remarkably similar to those of the Late Old Kingdom at Abydos. Tombs were of the shaft-and-chamber type, with the chamber at the foot of either the long or short side of the rectangular shaft. The chamber was often closed off with a wall of mudbricks. The shafts were generally short, when compared to Abydene examples, and there seems to be no evidence for lining the top of the shaft with bricks. No superstructures were found, except for a few traces of what Reisner took to be mudbrick *mastaba*s over the shafts, and he thought that the spacing of the shafts indicated that each shaft may have had a simple *mastaba*-like superstructure around it. The body was usually extended/partially extended with the head to the local north, and the partially contracted bodies have their faces to the left/east. The body was usually wrapped in linen, and coffins, where found, are comparatively tall. Interestingly, Reisner linked the development of his Old Kingdom cemetery 500–900 at Naga ed-Der to the presence of five nuclear tombs of local 'Headmen', with subsidiary graves sited around them (Reisner 1932: 186–9). While the precise identities of, and the relationship between, the 'Headmen' and the owners of the smaller tombs are uncertain, the subsidiary role of the one to the other has not been seriously questioned (O'Connor 1975: 23).

The other major cemetery excavation in Middle/Upper Egypt is Brunton's work at Qau and Badari (1927–30 (Vol. I)). Tomb-types at Qau were often difficult to determine because of the 'loose gravelly nature of the soil in which they are dug', while in some places the ground is 'very sandy' (Brunton 1927–30 (Vol. I): 43). In such circumstances brick reinforcement round the top of the shaft is not surprising. No superstructures over the shafts were noted. In all sub-periods of the Late Old Kingdom, simple graves were the most common, although these could be anything up to a remarkable 4.5 m deep. In Dynasty 6 a shaft with a chamber to the west was common, but became less popular and was replaced by a chamber to the east in Dynasties 7–8 and 9–10. Single chambers were the norm in all periods and there were no chambers at different levels 'as often found at Abydos. Probably the spaciousness of the cemetery made such crowding unnecessary' (Brunton 1927–30 (Vol. I): 45). Coffins were difficult to recognize because of the damp, but there does not seem to have been any damage through the activities of white ants. It is probable that all the bodies were wrapped in linen but the damp conditions made this difficult to ascertain. There was a 'striking variety' of attitude, but in the vast majority of cases the head was to the north and the face to the east. A number of wooden boxes were found with the average dimensions of a 23 cm cube. These contained 'toilet outfit, spare beads and amulets, and knick-knacks' (Brunton 1927–30 (Vol. I): 60). In one large example (*c*.43 cm long) was a mirror, an exception to the general rule that mirrors were found in front of the face. Legs of beef were not uncommon as offerings, but in only one case was an example found on the coffin; the provision of a dish of meat was more common.

CHAPTER 7

Ankhtify

A Time of Change

୮ᒣ୮ᒣ୮ᒣ୮ᒣ

A Time of Chaos?

Some of the literary production of the Middle Kingdom had a propagandistic bent which aimed to present the First Intermediate Period as a time of
(tautologically) kingless chaos. Within this genre of pessimistic literature,
chaos could be characterized by a variety of normative inversions: for
example, 'The poor of the land have become rich, (while) the man of
property is a pauper.' Some of these inversions, and generalized statements
of woe, relate to aspects of tombs, tomb-ownership and tomb-provisioning
for kings and private individuals alike. They refer to situations ranging
from the inaccessibility of good-quality materials for burial owing to the
collapse of overseas trade to the deliberate destruction of tombs and their
contents. A particularly full set is contained within the text known as the
Dialogue of Ipuwer and the Lord-of-All, or the *Admonitions of Ipuwer* (for a
convenient translation, see Lichtheim 1973: 149–63; for fuller study, see
Enmarch 2008):

> No-one sails north to Byblos today; what shall we do for cedar/pine trees for
> our mummies? . . .
> Those who were in the embalming-place are cast on high ground, embalmers'
> secrets are thrown away . . . .
> What the pyramid hid is empty . . . .
> He who could not make a coffin owns a tomb, and, see, those who owned
> tombs are cast on high ground . . . .
> Statues are burned and their tombs destroyed . . .

Ancient Egyptian Tombs: The Culture of Life and Death   By Steven Snape
© 2011 Steven Snape

There are aspects of these somewhat melodramatic statements which are worth consideration as possibly reflecting a historical reality, but there is also good reason to think that the changed situation of the First Intermediate Period was not necessarily an unmitigated disaster as far as tomb-provision was concerned, especially outside the major centres. In fact it has been argued that the level of wealth in local cemeteries, as displayed through the quantity and quality of grave goods, became significantly greater during the First Intermediate Period (Seidlmayer 1990). In addition, away from the royal influence, the First Intermediate Period and Middle Kingdom gave local dynasts the ability to do what, in the Old Kingdom, had been a royal prerogative: to create a tomb which was incised on the landscape, which became part of the landscape, which made royal/local power displayed forever in the landscape, visible to all future generations.

The First Intermediate Period at Saqqara

Perhaps the most obvious question to ask about this period is: what happened in the great Old Kingdom royal cemeteries of the Memphite necropolis? What filled the power vacuum of a disappeared royal authority, and what effect did that have on tomb building? For most of the period between the effective end of the Old Kingdom at the close of Dynasty 6 and the re-unification of the Middle Kingdom during Dynasty 11, the dominant regional power in the north of Egypt was the Herakleopolitans of Dynasties 9–10. The site of Herakleopolis Magna itself, strategically located at the entrance to the Faiyum, has had a somewhat patchy history of archaeological preservation, and if significant tombs belonging to the kings of the 'House of Khety' were built there, and survived whatever degradations the city suffered after the triumph of the Thebans at the end of the First Intermediate Period, they have still to be found (Pérez Die 1990, 2005; Spanel 2001 and refs cit.). The Herakleopolitan domain included the Memphite area, and the cemeteries there – especially Saqqara – continued in use during the period. But although the locations of the tombs of most of the 18 Herakleopolitan rulers named on the Turin Canon king list are as obscure as much else about them, there is one significant exception, that of Merikare, a ruler late in the sequence who is named as being active against the Thebans in the tomb of his vassal Khety at Asyut. Several of the officials who served the cult of Merikare, based at his pyramid, 'The Pyramid which is Flourishing of Places', were buried at Saqqara, suggesting that the pyramid is to be found there too. The most likely candidate for his royal tomb is an unexcavated mound near Teti's pyramid (Malek 1994). The significance of this structure is that it shows the desire of at least one Herakleopolitan king to follow the traditions of royal pyramid building in the most important royal necropolis of the Old Kingdom. Whether this was a personal initiative by Merikare (who, uniquely, had the resources to carry out this work?) or part of a general Herakleopolitan trend is unclear.

The development of specific favoured locations in the Saqqara necropolis included the clustering of burials around the tombs of local 'saints' (Malek 2000b; Wildung 1977). This phenomenon developed from the practice of deifying important local figures, including non-royals such as Hekaib at Aswan or Imhotep at Saqqara (whose tomb has not been found), and individual kings, including Unas (Altenmüller 1974) and Teti at Saqqara or Niuserre at Abusir (Schäfer 1908). The level of elevated respect given to these individuals is not always easy to define, particularly where private individuals are concerned, and it can sometimes be difficult to draw a clear distinction between deification/reverence and, indeed, worship/offering; the case of the Vizier Mehu, whose tomb was served by two generations of *ka*-priests of the family of a man named Bia, buried close to Mehu, is a good case in point (Fischer 1965). A relevant ethnographic parallel to the phenomenon of the prominent tomb of a local 'holy man' becoming the focus of both religious activity and the development of cemeteries can be seen in the presence of tombs of 'sheikhs' in Egypt today. It is therefore not surprising to see the cemetery close to the Teti pyramid, like other parts of the Saqqara necropolis, continuing in use during the First Intermediate Period and Middle Kingdom.

Town Cemeteries of the Late Old Kingdom

By Dynasty 6 a cemetery of local officials had developed at the Upper Egyptian town of Edfu. Tombs here included a mudbrick *mastaba* belonging to Isi which became the focus of a cult as he was regarded as a local 'saint'. Isi refers to his progress along the *cursus honorum* under the kings Isesi, Unas and Teti (Strudwick 2005: 340–2), but if royal patronage was at the heart of Isi's presented identity, the later Dynasty 6 tomb of Meryrenefer Qar at Edfu was much more individual in its content (Strudwick 2005: 342–4). Qar refers to his education at court under Teti and Pepi I, and his subsequent commission by Merenre to 'go south to the second nome of Upper Egypt as a Sole Companion, as Great Chief of the Nome, as Overseer of the Grain of Upper Egypt, and as Overseer of Priests'. Armed with this set of titles, giving him comprehensive powers in the nome, Qar was able to act in a way which would have been recognizable to

First Intermediate Period local rulers. The largest section of his tomb inscription is an extensive list of specific actions based on righting wrongs and acting appropriately, including: 'I buried every man of this nome who had no son with linen from the property of my estate.' Smaller, more modest tombs at Edfu, belonging to individuals who nonetheless considered themselves as worthy of a self-promotional autobiography, may be represented by stelae such as that of the 'Overseer of the Slaughterers of the whole house of Khuu', called Merer (Černý 1961), who claims to have served (or at least to have made temple offerings on behalf of) 13 rulers, possibly based at Edfu. The rectangular stela of Merer, 87 cm wide and 52.5 cm tall, and of definitely provincial craftsmanship, may have been erected in a now-lost superstructure to a simple shaft tomb of the First Intermediate Period, perhaps associated with a larger tomb belonging to one of the 'House of Khuu'.

It is notable that the Old Kingdom/First Intermediate Period cemetery at Edfu was close to the town itself (Bruyère 1937). Similar town cemeteries from this period have been found at other sites, particularly in the Nile Delta, which combined the extensive use of easily acquired mudbrick with a limited amount of the less-available limestone. In the eastern Delta, Bubastis was probably one of the largest towns of the Old and Middle Kingdoms, with a cemetery area to match (Bakr 1992; Farid 1964). In the central Delta during Dynasty 6 a cemetery of small, mudbrick *mastaba*s, some with stone elements, developed in the city of Mendes (Redford 2001). At Kom el-Hisn in the western Delta, the tomb of Khesu consists of a limestone core, within what was probably a substantial mudbrick *mastaba*, whose inner walls carried standard Old Kingdom scenes of hunting, butchery and offering (Silverman 1988). Similar town cemeteries occur in the valley too, including one at Memphis at Kom el-Fakhry (Jeffreys 1985: 69).

'A Man without Equal': Ankhtify at Moalla

If the pyramid of Merikare can be regarded as a genuine royal tomb, there are a number of tombs of the First Intermediate Period which straddle the divide between the royal and non-royal, not least because, to a significant degree, their form is based on the royal prototype of the pyramid complex. This is the case at Kom Dara in Middle Egypt (Weill 1958), where an enormous pile of mudbrick, sand and gravel (Figure 7.1), containing a central Burial Chamber, represents the remains of a pyramidal tomb with an unknown owner – possibly a Dynasty 8 king called Khui. But the most striking example of this phenomenon is the tomb of Ankhtify at Moalla

Figure 7.1 The 'pyramid' of Kom Dara

(Godenho 2007, from which the translations below have been taken). Ankhtify was one of the local rulers who emerged out of the political vacuum of the First Intermediate Period. An enemy of the ultimately triumphant Thebans, he controlled most of Upper Egypt south of Thebes. In this stretch of the Nile Valley he oversaw an efficient administration which served the needs of the distressed population at a time of crisis, he was a warlord who was victorious over his enemies, and a leader called to this role by the god Horus. We know all this because Ankhtify tells us so. In a time without kings, Ankhtify acted for himself and for the regions he controlled, answering only to his local gods, especially Horus and Hemen. Ankhtify may or may not have been acting in concert with the Herakleopolitans in the north – this is not made clear – but his enemies were certainly the Thebans and Coptites of Nomes 4 and 5.

The tomb of Ankhtify was discovered by chance in 1928 by quarrymen working on the East Bank of the Nile not far north of the city of Esna (Vandier 1950). The tomb itself (Figure 7.2) is cut into the west face of a distinct hill or *gebel* in the middle of a desert 'bay' formed by the high cliffs of the eastern desert, close to the edge of the cultivation which today is only a few hundred metres from the Nile itself. This is part of Egypt of which little is known before the end of the Old Kingdom; the most important regional centre, mentioned in the tomb of Ankhtify, seems to have been the now-lost town of Hefat. The tomb, as discovered, consisted of a wide shallow room cut into the face of the hill, about halfway up its height, filled with a series of 30 eccentrically shaped pillars, the result of natural fractures in the local limestone (Figure 7.3).

Figure 7.2   The tomb of Ankhtify at Moalla

The scenes on the interior walls of the pillared hall, badly damaged though they are, show a combination of the traditional and innovative. To the right of the doorway as one enters is the largest surviving section of painted decoration, Ankhtify spearing fish in the marshes, a theme directly lifted from Old Kingdom court scenes. The only reference to a king is the

Figure 7.3   The tomb of Ankhtify at Moalla (interior)

fragmentary cartouche of Neferkare (Pepi II) under this fishing and fowling scene, and the context of this reference is unclear. Images abound of Ankhtify himself, depicted in a manner which would not look out of place in an Old Kingdom *mastaba* at Memphis, and there are unsurprising scenes of offering-bearers and food-preparation, rendered in a lively provincial style. Reflecting the period, however, are the depictions of armed men with hunting dogs on the rear wall of the hall. On the central axis of the columned hall a short shaft leads to the simple Burial Chamber of the tomb.

While the interior walls of the pillared hall were used for figured paintings on a plastered surface, the pillars were carved with a long hieroglyphic text whose subject is the tomb-owner himself. But this is an (auto)biography which goes well beyond the limits of decorum of the Old Kingdom.

> Horus brought me to the (Horus-Throne) Nome ... in order to re-establish it, and I have done so. Moreover, Horus wanted it re-established because he brought me to it to re-establish it.
>
> I am the front of people and the rear of people because the like (of me) cannot exist and he will not exist. My like could not have been born and he was not born ... those who will come after me cannot match me in all I have done ... I am a man without equal.
>
> As for any ruler who will rule in Hefat and does an evil thing against this coffin ($d(r)it$) (or) any monument (mnw) of this tomb (pr), his forearm will be cut off for Hemen during his procession.

A similar fate awaited those who did a bad thing against any 'stelae' ($wḏw$), the 'eastern side' (i.e. the interior of the tomb where the false door was), 'funerary meal' ($ḥf3t$), or 'my Lord's person' (presumably the body of Ankhtify itself).

Ankhtify is insistent in stressing that this tomb, a concrete expression of his power and position, was created by him, from his own resources, and without his dismantling the tomb of anyone else. He is also quick to make identifications between elements of the tomb and a wider natural and mythological landscape, an idea which is close to aspects of the Pyramid Texts which relate parts of the royal tomb to a cosmic landscape. This is a theme which has had limited expression in the private sphere, apart from the regular identification of the lid of the coffin with the sky-goddess Nut.

> I acquired this coffin and all monuments of this tomb with my own money (*lit. copper*), because there is no door or pillar from another place in this tomb ... I placed eulogies on the strong doors, on the doors, and on the coffin, because I made this coffin from planks of wood from the trees of the Coptite nome. No other can say the same – I am a man without equal.

I made the door as high as the sky, the doorway is air and the ceiling is a sky
strewn with stars.
The frieze of its architrave is uraeus and its backbone Nekhebkau.
The pillars of cedar rise higher than the palm-trees of the two ladies of Imet.
Its threshold, brought from Elephantine, is like a hippopotamus which rages
against the lord of Upper Egypt.

In the statements he makes about himself, and the nature of his tomb,
Ankhtify seems to be coming close to presenting himself as a quasi-royal
figure, without ever directly claiming to be king.

But this is not all. Recent work by the University of Liverpool has shown
that the conception of the tomb complex was much greater than the
columned hall and Burial Chamber, with an open courtyard in front of
the columned hall and perhaps even a causeway leading to a valley
building. With the landscape-dominating pyramidal *gebel* (hill) itself, the
tomb of Ankhtify as a piece of royal emulation could hardly be clearer, not
least with the subsidiary tombs of individuals who may be related to, or
worked for, him running around the *gebel* in both directions from the
central tomb (Figure 7.4). This is a private tomb in Upper Egypt which has
taken and adapted the Memphite pyramid complex in a way which would
have been unthinkable in the Old Kingdom proper. A similar appropriation
of elements of the Old Kingdom pyramid complex can be seen in the elite

Figure 7.4   Subsidiary tombs at Moalla

Figure 7.5 The tomb of Wahka I at Qau

Middle Kingdom cemetery of Qau el-Kebir in Upper Egypt, but at Qau the tombs of the Dynasty 12 mayors Wahka I, Ibu and Wahka II (Steckeweh 1936) consist of valley building + causeway + mortuary temple leading to a rock-cut tomb in the cliffs (Figure 7.5), which does not have what, in the context of a period of a return to royal pyramid building, would have been a presumably provocative pyramidal form. The subsequent history of the tomb of Ankhtify is not yet well understood, although ongoing excavations are making the picture clearer. The courtyard in front of the pillared hall was certainly used as a place of offering for Ankhtify, and he may have achieved the status of a local 'saint'. However, directly on the floor of this courtyard were found the smashed contents of one or more First Intermediate Period tombs, with fragments of coffins, pottery, staffs and bows. It is tempting to relate this destruction to the activities of the vengeful and ultimately successful Thebans.

A Time of Chaos Revisited: Destruction and Restoration?

Destruction

Ankhtify's may not have been the only tomb to suffer from deliberate destruction during the First Intermediate Period. The *Instruction for*

Merikare (Lichtheim 1973: 97–109), a fictionalized account of a Herakleopolitan ruler giving advice to his (pyramid-owning) successor, seems to
refer to the events of the First Intermediate Period: 'Troops will fight troops
as the ancestors foretold; Egypt fought in the graveyard, destroying tombs
in vengeful destruction. . . . Lo, a shameful deed occurred in my time, the
nome of This was ravaged; though it happened through my doing, I learned
it after it was done.' Lichtheim (1973: 109) takes these two statements to
refer to a single episode, the destruction of tombs in the Thinite nome
(including Abydos?) in the First Intermediate Period, although, as in the
case of Ankhtify, the first statement may well have wider application.
Merikare's predecessor also refers to an abhorrent practice in tomb building: 'Do not despoil the monument of another, but quarry stone in Tura. Do
not build your tomb out of ruins, (using) what had been made for what
is to be made.' This concern with making clear that one's tomb was not
constructed to the detriment of another's has already been seen in
Ankhtify's tomb inscription and stands in stark contrast to, for instance,
the rather later use made by Amenemhat I in the building of his pyramid at
Lisht of blocks from Old Kingdom monuments at Giza, especially the
pyramid of Khufu (Goedicke 1971).

   Although it is tempting to dismiss both the *Ipuwer* and *Merikare* texts as
propagandistic fictions, some archaeological evidence supports the idea of
a significant amount of deliberate destruction in cemeteries, particularly
elite cemeteries, associated with the First Intermediate Period. At the end of
the Old Kingdom the *mastaba* cemetery at Mendes suffered an episode of
deliberate destruction which involved burning within tombs and the
exposure of bodies (Redford 2001). It is possible that the burning of Archaic
tombs on the Umm el-Qa'ab and the destruction within the tomb of Weni,
both at Abydos, took place at this time, and may have been the incident
referred to in Merikare (Leahy 1989: 56–7).

Restoration

An interesting aspect of increasing local autonomy in tomb provision
during the Old Kingdom/First Intermediate Period transition is provided
by the text from the tomb of Shemai at Coptos in Upper Egypt. The tomb of
Shemai (Strudwick 2005: 345–6) contains a text added by a man named Idi,
suggesting that he paid particular attention to providing for his ancestors
by having 'made pleasant with incense this *ka*-chapel of my father and my
ancestors'. Moreover, Idi notes that this chapel had become dilapidated
and so he 'refreshed and set up the statues of these noble ones, these
nobles, which I found in a state of disrepair'. As far as his father's tomb was
concerned, he 'executed everything which he had ordered in terms of works

for the necropolis'. Although there is no suggestion that this is post-destruction restoration, the idea that he as an individual made good for his father and ancestors what was found to be not good, and out of his own resources, brings together a number of topical themes. This is particularly interesting in that the sense of self-reliance from the tomb of Shemai contrasts with the provision made for the offering-cult of the self-same Shemai on a decree issued by King Neferkauhor, one of several which benefited the Shemai family which were set up in the temple at Coptos (Strudwick 2005: 119–20).

The cemetery of el-Bersheh is one of the more important elite cemeteries in Middle Egypt. Located on the East Bank of the Nile close to Beni Hasan, it became the main necropolis of nomarchs of the 15th Upper Egyptian (Hare) nome, whose capital was the city of Hermopolis Magna. The el-Bersheh necropolis (Griffith and Newberry 1894–5; Silverman et al. 1992) took on the role of local dynastic cemetery in the First Intermediate Period, succeeding the nearby cemetery of Sheikh Said (Davies 1901), which housed the tombs of local rulers of Dynasties 5 and 6. Nine of the largest and best-decorated rock-cut Old Kingdom tombs at Sheikh Said and el-Bersheh contain copies of the same text (De Meyer 2005), which were added to their doorframes or on the walls of their interior rooms, often quite low down. The author of the text describes himself as the 'Great Chief of the Hare Nome . . . Djehutynakht, son of Teti', who writes: 'A commemoration which he made for his fathers who are in the necropolis, lords of the desert plateau. Making firm that which was found destroyed, renewing what was found in ruins. Lo, the predecessors who had stood before had not done this.' Djehutynakht, who has been dated to the First Intermediate Period (on criteria discussed in De Meyer 2005: 133), does not seem to be related to the Old Kingdom nomarchs whose tombs he claims to have restored. Rather, he associates himself with an earlier local dynasty in order to establish his own position as the possible founder of an early Middle Kingdom dynasty of nomarchs at el-Bersheh. He does this by portraying himself as protector and restorer of the tombs of his 'ancestors'; Brovarski (1981) suggests that Djehutynakht may be the father of Ahanakht I, the first of the known Middle Kingdom nomarchs to be buried at el-Bersheh. Two further puzzles remain: firstly, it is not clear from the tombs themselves what the nature of the 'restorations' of Djehutynakht actually consisted of, and, secondly, the tomb of Djehutynakht himself is unknown.

Although much of the detail of the ways in which tombs were used as political and economic instruments during the First Intermediate Period is unknown, it is clear that developments which took place during this pivotal epoch had far-reaching consequences. Those consequences can be broadly divided into two strands which will be followed in the next two chapters: the first is the way in which the architecture, decoration and equipment of tombs developed during the Middle Kingdom, while the second is the significant shift in underlying expectations of a non-royal afterlife which affected mortuary provision, particularly the explosion in importance of the god Osiris.

CHAPTER 8

Osiris, Lord of Abydos

⌐⌐⌐⌐⌐

The Osirian Afterlife

Perhaps the most far-reaching development of the Late Old Kingdom/First Intermediate Period, one which would have a major impact on conceptions of a non-royal afterlife, was the extent to which possibilities of an afterlife beyond the tomb, previously the exclusive preserve of the king, became available to a wider section of society. This phenomenon has sometimes been called the 'Democratization of the Afterlife', but this is something of a misnomer. While the gap between royal and non-royal afterlife expectations had narrowed significantly from the yawning chasm it had been during the high Old Kingdom (although this view has also been challenged, see Smith 2009), there was, and would always be, a significant difference between what happened to the king and what happened to everyone else after death. Nevertheless, the expectation of an afterlife away from the tomb, which can first be seen towards the end of the Old Kingdom, undoubtedly gathered pace during the kingless years of the First Intermediate Period. It has already been noted that the afterlife expectations of the king, as represented in the Pyramid Texts of the Late Old Kingdom, were a veritable smorgasbord of possibilities, the three most significant of which were the stellar, the solar and the Osirian expectations. Of these, the one that was seized upon by non-royals was the Osirian, perhaps because it was the one which least claimed royal exclusivity in merging with a celestial body, but more modestly hoped for participation in the community of the blessed under the authority of the god Osiris. In order to understand the expectations of a Osirian afterlife and, especially, the way the tomb was equipped to make these expectations a reality, it is necessary to review the myths surrounding Osiris. Although the fullest articulation of the myth in narrative form is no earlier than the Classical author Plutarch (Griffiths 1970) writing early in the second century AD, references to different aspects of the myth, and the funerary iconography derived from it, are legion, most extensively in the *Great Hymn to Osiris* on a stela belonging to a Dynasty 18 official, Amenmose, now in the Louvre (Lichtheim 1976: 81–6).

The myth of Osiris

The origins of the cult of Osiris are obscure, but the development of his iconography and references to him in the Pyramid Texts show that by the end of the Old Kingdom he was recognized as a god whose basic identity was royal (he is regularly depicted wearing the white crown of Upper Egypt, or a feathered variant, the *atef*-crown; he carries the crook and flail royal regalia) and mortuary (his body, apart from his hands and head, is tightly wrapped in white linen). The origins of Osiris may be as a god of 'chthonic fertility' (Otto 1968: 24), the power of creation which is pregnant in the earth and can be activated to make crops grow and, by extension, the Nile rise during the inundation. His adoption of the role of god of the Dead, which seems at first to be the opposite of this concern with fertility, is perhaps not so surprising if one regards the Dead as being capable of rebirth. The myth-cycle of Osiris provides an extended narrative which also locates him firmly as a god of rebirth in the afterlife.

At a time before human kings, the gods ruled Egypt. Osiris, together with his sister-wife Isis and their siblings the god Seth and his wife Nephthys, made up the fourth generation of gods after the creation of the world (according to the Heliopolitan version of the creation myth). Osiris was regarded as a good and a wise king, but he was tricked by his jealous brother Seth into being locked in a closely fitting chest which was thrown into the Nile. Isis, the faithful wife, searched for the chest, found it, and returned with it to Egypt. However, her grief at opening the chest, and seeing Osiris within, led her to abandon the body momentarily, at which point it was discovered by accident by Seth, who cut up the body of his brother and scattered the different parts throughout Egypt. Once again Isis set out on her task of searching for the parts of her husband's body, aided by Nephthys. Once the dispersed members had been reassembled, Isis, 'powerful of magic', revitalized them so effectively that she became pregnant with her son Horus, who was to grow up to struggle, successfully, with Seth for the throne of Egypt.

The story has within it a number of themes and elements which have already been noted as being important to the Egyptians in their attitude to what was required for a successful afterlife, notably the importance of the integrity of the body. The role of Horus as one who vindicates his father's legacy is also important, although the Plutarchian version of the myth puts more stress on the role of Isis (and indeed Nephthys) as the immediate protectors of the body of Osiris with no obvious role for Horus as the one who buries his father, as one might expect. But the central importance of the Osiris myth lies in what happens at the end of the story: although revivified, Osiris is nonetheless dead. He continues to exist, and indeed to act as king, but king not of Egypt but of a parallel world, the *Duat*, which we have already encountered in the Pyramid Texts. Osiris is also associated with the place where the blessed Dead reside, the 'Field of Reeds/*Iaru*'. The nature of this world is not fully described in a form which is accessible to us until the New Kingdom, although aspects of it are present in funerary material from the Middle Kingdom, and especially in the 'Coffin Texts'. But the rise of the Osiris cult led to another important development: the identification of Abydos as the burial place of Osiris, and the subsequent importance of Abydos as a funerary cult centre. Osiris is, therefore, a god of national importance, but identified with specific locations in the tangible world and in the intangible cosmos, who is, as the *Great Hymn to Osiris* notes, the 'Eternal lord who presides in Abydos, who dwells distant in the graveyard, whose names endures in peoples' mouths' (Lichtheim 1976: 82).

The Development of Abydos in the Middle Kingdom

The importance of Abydos as the royal cemetery of Dynasty 1 and (to a lesser extent) Dynasty 2 has already been discussed in Chapter 2 as has its role as a regional centre suitable for the burial of significant individuals such as Weni in Chapter 6. The clustering of more modest burials around the tomb of Weni provides an early instance of cemetery growth at Abydos based on focal points and ideal locations, but the development of 'horizontal stratigraphy' at Abydos (Snape 1986: 86–99) in the Middle Kingdom was based on quite different points of reference to the local 'sheikhs' of the Late Old Kingdom and First Intermediate Period.

The original deity of Abydos seems to be the god Khentyamentiu, who was depicted in the form of a dog/jackal. Both the name and the iconography are significant. The former means 'Foremost of the Westerners' (i.e. the Dead), while the latter puts him in a group of canine deities (including Anubis and Wepwawet) who are associated with cemeteries and the transition between the world of the Living and that of the Dead; perhaps the Egyptians primarily encountered jackal-like creatures in desert-edge cemeteries and the association stuck. What is clearly the case, however, is that Khentyamentiu of Abydos had a distinct afterlife-orientation, perhaps understandably given Abydos' primary role in the Early Dynastic Period as a royal necropolis. The temple of Khentyamentiu increased in importance during the Old Kingdom; royal inscriptions of Neferirkare of Dynasty 5 and Teti of Dynasty 6 were set up at Abydos exempting the temple from a series of taxes (Strudwick 2005: 98–101, 102–3).

However, the real importance of Abydos came with the eruption of the Osiris cult in the late Old Kingdom. Osiris is a central figure in the Pyramid Texts, and appears in private tombs of the Late Old Kingdom (Bolshakov 1992). It seems that in the Fifth and Sixth Dynasties, while Osiris was linked mostly with his Delta cult centre of Busiris in private tombs, in royal tombs he was predominantly associated with Abydos and, especially, the Thinite nome (Griffiths 1982: 626). The initiative for the development of the importance of Abydos was probably a combination of factors, including the flowering of a popular cult at a time when the centre of that cult had a brief period of secular importance. The relationship between the importance of Osiris and the Late Old Kingdom burials of high-ranking officials, including Weni and his father Iww, and the Vizier Djau-Shemai (uncle of kings Merenre and Pepi II), is unclear. However, whatever specific combination of factors gave rise to the importance of Abydos as the main cult centre of the god most closely connected to the afterlife, two factors are worth noting immediately. The first is that, as Osiris became a god associated with the salvation of a wide variety of people throughout Egypt, his title 'lord of Abydos' gave the site a particular importance not shared by anywhere else in Egypt. Although Osiris was also regularly referred to as 'lord of *ḏdw*' (*Djedu* = Busiris), it seems unlikely that this Delta site (Abusir el-Bana) was the focus of such intensive piety as that seen at Abydos, although it is difficult to quantify this assumption given the extremely poor level of archaeological survival of that site (however, for a group of Old/Middle Kingdom monuments from the site, see Fischer 1976).

The second factor to note is what seems to be the disappearance from collective memory of the kings of the earliest dynasties and their tombs (Leahy 1989: 57). This is curious given the importance placed on Abydos by Ramesside kings (especially Seti I and Ramesses II) as a place associated with the proper transmission of kingship, and the desire of those same kings to restore the monuments of their earliest 'ancestors'. However, as the king list in the Abydos cenotaph temple of Seti I testifies, the identities of these earliest kings had become blurred with those of the divine and semi-divine rulers of Egypt before human kings took the throne. Nonetheless, the Dynasty 1 tombs on the Umm el-Qa'ab did have a crucial role to play in ideas about early kingship, not because their true nature was realized but, on the contrary, because the tomb of one of these Dynasty 1 kings – Djer – became identified with the tomb of Osiris himself. In this way Abydos became important in the history of Egyptian kingship not because it was the historical necropolis of the first rulers of a unified of Egypt, but because it was regarded as the resting-place of Osiris, who, as a sort of *ur*-king, was the source of royal authority which flowed from the dead god to his son, the living king Horus. Abydos was therefore a site which, for Egyptian kings, represented *par excellence* a place to demonstrate their Osiris and/or Horus nature.

The sacred landscape of Abydos in the Middle Kingdom

Abydos is a large and complex site. In terms of its orientation, although it is not strictly orientated north–south, there was a 'local' north based on the assumption that the line of cultivation/river was north–south and that the high desert cliffs and the 'Great Wadi' which led to the afterlife were to the west – Osiris was, after all, 'Foremost of the Westerners'. During the Middle Kingdom the sacred landscape of Abydos contained a number of key locations (Figure 2.2). Four of these formed a cross-axis: the plateaux of the Middle Cemetery and North Cemetery were divided by low ground which provided a natural route for most of the way between the Umm el-Qa'ab and the Temple of Osiris, which was close to the western flank of the North Cemetery in the ancient town. The nucleus of this landscape was the Umm el-Qa'ab. Although early archaeological opinion suggested that the tomb of Djer was not identified as that of Osiris until the reign of Amenhotep III, circumstantial evidence indicates that certainly by Dynasty 13, and more likely by Dynasty 12, and possibly by Dynasty 11, the Umm el-Qa'ab had become firmly established as the god's burial place (Leahy 1989: 56). Embellishments to the tomb of Djer to make it more appropriately Osirian included the installation of the so-called 'Osiris Bed', effectively a life-size (if a statue of a god can be said to be life-size) figure of the dead Osiris, lying on a bed, the goddess Isis, in the form of a bird, perched over him in the position of his erect penis. This black basalt statue was the work of the Dynasty 13 king Khendjer (Leahy 1977; but cf. Ryholt 1997: 217) and represents an important attestation of Late Middle Kingdom royal activity at Abydos.

However, the most obvious remnants of Middle Kingdom royal activity at Abydos are to be found not in the central area of Osirian activity, but over 2 km to the south of the Temple of Osiris where Senwosret III found the space for the construction of a massive mortuary complex. First excavated by Weigall and Currelly (Ayrton et al. 1904) and more recently by Wegner (2007, 2009), the buildings within this group included a rock-cut tomb, cut at the foot of the cliffs of the high desert, over 270 m long, accessed by a shaft 25 m deep, and leading to a Burial Chamber containing an enormous, although robbed, granite sarcophagus, and, at the edge of the cultivation, a mortuary temple comparable in size to that at Senwosret's pyramid complex at Dahshur. Scholarly opinion is divided over the function of this complex, whether it is the tomb of Senwosret III himself or whether it is something else, a 'cenotaph'. Certainly the distinction between a tomb which was intended to contain a body and one which did not is not as obvious as it might first appear. The containment of the body is just one of the functions of the tomb, and a body-less tomb could continue to provide many benefits for the Dead. As far as a Middle Kingdom monarch was concerned, the question of whether it was more suitable to be buried in an Old Kingdom-style pyramid in the north of Egypt or to seek a close and (as a dead king) appropriate identification with Osiris at Abydos did not have an obvious answer, at least not for Senwosret III, and also for his New Kingdom successors Ahmose (who owned a significant mortuary temple and, possibly, tomb at Abydos – see Harvey 1998, 2004) and Seti I, who also owned a tomb-like structure at Abydos, the 'Osireion', as well as a 'real' tomb in the Valley of the Kings. It may well be that Senwosret III was the first king since the earliest dynasties to be buried at Abydos, or it may equally be the case that the king, like many of his non-royal contemporaries, sought not burial at Abydos but a presence via what was, in effect, a body-less tomb.

Chapels and Stelae at Abydos

The close association between Abydos and the cult of Osiris in the Middle Kingdom gave rise to a version of what one might term 'pilgrimage' to the site by non-residents (Yoyotte 1960). 'Pilgrims' would wish to be commemorated at Abydos or, rather, would wish to obtain the benefits of being close to the god through the agency of a physical manifestation of themselves at the site. Like most pilgrimages there were particularly propitious times of year to visit the site, and for Abydos this was the occasion of what are today referred to as the 'Mysteries of Osiris'. There were also particularly propitious places to leave a permanent presence and this, too, was related to the 'Mysteries' in that the Temple of Osiris, the Umm el-Qa'ab and the route which linked them were the epicentres of cultic activity, and being able to 'see' this was important. As a consequence, visitors to Abydos left attestations of themselves in and around the temple and overlooking the route. Small statues were one method, and the reign of Senwosret III saw an increase in this type of object from Abydos, but the ideal permanent marker of one's presence was a stone (usually limestone) stela which was – for those who could afford one or more of them – a good way of preserving identity and the specific benefits expected of being close to the god.

Mahat *chapels*

These stelae were placed in a special chapel called a *mꜥḥꜥt* (*mahat*). These structures are often referred to as 'cenotaphs' (or, sometimes, 'memorial chapels') because, like the stelae they were designed to contain, although some of them are associated with burials, many are not. The size and complexity of the chapels and stelae allowed for multiple ownership and, ideally, they were placed in specific locations close to the processional route of the god Osiris as he made his way to his tomb at the Umm el-Qa'ab in the great annual festival.

Two types of *mahat* were particularly popular, both made of mudbrick. The first consists of a barrel-vaulted chamber, open at the front and with an open forecourt defined by a low wall. This type could vary in size from examples large enough to have tree pits, multiple stelae and even smaller, subsidiary 'cenotaphs' (O'Connor 1985: Figs 5 and 6), to examples just large enough to house a single round-topped stela (Figure 8.1). The other type is

Figure 8.1 Middle Kingdom *mahat* and stela at Abydos excavated by John Garstang in 1908 (© Garstang Museum of Archaeology, University of Liverpool)

Figure 8.2 Middle Kingdom *mahat* of Iy at Abydos excavated by John Garstang in 1907 (© Garstang Museum of Archaeology, University of Liverpool

a solid '*mastaba*' of brickwork into whose faces stelae were set (Figure 8.2). Both types of cenotaph could be plastered and/or whitewashed, and the courtyards make it clear that these were place where people were expected to come and perform cult for the benefit of the individuals represented on them.

The *mahat* is, in some ways, a curious structure. It is a tomb without a body, something which might seem meaningless in a Western context, but it is important in the Egyptian context because it fulfils several key roles of the tomb, specifically those played by the Offering Chapel. It is a specific location where the deceased can be remembered (like flowers by the side of the road where someone has been killed), it is a place for the self-presentation/autobiography of the deceased to be published, and it is a monument through which benefits for the deceased could flow. These benefits were most obviously of the *hetep-di-nesu* type, but also included the less well-defined privilege of being buried close to Osiris, with whom one would have a close personal identification after death: 'I made a *mahat* at the Terrace of the Great God . . . so that (I) might receive offerings in the presence of the Great God and that I might inhale his incense.' Despite the Egyptian emphasis on the corporeality of afterlife survival, these were crucial functions. To define the function of a *mahat* is not simple, but the most important thing does not seem to be the form of the building, nor whether it did or did not include a body (i.e. a tomb), but that it should act as 'an abode for the transfigured dead' (Lichtheim 1988: 92). The *mahat*-chapels are constructions made of mudbrick, within which stone elements were placed. These stone elements could include offering-tables and statues, but the most important category of object is the stela.

Stelae

Unfortunately, owing to large-scale pillaging of the site in the eighteenth and nineteenth centuries for collectable and saleable stelae, only a small proportion of stelae have been found *in situ* within their cenotaphs at Abydos. However, alongside the evidence from the relatively few chapels which have survived, the stelae themselves often contain useful self-referential information related to how they came to be placed where they were. Toponyms which appear on the stelae include the 'District Great of Fame' and the 'Terrace of the Great God', which can be identified with the eastern and southern slopes of the North Cemetery at Abydos. Some of the stelae from Abydos actually refer to themselves having been placed in a *mahat* which the stela-owner had made for himself. The difference in character between tomb-stelae and cenotaph-stelae is not obvious because each had the same purpose: to associate the person(s) represented on them with the god Osiris, whether they were actually buried at Abydos or not.

Their archaeological importance lies in the amount of information they convey; these are supremely self-referential documents, often relating in some detail the process by which they came to be exactly where they were set up. They are equally self-regarding in their purpose, and they spell out in some detail the benefits to be accrued by the person for whom the stela was erected.

The Abydos stelae are the single largest and most important source of personal information, including identities and occupations, on sub-elite ('middle class') Egyptians of the Middle Kingdom, and possibly of any other period (for a study of burials of sub-elite Egyptians of the Middle Kingdom, see Richards 2005). Some of the stelae bear specific year-dates within the reigns of specific kings, relating to the occasion of their erection, and most have a wealth of genealogical information. While most of the stelae from Abydos are fairly conventional in their content – and this is hardly surprising since they were all focused on obtaining afterlife benefits from a proximity to Osiris – there was clearly an attempt to individualize some of these stelae since they, as much as the larger tombs for elite Egyptians, were a vehicle for self-presentation.

The increased use of stelae in the Middle Kingdom (especially during the reign of Senwosret I and in late Dynasty 12 to early Dynasty 13) gave rise to the development of a small number of standard types and sizes. As far as size is concerned, of the three stelae discussed below, the Manchester stela of Sobek-khu, at 28 cm tall, is at the lower end of the 'normal' range, the Berlin stela of Ikhernofret, at 1 m tall, is at the upper end, and the Bolton stela of Iy, at 44 cm tall, is an approximate average. Two types of stelae were especially popular. The first was a roughly rectangular, taller than wide stela with a cavetto cornice and torus-moulding frame, a type which clearly continues the Old Kingdom false door tradition of stelae whose appearance reflects an architectural setting. The torus-roll moulding and cavetto cornice top are intended to reflect elements of primitive reed architecture which are also present in the walls of stone buildings from the Step Pyramid enclosure at Saqqara until Graeco-Roman temples. In stelae these features provide a convenient frame for the main rectangular panel, which can then be further sub-divided into registers. This type of stela remained popular in the Middle Kingdom, although it became eclipsed by the round-topped stela, which became the most popular form for both private and royal stelae from the Middle Kingdom onwards, used both in architectural settings and as freestanding objects. The format allowed substantial variation on a theme of text and image. The most basic version had the text written in horizontal lines in the lower part of the stela, while the rounded top – the lunette – enclosed the pictorial content, which usually consisted of a group of figures. The lunette might also contain symbols such as the *wdȝt*-eye, a winged sun disk or, from the reign of Amenemhat II, gods such as Osiris, Anubis and Wepwawet.

Why a round-topped stela was considered especially popular for text and figure combinations is not immediately apparent, since the semi-circular lunette imposed obvious limitations on the positioning of figures of the same height. One possible explanation is the way in which the eye is naturally drawn to the centre-line of a rounded lunette, emphasizing that this is the area where interaction between the depicted figures takes place, so that a simple group of a person offering to a deceased figure will have the nexus of interaction over the offering table between them. More complex groups can also show this interaction at a centre-line, or perhaps with a central line of text dividing two groups of figures. Whatever the relevance of these design features, it was also the case that the round-topped stela fitted very neatly into the barrel-vaulted type of *mahat* (Figure 8.1). At Abydos there seems no distinction between round-topped and cavetto-cornice stelae – although one might imagine rectangular stele would be better suited to solid *mastaba*-type chapels, and round-topped to vaulted chapels, this does not seem to be a consistent pattern, though one must admit that lack of surviving evidence makes broad conclusions dangerous.

The mahat *and stela of Iy at Abydos and Bolton*

A good example of the thousands of stelae erected at Abydos in the Middle Kingdom is that belonging to a minor official called Iy, discovered by Garstang in its cenotaph in 1907, and now in Bolton Museum (Figure 8.3). The simple mudbrick cenotaph, given the designation 321 A'07, consists of a solid rectangular mass, with niches on four sides for the placement of stelae (Figure 8.2). The Bolton stela is of good-quality limestone, carved with neat hieroglyphs and with three rows of human figures. In the top row

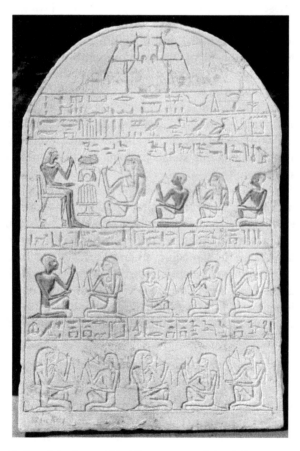

Figure 8.3 Stela of Iy from 321 A'07 excavated by John Garstang in 1907 (© Garstang Museum of Archaeology, University of Liverpool)

Iy sits facing his wife and three children, while the second row contains his parents, two *wab*-priests and a woman who, like the five women on the bottom row, has an unspecified relationship to him. On other stelae of this type, the lowest row or rows might consist simply of a list of names and with no figure. The personal names on 321 A'07 are typical of the town of Qau el-Kebir in Upper Egypt, and the people on the known five stelae in this group (four in Cairo, one in Bolton; Franke 1984: 51 [17]; Simpson 1974, 18) may be from this town.

Self-Presentation on Abydene Stelae

Stelae, like tombs, were designed to speak to the Living. A standard element of many of these Abydos stelae is the 'Appeal to the Living' (Collier and Manley 1998: 111–14; Garnot 1938), asking the passer-by to give offerings or speak the offering-formula, and a manner which would have been instantly understandable to an Old Kingdom tomb-owner. To be specific, it is the literate passer-by ('O living . . . who may pass by this tomb' – Collier and Manley 1998: 111) who is appealed to, as is obvious from the text on the stela of Ankhreni (Smither and Dakin 1939: 164, Pl. 21.4), which addresses 'O living who are upon the earth – every scribe, every lector-priest, every *wab*-priest . . .', but also goes on to specify that these individuals are intended to 'read aloud this stela', perhaps for the benefit of illiterate participants in the cult.

Part of this appeal is, as in tombs of the Old Kingdom, particularly the late Old Kingdom, the idea of self-presentation as a worthy individual. The Middle Kingdom saw the emergence of stelae which could act as a summation of a whole career of noteworthy achievements, or might commemorate one particular achievement. Typically the former is found at the tomb or Abydene cenotaph of the dedicatee, while the latter might be erected at the place where the achievement took place, such as those attesting mining expeditions in Sinai (Gardiner and Peet 1952–5). In some cases the two could be happily combined, as in the case of Ikhernofret.

Self-presentation on Abydene stelae (1): Ikhernofret and the 'Mysteries of Osiris'

Berlin 1204 is a fine round-topped stela a metre tall. It is one of eleven stelae from Abydos which belong to the royal official Ikhernofret or his family (Simpson 1974: 17). It contains a justly famous text (translated in Lichtheim 1973: 123–5) which describes Ikhernofret's activities at Abydos. This text begins with a speech of the king, Senwosret III, who sent the royal official

Ikhernofret to Abydos in order to 'adorn the secret image' of Osiris, choosing Ikhernofret because of his, extensively described, personal qualities. In fact Ikhernofret carried out two major activities at Abydos. The first was indeed to embellish and improve the image of the god and the sacred barque in which he was carried in procession. The second was to make sure that a series of processions at Abydos was carried out in proper order: 'I conducted the Great Procession, following the god in his steps ... in his beautiful regalia he proceeded to the domain of Peqer ... I made him enter the Great Barque ... it brought [Osiris] to his palace.' This ritual sequence, often referred to as the 'Mysteries of Osiris', appears to be a form of passion play, re-enacting the death and rebirth of Osiris in a mythical environment which is directly mapped onto the topography of Abydos. Peqer, where much of the action takes place, is probably the Umm el-Qa'ab, although this is by no means universally accepted (Leahy 1989: 58), while the processional route to/from the temple of Osiris would have included the low ground between the Middle and North cemeteries, giving the status of front-row seats to those edges of the cemetery plateaux which overlooked the procession, including, presumably, the site of the now-lost cenotaph (or tomb?) of Ikhernofret himself.

Self-presentation on Abydene stelae (2): the Good Soldier Sobek-khu

One of the most impressive of these self-presentations, approaching autobiography, is inscribed on the face of one of the less-impressive Middle Kingdom stelae from Abydos, a round-topped slab of limestone 44 cm tall, discovered by John Garstang in Cemetery 'E' at Abydos in 1900 (Garstang 1901; Peet 1914a) and now in Manchester Museum (Figure 8.4). The lunette contains a conventional *hetep-di-nesu* formula, below which are the crudely carved figures of Sobek-khu sitting before a table of offerings and six individuals, some of whom are specifically identified as members of his family. But most of the face of the stela is given over to a detailed autobiography. The text is rather cramped, and it seems as though the better-spaced lower text with vertical hieroglyphs was composed before the higher horizontal text. In whatever order the text is to be read it reflects on the stela itself and why it was there. 'I made this *mahat* for myself, it being an "akhifier" (*s3ḫ*) and its place established at the "Terrace of the Great God" ... so that I might smell the incense which comes forth.' Born in Year 27 of Amenemhat II, Sobek-khu became a soldier in the reign of Senwosret III. Fighting alongside the king with six other chosen men (a royal bodyguard?), he was promoted and given 60 men. Active on campaign in Nubia, he was once again promoted and given 100 men 'as a reward'. Fighting against the 'Asiatics' of Retenu, Sobek-khu showed

Figure 8.4   Stela of Sobek-khu from Abydos

conspicuous valour in close combat and was rewarded this time with
prestigious items including a staff of electrum. Sobek-khu is not known
merely from the stelae at Abydos; he also left rock-graffiti in Nubia itself
at Amada and at Semna (Franke 1984: 283 [455]), the latter as the leader of
a frontier patrol in Year 9 of Amenemhat III, by which time he must have
been in his late 60s. Within these texts, although they relate to historical
events, the wider significance of the events is not especially important,
but, rather, they provide the context by which the writer can display their
personal qualities, which would in turn lead to royal reward. Baines (1987:
59) suggests that the Sobek-khu inscription is a mixture of the convention-
ally private 'reward' texts, with a military narrative derived from royal

inscriptions somewhat similar to the later tomb-autobiography of Ahmose son of Ibana from el-Kab in Dynasty 18.

Acquiring a stela

One of the ways in which the self-referential nature of Middle Kingdom stelae at Abydos is useful is their description of the process by which they were produced. In these descriptions they give an insight into the 'funerary industry' at Abydos, an insight which is unmatched at any other Middle Kingdom site. The production of good-quality stelae was a skilled business, and probably involved several individuals. Two popular craftsmen's titles are 'outline-draughtsman' (*ss kdwt*) and 'sculptor' (*gnwty*), which suggests a two-stage process whereby the smoothed face of the stela (perhaps a task for an apprentice?) had its text and figures sketched in ink, followed by the carving out of those sketches. The best-attested examples of individual workmen employed in the 'funeral industry' at Abydos are those craftsmen who manufactured stelae for tombs and *mahat*-chapels, and who inscribed their names on some of these stelae. The names and titles of these crafts-men can occasionally be identified on stelae where they are not obviously part of the family-group which was the main subject of the stelae (Ward 1982; Wilson 1947: 235). Although the mechanics of this are not expressed on the stelae themselves, and we have no supporting documentation to compare with that regarding the production of funerary equipment at Deir el-Medina, it has been suggested that a craftsman may have been allowed to add himself to the *dramatis personae* of a stela (and therefore obtain the somewhat intangible benefits which flowed from that attestation) in return for a discount in the costs of his services (Leprohon 1978: 36). A good example of this phenomenon is a stela found by Petrie at Abydos in 1902–3 (Griffith 1903: 43, Pl. 30; Miller 1937) which mentions three individuals who seem to have been employed in the production of stelae. The most prominent, appearing on the left-hand edge of the stela, is the outline-draughtsman Sehetebibreseneb, who is described as *imakhu* before Ptah (the patron deity of craftsmen); on the rear of the stela is the journeyman-sculptor (*t3w s'nḫ* – for this term see Ward 1980: 172) Seneb, and on the front of the stela the sculptor Ankhtify. The stela itself is a variant derived from false doors, popular in the late Middle Kingdom after the reign of Ame-nemhat II (Pflüger 1947: 128).

This stela is far from being the only example of this practice. Other examples include an outline-draughtsman on a stela from the reign of Amenemhat III (Spiegelberg 1896: 1–2, Pl. 1), a sculptor called Iah on a Late Middle Kingdom stela now in Toulouse (Ramond 1977: 13, Pl. 3), an outline-draughtsman called Sasobek on a stela belonging to the Trea-surer of the King of Upper Egypt Senebsumai (Simpson 1974: 19) and an outline-draughtsman called Ibi on a stela, probably from the reign of Sobekhotep II, now in Leiden (Boeser 1909: Pl. 45; Franke 1984: 368). Such craftsmen were also, of course, in a position to create stelae for themselves (Dakin 1938; Faulkner 1952), and the number of these attestations seems to offer proof that the stela-maker himself believed in the efficacy of having oneself depicted on a stela on the Terrace of the Great God. Indeed, one of the largest *mahat*s in the portal cemetery belonged to the 'Overseer of Sculptors, Neby' (O'Connor 1985: 175).

But, while the evidence suggests that there was a flourishing trade in stelae at Abydos, there is some uncertainty in every case as to whether these craftsmen can be definitely said to be producing the stelae at Abydos or at some other site from where they were brought to Abydos. This question is relevant here in a way that it is not in the majority of other stelae from specific sites, given that Abydos was a place of pilgrimage where people came from different parts of Egypt – did they bring their *ex-votos* with them or buy them when they arrived? The self-referential nature of the texts on the stelae sometimes means that it is possible to detect whether a particular stela was a product of local manufacturers or was imported. The best example of this is probably the stelae of Nebipusenwosret, a royal official under Senwosret III and Amenemhat III whose large Abydos stela, now in the British Museum, specifically states that it is had been sent south to Abydos in the care of the senior lector-priest of the Abydene priesthood, Ibi, after the latter had 'come to see the King at his beautiful feast of eternity' (Blackman 1935; Lichtheim 1988: 122–4). Abydos as a place of pilgrimage is attested by stelae which refer to their owners as coming to Abydos deliberately to worship Osiris (for examples see Lichtheim 1988: 101), or on the way to other missions, taking advantage of the opportunity of being at Abydos to set up a *mahat* for themselves. Such individuals include the 'Commander of Recruits' Ded-Iku, who set up a *mahat* while on the way to 'secure the land of the oasis-dwellers' for Senwosret I (Lichtheim 1988: 93–4), and the Chamberlain Semty, who 'staked the mooring-post' of his boat at Abydos and then 'set my name at the place where the god is' (presumably a reference to the the stela itself) on the way back from a statue-restoration mission to Elephantine for Amenemhat II (Lichtheim 1988: 96–8).

It has been suggested that attribution studies of the hieroglyph- and relief-carving on these stelae might be fruitful in identifying the work or particular 'schools' of craftsmen, or even individuals (Freed 1996; Simpson 1974: 4 n.25). However, while there is good evidence to believe that schools of stela-carvers did exist at Abydos, craftsmen might be trained elsewhere and only them come to Abydos to seek their fortune; such is the case of the Master-Sculptor Shen, who worked as a sculptor at Amenemhat-Itj-Tawy (Lisht) before coming to work at Abydos under Senwosret I (Faulkner 1952; Lichtheim 1988: 90–2). Evidence for craftsmen who produced 'funerary industry' objects at Abydos apart from stelae is rather more difficult; the hand of a specific coffin-painter was recognized on examples from three separate tombs at Abydos (Peet 1914b: 60, Figs 88–9), and at least one group of similar, crude limestone statuettes seem to come from a common workshop (Snape 1994). Conversely, the popularity of Abydos as a 'national cemetery' could lead to groups of objects within tombs which seem to have had a primary origin outside the Abydos area, such as the collection of ceramic vessels in tomb 416 A'07 at Abydos which might indicate that the tomb-owner came from the Memphite/Faiyum region (Kemp and Merrillees 1980: 170).

The Spreading Cemetery at Abydos

The popularity of representation at Abydos in the Middle Kingdom seems to have led to efforts to regulate the area available for use. A granite stela found by Randall-MacIver and Mace (1902: Pl. 29) at the [local] south-west corner of the North Cemetery contains a royal decree, probably originally promulgated by Wagaf and later usurped by Neferhotep I (Leahy 1989), which effectively delineated which parts of the cemetery were available for use. The text of this stela states that it is one of four – two to the north and two to the south – which enclose the 'Sacred Land south of Abydos', and was probably intended to keep the area of low ground between the Middle and North Cemeteries free of interments in order to maintain an unimpeded processional way to the tomb of Osiris at the Umm el-Qa'ab (Kemp 1976: 36). It is likely that other decrees regulating the use of the cemetery at Abydos were in force at different times, although there is little surviving evidence for this – the Neferhotep stela itself may only have survived intact owing to its adoption as an ancient and venerable focus around which tombs were built in the early New Kingdom. That the necropolis itself was, in theory at least, well policed is attested by a Middle Kingdom stela found by Garstang in tomb 316 A'07 in the North Cemetery, which belonged to a 'Guardian of the Terrace of Osiris' (*s3w rwdw n Wsir*).

The need for these controls over burial at Abydos was a direct result of the popularity of its cemeteries, for reasons discussed above. Indeed it is possible to trace general trends in the use of the cemetery area at Abydos over considerable periods of time. Several of the archaeologists who have excavated in the Abydos necropolis have tried to relate the areas of their particular excavations to a general process of 'horizontal stratigraphy' at the site. Randall-MacIver and Mace (1902: 64) believed that the tombs in the North Cemetery were sited as close as possible to the temenos (enclosure) wall of the Osiris Temple. The limiting factor of available space meant that gradually the cemetery spread further and further to the [local] west. This theory was shared by Garstang, who believed that his Cemetery 'E' clearly illustrated this westward evolution, with tombs of the Middle Kingdom in the east and those of the Second Intermediate Period in the west (Garstang 1901: 2). However, Peet did not agree with this clear development of the cemetery, and denied any all-encompassing scheme of cemetery usage over long periods of time. He believed that 'Certain portions, determined by natural or artificial bounds, were marked out for burial at particular periods, and remained in use, as a rule, until full, when a move was made to a new part of the site . . . there was no attempt to fill up the space in a systematic method, starting from one part and spreading gradually in various directions' (Peet 1914b: xv). The cemeteries at Abydos do not present a clear or simple pattern of usage over a period of time. As much as any other cemetery from Dynastic Egypt, Abydos was subject to the use and re-use of any given spot. This seems to be largely because the actual place itself possessed innate qualities which made it a much to be desired place of burial or, if this was not possible, representation through *mahat* chapels. Certainly during the Middle Kingdom, and probably at other periods, different regions within the area available for interment had their own hierarchy of desirability; the most favoured positions were those most closely connected with the rituals of the Osiris cult. The constant overbuilding and re-use of tombs within this limited area led, in Peet's words, to 'utter confusion, partly because every cemetery contained tombs of most varying periods, and partly because there are so many tombs whose date cannot be accurately fixed' (Peet 1914b: ix).

The Abydos cemeteries also display both horizontal and vertical stratigraphy. Tombs were re-used, sometimes more than once (Peet 1914b: 73), and new funerary monuments were built on top of old ones; even without the intervention of human agencies, wind-blown sand could bury surface structures in a relatively short time (Ayrton et al. 1904: 11). Many earlier tombs were covered by later building work, such as the 'Portal' temple of Ramesses II, founded on top of Middle Kingdom *mahat*-chapels (O'Connor 1979: Fig. 3), or eradicated by the activities of later tomb-diggers, as is the case in Garstang's tomb 941-949 A'09, where the bottoms of Late Old Kingdom shaft tombs were visible in the floor of a Dynasty 18 chamber tomb (Figure 8.5). Another aspect of the confusion of the archaeological record at Abydos is a process which one might term 'diagonal stratigraphy', by which material of one period is re-used in a later period in a different

Figure 8.5 Abydos Tomb 941-949 A'09 excavated by John Garstang in 1909 (© Garstang Museum of Archaeology, University of Liverpool)

part of the cemetery. Stelae are particularly likely to travel around in this way, probably because they have the virtue of often being readily to hand in ground-level superstructures, and are conveniently shaped slabs of stone with applications limited only by the imagination of their user. These include their use as building materials for later structures, as in tomb 790 A'09; as lids of sarcophagi, in tomb 938 A'09; as battering stones used by robbers trying to break into stone sarcophagi (Peet 1914b: 91); and as stands for coffins (Ayrton et al. 1904: 50).

CHAPTER 9

'Lords of Life'

Coffins

⌐⌐⌐⌐

The Multi-Functional Coffin

The ancient Egyptian coffin (for an overview, see Taylor 1989) was not simply a container to convey a dead body to the tomb. It was a 'ritual machine' (Willems 1988: 293) whose shape and decoration indicated the ways in which it served a wider series of agendas related to the afterlife expectations of its owner:

1. Like the tomb, it could be a house for the *ka*, and early coffins have a house-like appearance.
2. The decoration of the coffin could emphasize the idea that the *ka* could leave the body and the coffin, via magical doors, and travel to the Offering Chapel.
3. The coffin could be a miniature version of the tomb in its internal depiction of goods and larger structures such as granaries.
4. The coffin could have texts and scenes which could guide the deceased to the afterlife: the Coffin Texts.
5. The coffin could be a model of the cosmos.
6. The coffin could be an item of magical protection through the idea of Osirian afterlife – it could become the mythological chest which contained the body of Osiris, and could have images of protective deities painted on it.
7. The coffin could be further identified with Osiris if its shape mimicked the wrapped, mummiform appearance of that god as an anthropoid coffin.

Ancient Egyptian Tombs: The Culture of Life and Death   By Steven Snape
© 2011 Steven Snape

8. The anthropoid coffin could, in effect, become an extension of the body on which rituals were carried out.
9. The coffin could be an object on which wider ideas of an Osirian afterlife could be depicted.

Naturally, these ideas did not all appear at once, but emerged as part of the gradual evolution of beliefs regarding the afterlife and the specific role of the coffin within the material response of the Egyptians to these shifting concepts. However, the developed role of the coffin, especially after the emergence of the outer box coffin and the inner anthropoid coffin, gave it a significant intermediary role which, like the statue, could be considered to be both part of the tomb and a substitute for the body.

Predynastic and Archaic Period Coffins

As has already been noted, the observation of naturally preserved bodies from desert burials may well have been a significant spur for the development of the idea that there was something particularly important about the need to preserve the human body; an idea which, at some stage, became part of the set of requirements for the *ka*. In this context it might well have been natural to wish to give the body a more dignified and comfortable resting place than a sand-filled pit, and the late Predynastic and Early Dynastic Periods saw the introduction of simple body-coverings, such as reed coffins, which developed into more elaborate wooden boxes. Crucially, these containers were designed to accommodate a body which continued to be buried in a contracted position. However, the barrier between the body and the desert provided just those conditions which would be detrimental to its survival, encouraging decomposition. The introduction of the coffin therefore hindered, not helped, the preservation of the body. This development happened at a time when experimentation with the grave itself was taking place: some cemeteries saw the introduction of a roofed wooden structure in the grave, effectively forming the first Burial Chambers with space around the body and coffin.

It is probably safe to assume that, at some stage, the prejudicial nature of the use of coffins and the development of Burial Chambers made itself known to the Egyptians. At this point it might have been sensible to abandon both developments and return to sand-burial. However, this was not the route down which the Egyptians chose to go, but instead they began to develop techniques which would create an artificially preserved body within the coffin. Perhaps the specific role of sand-desiccation had not been properly recognized, or perhaps the role of the coffin as something more than a container for the body had become too important to be abandoned. Whatever the case, by the Old Kingdom, both coffin use and artificial preservation of the body – mummification – had become firmly established as major elements of the mortuary repertoire, and both would continue to be used until they were effectively made redundant by the arrival of Christian burial practices.

The development of woodworking techniques in the late Predynastic was a major factor in the development of coffins. Indeed wood was the material for coffins *par excellence*, something which emerged in a number of different ways. Although ancient Egypt had an abundance of natural resources, good-quality timber was not one of them – the most commonly occurring and utilized species were tamarisk, sycamore fig and acacia, which only produce small sections of usable material, while palm-logs are too fibrous to produce carpentry-friendly wood. Although later coffins made use of large planks of imported timber, in the Predynastic and Archaic Periods this was not so much an issue, partly because of the relatively modest dimensions of a coffin for a contracted body, and partly because of the way in which the need to construct coffins from many small sections of wood made a virtue out of a necessity. Although some of these wooden coffins, which appear at sites such as Saqqara and Tarkhan in Dynasties 2 and 3, were simple, plain boxes, a more complicated type appeared whose sides were modelled in the 'palace-façade' style of contemporary *mastaba*s, and whose lids were vaulted with rectangular gable ends; these coffins were, like the tombs themselves, conceptualized as houses in which the Dead would reside. In this way one of the major functions of the coffin began to develop: the idea that it was a sort of mini-tomb, a house for the *ka*, which would provide immediate protection for the body, which was itself the ideal host for the *ka*, and from which the *ka* could leave in order to travel to the Offering Chapel. Therefore the coffin was integrated within the overall scheme of producing a tomb which would serve the *ka*. However, the potential of the coffin for decoration, and the different ways in which the coffin and its parts could be seen as metaphors for wider concepts, meant that it would achieve an even greater significance than protector of the body and home of the *ka*, and would connect to a different set of ideas.

Coffins in the Old Kingdom

A number of developments took place in the early part of the Old Kingdom which directly affected the design of coffins. The most obvious was the switch from the 'short-form' coffin, which housed a contracted body, to the 'long-form' coffin, which held an extended body. This change has been linked to the development of techniques of artificial preservation of the body, especially the removal of the internal organs of the abdomen and the subsequent bandaging of the limbs, which could only conveniently be carried out on a body which was stretched out and which would subsequently need to be buried in this extended state. The second development was the introduction of the stone sarcophagus.

To some extent, and depending on circumstance, the terms 'coffin' and 'sarcophagus' are interchangeable. Both words refer to an object which was used to contain the body, around which it had a reasonably tight fit. In Egyptian archaeology the terms are usually, but not always, used in a conventional way. The term 'coffin' is used for a container, usually of wood, which fits fairly tightly around the body. 'Sarcophagus' tends to refer to a container made of stone, usually of quite substantial size, and which may itself have been designed to contain a coffin. Indeed for elite burials of the Old Kingdom the configuration of an outer stone sarcophagus and an inner wooden coffin seems to have been an ideal 'set'. The advantages of a large, heavy stone sarcophagus are obvious. It protected the body from interference, particularly within the confines of a small Burial Chamber at the bottom of a deep shaft underneath an Old Kingdom *mastaba*. It could be manoeuvred into place during the construction of the tomb, ready for its intended occupant. It was also (as we have seen) an item denoting wealth and status. By contrast, the light and manoeuvrable wooden coffin could be made ready to receive the body as soon as it had undergone its necessary preparations in the embalming house. Encased within the wooden coffin, the body could be taken to the tomb, with all the rites of the funeral ceremony, before being placed within the stone sarcophagus, whose lid would then be manoeuvred into place creating (in theory) an impenetrable case which only the *ka* of its occupant could enter or leave. Although this 'nesting' of a wooden coffin within a stone sarcophagus seems to have been the ideal in the Old Kingdom, other variant practices occurred, including the use of a larger, outer wooden coffin as a sarcophagus. This prefigures the later variations in the use of multiple coffins in various configurations in the Middle Kingdom, New Kingdom and Late Period, each with their own specific requirements.

The origin for this use of wooden coffin/stone sarcophagus seems to be in royal practice. The thorough destruction of the interiors of Archaic royal tombs at Abydos means that we have little idea of the nature of the coffins/sarcophagi which housed the bodies of the kings of Dynasties 1 and 2, but the evidence from the Old Kingdom royal cemeteries of the Memphite necropolis indicates that long-form inner wooden coffins within stone sarcophagi were in use by the reign of Djoser. Although the Burial

Chambers of the great royal pyramids of Dynasty 4 have essentially been stripped clean of their original contents, the exception is the massive stone sarcophagi which still rest in the pyramids of, for example, Khufu and Khaefre. The materials chosen for royal burial were, unsurprisingly, the best available, so that the materials used for royal sarcophagi were typically hardstones such as granite, quartzite, basalt and alabaster. These royal sarcophagi were not heavily decorated; rather they were plain chests or had a 'palace-façade' exterior. For non-royal individuals, any sort of stone sarcophagus was a mark of status, wealth and (usually) royal favour. Limestone – ideally fine-quality limestone from the royal quarries at Tura– was the material of choice (or, rather, availability).

Coffins at the End of the Old Kingdom

Until the end of Dynasty 5 the decoration of coffins was little different to that of the Archaic Period, with the domination of 'palace-façade' decoration. Private coffins and royal sarcophagi were, in decorative terms, very similar. The major transformational period, as with the decoration of the Burial Chamber itself, was the end of Dynasty 5 and the beginning of Dynasty 6, specifically (as we have noted) the influence of royal Burial Chamber decoration at the pyramid of Unas. As we have seen, prompted by Unas' example, private individuals began to decorate the walls of the Burial Chambers of their tombs, but with a design scheme very different to that of the king. Rather than Pyramid Texts (which would, of course, have been deeply inappropriate), Burial Chambers of *mastaba*-tombs of Dynasty 6 developed scenes drawn from the main decorative scheme of the *mastaba* itself (Kanawati 2005). These themes would eventually and regularly find their way onto the coffin itself during the Middle Kingdom, but in the late Old Kingdom the decorative change to coffins was in the introduction of a range of motifs which would be the core decorative scheme for Middle Kingdom (and later) standard 'box' coffins.

The coffin can be seen as an item which is an interface between the body, the tomb and the cosmos. This is manifested in a number of different ways: it is made apparent through the developing decorative content of the coffin, but it is also evident in the way in which the coffin is placed within the tomb. In the Burial Chamber, the coffin is regularly orientated along a north–south axis, often within a stone sarcophagus whose north–south positioning is the most important design consideration of the Burial Chamber itself. The body within the coffin lies on its left side, with its head to the north, facing east. This positioning can be seen as having two distinctly separate but overlapping purposes. For the *ka*, if one assumes a burial to the west of the Nile Valley (as is the case in the Memphite cemeteries), the body looked towards the Offering Chapel within the tomb and, by extension, the direction from which the Living come with their offerings. This is, of course, a design principle which we have seen applied to other aspects of tomb design, most notably the positioning of the false door, but in this context the coffin, and body within, can be seen on the same terms: as part of a set of physical entities – the stone door, the wooden coffin, the dried flesh of the body – which all contribute to the idea of the tomb as the place where the *ka*'s needs are met. The eastwards orientation can also be seen as an attempt to place the body looking towards the horizon on which the sun will emerge every morning; although rather muted, ideas of rebirth from nature projected onto the tomb-owner will become more important and this is also reflected in the texts and images on the coffin as well as other parts of the tomb. This function brings the coffin within the realm of conceptualizing the cosmos within the tomb, and indeed the coffin itself became a mini-cosmos.

The Decoration of a Standard Box Coffin

The term 'box coffin' refers to a coffin which is rectangular in form, with a deep lower part (case) and a relatively thin, usually flat, lid (Figure 9.1). The standard elements of decoration are as follows:

1. The painting/carving of the *hetep-di-nesu* formula in a horizontal band close to the top of the case on both the exterior and interior of the coffin, beginning at the northern end of the east side of the coffin.
2. The painting/carving of a large pairs of eyes at the northern end of the exterior east (i.e. 'front') side of the coffin, i.e. on the outside of the coffin in front of the face of the deceased lying on his left side. The purpose of this 'eye panel' is to allow the *ka* to see out of the coffin without leaving it.
3. The painting of a false door on the interior of the coffin immediately in front of the face of the body, which would allow the *ka* to leave the coffin.
   In later coffins the eye panel and the false door became integrated as a large panel with the eyes painted above the false door, on both the outside and inside of the coffin, but the location at the north end of the east side of the coffin, in front of the face, was non-negotiable. Further elaborations to the decoration of the box coffin in the late Old Kingdom might include more elements on the inside of the coffin:

Figure 9.1   The box coffin of Userhet from Beni Hasan (© Garstang Museum of Archaeology, University of Liverpool)

4.   Lists of offerings.
5.   Materials used in the 'Opening of the Mouth' ceremony.

Box Coffins in the First Intermediate Period and Middle Kingdom

This description of box coffins in the late Old Kingdom is based on traditions which emerged in the Memphite area, partly influenced by royal innovations, and developed for use in elite tombs, especially those of Giza and Saqqara. As with the forms and decoration of tombs themselves, coffins developed to a significant degree with the onset of the First Intermediate Period. Partly this is for some of the same reasons: the accessibility to non-royal expectations of an afterlife by a much broader section of society; the influence of provincialism in the development of regional variations in major classes of burial equipment; and a greater level of self-awareness by individuals. But there is another important factor: while rock-cut tombs in the regions were still the possession of a small elite – albeit a local elite – the possession of a coffin, while not available to everyone, certainly brought the possession of an object which had many of the qualities of a tomb to a wider range of people. The simplest and earliest type is directly descended from the Late Old Kingdom/First Intermediate Period type described above, with eye panel and a horizontal text band running round the coffin near its lid, with *hetep-di-nesu* and *prt ḥrw* ('voice-offering') texts, stressing the central importance of offerings, chiefly food offerings, for the *ka* as one who is provided for, or *imakhu*. As such, these coffins are just one of a range of funerary objects, on which these texts can be appropriately inscribed. This type of coffin dominated the early part of the Middle Kingdom, until it was replaced by a greater variety of types during the reign of Amenemhat I.

Just as the regional elite tombs of the First Intermediate Period and Middle Kingdom display distinct regional variations within a broadly established pattern of functionality, so the different cemeteries of Middle Kingdom Egypt show the continuation of regional styles of other funerary objects coming out of the First Intermediate Period. Traditionally, two major traditions have been identified: a 'northern' (or 'Herakleopolitan') style, which includes the Delta, Memphite area and Middle Egypt (best represented by the cemeteries at Beni Hasan, el-Bersheh and Meir), and a 'southern' style with major centres at Asyut, Akhmim, Thebes, Gebelein and Moalla. A more detailed analysis of the material by Willems (1988) suggests that these two broad categories are unhelpful and that the problems of an already-recognized overlap in the neat north–south division (e.g. 'northern' types are not uncommon at Thebes) should be extended to regard individual sites as having their own local traditions within a broadly similar typology – based on the late Old Kingdom standard box coffin, which Willems terms the 'Middle Kingdom Standard Class Coffin'. Nevertheless, a number of general trends can be identified.

Coffins from the 'northern' group tend to have relatively limited decoration on the exterior (i.e. similar to that from the late Old Kingdom) but had elaborately and colourfully painted interiors. A panel depicting food offerings (sometimes referred to as the 'funerary meal') was regularly placed next to the false door. A horizontal band running round the interior of the coffin contained a series of painted and labelled objects – the *frises d'objets* – most of which were the type of personal possession the *ka* might need, such as toiletry items, staves, weapons, jewellery and clothing. The positioning of these objects in relation to the body was often very deliberate: headrests near the head and sandals near the feet. Some of the items in the *frises d'objets* look rather less domestic – royal regalia, for instance – and this may indicate that at least some of this material comes from a royal background. An origin in royal mortuary provision and expectations certainly seems to be present for the item which fills most of the space of the interior of the coffin: the Coffin Texts (Faulkner 1973–8). Derived originally from a series of expectations of a royal afterlife contained within the Pyramid Texts, the Coffin Texts provided a means by which the sub-elite of Middle Kingdom Egypt – those who could afford a coffin for their burial in an undecorated tomb – could access such an afterlife. Although, as their name suggests, the most obvious medium for the Coffin Texts are coffins, they could also appear in other contexts, such as the roofs of Middle Kingdom tombs at el-Bersheh (Silverman et al. 1992: 15–27). Regional variations in these texts are very marked, with el-Bersheh, Meir and Asyut particularly known for their distinctive local styles. At their most extreme, as at el-Bersheh, these coffins became vehicles for the transportation of the coffin-owner to an afterlife well beyond the tomb, with the floor of the coffin decorated as a road-map to a beneficial afterlife and guided there by the 'Book of the Two Ways'.

Coffins from the 'southern' group have their decorative content focused on the exterior. At Akhmim, this consists of an extended offering list running underneath the main *hetep-di-nesu* text band on the east side of the coffin, to the left of the eye panel, while at Gebelein and nearby Moalla, scenes of brewing beer and the depiction of the body on a bier are popular. One of the most recognizable of these regional traditions is the variant of Middle Kingdom box coffins which come from Asyut in Dynasty 12, whose recognizable characteristics include the use of double bands of both horizontal and vertical texts.

Osirian Features of Box Coffins

Another reason why the coffin is such an important funerary artefact for scholars of the Middle Kingdom is that it is the most informative object informing the religious background to the Egyptians' understanding of the afterlife – particularly as it relates to the changed circumstances after the Old Kingdom. This is partly because it is the main (although far from only) medium by which the Coffin Texts were conveyed, but also because of other religious and, possibly, liturgical aspects of the coffin. It is also the most complex and information-filled part of the tomb for the majority of significant (i.e. informative) Middle Kingdom burials, the only exceptions being large elite tombs such as the series at Beni Hasan. In many ways the coffin can be thought of as part of the tomb rather than an object within a tomb – the distinction is probably meaningless to the Egyptians as every element of the funerary provision had its particular role within the whole – and it is certainly the case that coffins could be conceived as mini-tombs, just as they could be conceived as models of the cosmos. One of the most important features of Middle Kingdom coffins is the extent to which they

Figure 9.2 The head of the anthropoid coffin of Khnum-Nakht from Rifeh

invoke divine protection for the deceased through imagery which is largely, although not completely, Osirian in both a very specific and broader sense. For the former there is the development of the 'anthropoid' coffin which is clearly designed to create an identity for the deceased *as* Osiris (Figure 9.2), while the 'box' coffin enlists the protection of a wider range of characters within the Osirian myth-cycle. The ideal set was, of course, an anthropoid coffin contained within a box coffin (Figure 9.3).

The most important development was the emergence of a series of vertical text bands on the outside of the coffin. Their purpose, and also sometimes that of a horizontal band with revised content, was to assemble a group of protective deities whose capabilities have already been demonstrated in Osirian myth and the Pyramid Texts. As such, these texts come

Figure 9.3   The box coffin of Userhet, containing his anthropoid coffin, in his tomb at Beni Hasan (© Garstang Museum of Archaeology, University of Liverpool)

from a radically different background to the offering-texts, and one where the deceased had significantly upgraded expectations of an afterlife, one where they could expect the protection of the gods. Chief among these protective deities was Nut, who, even before the end of the Old Kingdom, was associated with the coffin-lid as it was identified with the sky in the conceptualization of coffin-as-cosmos. Nut was doubly appropriate as being both a sky-goddess and, as the mother of Osiris, a natural protector of his body and also, as mother of Nephthys and Isis, one who would summon her daughters to care for their brother Osiris. Texts on the exterior of the short head end of the coffin often state 'Speech by Nut: I have placed Nephthys under thy head', with a similar speech referring to Isis at the feet.

Other phrases filling the short text bands down the front and back of the box coffin often begin '*imȝḫw ḫr*', 'provided for before . . .', followed by the name of a god. The standard arrangement of vertical text bands was two at each of the two shorter head and foot ends of the coffin, and four on the front and back. The gods who appear in these bands fall into the following groups:

1. Deities from the Heliopolitan Creation myth. These are referred to collectively as the 'Great Ennead', a group of nine deities who made up the first four generations of gods. The first generation of this group – the self-created Atum – does not appear individually on Middle Kingdom coffins, and neither does one of the members of the fourth generation, Seth, which is hardly surprising giving the overwhelming Osirian orientation of the coffin. Deities of the second and third generation of Heliopolitan deities – Shu, Tefnut, Geb and Nut – do appear individually, the former pair on the front of the coffin and the latter on the back. The reference to the collective Great Ennead appears at the head end of the coffin, as does reference to the Little Ennead, whose composition is unknown.

2. Immediate participants in the Osiris myth, which, in a broad sense, represents a continuation of the Heliopolitan Creation story. As we have already noted, Nephthys appears on the head end of the coffin and Isis at the foot, typically on the horizontal band. Osiris is, of course, the body itself.

3. Further protective deities and their 'patronesses'. The four 'Sons of Horus' are split between the front (Duamutef and Imset) and back (Hapy and Qebhsenuef) of the coffin, while vertical bands on the foot end refer to Selket and Neith. Together with Isis and Nephthys, these two goddesses make up a quartet of female deities who complement the Sons of Horus.

For most coffin-owning Egyptians of the Middle Kingdom the coffin itself was the most important part of their tomb assemblage, carrying the principal burden of decorative and textual content within an undecorated and physically unimpressive tomb. However, cemeteries containing such relatively modest burials also regularly featured tombs whose impressive size was matched by the extensiveness of their decoration. The relationship between tombs belonging to individuals of different social strata and their expectations for an afterlife in post-Old Kingdom Egypt is best examined using specific examples, two of the most informative of which are the Middle Kingdom cemeteries at Beni Hasan and Rifeh.

CHAPTER 10

Strangers and Brothers

The Middle Kingdom in Middle Egypt

ﭏﭏﭏﭏ

Continuity and Change

The locations and development of tombs in the Middle Kingdom show a much more diverse pattern than in the Old Kingdom, not least because, unlike the essentially court-centred monopoly of Dynasties 1–6, most of the regions of the post-First Intermediate Period Egypt had important elite cemeteries (Grajetzki 2006: 78–133), although their differential survival may have obscured some of this pattern. This is especially the case in the Delta, where tombs of this (and indeed every) period are rare; exceptions are the mudbrick *mastabas* with limestone-lined walls at Barnugi (Edgar 1907) and Kom el-Hisn (Silverman 1988) in the western Delta, and a continuation of the Bubastis necropolis in the eastern Delta. Other major provincial cemeteries which were established in the late Old Kingdom and First Intermediate Period continued to flourish in the Middle Kingdom, including Qubbet el-Hawa (Aswan), Meir and el-Bersheh. Abydos, as was noted in the previous chapter, took a different direction owing to its close identification with the cult of Osiris. Other regions had a less easy transition into the Middle Kingdom, including Moalla, Asyut and, presumably, Herakleopolis, on account of the anti-Theban political sympathies of their First Intermediate Period owners. By contrast, local cemeteries in other parts of the Nile Valley flourished in Dynasty 11 and the early part of Dynasty 12 in a way they had not done so previously. Perhaps the best example of this – indeed the best example of a multi-generational, socially stratified cemetery of the Middle Kingdom – is that at Beni Hasan in

Ancient Egyptian Tombs: The Culture of Life and Death   By Steven Snape
© 2011 Steven Snape

Middle Egypt, whose character is largely derived from a combination of local geographical and wider socio-political developments in the Middle Kingdom, particularly the relationship between the royal court and the provinces.

Local tombs for local rulers

Although it is common to refer to the most senior provincial officials as 'nomarchs', this term, which refers to the Graeco-Roman administration of the districts or 'nomes' of Egypt, had no direct equivalence in the Middle Kingdom, although it is used below for convenience. Some particularly prominent officials might have designated titles, such as 'Great Overlord' (*ḥry-tp ꜥꜣ*), but the most common title borne by these people is *ḥꜣty-ꜥ (haaty-aa)*, a term which means something like 'local prince' or (later) 'mayor'. The hereditary status of this title is ambiguous – although requiring royal affirmation the passage of local lordship from father to son was, as far as one can tell, the norm in Middle Kingdom Egypt.

The authority and wealth of these local officials depended on two factors which might be expressed in geographical terms: for the king their responsibility was the stewardship of the nome, while their local power was centred on their control of the nome capital. Often the most obvious manifestation of the latter was their controlling influence as 'Overseer of Priests' of the main deity of the nome capital, such as Hathor at Meir/Cusae or Khnum at Rifeh/Shashotep and Beni Hasan. This leadership role in the local priesthood was far from being a dogmatic proselytizing one; rather it was to do with the control of land owned by the temple and the income that land produced (Seidlmayer 2000: 127). The nomarch therefore had two income streams passing through his hands: that destined for the king and that applied for the benefit of the local temple; both provided opportunities for manipulation. There is a further factor at work here, which is not simply to do with cynical money-making opportunities. The nomarch as servant of the king and of the local god had a dual affirmation of legitimacy, and the tomb stressed this dual role. Ankhtify is at an extreme end of this scale, where he justified his position and actions by almost exclusive reference to the gods Horus and Hemen. Many Old Kingdom tombs, particularly those of Dynasty 4, are at the other end of the scale, where it was the king who provided the different levels of *imakh*, even to the extent of effectively being (through himself and his royal ancestors) the 'Great God' mentioned in offering texts. Middle Kingdom tombs are rather more balanced in their references to the dual authority of their owners, with the service of the local god providing a more royally acceptable alternative to statements of personal authority and initiative of the First Intermediate Period. This

combination of the possibility of quasi-independent action under an
umbrella of ultimate royal oversight was perhaps already detectable at
the end of the Old Kingdom in, for example, the texts from the tomb of Qar
at Edfu, which seem to 'express the growing importance of local authorities
as providers of goods for royal administration as well as enterprising
officers able to resolve local problems' (Moreno Garcia 1998: 160). The
extent to which these sentiments (and their overt statement on tomb walls)
suggest weakness in the royal position in its relationship to the regions,
both at the end of the Old Kingdom and early in the Middle Kingdom, is a
subject of intense academic debate.

The ability of local rulers to deploy local resources for their own benefit is
most clearly seen in the arrangements for their funerary cult. The most
remarkable and detailed example of this, indeed the most elaborate
example of the operation of the *ka*-priest system in the Middle Kingdom,
comes from the tomb of Djefai-Hapi at Asyut (Breasted 1906: 258–71
[§§ 535–93]; Devauchelle 1996; Griffith 1889; Reisner 1918), which
contains a series of extensive texts which are contracts made by Djefai-
Hapi with the priesthood of the local temples of Wepwawet and Anubis for
the provision of offerings, mainly for the benefit of his *ka*. The resources
that Djefai-Hapi gifted in these bequests were used to make offerings to the
gods of these temples on specific occasions but, more particularly, they
were directed towards the cults of a series of statues of himself which
Djefai-Hapi set up within these temples and in an outer, accessible part of
his tomb ('the lower steps/terrace of his tomb', *rwdw ḥr n is.f*). This
arrangement shows the varied routes by which the *ka* of an individual
might be given the offerings it requires, through the well-established locus
of the tomb (presumably a terraced courtyard at the front of the tomb) and
via a statue-cult within a local temple. This is a good example of a
phenomenon which was to become increasingly important, particularly
in the Ramesside period, of some of the functions of the tomb being
replaced or replicated in private statues within local temples. By a strange
coincidence, two life-sized statues belonging to Djefai-Hapi, and one
belonging to a woman, Sennui, believed to be a close family member,
have been found, not at Asyut, but hundreds of miles to the south in Nubia.
The broken base of one statue of Djefai-Hapi was found re-used in the
Nubian temple of Gebel Barkal (Reisner 1931: 80), while the other, along
with the shattered figure of Sennui, was found in tomb KIII (Reisner 1923:
Pl. 7), one of the Second Intermediate Period royal tombs of Kerma.
They had been smashed, as either execration or servant figures, a curious
echo of the use of servant statuary in Egyptian tombs or, perhaps, the
sacrifical burials of Dynasties 1–2, since sacrificial burial was part of the
Kerma burials.

The theme of self-reliance in funerary arrangements, which the Djefai-Hapi contracts represent, is also attested at Asyut in relation to tomb building itself: Anu, one of Djefai-Hapi's predecessors, states on the walls of his tomb that 'I completed this tomb, because I myself caused its inscriptions to be made while I was still alive' (Grajetzki 2006: 105). There is at least one further possible link between elite tombs and temples in the nomes. In his work at the Rifeh cemetery, Petrie (1907: 11) noted that unfinished parts of some of the larger rock-cut tombs suggested that the removal of limestone during their construction was in the form of usefully sized blocks of stone, rather than builders' rubble. His explanation for this was that the stone removed could have been taken to build the nomarch's palace at the nome capital, Shashotep. While the limited state of the archaeology of Middle Kingdom towns in the provinces does not allow this theory to be confirmed or denied, the extent of mudbrick and comparatively small quantities of stone used within vaguely comparable buildings of the Middle Kingdom might suggest that the quantities of stone removed from the massive Rifeh (and indeed Asyut) tombs may have been used in other ways. One might also compare the scenes of stone-quarrying in the Middle Kingdom tomb of Djehutynakht VI at el-Bersheh (Griffith and Newberry 1894–5 (Vol. II): 24; Silverman et al. 1992: 36). A project which created a tomb for a nomarch and also provided building material for the temple of the local god would create a pleasingly neat connection between the nomarch's tomb and the temple of the god from whom he sought favour.

Beni Hasan: The Archetypal Middle Kingdom Necropolis

Beni Hasan is the name given to the cemetery of the Oryx (16th Upper Egyptian) nome. It is remarkable in the way in which it, as a regional centre not directly connected with the seats of national power and royal influence, retained its own distinctive regional traditions as an area governed by families of local dynasts who displayed their power through self-created elite tombs. It is also important because its Middle Kingdom necropolis contains, in an integrated funerary landscape, both the tombs of the ruling elite and those of the less-powerful members of society, who, nonetheless, had their own aspirations for a comfortable afterlife and at least some wealth to deploy to help them achieve that aspiration. In the desert cliffs overlooking the modern village of Beni Hasan the ancient tombs are arranged hierarchically to mimic the status of their owners in life: the 'Upper Cemetery' a typical *Felsgräbernekropole* – a terrace of impressive rock-cut tombs (Figures 10.1 and 10.2) – and, on the sand- and gravel-covered slopes running down to the cultivation from the Upper Cemetery,

Figure 10.1 View of the Beni Hasan cemetery

Figure 10.2 Elite tombs at Beni Hasan

the 'Lower Cemetery' – a *Gräberfeld* containing the simple shaft-and-chamber tombs of the sub-elite of the Oryx Nome.

Architecture and decoration in the 'Upper Cemetery' at Beni Hasan

The first thing to note about the tombs of the Upper Cemetery at Beni Hasan is their elevated position. Like many contemporary elite tombs, their specific location in the cliffs overlooking the Nile Valley was partially determined by the quality of the rock – finding a good seam of limestone which was suitable for the cutting of large-chambered tombs was essential. But position was also determined by visibility, which could work in two ways. The first was the visibility *of* the tomb itself from the valley below, and its continued presence as part of the sacred landscape of the region in the minds of succeeding generations who lived in the area. The second was the visibility *from* the tomb; it is tempting to think of many of these elite cemeteries being located in positions which commanded a significant vista over territory controlled by the tomb-owner in life, and now from which offerings would, hopefully, flow towards the tomb for the benefit of its owner.

In terms of their external appearance, the tombs of the Upper Cemetery have the appearance of a row of elaborate façades belonging to a group of large and impressive upper-class villas (Figure 10.3). Some of them have

Figure 10.3 Tomb façade at Beni Hasan

carved porticoes which deliberately mimic in stone the wooden columns and roofing-beams of real houses. Not only was this an extremely effective means of creating a tomb exterior which would be visible for some considerable distance, but it was also a further reminder of the continuing role of the tomb as the house of the *ka*. Even more than is the case in the (probably) house-like tombs of the Old Kingdom, form followed perceived function. The 39 large tombs in the Upper Cemetery show a general evolution towards increased architectural sophistication: the earliest have simple rock-cut chambers, roughly square, but with no internal columns or external portico; a middle group lack external porticoes, but have interiors divided by rows of columns running transversely across the chamber; and the most complex group has external columned porticoes, internal chambers divided by rows of columns, and rock-cut shrines at the rear of the main chamber (Newberry 1893–1900 (Vol. I): 3).

The location (on the East Bank of the Nile) and form of these tombs required a certain amount of architectural adaptation in their desire to incorporate traditional, standard elements of tomb design which survived from the Old Kingdom. A decision had to be made concerning false doors within these tombs – should they be orientated so that they faced east, with the west behind them, or should they be located in the innermost part of the tomb? In an East Bank cemetery, with the tombs orientated so that they were approached from the west, it was not possible to do both. At the East Bank cemetery of Sheikh Said, the tendency was to have false doors on the west wall of the tomb (Fischer 1996: 5). At Beni Hasan the situation is more complex: the compromise in some tombs (e.g. Amenemhat and Khety) was to have the false door on the western wall of the tomb, which is to say on the wall close to the entrance, while Baket III came up with a different solution, by cutting a small offering-room in the south wall of his tomb, the west wall of which contain an offering list and a false door orientated towards the west.

Twelve of these tombs have a significant amount of decoration on their internal walls, eight of which belong to 'Great Overlords of the Oryx Nome'. The themes depicted on most of the wall-space in all of these tombs would not have been out of place in an Old Kingdom tomb: scenes of offering to the tomb-owner, of craft and agriculture, or hunting and fishing. But there were also new themes which reflected some of the things which had changed since the Old Kingdom. An emphasis on an Osirian afterlife is apparent in scenes of boat journeys described as going to and from Abydos. A greater interest in historical events is also evident in a number of ways, including some of the tombs which have been dated to late Dynasty 11 and early Dynasty, which are remarkable in depicting scenes of conflict. The tomb of Khety (Tomb 17) is notable for a huge tableau depicting pairs of wrestlers (a motif copied in some later tombs at Beni Hasan), while the tomb of Khety's father (Tomb 15), Baket III, depicts a siege. The reasons behind these violent images coming to be depicted in a context – the tomb – which generally avoids the importation of negative elements such as human conflict are not clear. Too late in date to sit comfortably within the genre of (largely textual) triumphalism of the First Intermediate Period, as at Moalla and Asyut, these scenes may reflect internal difficulties within the unified Egyptian state late in Dynasty 11 and/or early in Dynasty 12. However, although the specific historical inspiration is contentious, it was obviously considered an appropriate and significant element within tomb decoration at this time at Beni Hasan. Other surprising elements within the canon of depiction in the tombs of Khety and Baket III include non-naturalistic subjects, such as mythical creatures, which, like the scenes of conflict, appear without accompanying textual explanation.

There is much less evidence for funerals in Middle Kingdom tombs than those of either the Old or New Kingdoms. There are no extensive scenes showing the multi-part rituals of procession and activity at the tomb, although it may be that scenes which have been interpreted as depicting offering-cults at the tomb (for instance on the south wall of the tomb of Khnumhotep II) actually represent funeral ceremonies. There are a few other pieces of evidence which are suggestive of ritual carried out at the time of funeral. One comes from a group of Dynasty 13 (although the date is disputed) papyri found beneath what was later the Ramesseum at Thebes, where a fractured account of what seems to be a funerary liturgy refers to the sacrifice of 40 bulls and a group of participants, including mourning women, involved in 'circulating round the *mastaba* (*i*ⁿ) four times' (Gardiner 1955).

The three most impressive tombs in the late group at Beni Hasan belong to local dynasts who can be dated with some confidence owing to their inscriptions referring to kings whose reigns (and sometimes individual year-dates) were contemporary with the lives of the tomb-owners. These are the tombs of Khnumhotep I (Tomb 14: appointed by Amenemhat I), Amenemhat (Tomb 2: Year 25 of Senwosret I and refers to Amenemhat II) and Khnumhotep II (Tomb 3: Year 19 of Amenemhat II and Year 6 of Senwosret II). The tomb of Khnumhotep II in particular represents a high-water mark in tomb construction and decoration at Beni Hasan. It contains a long and interesting (auto)biographical text which appears to be a natural descendant – perhaps a country-cousin – of similar texts of the Old Kingdom, particularly in its reference to named kings in the organization of the nome and the appointment of Khnumhotep to office. Intriguingly, the same tomb depicts a group of *Aamu*-Asiatics in their distinct and colourful robes coming into Egypt, a record of an incident which has often been taken as early evidence of the penetration of Middle Kingdom Egypt by Near Eastern nomads well before the onset of the Second Intermediate Period, possibly to seek employment as mercenaries (Bietak 1996: 14). In the context of the tomb of Khnumhotep II this vignette seems to be part of a 'notable things which happened in my time' *topos*, although its role as part of a more sophisticated, coherent decorative scheme for the whole tomb cannot be discounted (Kamrin 1999).

The last major tomb in the Upper Cemetery at Beni Hasan seems to have been started for Khnumhotep III, but only the portico was completed. The fate of Khnumhotep III is much debated, since it seems to be a marker for the decline of the elite cemetery at Beni Hasan, and indeed the contemporary decline of similar cemeteries in Upper Egypt. This is because a man called Khnumhotep who was buried at Dahshur in the cemetery associated with the pyramid of Senwosret III is believed to be Khnumhotep III. A long-held theory within the study of Egyptian history (for review, see Franke 1991) holds that Senwosret III brought about a series of reforms of provincial administration during his reign which limited the power of local dynastic families such as that at Beni Hasan. The structure of government was brought much more closely in line with that of the Old Kingdom and, as a result, elite burial was to be sought in royal court cemeteries rather than the mini-court cemeteries of the regions. Direct royal favour was to replace local autonomy, which had been constructed through local power-bases and economic control. A more nuanced view of events at Beni Hasan suggests that the owner of the unfinished tomb at Beni Hasan was not the obvious heir of Khnumhotep II, but rather another son, Khnumhotep IV. The fate of Khnumhotep III was to be educated at court, to have a career of service to the king, and to be buried in a royal cemetery (Franke 1991). Thus the end of important regional cemeteries may have come about not through crude restrictions on provincial power by Senwosret III, but by a more gradual process of bringing the sons of important regional families to court to acculturate them in court ways, just as was to become a regular process for foreign princes in the New Kingdom. Whatever the specific detail, we are reminded of the role of the tomb as a marker for shifts in political and economic power as much as religious innovation. Moreover, whatever the specific personal history of Khnumhotep III, it is clear that the sequence of great regional tombs at Beni Hasan, Meir, el-Bersheh, Asyut and Qau comes to an end during or immediately after the reign of Senwosret III.

Elite Tombs at Asyut and Rifeh

The important Upper Egyptian city of Asyut is immediately overlooked to the west by the cliffs of Gebel Asyut el-Gharbi, part of the extensive Gebel

Durunka range. These cliffs provided the perfect preconditions for rock-cut tomb placement, and the Gebel Durunka is honeycombed with tombs at Asyut itself and further to the south at Rifeh. The largest and most important of these tombs are those of the late First Intermediate Period, at a time when the princes of Asyut were important allies of the Herakleopolitans. Indeed, it seems that the capture of Asyut by the Thebans effectively brought Herakleopolitan resistance, and the First Intermediate Period, to an end. From this period, the most important tombs at Asyut are those of Iti-ibi, his son Khety II and Iti-ibi-iker (Kahl 2007).

Iti-ibi's tomb was provided with a courtyard in front of a large hall (at 600 m^2, the largest of any tomb of the period) divided by two pairs of pillars, and containing four shafts. The tomb of Khety II, next door to that of Iti-ibi, has the same format, although at a smaller scale, and with just two shafts. The nearby tomb of Iti-ibi-iker is particularly notable not only because it, too, dates from the later part of the First Intermediate Period – and has illustrations of marching soldiers – but also because its walls carry dozens of graffiti of the early part of the New Kingdom; not just simple drawings but sections of literary texts, suggesting that this ancient tomb may have been used as the educational venue for school trips in Dynasty 18 (Kahl 2006). The autobiographical inscriptions from these tombs are, alongside those of Ankhtify, the most informative regarding the political situation during the First Intermediate Period. Unlike Ankhtify, the princes of Asyut clearly identified themselves as allies of the Herakleopolitans on the walls of their tombs. One interpretation of the evidence suggests that sections of Iti-ibi's tomb were decorated with scenes/texts referring to warfare against the Thebans, sections which were plastered over and repainted in a less bellicose fashion occasioned by the Theban capture of Asyut. Texts from the tomb of Khety II suggest that the Thebans were repulsed by the returning Asyuti leadership backed by Herakleopolitan troops; in his tomb the Herakleopolitan king Merikare is addressed in these terms:

> You conveyed him (i.e. Khety II) upriver, heaven was cleared for him, the whole land was with him, the princes of Middle Egypt and the great ones of Herakleopolis. The district of 'Queen of the Land' came to repel the evil-doer (i.e. the Thebans) ... 'Welcome' the town cried jubilantly to its ruler. ... The ruler's son reached his town, he entered his father's territory, he brought back the refuges to their homes and he buried his old people.

A concern with military matters is evident in elite tombs at Asyut even after the re-unification of Dynasty 11: the tomb of Mesehti, who probably administered Asyut for the Thebans in late Dynasty 11, contained a large and impressive set of model soldiers (Grébaut 1890–1900). Early in Dynasty

12 some semblance of local dynastic power/tomb building had returned. From early in Dynasty 12 to the reign of Amenemhat II a series of three local rulers, each called Djefai-Hapi, built important rock-cut tombs. All are characterized by their impressive size: that belonging to Djefai-Hapi I (actually the second in the series) runs for a distance of 55 m into the mountain, with interior walls up to 11 m high, and with equally notable façades, although the frontage of these tombs is now in a poor condition (Edel 1984). The core of Djefai-Hapi I's tomb is a transverse hall measuring 23 m × 10.5 m whose walls bear the text of a series of 10 legal contracts discussed above. Another important aspect of the Djefai-Hapi tombs is the way in which they seem to have been used as a cultural resource, being especially influential in providing motifs for the decoration of Dynasty 18 Theban tombs some 500 years later (Kahl 1999). The material from the Djefai-Hapi tombs may well have been appealing to the elite of early Dynasty 18 because of their combination of 'Self-confidence and direct responsibility on the one hand and confidence in the gods and loyalty to the king on the other' (Kahl 2007: 18). The Asyut cemetery also provides, in the tomb of Nakhti (Chassinat and Palanque 1911), one of the limited number of intact tombs which allow a general appraisal of what might be considered a standard set of burial equipment in an elite tomb of the Middle Kingdom.

Subsidiary burials at Rifeh and the contents of Middle Kingdom tombs

The necropolis at Asyut was not the only part of the Gebel Durunka formation to be used for private tombs. The city of Asyut, and its cemetery, is close to the southern border of the 13th Upper Egyptian nome, while the neighbouring 11th Upper Egyptian nome had its capital, the town of Shashotep (probably in the vicinity of the modern town of Shutb), and its cemetery at the northern end of its nome. Therefore the cities of Asyut and Shashotep were no more than 5 km apart, and their respective cemeteries are neighbouring localized concentrations. The cemetery of Shashotep is at the site of Rifeh, an important but somewhat under-explored necropolis which, because of the obvious potential of the cemetery, indicated by the Beni Hasan-like façades of its larger rock-cut tombs (Figure 10.4), was the object of Petrie's interest for a season of fieldwork in 1906 (David 2007; Petrie 1907). The rock-cut tombs at Rifeh, as much as any other cemetery, had suffered from later re-use, not least by very active Coptic activity in the region which turned one of the tombs into a church, a fate shared by several rock-cut tombs in Middle Egypt.

As we have seen with the tomb of Ankhtify and at Beni Hasan, a significant function of these tombs was to display the authority and status

Figure 10.4   Elite tombs at Rifeh

of a local dynast through the visible physicality of the tomb itself and by the way its decoration celebrated his specific achievements. But these structures could also function as family tombs where more junior members of the local dynasty could be buried. The courtyards in front of the larger examples of these tombs, like that of Ankhtify at Moalla, provided a suitable venue for the offering-cult of the *ka*-spirit of the tomb-owner, but they were also obvious locations for shafts which could be cut to provide places of burial for the family or retainers of the main tomb-owner.

One of the best examples of these subsidiary shafts in the courtyard of a large tomb is the so-called 'Tomb of the Two Brothers' from the cemetery of Rifeh, which was discovered by Petrie's team in 1906 (David 2007). This interment is famous because, although the burial chamber is modest in size, particularly for one containing two burials, and undecorated, it was discovered undisturbed and packed with a set of grave goods comparable in quality with those of the limited number of individuals of a similar status from other parts of Middle Kingdom Egypt (see below). It was a double burial for two individuals named Khnum-Nakht and Nakht-Ankh, who may well have been related, although the genealogical information contained in the burial is not enough to confirm their relationship to each other, or to the un-named owner of the large rock-cut tomb in whose courtyard they were buried. They were both provided with a well-decorated rectangular box coffin, each of which contained an anthropoid coffin. A single canopic chest inscribed for Nakht-Ankh contained four canopic jars. The mortuary assemblage also included three wooden statues (two inscribed for Nakht-Ankh and one for Khnum-Nakht), two wooden statues of offering-bearing female servants, and two large model boats. Two simple ceramic vessels, a jar and a bowl, may have contained food offerings made at the time of interment.

This set of objects is not unusual for a tomb of this type from the Middle Kingdom. A detailed study of the position of 'funerary furniture' within private tombs of this period has been carried out by Podvin (2000), who has examined 30 substantially undisturbed tombs from cemeteries ranging from Abusir in the north to Thebes in the south. Although the sample is extraordinarily small considering the total number of known burials from the Middle Kingdom (e.g. the 888 excavated by Garstang at Beni Hasan), a number of general conclusions might tentatively be drawn from this possibly unrepresentative sample. Of the 30 tombs, 23 were single inter-ments – 14 men and 9 women – and 24 of the tombs possessed a single Burial Chamber. The objects recovered can be divided into two classes: those made specifically for the tomb and those used in daily life and taken to the tomb. The identification of the former is usually less problematic than the latter, which might have been made for the tomb although appearing to be items of quotidian utility. In the former category the percentage of total objects recovered is, unsurprisingly, dominated by coffins (46.5%), followed by wooden models (28.5%) and amulets/jewellery (14.5%), with the remaining items of the funerary assemblage being largely made up of canopic containers, face-masks and statuettes. Of the objects of daily life, the principal categories are toilet objects (37%), furniture (20%), sticks and staves (15%) and clothing/sandals (12%). Within this general pattern there are a number of interesting local variations: there are, for instance, no known canopic containers from Beni Hasan. There is also a general standardization about how and where the coffin is placed in the tomb; usually feet first (i.e. the head is left near the entrance to the chamber). Of the 41 coffins from Podvin's study, 29 are aligned north–south with the head to the north; since the Burial Chambers are usually just big enough to accommodate the coffin, this means that there was a deliberate policy of cutting Burial Chambers on the south side of a shaft, so that the head would end up to the north.

Sub-elite tombs of the Middle Kingdom (1): the 'Lower Cemetery' at Beni Hasan

The 'Lower Cemetery' at Beni Hasan is an extensive graveyard which is broadly contemporary with the elite 'Upper Cemetery'. The extent of this

Figure 10.5 Coffins in a shaft tomb at Beni Hasan (© Garstang Museum of Archaeology, University of Liverpool)

'Lower Cemetery' has not been fully explored but, between 1902 and 1904, as noted, John Garstang excavated 888 tombs there. An average tomb in the 'Lower Cemetery', as described by Garstang (1907: 45–6), consisted of a shaft, 1 m square, cut vertically through the rock to a depth of 5–7 m. At the foot of the shaft, on its south side, was a burial chamber whose dimensions –2 m long and about 80 cm in width and height – were just large enough to accommodate one (although occasionally more than one – Figure 10.5) box coffin and a few other graves goods placed around or on top of that coffin (Figure 10.6). When these tombs had larger Burial Chambers, it was in order to accommodate more burials, not to provide additional space for a single interment.

The extent to which these shaft tombs were cut in tightly packed group is remarkable (Figure 10.7), perhaps indicating (along with their standard form) the speculative cutting of tombs for later use, although we really have no idea about the organization of work on these cemeteries. Perhaps associated with this tight packing is the lack of stelae (only 10 were excavated from the 888 tombs), which one might have expected to have been placed within superstructures to these shafts. The range of titles and occupations preserved in these tombs, mainly on the coffins they contained, suggests 'middle-class' occupations – stewards and soldiers, priests

Figure 10.6 Wooden models on a coffin inside a shaft tomb at Beni Hasan
(© Garstang Museum of Archaeology, University of Liverpool)

and doctors (Garstang 1907: Pl. 7). There are also a notable number of
women buried at Beni Hasan who have objects identifying each as a *nbt pr*
(*nebet per*), a title which literally means 'Lady of the House', whose
importance at later periods is uncertain, but which at its emergence in
the Middle Kingdom seems to suggest some level of social status for its
owner (Orel 1994: 236). Garstang's analysis of the tombs (Garstang 1907:
211–44, Pl. 7) suggests that, of the *nbt pr* women, five were buried with a
single male, eight as part of a family group of three–four individuals, and 11
as single burials.

The most striking element in these tombs is the quantity of wooden
models, ranging from individual servant figures, to groups of workers,
models of whole workshops/granaries, and fully rigged boats (Tooley
1995). The tombs in the Lower Cemetery at Beni Hasan, although they
appear at first sight to be very different in form and contents to those in the
Upper Cemetery, are not as different as it first might seem. The same
concerns drive both; indeed the Lower Cemetery tombs give the impression of being more concentrated and economical versions of the Upper

Figure 10.7   Shaft tombs at Beni Hasan (© Garstang Museum of Archaeology, University of Liverpool)

Cemetery tombs. The notions of offering and food production are catered for by wooden models rather than scenes on the walls of a large tomb, while the Osirian boat journey to and from Abydos is catered for by (ideally) two boats.

Sub-elite tombs of the Middle Kingdom (2): 'soul-houses' at Rifeh

Although the largest and richest tombs of Rifeh were located in the cliffs of the Gebel Durunka, the gravel terrace below those cliffs contained many contemporary 'graves about three or four feet deep originally, with the head to the north' (Petrie 1907: 12). Grave goods were sparse in this cemetery, which housed the burials of a population whose ability to put economic resources into their burials was significantly lower than the burials of the 'Lower Cemetery' at Beni Hasan, which we have already broadly classified as 'middle class'. However, one notable type of object was recovered in significant numbers in this cemetery at Rifeh: the so-called 'soul-house' (Niwinski 1984). The origin of this class of funerary object is in the development of small ceramic trays, usually no more than 30–40 cm in diameter, with food offerings modelled on them, which were effectively smaller, cheaper versions of the large stone offering tables found in elite tombs. This idea developed into the tray becoming a model Offering Chapel, or the columned façade of a rock-tomb, or a detailed model of a house. These objects have been found in several Middle Kingdom cemeteries in Egypt, but the largest single group are the 150 found by Petrie at Rifeh, where they appear to have been 'sealed' in place by a later wash of gravel over the cemetery. The evidence from Rifeh indicates that these 'soul-houses' were placed on the surface of the grave, or very close to the surface (Figure 10.8). They appear to be an attempt by the owners of these very modest graves to provide some sort of superstructure

Figure 10.8 'Soul-house' from a Middle Kingdom tomb at Abydos (© Garstang Museum of Archaeology, University of Liverpool)

which might emulate the Offering Chapels of elite tombs as places of offering and, perhaps, residence by the *ka*. It is therefore more appropriate to think of these 'soul-houses' as actually part of the tomb itself, rather than an object within it, although, as we have seen with coffins, the distinction between tomb apparatus and tomb contents is not always an easy one to draw.

CHAPTER 11

North and South

Middle Kingdom Tombs at the Royal Residence

〔﹃﹄〕﹃﹄

Court Cemeteries of the Middle Kingdom

The previous chapter has suggested that the largest and most interesting private tombs of the Middle Kingdom were built away from the royal residence. Unlike the Old Kingdom and, to a significant degree, the New Kingdom, it was burial away from the royal tomb and without the support of royal resources which allowed the development of individual, regional traditions. However, this is only the most important trend of the period and the Middle Kingdom did produce some very noteworthy tomb developments, particularly in Dynasty 11. A provincial backwater in the Old Kingdom, with none of the regional importance of a site like Aswan/ Elephantine or Abydos, the emergence of Dynasty 11 as the victorious unifying force at the end of the First Intermediate Period gave Thebes a national prominence. This emergence of Dynasty 11 can best be seen in its 'royal' tombs, culminating in the extraordinary tomb of Nebhepetre Montuhotep II at Deir el-Bahri.

Montuhotep II and Dynasty 11 at Thebes

Montuhotep's predecessors – local rulers of early Dynasty 11 – had been buried in distinctive tombs in the el-Tarif district of the Theban necropolis. This comparatively low-lying part of the desert edge was transformed into a suitable location for appropriately impressive tombs by the digging of sunken courtyards. At the rear and sides of these courtyards, broad and shallow rock-cut colonnades were cut which provided porticoes at the rear

Ancient Egyptian Tombs: The Culture of Life and Death   By Steven Snape
© 2011 Steven Snape

of which a series of rooms housing the cult rooms for the putatively royal tomb-owner were excavated. These structures are referred to as *saff*-tombs, from the Arabic for 'row', reflecting their external appearance; the term is also applied to similar, though more modest, elite tombs cut into the lower hills of the Theban mountain. The largest of the el-Tarif *saff*-tombs belonged to Intef I and Intef II (Arnold 1976).

In contrast, the tomb planned by Montuhotep II was much more ambitious in its complexity and scale, and in its location in the natural amphitheatre of the Deir el-Bahri 'bay' in western Thebes. This tomb (Arnold 1974–81) reinterpreted the traditional Old Kingdom royal pyramid complex elements of monumental tomb + mortuary temple + causeway + valley building to fit its specific location. The resulting terraced, colonnaded structure, with burial apartments cut into the bedrock below and behind the temple and (possibly) crowned by a pyramid (Figure 11.1), expressed a vitality and imagination in royal tomb design, offering the possibility that the West Bank at Thebes might develop into a royal necropolis for the newly unified Egyptian state. In this Montuhotep was 500 years ahead of his time, and it would only be with the New Kingdom that Thebes would house the royal necropolis of the Valley of the Kings, in a form quite different from the highly visible Deir el-Bahri temple-tomb. Instead, with Dynasty 12, there was a shift back north to a (basically)

Figure 11.1   The 'temple-tomb' of Nebhepetre Montuhotep II at Deir el-Bahri

Memphite and definitely pyramidal form of tomb directly derived from the Old Kingdom – the first pyramid of the Middle Kingdom, that built by Amenemhat I at Lisht in *c*.1930 BC, appears to take as its blueprint the last substantial pyramid of the Old Kingdom, that built by Pepi II 25 km away at South Saqqara, in *c*.2200 BC.

Elite tombs of Dynasty 11 at Deir el-Bahri

The bay of Deir el-Bahri was also the location of the tombs of some of the royal officials of Dynasty 11, built to look down upon the approach to the temple-tomb of Montuhotep II. These were cut high in the cliffs on the steep, northern side of the bay, with large, impressive causeways running up to them (Figure 11.2). Other Dynasty 11 tombs which look down on the Deir el-Bahri 'bay' were located to the south-west of Montuhotep's tomb. Although not now in the best of conditions, these tombs have provided interesting examples of both the architecture and contents of tombs of this period. A good example of a 'standard' tomb of this period, in architectural terms, is that of the earliest of the royal treasurers of a newly unified Egypt, Khety (TT 311; Winlock 1923), who appears to have died during the reign of Montuhotep II and was probably succeeded in his post by Meketre. Khety's tomb required the modelling of the hillside to form a broad, open façade, pierced by a central doorway leading to a long, narrow hall cut into the rock perpendicular to the façade,

Figure 11.2 Dynasty 11 tombs at Deir el-Bahri

at the rear of which a two-stage sloping stairway led to two chambers, which have been interpreted as the real and 'dummy' Burial Chambers.

Although already in a badly damaged condition when it was discovered by Winlock in 1920, the tomb of Meketre (TT 280; Winlock 1920) is still impressive. Meketre's career was that of a successful Theban official at the time of the unification. He first appears as a humble seal-bearer late in the reign of Montuhotep II but, three decades later, had risen to be Royal Chief Steward under Amenemhat I, making him one of the most senior royal officials of early Dynasty 12 (Allen 2003). His tomb consists of a wide portico cut into the cliffs at the top of a broad causeway, a passageway cut into the cliffs at the rear of the portico, an Offering Chapel and a Burial Chamber. Little of the original relief-carving now survives and the Burial Chamber only preserved fragments of the smashed outer sarcophagus and gilded inner coffin. However, the tomb is famous for preserving the best example of what would become a major element of many Middle Kingdom burials: a set of wooden models placed in the tomb's *serdab*, which had been ignored by the tomb's robbers and were still *in situ* at the time Winlock excavated the tomb.

It seems likely that wooden models for burial within tombs were a suitable and efficient substitute in response to demands from owners of relatively modest burials who could not afford to have elaborate super-structures with reliefs depicting the production of food for them in the afterlife. Small wooden models showing servant-figures producing the things which the tomb-owner might need became common, particularly at sites such as Beni Hasan, where, along with the coffin and its contents, they provided the basic repertoire of equipment within the Burial Chamber of seemingly superstructure-less tombs. However, the Meketre models are not small, nor do they restrict themselves to individual or small groups of figures. Instead the 23 models, now divided between Cairo Museum and the Metropolitan Museum of Art in New York, consist of large three-dimensional tableaux of figures or large rectangular boxes forming the workshops within which the activities took place (Winlock 1955). In the former category are multi-figured groups showing, for instance, Meketre and his officials watching a bovine procession at the cattle-count, and a pair of fishing boats, fully crewed, with a fish-filled net slung between them. The latter category includes the fully equipped workshops for car-penters, for textile-workers and for butchers, and also models of a house set within a walled garden. The models seem to offer not only the facilities for production for the *ka*, but also a secure and pleasant residence for it.

In 1920, while working on the tomb of Meketre, Winlock discovered a small undisturbed burial, a roughly shaped corridor cut into the upper terrace of Meketre's tomb which had been sealed with a wall of mudbricks.

The undecorated tomb contained a wooden rectangular box coffin of imported fir or cedar, inscribed for a man named Wah (Hayes 1953: 303–5). In front of the eye panel of the coffin was a buffet of food offerings – a beer jar and a series of small conical loaves making up the basic requirements of the 'bread and beer' funerary offerings, plus a complete foreleg of beef – the ideal food offering, as demonstrated in the tomb scenes of much larger and more elaborate tombs of the Old Kingdom onwards. On the ground near the coffin were a few linen sheets which had, presumably, been used to protect the coffin as it was manoeuvred into place within the tomb; what faced the excavators was the state of the tomb exactly as it had been left by those burying Wah. This first impression – the size and roughness of the tomb, the sparse grave goods, the name without a title – suggested that the burial belonged to a man of modest means and position. However, when the coffin was opened it was found to contain rather more indications of wealth and status. This included a fairly standard range of funerary equipment: a copper mirror, a wooden headrest, a set of acacia staves and a wooden statuette of Wah. The mummy itself appeared as a massively wrapped bundle, from the top of which peeped a gilded mummy-mask, a standard element of burials of this period, depicting the bearded Wah. But the most striking aspect of the coffin's contents was the amount of linen which wrapped the body: 40 sheets, some over 25 m long, totalling over 800 m^2 of cloth. One of these sheets, wrapped closely around the body itself, had been dyed red with henna and labelled 'Linen of the Temple that protects … the justified'; the linen might therefore be seen as having three separate functions: as a practical element in Middle Kingdom mummification, as an expression of wealth and status, and as a specifically magically protective element within the tomb.

The jewellery on the mummy of Wah included necklaces of gold and silver beads and a group of scarabs, one made of lapis lazuli and, the most spectacular, one made of silver inlaid with gold hieroglyphs naming the 'Overseer of the Storehouse, Wah' and his employer, Meketre. The connection with Meketre was therefore established and Wah's burial in the courtyard of his master's tomb more understandable. It was also clear that, contrary to first appearances when the tomb was opened, Wah was actually a reasonably wealthy man who, presumably through the patronage of Meketre, could afford not just Egyptian products (linen, copper, local wood), but also foreign imports (silver, lapis lazuli and imported wood). Wah's burial is also an important piece of evidence for the state of the developing art of mummification in the early Middle Kingdom. The Old Kingdom emphasis on wrapping the body to present an externally coherent unit is still evident, although in a somewhat shapeless manner. The body itself shows signs of the continued, albeit limited, removal of soft internal organs: the liver and intestines had been removed through a slit cut in the abdomen, but the other two 'canopic' organs – the lungs and stomach – had been left in place. The destination of the liver and intestines is not known since the tomb did not contain any canopic equipment.

Dynasty 12 at Thebes

The abandonment of Thebes as a royal capital by kings of Dynasty 12 meant that the southern city was no longer the residence for the very highest governmental officials, who moved with their king to the new northern capital of Itj-Tawy (whose exact location is not known, but was probably near Lisht), and, like him, were buried there. Moreover, the re-establishment of *mastaba* cemeteries around the new royal pyramid complexes meant that the highest elites in Egypt not only sought cemeteries near their new residences, but were also locked into, or actively sought, burial in one of these *mastaba*s. This process (and the importance of developing phenomena such as the Osirian afterlife) can be seen in what we know of officials such as the royal steward Sobeknakht, attested by a statue at Thebes, where he probably began his career, a stela at Abydos and a *mastaba*-tomb at Lisht North, or the Theban Intefiker (Antefoker), who served as vizier under Senwosret I, and who appears on the walls of his mother's tomb at Thebes (TT60), but was also provided with a *mastaba* at Lisht North. With this shift the opportunity for Thebes to develop an elite cemetery for officials associated with the royal tomb was lost. However, Thebes did receive a boost to its prominence in a number of ways: it seems to have become the major administrative centre for the south of Egypt and, crucially, Egypt's newly acquired Nubian empire, while the temple of Amen at Karnak started its growth through royal patronage which would reach its apogee in the New Kingdom. There were, therefore, enough elite officials based at Thebes to provide a market for an elite cemetery. Remarkably, the evidence for this cemetery is much less obvious than the regional centres in Middle Egypt. Perhaps the specific topography of the Theban West Bank, which does not provide the same obvious cliff-terraces for tomb building as does, say, Beni Hasan, discouraged the development of a concentrated group of tombs from a similar period. Perhaps the strong multi-generational regional traditions were lacking in what was still a royal centre. Whatever the case, the number of elite tombs which can be firmly dated to the Middle Kingdom at Thebes is surprisingly low. Exceptions include the tomb of the mother of Intefiker – a rock-cut tomb which essentially consisted of a straight corridor cut into the cliffs and which, although badly damaged, contained painted scenes showing the transport of the coffin to the tomb, a precursor of what would, in Dynasty 18, become the elaborate multi-stage ritual of the Theban funeral. Another reason why there are so few well-preserved tombs from the Middle Kingdom at Thebes is their usurpation and remodelling in the early New Kingdom (see below p. 187).

The Return to the North: Court Cemeteries of Dynasty 12

The evidence for elite burial associated with the major royal pyramid complexes of Dynasty 12 is as follows:

- *The pyramid of Amenemhat I at Lisht North.* Princesses and particularly favoured courtiers were buried within the enclosure wall of the upper enclosure of the pyramid complex. These included Intefiker, the Chief Steward Nakht and the Vizier Senwosret. But the most impressive tomb from this court cemetery is one which was subsidiary to that of the Vizier, belonging to the Lady Senebtisi (Mace and Winlock 1916) and remarkable because of its intact Burial Chamber and contents (Figure 11.3). Arnold (2008: 13) suggests that Lisht North was used for elite burial in the latter part of reign of Amenemhat I, which may have overlapped with that of Senwosret I in a 10-year co-regency, which resulted in Lisht South only being used late in reign of Senwosret I and into the reign of Amenemhat II.
- *The pyramid of Senwosret I at Lisht South.* Mastaba-tombs were built for high-ranking courtiers around the royal pyramid (but outside the upper enclosure, which had small pyramids for royal women). These included those of the Vizier Montuhotep, the High Priest of Ra at Heliopolis Imhotep and the High Priest of Ptah at Memphis Senwosretankh. The last tomb is the largest and most impressive, consisting of a solid *mastaba*, cased in fine limestone, carved into a 'palace façade' exterior, surrounded by a double enclosure with a pylon entrance and a court in front of the *mastaba*, and with the burial underneath the *mastaba* itself (Arnold 2008: 13–24, Pls 2–7, 9–25). It is remarkable because of its use of Pyramid Texts, which appear to have been copied wholesale from the pyramid of Unas.
- *The pyramid of Amenemhat II at Dahshur.* The upper enclosure of the pyramid contains rock-cut gallery tombs for the burials of the royal daughters Iti, Khnemet, Itiweret and Satmerhut, and the later (Dynasty 13) burials of the royal wife Keminub, and the treasurer Amenhotep. There are no significant burials of elite officials, apart from the *mastaba* of the Vizier Siese.

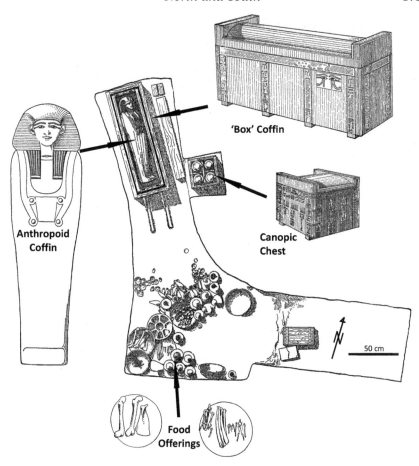

'Box' Coffin

Anthropoid
Coffin

Canopic
Chest

50 cm

N

Food
Offerings

Figure 11.3 Plan of the tomb of Senebtisi at Lisht, and its most significant contents (adapted from Mace and Winlock 1916: Figs 1, 9, 18, 23, 83 and 84.)

- *The pyramid of Senwosret II at Kahun.* A series of underground princesses' tombs was located immediately to the south of the king's pyramid, including the 'treasure' from the burial of Sat-Hathor-Iunet (Brunton 1920). Eight solid rock-cut *mastaba*s in a row immediately to the north of the king's pyramid may be the superstructures of the princesses' tombs. No tombs of elite officials were built close to the pyramid, and the only substantial tomb of this type in the vicinity is the *mastaba* of the 'Overseer of Every Work of the King' Inpy.
- *The pyramid of Senwosret III at Dahshur.* There is a question as to whether this pyramid was used for the burial of the king, or whether Senwosret III was buried at Abydos. As far as the tombs of elite

officials are concerned, there are very few associated with this pyramid, which is particularly striking in view of the general perception of the demise of major provincial cemeteries during his reign. Exceptions, in the cemetery north of his pyramid enclosure, include the relatively modestly sized *mastaba*s of the viziers Sobekemhat, Nebit and Khnumhotep, which also had 'palace façade' casings.

- *The (first) pyramid of Amenemhat III at Dahshur.* North of the pyramid is the tomb of the king's daughter Nubheteptikhered.
- *The (second) pyramid of Amenemhat III at Hawara.* A substantial *mastaba* cemetery to the north of the pyramid complex was subject to extensive re-use, most notably for the burials of sacred crocodiles in the Graeco-Roman Period, which erased much of the information regarding its Middle Kingdom occupants.

Arnold (2008: 13) explains the pattern of elite tomb distribution in the later part of Dynasty 12 by suggesting that there was a significant overlap in the building of the pyramids of Senwosret III and Amenemhat III at Dahshur on account of their co-regency. Because of this co-regency, significant numbers of officials were buried near the pyramid of Senwosret III (*c.*50 but mainly to the north of the pyramid owing to building work and an existing Old Kingdom *mastaba* cemetery to the south), but none near Amenemhat III's pyramid at Dahshur. However, the foundation of a new pyramid for Amenemhat III at Hawara attracted the tombs of officials who were active later in his reign.

In the Middle Kingdom the use of other parts of the Memphite necropolis resumed (if they had ever discontinued), although on a significantly smaller scale than in the Old Kingdom. There was in some instances an attempt to re-create Old Kingdom traditions in funerary architecture (such as the Offering Chapel focused on the false door) in parallel to the royal reinstatement of the pyramid. An important cluster of these Middle Kingdom tombs developed within the Teti Pyramid Cemetery at Saqqara, where traditional architectural forms (and indeed the desirability of ancient locations) were mixed with more innovative forms; the tombs of Ihy and Hetep (Silverman 2009) do not follow the solid, multi-roomed *mastaba* form, but consist of open columned courts with Offering Chapels to their rear. This is a form of tomb eminently suitable for the Saqqara plateau, and which which would fully come into its own during the New Kingdom. It was also an ideal location for what are probably the earliest examples of the archetypal Middle Kingdom private sculpture, the block statue, a form which would be particularly used within temples, rather than tombs, for elite self-projection. Interestingly, both tombs have a sloping shaft leading to a Burial Chamber which was deliberately located under the temenos wall of Teti's pyramid.

Despite the somewhat patchy archaeological recovery of elite tombs in court cemeteries, burial close to the king and the royal family seems to have retained its theoretical cachet in the Middle Kingdom, as is suggested by the account of Sinuhe being tempted by such a form of burial:

> Think about the day of burial, the passing over to an honoured state ...
>
> A procession will be made for you on the day of interment, the anthropoid sarcophagus (overlaid) with gold [leaf], the head with lapis lazuli, and the sky above you as you are placed in the outer coffin and dragged by teams of oxen preceded by singers.
>
> The dance of the Muu will be performed at your tomb, and the necessary offerings will be invoked for you.
>
> ...
>
> A pyramid of stone was built for me in the midst of the pyramids. The overseers of stonecutters of the pyramids marked out its ground plan. The draughtsmen sketched in it, and the master sculptors carved in it. The overseers of works who were in the necropolis gave it their attention.
>
> Care was taken to supply all the equipment which is placed in the tomb chamber.
>
> *Ka*-servants were assigned to me, and a funerary estate was settled on me with fields attached ...
>
> My statue was overlaid with gold ... (Trans. after Simpson et al. 2003: 62–6)

CHAPTER 12

Ineni, Senenmut and User-Amun

New Tombs for Old

卍卍卍卍

The Middle Kingdom to New Kingdom Transition at Thebes: Tradition and Innovation

As we have already seen, the Middle Kingdom at Thebes presents a somewhat mixed picture in terms of private cemeteries. The Dynasty 11 elite cemetery at Deir el-Bahri, associated with the tomb of Montuhotep II, is not repeated by an important series of Dynasty 12 tombs, nor perhaps should we expect it to be given the move north and pyramid building by kings of the high Middle Kingdom. Nevertheless, Middle Kingdom Thebes does throw up a few interesting individual tombs, such as the rock-cut tombs of Intefiker's mother and that of Khety, which prefigure in their architecture (corridors cut horizontally into the Theban cliffs) and decoration (scenes of funeral) some of the major trends in later Dynasty 18 tombs in the region. As well as the Theban cliffs, the low-lying desert plain between the cliffs and cultivation was also used, although many of these tombs would later be swallowed up by the major New Kingdom mortuary temples built here. Most known tombs of the latter part of the Middle Kingdom at Thebes consist of very deep, single-occupant shaft tombs, although their lack of obvious Offering Chapels has led at least one scholar to speculate that this might be connected with the huge number of Middle Kingdom stelae at Abydos at this period, with the Abydene *mahat* acting as Offering Chapels (close to Osiris) which were far away from, but acted effectively for, the Theban burial chambers (Polz 2007: 308–9).

The Second Intermediate Period brought with it the necessity to provide appropriate tombs for the Theban Dynasty 17, which had royal pretensions

Ancient Egyptian Tombs: The Culture of Life and Death   By Steven Snape
© 2011 Steven Snape

mirroring those of the earlier Theban Dynasty 11. Indeed the 'royal' tombs of Dynasty 17 copy the Dynasty 11 tomb of Montuhotep II in that they do not directly derive from a clear developmental line, but are composed of a cluster of traditional and innovative elements which would, ultimately, have no future. The locations and forms of the burials of the late Dynasty 17 and early Dynasty 18 kings are very contentious, but it seems on present evidence that tombs numbered K94.1 and K93.11 at Dra Abu el-Naga – both of which make use of small pyramids above in their freestanding super-structures which were not dissimilar to Abydene cenotaph chapels (Polz 2007: 239–45) – should be attributed to Kamose and Amenhotep I (although it has been suggested that the latter may have been the original owner of tomb KV39 in the Valley of the Kings). The tombs of Ahmose and Tuthmosis II, and the original tomb of Tuthmosis I, are unknown.

For non-royal and royal individuals the reign of Hatshepsut was a major period of change: for the former the *saff*-tomb evolved into the standard Theban T-shaped tomb of Dynasty 18, while for the latter the royal burial became established in the Valley of the Kings. Indeed, the reign of Hatshepsut is so significant as one where a variety of culturally important aspects of New Kingdom culture develop, particularly in respect to royal mortuary provision, that Polz (2007: 380) has noted that, in these terms, it 'marks the beginning of the New Kingdom'. This beginning was linked to a number of other significant political and cultural factors.

The Rise of Thebes

However, in political terms it was the expulsion of the Hyksos by Theban rulers of Dynasties 17/18 which was the defining act which brought about the foundation of the New Kingdom. The nature of this re-unification – achieved by an aggressively militaristic state with a strong sense of root-edness in the Theban area – had a whole series of consequences which directly affected the development of royal and private tombs. On the one hand, the development of a Nubian and Western Asiatic empire, which was a natural extension of the northern and southern wars of 'liberation', gave Egypt imperial control over a region which stretched, as Amenhotep III would later put it, 'from Naharin to Karoy' – from the Euphrates in Syria to the fourth cataract of the Nile in the Sudan. This resulted in Egypt becoming a supremely confident expansionist state, wealthy through the economic exploitation of its imperial possessions, in addition to its own natural agricultural abundance. Royal military victories demanded commemoration, which took the form of gift-giving to the gods who made those victories possible. Temple building, on a massive scale, in stone, was a defining feature of the New Kingdom, partly funded by the fruits of military success; a scene in the tomb of Ineni is captioned: 'Nubians given as selected war-captives to the divine offering of Amen after the defeat of wretched Kush, and the tribute (*inw*) of all desert countries which His Majesty has given to the temple of Amen as a yearly allowance' (Dziobek 1992: 33; Haring 1997: 135). Temples were built for the gods who assured the military success of the king, while the external walls and pylon gateways of these temples were used to depict and describe the specific victories and the generality of divine approval of royal activity.

The principal beneficiary of this royal gratitude was the god Amen. As with the early Middle Kingdom, a Theban dynasty had achieved the unification of Egypt and had therefore been given the opportunity to project its parochial concerns on a national stage. The most important of these concerns was the promotion of Amen to be a state deity rather than a local god. The kings of Dynasty 18 patronized their Theban protector deity by embellishing his Theban temple at Karnak. However, unlike the Middle Kingdom, rulers of the early part of Dynasty 18 did not find it necessary to subscribe to traditional established forms of royal conduct – specifically the re-activation of the northern pyramid cemetery as the form and locus of royal burial. The issue of what was the capital city of Egypt in the New Kingdom is much more complex than that of the Old Kingdom (when all principal royal and elite functions – including royal and elite burial – were concentrated in Memphis), but as far as Dynasty 18 was concerned, and apart from the Amarna Period, it is probably accurate to say that there were two cities which between them had most of the attributes of a capital city: Memphis was almost certainly the largest and most populous city in Egypt, and was the economic and administrative hub for northern Egypt, while Thebes served as the administrative centre for southern Egypt and Nubia but, more importantly, it became a 'religious capital'. Amen, by his association with the paramount Old Kingdom deity, became Amen-Re, an *übergott* who was the patron deity not of merely Thebes, but of the Egyptian empire. His home, and that of his divine family, in the Karnak complex at Thebes became the place where Egyptian kings wished to build to show their allegiance to this prime god. Karnak became one of the largest religious complexes in the world, and even today in its ruined state is an impressive collection of columned halls, monolithic granite obelisks and pylon gateways, all built on a colossal scale.

But another development was even more important for the development of royal and private tombs. Such was the importance of Thebes to Egyptian kings that they wished to be buried within the 'Domain of Amen-Re', to be in the god's presence for eternity. This led in turn to the abandonment of the northern pyramid cemeteries as the prime spot for royal burial. It also

Figure 12.1   View of the Valley of the Kings

led to the abandonment of the pyramid complex as a form of royal tomb, partly because the topography of Thebes did not lend itself to pyramid building, since the West Bank at Thebes is dominated by a valley-gouged mountain (Figure 12.1) which rises from the edge of the cultivation, rather than the low desert plateau of the Memphite West Bank.

Other factors also need to be considered. The abandonment of the pyramid as a royal tomb might have been a necessity owing to the specific topography of Thebes, but it also seems to have been stimulated by a growing recognition of the unreliability of the pyramid as a secure form of burial. Pyramids were, very obviously, self-advertised stores of valuable treasure – real or imagined – and it seems likely that, by the beginning of the New Kingdom, they were as empty as they are today. Security of royal burial was to be sought not in the quantity of stone which needed to be tunnelled through in order to get to the Burial Chamber (e.g. Khufu of Dynasty 4), nor in a cunningly designed series of internal passageways designed to mislead potential robbers (e.g. Amenemhat III of Dynasty 12 at Hawara), but in complete secrecy. The twin factors of Theban burial and desire for secrecy led directly to the development of the Valley of the Kings as *the* royal cemetery for the next 500 years.

The early New Kingdom brought with it a series of social changes which also directly affected tomb development, particularly for private tombs.

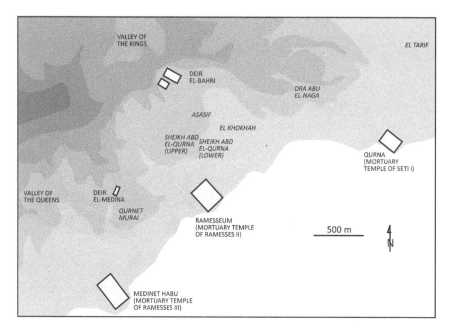

Figure 12.2   Plan of the West Bank cemeteries at Thebes

One of these changes was the emergence of an elite who came from provincial backgrounds, did well in the imperial administration of the newly founded Egyptian empire – as soldiers, bureaucrats, priests, or all three – and, like the elites of the Old and Middle Kingdoms before them, desired personal commemoration through their tombs. The nature of the royal tomb itself meant that private tombs could not now be arranged around it as part of the extended complex of royal nucleus and elite subsidiaries, but burial at Thebes had the threefold impetus of being the local cemetery for elites who worked in the principal urban centre of southern Egypt (including the Karnak complex itself), being, like the royal tomb, within the Domain of Amen-Re, and being reasonably close to the royal burial. As a result, the West Bank at Thebes became what the desert to the west of Memphis had been in the Old Kingdom: the most concentrated collection of high-quality tombs in Egypt (Figure 12.2).

Ineni, Tuthmosis I and the Valley of the Kings

One individual, more than any other, illustrates these trends. The 'Overseer of the Double Granary of Amen' and 'Overseer of Works in Karnak' Ineni ranks as one of history's most productive palindromes. The career and monuments of Ineni (Dziobek 1992: esp. 122–44) illustrate in remarkable detail the developments in royal and private tomb building at Thebes in the early part of Dynasty 18. He was one of a series of extraordinarily capable (or so they tell us!) individuals who acted for their royal masters in bringing major royal projects at Thebes to completion. He served under Amenhotep I, Tuthmosis I, Tuthmosis II and Hatshepsut, but his most significant work was under the second of those kings. In particular he makes reference (in the autobiographical text in his own tomb) to his leading role in creating a tomb for Tuthmosis I: 'I oversaw the excavation of the cliff-tomb (*šȝd ḥrt*) of His Majesty all alone, no-one seeing, no one hearing … I created fields of mud (*kȝḥw*) to plaster their tombs of the necropolis.' This passage has been much debated, especially in the context of the question of which was the earliest tomb in the Valley of the Kings. Although this text offers no definitive conclusions, a number of points are worth making. First, that the location of the royal tomb was to be hidden – far from being an advertisement of royal power, as the pyramids were, it was to be a secret. Secondly, the hidden location of the tomb meant that a different form of royal tomb needed to be developed, one which was embedded within the environment – specifically the wadis of the Theban mountain – rather than adding to and dominating the landscape. Thirdly, the text itself tells us that, although the location of the royal tomb was secret, the fact that it was secret was not itself secret, and that Ineni, as part of his own self-presentation, wished to boast about it as a special mark of royal regard in being trusted with something which was so important to the king – his eternal resting place. Each of these three elements brought with it a series of problems. How was the royal tomb to be hidden? If the royal tomb was hidden, how was the dead king to be offered to, and how were his personal achievements to be celebrated? Where could Ineni boast about his particular royal favour in a fact-based way which would impress future generations?

The best-established candidate for the tomb referred to by Ineni is KV38, a small, almost completely undecorated tomb cut into the foot of the cliffs at the western end of the Valley of the Kings, with a cartouche-shaped Burial Chamber containing a sarcophagus inscribed for Tuthmosis I. Although the presence of the sarcophagus, and the size of the tomb, make an identification with the earliest tomb in the valley a possibility, it has been argued (e.g. Romer 1974, 1976) that KV38 was modelled on KV34, the tomb of Tuthmosis III, not the other way round. In this version of events, KV38 was prepared by Tuthmosis III for the re-burial of his grandfather, Tuthmosis I, after he had removed his body from KV20, the original 'no-one seeing, no-one hearing' tomb, after that tomb had itself been remodelled during the reign of Hatshepsut for the joint burial of Tuthmosis I, the original owner, and Hatshepsut herself. Whatever the specifics of the chronology, the basic nature of the Dynasty 18 royal tomb in the Valley of the Kings emerged as a sepulchre of relatively modest size, rock-cut, designed to be hidden, and whose major emphasis was not on its external appearance, as had been the case with Old and Middle Kingdom pyramids, but on its internal decoration.

The decoration of royal tombs in the New Kingdom

An insight into the afterlife expectations of Dynasty 18 kings can be found in the New Kingdom successors to the Old Kingdom Pyramid Texts, the 'Books of the Underworld'. These texts, with their accompanying pictorial illustrations, essentially make up the entire decorative scheme of royal tombs of the New Kingdom (apart from the Amarna Period). Although they can be classified into a small number of discrete texts – the most important being the *Book of What is in the Underworld* (also known as the *Amduat* from the Egyptian *imy-dw3t*), the *Book of Caverns* and the *Book of Gates*; Hornung 1999) – their essential subject matter is the same, namely the perilous night journey of the sun-god Ra through the underworld. Assailed by dangerous negative forces, Ra's task is to unite himself with Osiris, allowing him to be regenerated and reborn come the dawn. The reason that these themes were of paramount importance to the dead king is that, at death, he was united with the sun-god, as well as with Osiris, or was seen as one of the deities who journeyed in the barque of Ra across the sky by day and through the underworld by night. The night journey was the most dangerous as it was here that the sun-god was most vulnerable and open to attack by the chaotic forces of the underworld, including the snake Apophis and, to a leser extent, the confederates of Seth in his role as murderer of Osiris. The allies of these chaotic elements could include the damned, the *mutu* (*mwtw*), whose fate is the exact opposite of the blessed Dead, the *akhu* (*3ḫw*); they are shown with mutilated bodies, being tortured by fire-spitting serpents, and forever banished from the life-giving light of Ra.

The earliest of these books is *Book of What is in the Underworld*. It was, essentially, a nautical chart which allowed a pilot – the king – to steer the boat of the sun-god Ra across the night sky. Sometimes the king is identified with Ra and with Osiris. Most of the oldest versions of the *Amduat* appeared on the walls of the tombs of early kings of Dynasty 18 (for a private exception, see below), and the manner in which they were painted indicates their origin. In the tomb of Tuthmosis III, for instance, the unbroken curved walls of the Burial Chamber were covered with texts and stick-figures in black ink on a light-brown background, evoking the papyrus rolls on which the originals of these texts were kept. The text further evoked the night-time journey by being divided into twelve, representing the hours of the night. Later royal tombs, particularly the long straight-axis tombs of the Ramesside period, conveyed the journey in greater pictorial detail, showing the defeat of the enemies who nightly try to halt the passage of the sun-god, especially the snake Apophis, who attempts to swallow the sun.

Senenmut, Hatshepsut and 'Mansions of Millions of Years'

One of the more controversial figures of the early New Kingdom was Senenmut, an official who, like Ineni, had a relatively humble background; the titles of his parents Ramose and Hatnofer suggest a non-elite origin, probably from the town of Armant, just to the south of Thebes (Dorman 1988: 165ff.). The route of his rise to influence at court is unknown, but the later stages were marked by his close association with Hatshepsut, not least as tutor to her daughter Neferure. However, Senenmut seems to have been an able administrator in a variety of roles. His most significant title was Chief Steward of Amen, which would give him control of the most important estates in Egypt after the Crown itself, although his real power-base was as favourite and factotum of a ruler who had unusual needs – the projection of appropriate authority by a female ruler in an office which was designed for a male office-holder. Senenmut was involved in a number of building projects for Hatshepsut, including the extraction and transport of a pair of granite obelisks from the Aswan quarries, while a chapel he made for himself at Gebel es-Silsila might attest to his presence there on a royal building project, since Gebel es-Silsila was the main source of building stone – sandstone – for temple projects at Thebes, especially in Karnak. Senenmut's role as an architect is more problematic. He describes himself as the responsible official, 'Overseer of Work of Amen', for the construction of Deir el-Bahri (*imy-r k3t n 'Imn m ḏsr ḏsrw*) in his TT353 tomb and on two of a series of hard stone statues which were carved for him (Dorman 1988: 172), although most of these simply list administrative titles. His image appears several times in the Deir el-Bahri temple of Hatshepsut (unusual for a non-royal), although whether this indicates his closeness to the temple, to Hatshepsut, or to both is unclear. However, whatever the specific role of Senenmut in the creation of the Deir el-Bahri temple, its importance in the development of a multi-faceted royal funerary provision is undoubted.

The royal tombs in the Valley of the Kings were, in one sense, the antithesis of the pyramid: pyramids were visible from many miles away, Valley of the Kings tombs were hidden; pyramids were very limited in their internal decoration, Valley of the Kings tombs had their walls covered with painted scenes; pyramids were physically connected to structures where cult ceremonies for the benefit of the dead king could be carried out by the living for eternity, tombs in the Valley of the Kings were sealed, hidden and intended to be forgotten. This is something of a generalization, but one which holds good for much of Dynasty 18. Ramesside tombs in the Valley of the Kings made little effort to conceal their location, with impressively sculpted and decorated doorways, and with evidence of different levels of access to the interior parts of the tomb. On the other hand, the basic intention of the New Kingdom royal tomb was essentially the same as the Old Kingdom pyramid: to provide a means by which the king could achieve an afterlife with the gods, while still being provided for, by offerings from the living, and providing a permanent memorial to his royal achievements. The difference now was that, at Thebes, these functions, rather than being integrated within a physically connected complex as in the Old and Middle Kingdoms, were now fragmented across the Theban landscape. The royal tomb might be hidden, but the mortuary temple could not be; instead of being built next to the tomb – which it could not be because of reasons of space in the Valley of the Kings and the very obvious factor of secrecy – the mortuary temple was now built on the edge of the cultivation on the West Bank of Thebes, within sight of Karnak. This last factor was no coincidence, since the mortuary temple was now regarded not just as a place of offering by the Living to the dead king (not that it ever had been merely that), but as part of an integrated series of structures at Thebes.

Almost every king of the New Kingdom after Hatshepsut wished to do three things at Thebes: to add to and embellish the house of the god Amen-Re at Karnak; to excavate a tomb in the Valley of the Kings; and to build a mortuary temple/memorial temple/'Mansion of Millions of Years' (*hwt nt hh n rnpwt*; for the varied means of referring to these structures, see Haeny 1997) for him- or herself which would in some senses act as a bridge between the two. The god Amen-Re would visit the king's 'Mansion of Millions of Years' during the appropriate festivals – indeed the central sanctuary within these 'Mansions of Millions of Years' was designed to house the visiting barque of Amen-Re and those of his wife Mut and son Khonsu, stressing the primary function of this visit. The 'Mansion of Millions of Years' would also contain suites of rooms where the dead king would be associated with Osiris and Re – the main deities concerned with royal (and increasingly private) afterlife. However, since the 'Mansion of Millions of Years' was largely based on the format of the 'standard plan' New Kingdom temple, there was plenty of space on the pylon gateway(s), external walls and internal walls in the accessible courtyards for the king to depict the specific achievements which would bring him divine favour – primarily successful military campaigns. These scenes would, ideally, have real historical content. Particularly important examples of this genre are the expedition to Punt and obelisk-transportation by Hatshepsut at Deir el-Bahri, the Kadesh campaign scenes of Ramesses II in the Ramesseum, and the Libyan and 'Sea-Peoples' campaigns of Ramesses III at Medinet Habu.

Whatever the specific historical subject matter, the overarching consideration was the display of divine approval for royal action. An extraordinary and non-historical display of divine favour may be cited in the (tastefully rendered) scene of the impregnation of Hatshepsut's mother by the god Amen-Re, giving rise to the 'divine birth' of Hatshepsut herself. The 'Mansion of Millions of Years' was, therefore, a building which contained not only depictions of 'real' events and people, but also scenes which showed the king with the gods in exactly the same terms. There is no essential difference in scenes at Medinet Habu where Ramesses III is shown with his own family and those where he is shown with the divine family of Thebes, Amen-Re, Mut and Khonsu; both have an equal 'reality' in the context of this building and its purposes. The same is, of course, true of private tombs of this period as well, where the real and historical merge with the imagined.

Designed for Afterlife: Ineni, Senenmut, User-Amun and Private Tombs at Thebes

Clearly Ineni and Senenmut were individuals who had a more than usual interest in the ways in which innovative physical structures were developed in early Dynasty 18 to serve changed needs of royal burial and commemoration within the specific landscape of Thebes. It would be odd if they did not, while contemplating the problems of their royal masters and mistress, consider their own tombs, both as physical structures and as arenas for personal presentation, especially as they both had careers which would give them much to present. Unsurprisingly, as the earlier official, it is Ineni who seems to have been principally responsible for the development of a specific type of tomb at Thebes which was, with minor variations, to become the norm for private individuals during the same period as that of the royal tombs in the Valley of the Kings. The most important aspect of Ineni's work was the way in which he did not completely invent New Kingdom tombs at Thebes from scratch, but rather developed existing forms to create a new type.

Ineni's tomb (TT81; see Dziobek 1992) is located halfway up the hill of Sheikh abd el-Qurna (Figure 12.3) in the so-called 'Upper Enclosure', which was to become the most important non-royal elite cemetery during the first half of Dynasty 18. The tomb (Figure 12.4A) is today visible from some

Figure 12.3   View of the cemetery of Sheikh abd el-Qurna at Thebes

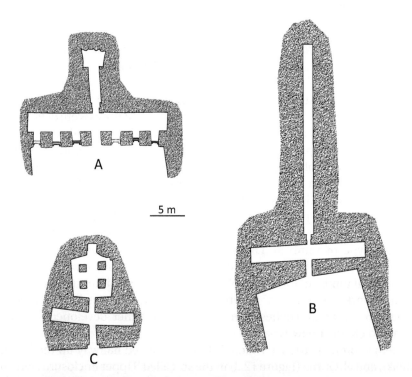

Figure 12.4   Plans of three Dynasty 18 tombs: A – Ineni; B – Rekhmire;
C – Amenhotep-Huy (all to scale)

distance because of its striking wide façade of six pillars (and two attached half-pillars at each end of the colonnade), forming the front of a shallow portico which was pierced by a central doorway leading to a corridor and rear hall. As has been noted by Dziobek (1987: 72), the external appearance of TT81 is remarkably similar to that of a *saff*-tomb. In fact Dziobek believes that the tomb, like others from late Dynasty 11 at Thebes, was abandoned when the court moved north to Itj-Tawy, and was later adopted by Ineni. However, Ineni did not simply embrace the *saff* design, but adapted it by adding inter-columnar walls of (now largely lost) mudbrick to create a tomb which had a subtley niched façade, fronting a transverse hall. Ineni had created a new tomb design whose interior resembled a letter 'T' (Dziobek 1987, 1992, 19–20). This inverted 'T'-shape was to become the standard form for Dynasty 18 at Thebes, perfectly designed for the topography of Thebes and with obviously distinct internal elements which could themselves be used for the depiction on their plastered and painted walls of scenes of a similarly distinct thematic separation. The façade of the tomb also developed to include a number of additional elements to make the exterior of the tomb even more visibly striking. These elements included rows of baked clay 'funerary cones' stamped with the name of the tomb-owner or his family/associates (Davies and Macadam 1957), stelae and small mudbrick pyramids constructed above the façade (Figure 12.5).

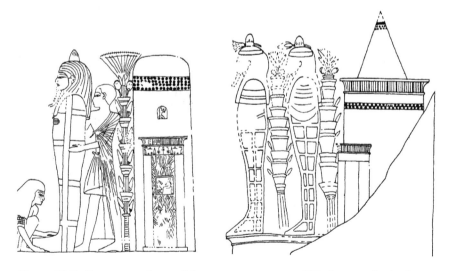

Figure 12.5 Representations of the superstructures of Theban tombs in the tombs of (left) Nebamun and Ipuky – TT181; and (right) Rai – TT159 (adapted from Borchardt et al. 1934: Figs 4 and 1)

By the time Senenmut was active, the T-shaped tomb had been well established as the norm. That is not to say that it was incapable of variation, and Senenmut's tomb or, rather, tombs, are good examples of this. Senenmut was unusual in that he had a bipartite tomb which, like the Valley of the Kings tomb and 'Mansion of Millions of Years' of his royal mistress, was in two separate locations, and two extraordinary locations at that. The first part of the tomb, the Burial Chamber, designated TT353 (Dorman 1988: 80–4; 1991), was excavated at Deir el-Bahri. It was, in essence, a sloping stairway over 90 m long which began in a quarry used in the construction of Hatshepsut's Deir el-Bahri temple, and ending in two chambers underneath the forecourt of that temple; whether this was a deliberate attempt to place the Burial Chamber of Senenmut within the precincts of Hatshepsut's temple, or whether the aim was to dig down to a later of good-quality limestone, is not clear (Dorman 1988: 105–6). The stairway was punctuated at its lower levels by three small rooms, although only the upper room, Chamber A, was decorated – with an astronomical ceiling (unique until the tomb of Seti I) and wall decoration of passages of funerary literature which are exceptional for the early New Kingdom, including an early version of the Chapters of Coming Forth by Day (often referred to by the modern designation the Book of the Dead; for details, see Dorman 1988: 82–4). The length of this tomb and its emphasis on funerary literature seem more reminiscent of contemporary royal, rather than private, tombs (not least KV20, as has often been noted; Dorman 1988: 101, n. 153), as does its unusual astronomical ceiling. The second part of the tomb, the Offering Chapel (TT71; see Dorman 1988: 84–95; 1991), was cut into the now-established elite burial ground of the early Dynasty 18 high on the slopes of Sheikh abd el-Qurna. Senenmut's was one of the earliest of the New Kingdom tombs in this cemetery, and so he chose the highest, most obvious location; he was quickly followed by other contemporary or near-contemporary high-ranking officials so that this became the cemetery of choice for the Theban elite during the reign of Tuthmosis III. Dorman (1988: 85, n. 79), notes that 41 tombs of this period were packed onto this hillside. Perhaps as an official with access to the best royal craftsmen, Senenmut could ensure that his tomb(s) would surpass in size and quality of workmanship anything that had been built before. It is also notable that Senenmut's mortuary provision consisted of two well-established elements – the Offering Chapel and the Burial Chamber – but that there was a striking distinct physical separation of the two so that each could be placed in its ideal location.

However, this separation of a bipartite tomb into two physically separate elements is not unique to Senenmut. The Vizier User-Amun, who was active under Tuthmosis III, had a similar arrangement. Tomb TT131

(Dziobek 1994, 1995) is a conventional broad-façade tomb (topped by a pyramid an impressive 6–10 m tall) at Sheikh abd el-Qurna, with a 'broad hall' whose scenes of public activity by User-Amun include the depiction of the tomb-owner involved in the reception of foreigners bearing 'tribute', a text describing his installation as Vizier, and a processional scene including Tuthmosis III itself. This tomb has neither a 'long hall' nor a Burial Chamber; these are to be found in TT61 (Dziobek 1994, 1995), which is also at Sheikh abd el-Qurna, but higher up the hill in the 'Upper Enclosure'. The walls of this tomb are decorated with scenes depicting the funeral of User-Amun and a complete set of *Amduat* texts (and an almost-complete copy of the *Litany of Re*), which may be the earliest from any tomb and are all the more remarkable since these are primarily royal mortuary texts.

It would appear that Senenmut and User-Amun were particularly well blessed in their mortuary provision, as owners of tombs which were truely bipartite and also contained texts and scenes which were normally associated with royal burial. However, there are other situations by which particularly well-favoured private individuals could come to own more than one 'tomb', and this may provide a clue as to why several large Offering Chapels in the Theban necropolis seem to lack obvious burial provision, while other modest burials of especially favoured private individuals within the Valley of the Kings seem to lack (as yet) an obvious Offering Chapel. (Dorman 1995).

CHAPTER 13

Rekhmire and the Tomb of the Well-Known Soldier

Foreigners and Funerals in the Age of Empire

рրրր

Wall-Scenes in Theban Tombs of Dynasty 18

Throughout Dynasty 18, a period of some 200 years, the West Bank at Thebes was the most important necropolis of elite tombs in Egypt. It came to contain hundreds of rock-cut tombs, some of whose walls were covered with painted scenes of exquisite delicacy. A thorough compendium can be conveniently found in Kampp (1996). One of the most important, and certainly one of the largest, of these tombs belongs to Rekhmire. Unlike Ineni and Senenmut, Rekhmire came from an established court family – his uncle was User-Amun and his was the third generation to achieve the office of Vizier, the most important civil office in Egypt. His career spanned the reigns of Tuthmosis III and Amenhotep II, a period which saw the end of the most important phase of territorial expansion through aggressive military activity in Western Asia and Nubia, and the consolidation of political and economic control over the empire and peace with its rivals, most importantly the Western Asiatic state of Mitanni. This was an era of wealth and confidence for Egypt, which was reflected both in the continuation of royal building projects and in the desire of the servants of this empire, Egyptian elites, to display their own wealth and status through their tombs. This desire was, of course, nothing new, but the particular emphases given in Theban tombs of the middle part of Dynasty 18 lend tombs of this period a flavour all of their own. The decoration in later Dynasty 18 tombs – those from the reigns of Tuthmosis IV to Amenhotep III – come from

Ancient Egyptian Tombs: The Culture of Life and Death By Steven Snape
© 2011 Steven Snape

an age of empire and luxury which were rather different from the more austere paintings of the earlier part of dynasty. Deliberate attempts to produce sensuous effects include the textures of the natural world in hunting and pool scenes, and diaphanous drapery as part of an atmosphere of louche eroticism in banqueting scenes (for a discussion of what might be called 'coded sexuality' within Dynasty 18 tomb scenes, see Manniche 2003). An especially good example of a tomb with decoration of this type is that of Nebamun, now in the British Museum (Parkinson 2008).

However, tombs from the early part of the dynasty, such as those of Ineni and Senenmut, had set the standard. The basic form of the tomb was the inverted T-shaped chapel cut into the cliffs of the Theban mountain, and the range of scenes depicted on its walls emphasized both the activities of the tomb-owner in his lifetime and his expectations for the afterlife. The tomb of Rekhmire (TT100; see Davies 1943) is an outstanding example of the conventional arrangement of these scenes within the tomb, but, because of its size, with more extensive detail in their depiction than any other (Figure 12.4 B). More specifically, its size is based not on the removal of stone to create significant interior space, but on the maximization of this stone removal to create long narrow corridors in both the transverse hall and long hall, the aim being to generate decoratable wall area. The arrangement of the scenes within the tomb followed its architectural divisions. The outer part of the tomb, the transverse (or 'broad') hall, depicted the activities which Rekhmire would have undertaken during his working life, while the long hall (or 'corridor') has the most complete set of funeral scenes of any tomb in Egypt. This thematic division holds good until late in Dynasty 18, when it was changed by developments during the Amarna Period. However, even some post-Amarna tombs at Thebes followed this earlier pattern, so that a much later tomb, that of Amenhotep-Huy (TT40; Davies 1926), who was active during the reign of Tutankhamen, although it has an inner room in the form of a pillared hall rather than a narrow corridor, nevertheless has an outer transverse hall decorated with scenes which bear comparison in their content and arrangement to those of Rekhmire (Figure 12.4 C).

Scenes of daily life?

It is common to refer to scenes in the transverse hall in the same terms as most of the content of the decorated walls of Old and Middle Kingdom tombs, as 'scenes of daily life'. They show, and describe, the tomb-owner relating to a wider world which seems to be embedded within his (or her) experience. The tomb of Ineni is a good example in that not only does the text talk about his activities for Hatshepsut, but the illustrative scenes show him carrying out wider duties, including the inspection of measuring of incense to be used in various temples at Thebes (Haring 1997: 134–5). Rekhmire and Amenhotep-Huy show and describe similar themes, creating a room which expresses some aspects of their lifetime experience, especially as it relates to activities and situations which emphasize their status, particularly their closeness to the king (Figure 13.1). One of the most striking themes is that of the reception of foreign 'tribute' by the tomb-owner, as an agent of the Egyptian state, giving particular visual interest in the depiction of rows of foreigners, eminently recognizable in their specific ethnic identity through the way they, and the objects they bring, are depicted. One suggestion regarding the particular role these depictions play within these private tombs is that they represent 'the functioning of the tomb-owner in his official capacity before the king "who made him" at the moment of that monarch's first ceremonial appearance when he received the homage of all his subjects' (Aldred 1970: 113), although it might also be that at least some of these scenes do not primarily represent a specific historical event but a cumulation of such events at which the tomb-owner played a leading role.

Funerals in Theban tombs

The tomb provided the venue where the funerary rituals which would transform the tomb-owner into an effective entity, ready to participate fully in the opportunities that the afterlife would afford. It was also the locus where the graphic depiction of those rituals and their textual description were displayed. It is unclear whether this was simply to emphasize this particular role of the tomb, to ensure their magical guarantee whatever the real nature of the interment, or to provide the means by which they might magically be said to be constantly repeated. Whatever the case, these scenes in Theban tombs of Dynasty 18 provide the most detailed evidence of what went on at an Egyptian funeral (Assmann 2005: 299–329). However, it must be noted that these Theban scenes have a particular context in both time and place – they differ quite markedly from what we know of Memphite funerals of the Old Kingdom and from later Dynasty 18 funerals at Memphis and, probably, Thebes itself, which emphasizes the dynamic and localized nature of these rituals.

The most complete textual description of a Theban funeral comes from the tomb of Djehuty (TT110; Davies 1932), which dates to the reign of Hatshepsut/Tuthmosis III:

> A beautiful burial comes in peace after your seventy
> days are completed in the *wabet*.

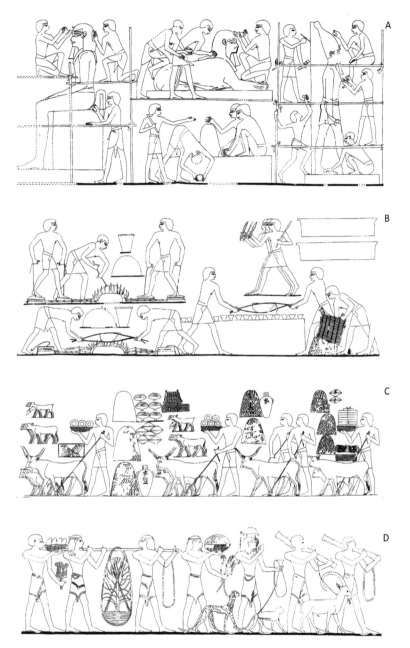

Figure 13.1 Selected scenes of royal service from the tomb of Rekhmire: A –
workshops producing royal stone statuary; B – workshops producing copper/
bronze and casting parts of temple doors; C – receiving taxes from the northern
part of the area overseen by Rekhmire (Asyut to Coptos); D – receiving 'tribute'
from the land of Punt (adapted from Davies 1943 (Vol. II): Pls 17, 34, 52 and 60)

> May you be placed on a bier in the house of rest and
> drawn by white oxen.
> May the ways be opened with milk, until you reach
> the entrance of your chapel.
> May the children of your children be gathered in an
> unbroken circle and weep with an affectionate heart.
> May your mouth be opened by the Chief Lector-
> Priest and your purification performed by the
> *sm*-Priest.
> May Horus adjust your mouth and open for you your
> eyes, your ears, your limbs and your bones so that all
> your natural functions are complete.
> May the transfiguration-spells (*s3ḥw*) be read for you,
> and the offering-spell (*ḥtp-di-nsw*) be performed for
> you . . .

The ritual actions which are described here are illustrated within the elite Theban tombs of Dynasty 18, especially in the long hall, the fullest set being in the rising corridor of the long hall in the tomb of Rekhmire (Figure 13.2).

Theban funerals: an Ostracon in Manchester

Another, less formal, image of a funeral survives as an ink sketch on a limestone ostracon from Thebes (see cover illustration). This remarkable object was purchased by Alan Gardiner in Luxor and published by him (Gardiner 1913). It now resides in the Egyptology collections of the Manchester Museum. We do not know why this sketch was made. It is unlikely to have been a preparatory or practice drawing for a depiction on the wall of a tomb since, unusually, the scene on the ostracon is not a standard funeral scene showing ceremonies performed immediately out-side the tomb, but shows the subterranean interior of a simple shaft-and-chamber(s) tomb with no evident superstructure. It would be nice to think of this sketch as a piece of accurate reportage showing the deposition of a body within a tomb by a Deir el-Medina workman with a little time on his hands and a recent funeral on his mind.

The ostracon shows a family tomb which is entered via a vertical shaft which has been provided with a series of hand-holds to allow the somewhat difficult descent of the coffin and its bearers. The lack of any illustrated superstructure may be significant, not in indicating that the tomb had no superstructure but in the separation of Burial Chambers from Offering Chapel. On the surface a funeral is in progress – to the right a priest pours libations and burns incense in front of a group of four mourning women.

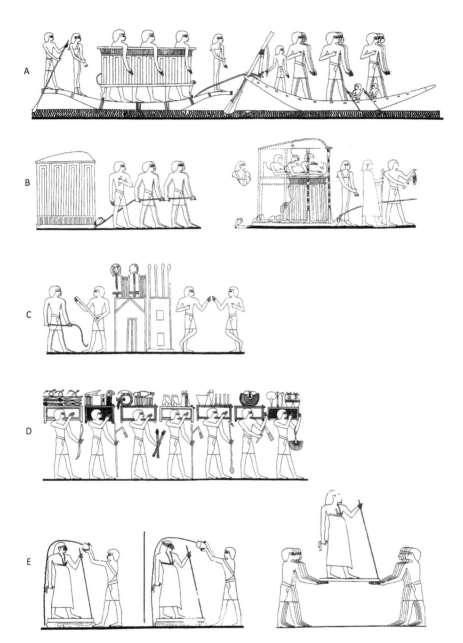

Figure 13.2 Selected scenes of funeral from the tomb of Rekhmire: A – ferrying the coffin across the river; B – dragging the coffin to the tomb (two examples); C – on arrival at the necropolis the cortège is greeted by the lector-priest and the *muww*-dancers; D – mourners carrying Rekhmire's burial equipment; E – purifying (left) and transporting (right) the statue of Rekhmire into his tomb (adapted from Davies 1943 (Vol. II): Pls 87, 90, 92, 93, 100 and 107)

Within the tomb itself are four human figures, all of whom appear to be male – one descending (or ascending?) the shaft, one manoeuvring the coffin from the bottom of the shaft into a burial chamber to the left at the base of the shaft, and two further individuals kneeling in the corner of that chamber. The other figure in the left-hand chamber is shown with a jackal's head – whether this is meant to represent Anubis taking charge of the body or a masked priest playing the part of Anubis is, as with more elaborate, 'official' depictions of funeral ceremonies, difficult to say. The left-hand Burial Chamber seem to be connected, via a set of stairs, to another chamber(s), while a further chamber at the right of the bottom of the shaft contains two bodies which have already been interred, along with a schematic rendition of a modest set of grave goods.

A Guide to the Afterlife: The Book of the Dead

The ultimate aim of the funeral ceremonies was to activate a beneficial afterlife for the tomb-owner. One of the ways this was done was to use the tomb as a route to an afterlife beyond the tomb, with the gods. The very heart of the tomb, the shrine/chapel with its sculpted figure of the tomb-owner (and, perhaps, members of his family), was regularly decorated with scenes showing the deceased meeting the gods. Increasingly, the inner parts of these tombs also depicted scenes showing the natural continuation of the funeral ceremony, the passage through the afterlife to vindication before Osiris. The natural descendant of the Middle Kingdom coffin texts, as an extensive set of funerary literature which guided the non-royal Dead to an Osirian afterlife and helped him/her to achieve that afterlife, is the *Chapters of Coming Forth by Day*, whose title is somewhat more optimistic in tone than that by which it is more popularly known today, the Book of the Dead (for good introductions and overviews to this and related funerary literature, see Hornung 1999; Kemp 2007). The Book of the Dead, rather than being a well-defined piece of writing with a central theme, is, somewhat like the Pyramid Texts and the Coffin Texts, a fairly loose collection of texts brought together to form individual collections of varying numbers of sections. These sections, or chapters, provide the information required to achieve an Osirian (or, sometimes, solar) afterlife, but this information might consist of ritual texts to be recited at the funeral, or a guidebook to the regions which, immediately after death, the deceased needs to journey through, or a set of examination cribs to allow the deceased to answer correctly the questions set by the demons who are there to impede his progress, or, ultimately, a guarantee of the success of his journey and ultimate judgement. The length of an individual Book of the

Dead depended on the wishes, or perhaps wealth, of the commissioning owner – a full text could consist of 180–200 sections, filling a papyrus roll over 40 m in length – and on its location – some elements of the Book of the Dead could appear on the walls of the tomb itself or on coffins. In the papyrus versions the texts were written in black ink with especially important sections, such as titles of extra-textual instructions, sometimes referred to as rubrics, in red ink. Pictorial accompaniments, referred to as vignettes, were a means of emphasizing the meaning and content of the texts, and the best copies – such as that belonging to the royal scribe Ani in the British Museum (Faulkner and Andrews 1989) – were miniature works of art in their own right.

Some of the sections specifically related to making effective various items of funerary equipment within the tomb, such as Chapter 6, which was the *shabti*-spell (which magically activated small figurines included in the burial equipment as effective substitutes for the deceased if Osiris called upon him/her to perform work), or Chapter 30, which was inscribed on the base of heart-scarabs, ensuring that the heart did not testify against the deceased in the court of Osiris. Perhaps the most important section of the Book of the Dead was Chapter 125, which described a defining moment: the judgment of the deceased in the court of Osiris. Judgment is a concept which has not figured very heavily in our overview of the Egyptian view of the afterlife and how to achieve it, nor has there been an emphasis on the need for a particular religious adherence or even a strong sense of moral worth. The equipping of a tomb and provisioning it for eternity seem to have little to do with any sense of right and wrong, or divine approval in any specific way. But the idea of eternal joy through wealth is one based on an afterlife within the tomb, and an Osirian afterlife, although needing the tomb as a necessary vehicle to get to that afterlife, conceives of an afterlife where blessings flow from being in the *sḫt-ḥtpw* (*sekhet-hetepu*), the 'Field of Offerings', overseen by Osiris. However, even here the ideas of divine provision link back to those within the tomb: the blessed Dead are described as *imakhu*, (in Chapter 110 of the Book of the Dead), being provided with everything they need, and able to do 'everything that is done on earth'.

So what was required to get here? Knowledge is one thing, including the knowledge necessary to pass through gates guarded by ferocious demons, being able to identify them, and even the different parts of the doorways themselves which call out to the deceased 'What is my name ...?' Some sense of moral worth is also required, ideally reflected in moral acts in one's lifetime. The so-called 'negative confession' gives a sense of divinely approved behaviour, whether in relation to other humans or to the gods, but perhaps the most important idea here is not that the flawed human confesses his/her failings before the gods and asks for forgiveness; rather the idea is to deny all wrongdoing. Presumably, the power of the written and spoken word will make it so and any sins will be washed away by the convincing show of denial.

The judgment scene of Chapter 125 shows the court of Osiris, with Osiris himself a major figure, sometimes accompanied by a row of other gods who also sit in judgment. Approaching Osiris is the deceased, usually led by the god Anubis in his role as god of the liminal space between life and death. Between them is a large pair of scales, often operated by another figure of Anubis. A feather, representing *maat*, sits on one pan of the scales, the heart of the deceased sits on the other. The judgment of the deceased is visually conceived as the weighing of the heart – the seat of both emotions and intellect – and the feather of *maat* as representing, in this context, the concepts of truth and rightness. The god Thoth records the result and the creature Ammit (*3mt mwtw*, 'Swallower of the Dead'), with its crocodile head, lion's forequarters and hippopotamus's rear parts, waits to devour the unsuccessful examinee. However, since the Book of the Dead is a guarantee as well as a guidebook, Ammit is always left hungry. The deceased is always successful and, avoiding the Lake of Fire of Chapter 126, is shown being led by Horus to Osiris (and, often, Isis) to be received into the Field of Offerings. Although a more extensive and elaborate exposition of the transition to a beneficial afterlife, the Book of the Dead is an obvious descendant of the Coffin Texts, both in the overarching concept of a journey to the afterlife which is fraught with danger, and in a number of its key details: the Lake of Fire appears in the Book of the Two Ways (CT 1054 and CT 1166), while the place of damnation is overseen by the 'Swallower of Millions' (CT 335). The length of the Book of the Dead compared to the Coffin Texts is, rather obviously, as much to do with format as anything else – a papyrus roll which could be any length has much greater potential than the physical limits of a coffin or indeed the walls of a tomb.

As far as the function of the tomb is concerned, one copy of the Book of the Dead is particularly informative, that belonging to the Dynasty 18 official Nebqed. One vignette from his copy of the text shows a sequence of critical roles and actions around the tomb (Figure 13.3): the arrival of the funeral procession at the tomb; the 'Opening of the Mouth' in front of the tomb; the encoffined body surrounded by its funerary 'kit' within the Burial Chamber; the *ba* (see below) travelling down the burial shaft carrying food and drink; and the 'coming forth by day' of the deceased. It is as neat and effective an image as any to convey the physical form of the tomb, its role as a venue for ritual action, and its function as both a home and a gateway for the non-corporeal forms of the dead tomb-owner.

Figure 13.3   The tomb of Nebqed, as illustrated in his Book of the Dead (adapted from Naville 1886: iv)

Local Elites at el-Kab

The town of Nekheb, lying on the East Bank of the Nile 100 km south of Thebes, seems to have been an important centre in the late Predynastic and early Dynastic Period. It was on the opposite bank of the river to Hierakonpolis; its principal deity, Nekhbet, was the titular deity of Upper Egypt; and its cemeteries contain tombs from the Predynastic to the Graeco-Roman Period. However, Nekheb, now better known by its modern name of el-Kab, never achieved significant prominence at any period of its history. It seems to have been a reasonably affluent regional centre which occasionally benefited from royal largesse, such as the temple of Amenhotep III in the nearby Wadi Hillal, or the great enclosure wall around the town's temple enclosure, probably the work of Nectanebo II. There appears to have been a *mastaba* cemetery close to the town during the Old Kingdom, with tombs made of mudbrick and containing false doors and statues along the Memphite model, including the *mastaba*s of the local officials Kaimen and Neferseshem (Quibell 1898). In the Middle Kingdom the cliffs overlooking the town began to be used for rock-cut tombs, the most important of which was that belonging to the Dynasty 13 Overseer of Priests, Sobeknakht (Tylor 1896). However, el-Kab is best known today for its later rock-cut tombs, which, like those of Ineni and Senenmut at Thebes, can be dated with some confidence to the early part of Dynasty 18.

Unlike the largest contemporary elite tombs at Thebes, and partly owing to the lack of space, the el-Kab tombs do not have wide façades. Instead, they share a terrace of the limestone cliffs in the manner of some of the Middle Kingdom tombs in Middle Egypt, such as Beni Hasan, and each has a relatively modest entrance. Nonetheless, and especially when taken as a group, the visible presence of these tombs is obvious from the town below. Because these tombs are, when compared to contemporary Theban examples, grouped closely together they do not have the luxury of a broad transverse hall; instead their interiors are much simpler. The layout of most of these tombs is a main hall which is approximately twice as deep as it is wide, and usually with a separate room opening off this hall which contained the burial shaft. Comparisons between elite tombs at el-Kab and Thebes may be a little unfair, given that the former are the work of regional administrators and the later the work of some of the most powerful non-royal individuals of New Kingdom Egypt. However, comparing the tombs is useful for a number of reasons, the first being that trends in the decoration of Theban tombs were clearly being copied at el-Kab, especially in the use of the tomb as a place for overt self-presentation with, ideally, a good level of historical detail. The second reason is that this factor of detailed self-presentation has given us, at el-Kab, one of the most important tombs in Egypt, when judged in terms of its contribution to our understanding of dynastic history.

Ancestors and identity at el-Kab (1): the tomb of Pahery

The most interesting and impressive of the rock-cut tombs at el-Kab belong to the family of Pahery (Figure 13.4). His tomb contains, in a somewhat more concentrated form, expressions of the concerns found in more detail in the elite tombs of early Dynasty 18 at Thebes: a combination of the depiction of personal achievement and ceremonies connected with the funeral as seen in the tomb of Rekhmire. The tomb contains scenes stressing Pahery's role as the Mayor of el-Kab and therefore a trusted provincial official, including a standing figure of Pahery overseeing

Figure 13.4   The interior of the tomb of Pahery at el-Kab

agricultural activity, especially the production of grain and flax, and using that produce to fill granaries and transport barges. Underneath this scene Pahery carries out two more important economic activities: counting cattle and registering the receipt of gold, the latter possibly from the desert east of el-Kab. The centre of the wall shows scenes of fishing, food-preparation and wine-making, but the central scene here shows Pahery as tutor to the infant Prince Wadjmose on his knee – Pahery may have been a provincial official but he was clearly one who was connected at court and, just as any Theban official, used his tomb as a way of proclaiming royal favour through specific roles connected to the king and his family. The tomb also has a substantial set of scenes of funeral which could have been taken directly from a contemporary Theban tomb, including the sequence of ritual actions, and the participants (the *muw*-dancers, the *djeryt*-mourners) appear as though they have been directly lifted from a Theban tomb, while on the opposite wall are scenes of Pahery offering, being offered to, and of banqueting. But the most interesting part of the tomb is the rear wall, where the vaulted roof of the tomb creates the appearance of a round-topped stela (as noted by Lichtheim 1976: 15), in the centre of which is a rock-cut statue group of the seated figures of Pahery flanked by his mother and wife and acting as an obvious focus for offering within the tomb, and representing yet another Theban feature.

The Human Spirit (3): the ba

Pahery's tomb is also interesting in the statements it makes regarding different aspects of the afterlife which he expected. An important series of statements describe the potential and limitations of the *ba*, another spiritual aspect of an individual which achieved a semi-independent existence after death, and sometimes is depicted as a human-headed bird (Žabkar 1968). Pahery is described as 'Becoming a living *ba*, having control of bread, water and air' and told that his *ba* 'shall thrive on bread, water and air, assuming the form of a phoenix, a swallow, a falcon or a heron, as you wish', that it is 'divine among the spirits (*ȝḥw*) and the worthy *ba*s converse with you', and that 'Your *ba* will not abandon your corpse' (Lichtheim 1976: 15–21). The corporeality of his existence after death is stressed by the statement 'Your eyes are given to you to see, your ears to hear what is spoken, your mouth to speak and your feet to walk. Your hands and your feet have motion. Your flesh is firm and your muscles smooth – you delight in all your limbs', but an existence beyond the tomb is guaranteed by the affirmations that

> You are not turned back at the gate of heaven (*duat*). The doors of lightland open for you . . . You reach the Hall of the Two Truths and the god who is in it welcomes you . . . Your heart rejoices as you plough in your plot in the Field of Reeds. You are rewarded by what you have grown and you gather a harvest rich in grain.

Ancestors and identity at el-Kab (2): the tomb of Ahmose son of Ibana

The tomb of Ahmose son of Ibana is close to, and constructed in the same form as, the tomb of his grandson Pahery. But while the interior of the tomb of Pahery is covered with an abundance of varied scenes and texts, the tomb of Ahmose has one dominating feature: virtually the whole of one long wall of his tomb (Figure 13.5) is covered with columns of hieroglyphic text which tell the reader in some detail of Ahmose's active participation in the wars of Theban kings at the end of Dynasty 17 and the beginning of Dynasty 18. This text is one of the most important historical documents for the expulsion of the Hyksos and the foundation of Egypt's New Kingdom empire, although its role in this tomb was a thematically specific self-presentation. It is striking that this is an unillustrated text. This in itself is not unusual since it was clearly undecorous to depict scenes of warfare within a private tomb; perhaps because it would be introducing discordant, violent and potentially harmful elements within a tomb and perhaps also it would presume to a royal prerogative. But if the idea of a military career and persona being conveyed in text is not in itself unusual, the level of detail is.

Figure 13.5   The 'autobiography' of Ahmose son of Ibana at el-Kab

It is unprecedented in its scale, perhaps because Ahmose is unusual in being a successful career soldier rather than a member of the new Dynasty 18 elite who may have had some military experience but a range of other activities to celebrate in their tombs. Perhaps this is because of the wealth and status which military success brought Ahmose, and was displayed here in an impressive tomb in his native town. It is interesting to speculate whether Ahmose son of Ibana himself would have been able to read the extensive autobiography in his tomb – there is nothing in his autobiography to suggest that his background would have provided him with a literate education.

This stands in very marked contrast with Pahery, who describes himself as a scribe and depicts himself in the act of writing. There is nothing in Pahery's record to suggest he had any sort of military career, which would have been a real possibility since he was living at a time of great imperial expansion. Instead Pahery presents himself as a representative of the *novi homines* of the Egypt of the early Tuthmosides – not one of the new court *arrivistes* like Senenmut and Ineni, but an important regional administrator of Egypt's agricultural and mineral wealth. Closeness to the court is stressed by his role as tutor to Prince Wadjmose, and his tomb contains scenes showing his attachment to contemporary metropolitan mores, whether those are banquets, the detailed ritual of the Theban funeral or a sophisticated approach to the possibilities of a personal afterlife within and beyond the tomb. Interestingly, too, Pahery stresses his connection with his grandfather, particularly claiming responsibility for the provisioning of his tomb, and it is likely that it was the wealth and status accumulated by Ahmose which provided the basis for advancement by his descendants. It is a pleasing picture, the hoary old soldier Ahmose recounting his wartime exploits to his posh grandson.

The Contents of Dynasty 18 Tombs

Although the architectural and decorative survival of many elite New Kingdom tombs at Thebes provides us with a wealth of data on how the Offering Chapels were designed for the memorialization and afterlife-expectations of their owners, our understanding of the range of equipment buried with them is less clear. Although many museums are filled with objects which derive from ancient Egyptian cemeteries, most of the tombs they come from were already robbed long before their excavation, or indeed derive from illicit diggings themselves. Intact burial chambers are a real rarity in Egyptian archaeology, not least for the reason that their often-valuable contents made them attractive targets for ancient robbers. However, a certain number of elite tombs from New Kingdom Thebes have been discovered with their burials intact, or only slightly disturbed, and these provide a sound basis to describe a typical assemblage of funerary material from the period. A full examination of this issue can be found in Smith (1992), who describes 36 tombs which he considers to meet his definition of being 'substantially intact'. The most high-status examples of these tombs are the Valley of the Kings burials of Maherperi (KV36; Daressy 1902; Reeves 1990: 140–7) 'Fan-Bearer at the right hand of the King' from the reign of Tuthmosis IV, and that of the parents-in-law of Amenhotep III, Yuya and Thuyu (KV46; Quibell 1908). 'Family tombs' from the reigns of Hatshepsut/Tuthmosis III (Dorman 2003) include the burials of Hatnefer and Ramose (Lansing and Hayes 1937), the parents of Senenmut, buried in front of his tomb at Sheikh abd el-Qurna and that of the family of Neferkhewet from Khokha (Figure 13.6) (Hayes 1935); that of Kha and Meryt (TT8; Schiaparelli 1927; Smith 1992: 226, Fig. 4) from the East Cemetery at Deir el-Medina dates to the reigns of Tuthmosis IV/Amenhotep III. Most intriguing is the undisturbed burial of a royal lady of Dynasty 17 found by Petrie (1909) near the entrance to the Valley of the Kings; the entire assemblage is now in the Royal Scottish Museum in Edinburgh.

There is an obvious and unsurprising correlation between a tomb-owner's status and the quality and quantity of grave goods; all the

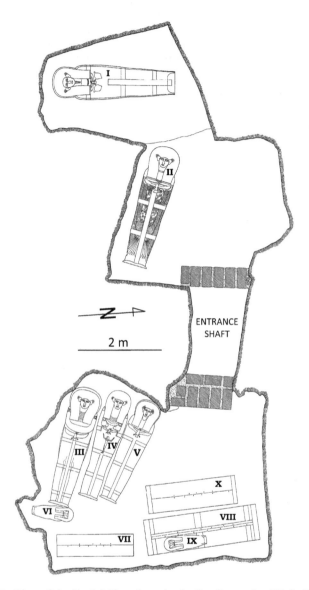

Figure 13.6 Plan of the Burial Chambers in the family tomb of Neferkhewet and Rennefer at Thebes (adapted from Hayes 1935: Fig. 1). All the contents have been removed, apart from the coffins, to illustrate the phases of burial in the tomb, during a period of about 60 years during the reigns of Tuthmosis I–Tuthmosis III. The order of interment appears to be: (I) Neferkhewet in the far western chamber, then (II) his wife Rennefer in the nearer western chamber, then the three burials of (III) their son(-in-law?) Bak-Amen, (IV) their daughter Ruyu and (V) their son Amenemhat in the eastern chamber. All the burials I–V are in anthropoid coffins and it appears that they were intended to be buried in these rooms. The relationship to this family of the owners of the miniature anthropoid and box coffins – (VI) a girl *c.*1 year old, (VII) a boy *c.*6 years old, (VIII) an adult woman, (IX) a child of less than 6 months old and (X) a boy *c.*10 years old – is unknown

individuals who were found within intact or near-intact tombs at Thebes had been provided with a basic funerary set which consisted of a coffin, jewellery, toilet set and a numbers of boxes/baskets. With a rise in status and wealth came additional elements, including personal possessions from life, and equipment produced for the tomb, including amulets, *shabtis*, canopic jars, funerary papyri and statuary.

CHAPTER 14

Huya and Horemheb

Amarna and After

ᒋᒋᒋᒋ

Life and Death at Amarna

The Amarna Period is perhaps the most extraordinary episode in the history of religious development in ancient Egypt. The most significant issue for debate among students of this period has traditionally been its differentness – to what extent does it represent a break with what went before? On one level a break is obvious enough, particularly the foundation of the city of Amarna as a new capital city for Egypt, which could be designed from scratch by Akhenaten to cater for whatever he wanted to do there. Exactly what it was that he wanted to do is rather more problematic, with perceived views of his intentions ranging from a full-blooded mono-theism and total rejection of the traditional polytheism of Egypt, to a more nuanced emphasis on solar religion (something with which his father Amenhotep III had experimented; Baines 1998), perhaps combined with a more political aim of sidelining the powerful Theban Amen cult and its priesthood. It seems that the central pillar of active 'Atenism' (if there can be said to be such a thing) was the cult worship of the Aten by Akhenaten and Nefertiti within structures which were specifically designed for solar worship – temples whose open courts contrasted with the dark hidden sanctuaries of Egypt's traditional gods. However, this was not itself a radical innovation since solar worship had been practised in open-court temples from at least as early as the Old Kingdom in the so-called 'sun-temples' of Dynasty 5 at Abu Ghurob, but it is obvious that the cultic landscape of Amarna/Akhetaten was primarily designed with this specific purpose in

Ancient Egyptian Tombs: The Culture of Life and Death   By Steven Snape
© 2011 Steven Snape

mind, since Akhenaten tells us as much on the boundary stelae that he had carved onto the cliffs of the desert edges of his city. The extensive texts on these stelae, particularly those of the 'Early Proclamation', list the crucial structures which the city was intended to contain (Murnane and van Siclen 1993: 40–1) – most importantly temples for the Aten, palaces for the royal family, a royal cemetery and a sacred animal necropolis for the Mnevis bull. At the end of the list there is a reference to tombs which are to be constructed for priests who served the Aten cult, in the mountain to the east of the city. So this prospectus for the new city provides a description of how the king, his immediate family, the god Aten and those officials who are specifically involved with the operation of the cult of the Aten will be provided for in this specific place. What it ignores are the needs of the rest of the population of the city, who would have to cope with being moved from their homes.

In one sense this did not really matter since the normal and exclusive relationship between king and god had not changed; the only difference was that the god was now Aten rather than Amen, and the specific mechanisms by which the king worshipped the paramount god of Egypt could hardly be of overwhelming concern to most people. As far as their own religious practice was concerned, the elite population of Amarna 'pray at home, in front of an altar that contains a picture of the king and his family . . . Akhenaten is the sole intermediary' (Hornung 1983: 248), while the majority of the population of Amarna seems to have continued with their 'household religion' at Amarna as they had at Thebes, or wherever else they came from (Stevens 2006). But another, connected issue was that of the provision for the burial of Amarna elites, and the expectations of an afterlife which were served by these tombs. For the majority of the population, the influence of 'Atenism' is not immediately apparent in the modest, usually robbed, simple burials within those portions of cemeteries of the Amarna non-elite which have been recovered to date (Kemp 2006: 27–45).

However, an 'Atenist' agenda was more of an issue for the Amarna elite, the Late Dynasty 18 equivalents of the Inenis, Senenmuts and Rekhmires of early Dynasty 18. These were people who had a firm idea of what was needed to ensure a beneficial afterlife, principally a well-equipped and properly prepared tomb. However, there was a problem. Although tomb building for the Amarna elite was an obvious aspect of the creation of a new city in which people were intended to reside forever, a major question needed to be answered: what could a person expect to happen to them after death in the brave new netherworld of 'Atenism'? This is a question which does not seem to have developed a satisfactory resolution and our main evidence base – the tombs themselves – provides us with somewhat unsatisfactory answers. Perhaps the best way to approach this problem is to ask the same question about Amarna tombs as has been asked about the period itself: what is the same and what has changed?

Tombs at Amarna

There is much about the Amarna private tombs (Davies 1903–8) which would have been familiar to Ineni or Rekhmire. They were cut high in the cliffs above Amarna in two groups, at the northern (17 tombs) and southern (27 tombs) ends of the 'bay' which defined the eastern limits of the city of Amarna, apart from the tomb of Akhenaten himself. Differences between the two groups of tombs are not obvious, although one suggestion is that the northern group is made up of tombs of 'Advisors and Intellectuals' and the southern group those of 'Pharaoh's Executive Arm' (Reeves 2001: 134–7). The northern group includes the tombs of those officials whose titles suggest that they were the most closely involved with the operation of the Aten cult at Amarna, especially those of Meryre I ('Greatest of Seers of the Aten in the House of Aten'), Panehesy ('First Servant of the Aten in the House of Aten in Akhetaten') and Pentu (Chief Physician of the king, but also bearing the title 'First Servant of the Aten in the Mansion of the Aten in Akhetaten').

Both sets of tombs, grouped in terraces with their obvious façades, would have looked rather similar to the Theban cemeteries at Sheikh abd el-Qurna or other provincial cemeteries such as el-Kab. The basic format of the tomb was not dissimilar to those built at Thebes during the reign of Amenhotep III, such as Ramose and Kheruef, with their configuration of two principal rooms, one a transverse hall with 12 or 24 papyriform columns, and an inner hall, with a niche-shrine at the rear containing a rock-cut statue of the tomb-owner. There was, in fact, nothing intrinsically innovative about the architecture of the tombs of the Amarna elite, just as there was nothing essentially innovative (apart, perhaps from its multiple occupancy) in the form of the royal tomb which Akhenaten cut for himself in the 'royal wadi' to the east of the city. The crucial difference is in the decoration on the walls, which conveys the specific intent of the tomb – its underlying belief system and how it is intended to be used. We have seen that elite tombs of Dynasty 18, like those of most periods of Egyptian history, have two dominant themes: how does the decoration of the tomb convey the specific status of the tomb-owner, and how does the tomb act as a machine to bring about a beneficial afterlife for its owner.

Whereas tombs at places like Thebes and el-Kab showed the tomb-owner going about his business, particularly stressing how these activities attracted the notice and favour of the king, tomb-owners at Amarna seem

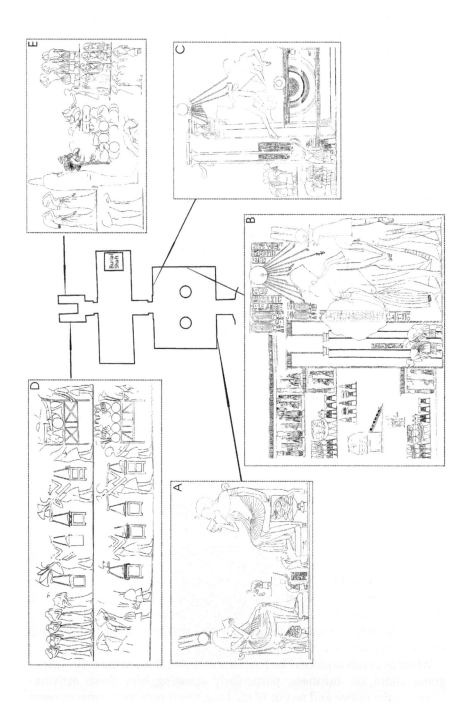

to be relegated to the role of spectators of royal activity. The main themes depicted in Amarna private tombs, often as giant single scenes filling entire walls, are, in descending order of importance and extent of depiction: (1) the relationship between the royal family and the Aten; (2) the city of Akhetaten itself; and (3) the tomb-owner. Closeness to the king is a crucial theme, but it is as an observer or a minor figure within royal tableaux that the tomb-owner appears in his own tomb (Figure 14.1 A and B). Scenes such as chariot-processions by Akhenaten while being blessed by the life-giving rays of the Aten or scenes of the arrival of foreigners to bring tribute to Akhenaten in his great imperial *durbar* of Year 12 focus on the royal presence and royal activity. The best that the tomb-owner could hope for was to appear as a tiny figure being rewarded by the king by having some piece of jewellery thrown down from the 'window of appearance' (Figure 14.1 C).

In terms of technique there is one aspect of the decoration of these tombs which is worth particular comment. Whereas most New Kingdom tombs at Thebes were decorated with scenes painted onto a flat, prepared surface, those at Amarna were carved as sunk-relief into the faces of the walls of the tomb. Partly this is due to the nature of the limestone at Amarna, which, with supporting plasterwork, was of a sufficiently compact consistency to make relief carving (which was subsequently painted) a possibility; sometimes the potential of 3-D relief carving could be used with specific impact, such as the deeply cut depiction of a garden well in the tomb of Meryre I (Davies 1903–8 (Vol. I): Pl. 32). However, the use of relief and the thematic content of these tombs were not entirely new; like much which is taken as typical of the Amarna period – the grotesque colossal statues, the new temple-type with reliefs showing the distorted images of Akhenaten and Nefertiti – this aspect of the artistic innovation of the Amarna Period is first seen early in the reign of Akhenaten, at Thebes.

The change in style and technique can be seen in a single Theban tomb, that of the Vizier Ramose (TT55; Davies 1941). The east wall of the tomb depicts a banqueting scene, a common enough theme in Dynasty 18 tombs, but one rendered in delicate raised relief, using a combination of limestone and plaster, and with only the occasional detail, particularly the

Figure 14.1 Plan and selected scenes from the Tomb of Huya at Amarna: A – Huya serves Akhenaten and Queen Tiy; B – Huya accompanies Akhenaten and Tiy in a visit to the Aten temple at Amarna; C – Huya is rewarded from the 'window of appearance'; D – part of Huya's funeral procession; E – rites performed before the body of Huya (adapted from Davies 1903–8 (Vol. III): Pls 1, 6, 8, 17, 22 and 23)

eyes of the figures, painted with simple black outline. This scene is often regarded by modern viewers as one of the most sensitive and accessible pieces of Egyptian art. Although perhaps the best, it is not the only example of the technique: other near-contemporary tombs with similar scenes from Thebes dating to late in the reign of Amenhotep III include that of Kheruef (TT192; Epigraphic Survey 1980), Steward of Queen Tiy. However, Ramose's tomb is important as the latest in this group, and one whose decoration spanned the transition from Amenhotep III to Amenhotep IV (Akhenaten). While the east wall of the tomb shows the figures in 'traditional' mode, the unfinished west wall bears a scene which will become commonplace at Amarna: the tiny figure of Ramose is shown bowing before a 'window of appearance' from which Akhenaten and Nefertiti, blessed by the spreading rays of the sun disc of the Aten, look down on the now-marginalized tomb-owner. There is, however, a coda to this tale of transition from one style and theme to another: the south wall of the tomb bears an image of a funeral cortège making its way to the tomb accompanied by mourners. The important aspect of this scene is that it was painted on a flat surface, and is entirely conventional in its depiction of a traditional Theban funeral, including rituals at the tomb and the deceased before Osiris. Although it is assumed that this scene was speedily added to a yet-unfinished tomb at the time of Ramose's death, the painting is of extraordinary quality. Another important transitional tomb from this period is that of the Royal Butler Parennefer, owner of tombs in both Thebes and Amarna. His Theban tomb (TT188; Davies 1923) has a damaged scene showing Amenhotep IV and a queen before an altar on which the rays of the Aten cascade down which is carved, unusually but appropriately, on the façade of the tomb at the rear of its open courtyard. The tomb also contains texts which specifically refer to Osiris and Anubis.

The Amarna afterlife

As we have seen, the prime function of an ancient Egyptian tomb is to act as a vehicle for salvation in the afterlife, whatever the specific nature(s) of that afterlife. In the context of the Amarna Period it might be asked: to what extent does the Amarna private tomb retain the traditional functions of a locus for offerings for the *ka*, and a portal to the Osirian afterlife? More broadly, what exactly were the expectations of an afterlife in the theology of the Amarna Period? The situation is actually rather confused (von der Way 1996).

An afterlife in 'another place' is not overtly mentioned in the private tombs at Amarna. Nor, for that matter, is it mentioned in the royal tomb itself, although that is a tomb whose decoration has been substantially destroyed. Most of the surviving scenes seem to be repetitious depictions of the king/royal family being showered with the rays of the Aten, although the side-rooms of the tomb were decorated with scenes which would be extraordinary in any context, let alone a New Kingdom royal tomb: the depiction of what may be the death in childbirth of two separate royal women who may have been buried within the tomb (Martin 1974–89). The intention, in a rather ill-defined way, seems to be that the king would somehow merge with the Aten after death. For ordinary mortals the options were rather more limited and seem to go back to the Old Kingdom limitations of an afterlife only within, or in the close environs of, the tomb itself.

There was one crumb of comfort for the recipients of what appears to be a centrally controlled and dictated tomb-building programme. Most of the tombs were unfinished (Owen and Kemp 1994) and the suspicion is that most of their intended occupants were still alive by the time Amarna was abandoned and could therefore return to the safety of their previous dispensation. This, of course, makes a huge assumption about the enthusiasm which the elite members of the Egyptian court had felt for the 'Amarna Experiment', at least to the extent it affected their own afterlives. Unfortunately, for at least one individual, Huya, the Steward of the Dowager Queen Tiy, this was not an option. Probably already far from young when he came to Amarna, Huya's tomb seems to have been the only one to be fully completed at Amarna. The actual use of this tomb may have made more pressing the need for the tomb to reflect both the act of burial itself and a clear sense of what a non-royal, elite afterlife at Amarna actually involved. The former was catered for by scenes of funeral (Figure 14.1 D and E), unique in one of the private tombs at Amarna, albeit a rather abbreviated funeral compared to earlier Dynasty 18 depictions. Completely absent are scenes reflecting a transition to an Osirian afterlife; instead the emphasis is placed on a variant of an afterlife lived within the tomb, or, more specifically, in and around the environs of the tomb at Amarna. A request for offerings comes at the end of a speech of praise by Huya to the rising sun in his tomb:

May you cause me to be continually in the place of favour, in my tomb of justification. May my *ba* come forth to see your rays and receive nourishment from its offerings. May one be summoned by name and come at the voice. May I partake of the things which issue [from the presence, that I might eat *shenes*-loaves, *bit*-pastry, offering-loaves, jugs of beer] roasted meat, hot food, cool water, wine, milk, everything which comes forth [from the Mansion of the Aten in Akhetaten]. For the *ba* of ... Huya, the justified.

(Translation based on that of Murnane 1995: 131)

Although Huya's tomb is the one with the fullest set of scenes and texts referring to specific expectations of funeral and afterlife at Amarna, other tombs also contain insights into what was on offer. The tomb of Panehesy contains a series of *hetep-di-nesu* formulae including one which refers to Akhenaten granting the tomb-owner 'the receiving of offering loaves which come forth from the presence in every festival of the living Aten in the Mansion of the Benben, for the *ka* of ... Panehesy, the justified' (Murnane 1995: 173). The role of the tomb itself is referred to in a text from the tomb of Pentu in which the tomb-owner asks the Aten to be allowed to 'rest in my place of continuity, that I be enclosed in the cavern of eternity; that I may go forth and enter my tomb without my *Ba*'s being restrained from what it wishes' (Murnane 1995: 181). The general pattern seems clear enough: the Amarna afterlife for an elite individual is based on royal patronage, for the allocation of a tomb which is decorated in appropriate style, a funeral which uses those elements of established liturgy which refer to the activation of the body, and an existence for the *ba* and the *ka* within the tomb and in the city of Amarna itself, where they are fed through royal patronage on the reversion of offerings in the temples of the Aten. Whether those reversions are physically transported to the tomb or, as may be more likely, thought of as being fed upon in the city itself by the *ba* is not obvious.

Nonetheless the tomb as a locus for individual relationships seems to continue. Perhaps the best evidence for this comes from a tomb in the southern group which was actually used, that of the 'Scribe of the Offering-Table of the Aten' Any (who was 'justified in a good funeral' – Murnane 1995: 123). The façade of his tomb was provided with a series of niches to contain stelae, six of which have been recovered (Davies 1903–8 (Vol. V): Pls xxi–xxiii; Murnane 1995: 124–5). These stelae bear simple scenes, mostly showing offerings being made to Any by named individuals, all of whom seem to be his employees, friends or relatives. The importance of these stelae is that they indicate that tombs could be used as places of interaction between the Living and the Dead, and genuine personal sentiment, during the Amarna Period.

However, the impression given of the view of the afterlife during the Amarna Period is one of lack of consistency or, perhaps more accurately, a lack of clear articulation of a well-formulated and consistent view of the afterlife within 'Atenism'. Part of this view may be derived not just from the tombs themselves, but also from their contents, specifically the continued inclusion of *shabti*s within the burial equipment of Akhenaten, Nefertiti and private individuals during the Amarna Period (Martin 1986). While these supremely Osirian objects were largely stripped of their overtly Osirian textual identification in favour of an orientation towards the Aten, the very existence of these figurines suggests a lingering traditionalism in sometimes unexpected places. This is perhaps best expressed in the *shabti* belonging to the Lady Ipy, which bears a text referring to following the Aten, yet also has an abbreviated version of the summoning-spell (Murnane 1995: 181) – although who might be summoning the *shabti* to do what, and where, is left tactfully ambiguous.

New Kingdom Tombs at Saqqara

Our view of New Kingdom private tombs is skewed by differential survival. Rock-cut tombs, such as those at Thebes, el-Kab and Amarna, naturally lend themselves to longevity, while tombs which are not so embedded in the landscape, being constructed of masonry or mudbrick, have not survived so well. This latter situation is the case at sites which also saw the construction of important tombs of the New Kingdom, such as Saqqara and Abydos. Monuments might also have differential survival of different elements, such as mudbrick/masonry elements added to basically rock-cut tombs, whose later disappearance may give a distorted impression of the original appearance of these tombs which we think we know well. A good example of a specific element are the finds of small stone pyramidia which topped now-disappeared mudbrick pyramids that were part of New Kingdom tombs (Rammant-Peeters 1983), including those of early Dynasty 18 (Malek 1990). At Thebes these may be in imitation of Dynasty 17–18 royal tombs, but the underlying solar aspect of these objects becomes increasingly obvious through the texts they bear.

Although it is tempting to see the re-establishment of the unified Egyptian state of Dynasty 18 in terms of the building of temples, royal tombs and private tombs at Thebes, early Dynasty 18 also saw a revival in the importance of Memphis as a royal centre. This revival, although less immediately visible in the archaeological record today than that of Thebes, included temple building and elite burials (Malek 1989). Given the importance of Memphis as the largest city in Egypt and the most important administrative centre during late Dynasty 18, it is not surprising that its cemeteries should accommodate the tombs of important officials based there. What is surprising, when compared to tombs of the Old Kingdom, is the extent to which these New Kingdom tombs became lost and have only comparatively recently begun to be recovered. More specifically, Saqqara became used as the principal cemetery for Memphis on the abandonment of Amarna by Tutankhamen in or around his Year 3 (no significant tombs of this period have been recovered from, for instance, Giza; Malek 1981: 156–7). This situation continued until the reign of Ramesses II, which was the last in which significant numbers of substantial, well-decorated tombs were constructed at Saqqara, perhaps because of the foundation of the new capital of Pi-Ramesse (Qantir) and a concomitant shift of elite burial away from the Memphite region (Malek 1985: 45). Apart from the role of Memphis as a royal administrative centre, other factors may also have played a part in the growing importance of the Saqqara necropolis in the post-Amarna Period, including the increasing emphasis, even at Thebes, put on the cult of Ptah-Sokar-Osiris, the Memphite form of Osiris (van Dijk 1988: 44). Two other factors may be relevant in the post-Amarna period, one being the increasing disconnec-tion between the place of the royal tomb and that of other elite groups, and the lack of correlation between the place of one's work and that of one's burial, with some important Theban officials being buried at Saqqara (van Dijk 1988: 39–40).

One of the problems with these New Kingdom Saqqara tombs is the very fact that they were masonry constructions, rather than primarily rock-cut, which means that it was relatively easy to dismantle them, and particularly to remove the slabs of fine-quality limestone from the mudbrick body of the superstructure – i.e. the carved scenes were not on well-established walls in the same way as in the best tombs of the Old Kingdom. The normal chances of being robbed of stone in this way were exacerbated by the foundation of the Monastery of Apa Jeremias close to the Unas Valley Temple and the adjoining New Kingdom cemetery, which had a seriously prejudicial influence on the survival of both.

Virtually all the now-known decorated tombs come from a relatively limited period, with a 'core' from the reign of Tutankhamen to that of Ramesses II (Malek 1985: 46–7). The tombs on the Saqqara plateau itself cluster in two known groups, one south of the Teti pyramid and the other above the Valley Building of the Unas pyramid complex (Malek 1981, 1985). Very few pre-Amarna Dynasty 18 tombs have yet been excavated at Saqqara, and it is likely that these would have been rock-cut tombs, somewhat similar to those at Thebes, cut into the face of the scarp of the Saqqara plateau, where known examples include the tomb of the late Dynasty 18 vizier Aper-El (Zivie 1988, 1990) and, remarkably, that of Nehesy, who may have been the official who led Hatshepsut's expedition to Punt (Zivie 1984; Malek 1989: 61 n. 3).

Temple-Tombs at Saqqara

The second type of New Kingdom tomb found at Saqqara is the so-called 'temple-tomb', which was built on top of the Saqqara plateau. The two locations which seem to have been particularly favoured were the already-full area of the Teti Pyramid Complex (perhaps because of a revival of the cult of King Teti as a local 'saint' during the New Kingdom; Martin 1989: 2) and an area to the south of the causeway of the Unas Pyramid Complex, which probably offered more space for the construction of large tombs. Although, in general form, these 'temple-tombs' may have had earlier variants (Malek 1985: 44 n. 2), the fully developed freestanding 'temple-tomb', with extensive relief decoration, was a phenomenon which only began late in Dynasty 18. As with the Archaic Period and the Old Kingdom, the presence of high state officials of the reign of Tutankhamen means contemporary high-status tombs, the most important being in the military domain the tomb of Generalissimo Horemheb and Chief Treasurer Maya.

One of the earliest of these 'temple-tombs' to be excavated is that of Apuia, who was 'Overseer of a Workshop' and 'Head of Goldworkers' during late Dynasty 18, which was discovered by Quibell in the Teti Pyramid Cemetery as part of his work at the site from 1912 to 1914 (Quibell and Hayter 1927). This tomb (Figure 14.2 A) has long provided a model for a 'standard plan' tomb of this period and place, although, as more recent discoveries of New Kingdom tombs have been made at Saqqara, it must be noted that the Apuia model (as described in Kitchen 1979) is really applicable only to medium-sized, regular tombs within the group, and that both much larger and much smaller tombs, each with their own morphological considerations, represent significant variants. Nonetheless, the tomb of Apuia provides a good starting point for understanding the nature of these New Kingdom Memphite tombs.

The basic structure of the tomb's superstructure is a rectangular court-yard, surrounded by an enclosure wall of mudbrick, orientated east–west. The courtyard is floored with limestone slabs. More elaborate versions of this type of tomb may be peristyle in form, i.e. it may have a colonnade running along one or more walls. The entrance doorway to the tomb is at the east, while the western end of the courtyard has a set of three 'cult rooms'; in larger tombs there is a separate 'stela room' behind the central cult room. The internal walls of the superstructure are lined with limestone slabs bearing relief decoration; in the case of Apuia these show activity in the workshops which Apuia supervised, including the production of royal statues, stelae and chariots (Figure 14.2 C). The tomb contained two freestanding stelae. One of these was round-topped, solar in content, and stood in the courtyard of the tomb. The second, which was more Osirian

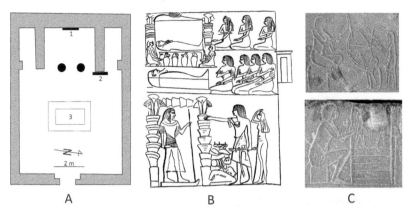

A   B   C

Figure 14.2   Plan and selected scenes from the tomb of Apuia at Saqqara. A: Plan
of the tomb, noting the position of 1 – stela in the central chapel with scenes
of Apuia worshipping Osiris, and of Apuia receiving offerings from his family;
2 – round-topped stela with a hymn to Ra-Horakhty and a scene of funeral before
the tomb; 3 – shaft (11 m deep) to the burial chamber. B: Scene of funeral on a
block from the tomb (adapted from Quibell and Hayter 1927: 34) – the upper
register includes depictions of the coffins and canopic chests, and the mourning
figures of his wife Nefertari and their daughters Iwy and Nefertiti, while the lower
register shows offerings being made to a statue of Apuia by his son Huy and an
unidentified female. C: Two depictions of craftsmen from the tomb of Apuia – the
lower carving a royal stela, and the upper a wheelwright working on a chariot

in its themes, was (probably) flat-topped and stood at the rear of the central
cult room. Some of these tombs were provided with small pyramid, usually
a separate, freestanding element. This basic plan could easily be expanded
for larger tombs. The tomb of Horemheb (Martin 1989) is the most
significant example of this: his tomb grew into a substantial structure
which included an entrance pylon, a colonnaded court, a sub-pylon
containing a statue room and flanking storerooms, a second colonnaded
court, and three cult rooms, including a central room surmounted by a
small pyramid (Figure 14.3).

Precursors to the temple-tomb?

Although it is tempting to regard the 'temple-tomb' (probably more
accurately described as a 'courtyard tomb' – Martin 1989: 12 n.6) at
Memphis as an architectural innovation in tomb design, particularly as
it seems radically different to contemporary Theban tombs, and obvious
existing models at Memphis – the *mastabas* of the Old Kingdom and the
Theban-like rock-cut tombs of Dynasty 18 – it would be wrong to think of

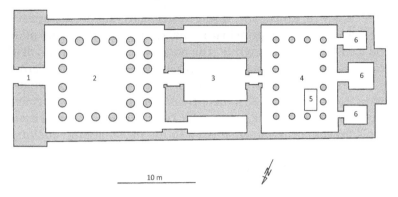

Figure 14.3 Plan of the tomb of Horemheb at Saqqara: 1 – entrance pylon;
2 – first court; 3 – statue room; 4 – second court; 5 – main shaft to burial
apartments; 6 – chapels, the central one of which was topped by a small pyramid

this form of tomb as being unprecedented. The 'temple-tomb' form –
essentially an open courtyard with a single or group of enclosed cult rooms,
and subterranean burial – lends itself well to a location where a flat plateau
surface, poor-quality rock, difficulty in obtaining large quantities of building stone, or any combination of these factors, prevails. It is a form of tomb
not dissimilar to the late Dynasty 17–early Dynasty 18 royal burials at
Thebes. In a private context, parallels can be found in the New Kingdom at
el-Amrah, near Abydos (Randall-MacIver and Mace 1902: Pls 23–6). The
difference at Memphis seems to be that these tombs were being produced
for the highest officials of the state and their entourages, so that the size,
complexity and level of decoration within these tombs are significantly
greater than at any other location in Egypt.

Decoration in Memphite tombs

An understanding of the decorative scheme of New Kingdom Memphite
tombs is hampered by the somewhat patchy survival of both tombs and
individual elements within those tombs when compared to those of the
Theban necropolis. Nevertheless, enough material has survived to indicate that the themes of tomb decoration at Memphis were not considerably different to those at Thebes, although with some local variation.
Relief is the mode of decoration, perhaps echoing the relief decoration of
some of the late Amenhotep III tombs at Thebes, such as Kheruef and
Ramose, although it has been noted that the relief carving in the later
Memphite tombs is 'altogether more mannered and adventurous' (Baines
1998: 304 n. 134).

In the tomb of Apuia, the reliefs which have survived suggest the predominance of the two principal Theban concerns: self-presentation in life and translation to the afterlife. The north wall of the courtyard depicts scenes of industry, including chariot-production, while the southern wall bears scenes of funeral. In the tomb of Horemheb, the comparatively extensive wall-space allowed a fuller treatment of the chosen themes. As Commander-in-Chief of the Army under Tutankhamen, Horemheb would want this aspect of his career stressed in the personal presentation elements of the tomb, but this needed to maintain a balance between what was decorous for a non-royal to claim in warfare – the same factors which restrained Sobek-khu in the Middle Kingdom, and the tombs of military men at Thebes. The solution to the problem was to show the prologue to battle (scenes of military camps, 'on campaign'), its aftermath (rows of foreign captives) and its personal relevance to the tomb-owner (the reward of Horemheb by the king). These scenes fill much of the (surviving) wall-space of both the first and second courts of Horemheb's tomb. But the second court also shows scenes of transition from this world to the next, particularly depictions of funerals, which naturally lead to scenes of Horemheb in the 'Fields of Iaru' which decorate the walls of the Offering Chapel. Within a generally shared New Kingdom background of expectations of an afterlife, and the role of the funeral in ensuring a smooth transition to that afterlife, there are distinctive regional variations at Saqqara. This is most extensively shown in Horemheb's tomb, which has notable scenes of mourning, the erection of booths for the funeral, and the 'smashing of the red pots'. Other notable, specifically Memphite themes include depictions of the tomb-owner holding up a *djed*-pillar, while a small number of Memphite tombs of the Ramesside period have king-lists on their walls. This latter feature is more usually associated with royal temples (van Dijk 1988: 44), and may be an indication of the way in which Ramesside tombs were increasingly regarded as mini-temples, with royal temples, to some degree, being regarded as appropriate models.

Ramesside tombs at Saqqara

Ramesside tombs at Memphis are capable of much greater variation in form than the late Dynasty 18 versions. They are usually somewhat larger (cf. the tomb of Tia and Tia, from the reign of Ramesses II – Martin et al. 1997) and more individual than the earlier versions, sometimes showing an improvisation in form forced upon them by the constraints of location. A good example of this is the tomb of Mose, who lived during the reign of Ramesses II, in the Teti Pyramid Cemetery. Although possessing the requisite courtyards and offering rooms, it seems as though restrictions on space in this part of the cemetery forced an unusual L-shaped plan on the tomb (Gaballa 1977; Malek 1981). One of the most striking features of these tombs is the presence of a pyramid within the tomb complex. The inclusion of this architectural element represents a return to a notable feature of the Memphite skyline, but in a private rather than royal context. In a sense the pyramid should not be considered surprising because we have already seen it used as a solar symbol in Theban tombs of the New Kingdom, but the size of the pyramids at Saqqara is perhaps notable. The Dynasty 18 practice of constructing small mudbrick pyramids on top of tomb superstructures, as shown on depictions of tombs at both Thebes and Memphis, was replaced in the Ramesside period, at least for elite tombs, with more substantial pyramids built of limestone masonry which were too large and heavy for roofs and so became a separate element at the rear of the tombs – the pyramid of the tomb of Tia and Tia (sister and brother-in-law of Ramesses II) was, including its base, *c*.7 m tall (Martin et al. 1997: 6). A concern with a solar afterlife may also be seen in the decoration of the underground rooms of the larger Saqqara tombs, where there is a preference for monochrome yellow decoration, probably to show the figures depicted as bathed in the golden light of the sun, a feature also seen in underground rooms of some contemporary tombs at Thebes (e.g. in the Deir el-Medina tomb of Nakhtamen – Bruyère 1926).

Although the evidence is not extensive enough to come to any firm conclusions, Malek (1985: 50) suggests that tombs in the Memphite necropolis during the New Kingdom can be classed as large 'nucleus' or smaller 'subsidiary' tombs and that the arrangement of the smaller tombs in relation to the larger tombs, at least in the Teti Pyramid Cemetery, may be based on groupings by profession. Susidiarity could take other forms. The tomb of Paser (Martin 1985), an 'Overseer of Builders' during the reign of Ramesses II, falls within the class of 'standard type' Memphite New Kingdom tomb. Like that of Apuia, it contained the two variants of stelae. Built against the southern wall of Paser's tomb is the tiny chapel of Raia (Martin 1985), a Singer in the Temple of Ptah. This is an excellent example of the 'small chapel' category, consisting of a simple, open-fronted room, with two papyriform columns and walls lined with limestone. The back wall is an essential concentration of some of the most important themes in tomb decoration compressed onto a single panel of three registers: Raia the singer performing before the god; Raia in a shrine-coffin being dragged by cattle to the tomb; Raia the mummy supported by Anubis during the funeral ceremony. The poorly preserved side walls show Raia receiving offerings and, probably, in the presence of Osiris. A different case of subsidiarity is that of Iurudef (Raven 1991), servant of Tia and Tia, who, as well as appearing in scenes of the walls of the tomb of his masters, had a small chapel in the corner of the first court of their tomb. He was also allowed to bury his family in tomb shafts within the temple-tomb; these shafts contained an astonishing *c.*70 individual interments, about half in wooden coffins, jammed into a small group of chambers which open off the shafts. Perhaps only 17 of the bodies recovered belong to Iurudef's family as the tomb was re-used at the end of the New Kingdom/Third Intermediate Period.

Post-Amarna Tombs at Thebes and Elsewhere

With the highest state officials buried at Memphis (and then Pi-Ramesse?) in the post-Amarna Period, Thebes became, oddly, something of a second-class elite cemetery. Nevertheless, it, too, felt the effects of the post-Amarna changes, particularly in the development of features which would become more standard in Ramesside tombs there. It has been argued (Strudwick 1994) that the post-Amarna Period to the reign of Seti I was one of transition from 'Dynasty 18' to 'Ramesside' tomb types, including the continued use of some features which had begun to appear in the reign of Amenhotep III. Perhaps the most important example of this transitional type is TT41, belonging to the multi-titled official Amenemope (Assmann 1991).

One remarkable tomb of the immediate post-Amarna Period comes from Sohag in Upper Egypt, where the 'Fan-Bearer on the Right of the King' and 'Overseer of Tutors' was the owner of an impressive rock-cut tomb which had a broad façade, a pillared portico, a columned inner hall and a transverse hall leading to a small central shrine and two set of burial apartments (Ockinga 1997). The tomb is in poor condition, but the walls of the portico have survived well enough to reveal a scene of chariot-procession, in strikingly Amarna style, by Tutankhamen. The inner hall is in rather worse condition, but it is possible to detect scenes of funeral, which seem to owe rather more to depictions of contemporary Memphite funerals, rather than Theban ones.

The tombs of Egyptian imperial administrators in Nubia are based on those from Egypt itself, so that the late Dynasty 18 'Scribe of the Treasury and Overseer of Foreign Lands' Siamen and his wife Weren were buried at the administrative centre of Tombos, on the third cataract of the Nile, in a tomb with a mudbrick courtyard-and-pyramid superstructure which would not have looked out of place at Saqqara (Smith 2003: 137–43). This style of tomb was also emulated by some Egyptianized Nubian elites of the New Kingdom (Simpson 1963).

CHAPTER 15

Samut and the Ramesside Private Tomb

Standard Tombs of the Ramesside Period

For whatever reason – perhaps stimulated by the disruption of the Amarna Period (Strudwick 1994: 330), perhaps as a result of the rise in 'personal piety' for which the Ramesside period is well known (Frood 2007: 16–17) – private tombs of the Ramesside Period, Dynasties 19 and 20, are significantly different from those of Dynasty 18. This difference is most noticeable at Thebes, where there is a shift away from the traditional T-shaped private tomb, with its strong emphasis on presenting the detail of personal autobiography in brightly coloured scenes. The general conception of the tomb underwent an important change which can perhaps be summarized by noting that the most significant difference in conceptual terms between tombs of Dynasty 18 (and indeed earlier), on one hand, and those of the Ramesside Period, on the other, is that the former are primarily 'houses of the dead' while the latter are first and foremost 'private mortuary temples' (Kampp-Seyfried 2003: 10). The depiction of the tomb-owner acting in life, emphasizing his social position and status in relation to the king, was no longer a dominant image in the tomb chapel. Instead there was a much greater emphasis on religious themes and depictions of the gods.

Expectations for the afterlife are fully catered for in scenes showing the funeral and the successful attainment of an Osirian afterlife – themes which would not be out of place in Dynasty 18 tombs – but a new element is introduced in the enhanced emphasis on the possibilities of a solar afterlife. The canon of royal expectations, as expressed in the now-ancient Pyramid Texts and in contemporary royal tombs, slips even further into this sphere.

Ancient Egyptian Tombs: The Culture of Life and Death   By Steven Snape
© 2011 Steven Snape

This new element is expressed in three ways: architectural elements (small pyramids/funerary cones/stelophorous statues with solar hymns), graphic elements (scenes of the deceased shown with the solar barque crossing the sky and images of the deceased bathed in golden light) and textual elements (e.g. hymns to the sun).

The architecture of Ramesside private tombs

Before the Ramesside Period the dominating design feature in private tombs might be said to be 'axiality' (Assmann 2003: 47). The different elements of a tomb, the rooms which have their specific functions, are arranged on a horizontal axis, theoretically moving from the east to the west. In, for example, a Dynasty 18 private tomb at Thebes, a progress through the tomb involved moving from the entrance through the transverse hall, with its concern with the realm of the living tomb-owner, through the 'long hall', with its concern with the funeral and transition from one state to another, to the shrine, where the statue awaited offerings. This format was broadly reflected in earlier tombs, which were concerned with the dichotomy of the inner and outer, the more public and the more private, the coming closer to the point of interaction between the Living and the Dead, this world and the afterlife. Although the Burial Chamber tended to be underground, and therefore at a physically lower level than the Offering Chapel, the tomb basically existed on a single horizontal plane – there seems little significance in whether scenes were depicted at the top or at the bottom of tomb walls. This is, of course, something of a simplification, but one which holds good if we compare it to the concern with differentiated vertical zoning in Ramesside tombs. This vertical zoning has two principal aspects: the architecture of the tomb and its internal decoration.

As far as the former is concerned, the governing architectural template was what Seyfried (1987) has termed the '*Drei-Ebenen-Grab*' or 'Tomb of Three Levels'. The central level (B on Figure 16.2) was based on a traditional Theban T-shaped tomb, but with the transverse hall sometimes expanded to form an enclosed court, a development which had already taken place in the reign of Amenhotep III and which was also part of the design scheme of private tombs at Amarna. The upper level (A on Figure 16.2) was the superstructure built above the main rock-cut chapel. The most striking element here was a small pyramid, whose presence can be reconstructed from depictions of the exterior of these tombs within the tombs themselves. These pyramids are standard on Ramesside examples of tomb-illustration, which make up 20 of the 24 examples cited by Davies (1938) in her discussion of this material (see also Seyfried 1987: 222–8). The lower level (C on Figure 16.2) consisted of the subterranean rooms of the tomb, including the Burial

Chamber and the sloping passage which led to it. These three levels are specifically identified with particular aspects of the afterlife of the tomb-owner. The upper level is clearly orientated towards a solar afterlife. The lower level, which is much more accessible and decorated than in a Dynasty 18 tomb, is associated with an Osirian afterlife, although in some examples scenes in the Burial Chamber which depict the deceased painted in yellow, bathed in the light of the sun, also suggest a solar orientation. There is nothing particularly new in these ideas, since solar and Osirian expectations of an afterlife have a long history, even for private individuals, and the reorganization of space within the tomb to express such concerns more appropriately hardly seems radical, although it does give a particular appearance to the Ramesside private tomb, certainly at Thebes.

The most significant shift in emphasis is in that part of the tomb which, architecturally, appears to have changed the least: the middle level. In fact this part of the tomb indicates an important change in function and especially in the role of painted wall-scenes. In marked contrast to the practice in Dynasty 18, Ramesside tombs at Thebes show little interest in depicting and describing the range of activities which might be said to make up the public identity of the tomb-owner; instead the decoration is primarily concerned with the tomb-owner worshipping the gods. It may be that the desire for 'personal presentation' found other outlets, particularly in the use of statues bearing autobiographical texts placed in temples (Frood 2007: 6–7, and *passim* for examples). The desire to be close to the gods, which appeared as a minor concern in pre-Ramesside tombs and was best expressed in material (such as the Coffin Texts and Books of the Dead) placed within the hidden Burial Chamber, was now given full expression on the walls of the accessible parts of the tomb. As Assmann (2003: 49) has noted, the wall-space of Ramesside tombs is divided vertically into an upper and lower register. This is unlike the organization of space on the walls of Dynasty 18 (and, of course, even earlier) tombs, which also use horizontal registers, but primarily as a means of deploying the scenes in horizontal strips. In Ramesside tombs, by contrast, the bipartition of the wall-space is determined by a thematic distinction: the lower sections are concerned with the funerary cult and well-being of the tomb-owner, including scenes of funeral (Barthelmess 1992), but the upper registers are concerned with the tomb-owner worshipping the gods.

The Ramesside Afterlife

The accretion of different possibilities for the afterlife which had accumulated up to the Ramesside Period is well demonstrated by a passage from a model letter, probably designed for the training of scribes, written in the Memphite area, during the reign of Ramesses II. In Papyrus Anastasi I the writer expresses good wishes for the well-being of the recipient of the papyrus, including a list of what would make up an ideal afterlife:

> May you spend lifetime with your gods, pleased with you without displaying anger.
>
> May your reward be received after old age.
>
> May you be salved with fine-quality unguents like the blessed ones.
>
> May you enter your tomb of the necropolis and mingle with the excellent *Ba*s.
>
> May you be judged among them and be declared righteous in Busiris before Wennefer and be well established in Abydos before Shu-Onuris.
>
> May you cross over to the district of Peqer in the god's retinue and cross the divine region in the retinue of Sokar.
>
> May you join the crew of the Neshmet barque without being turned away.
>
> May you see the sun in the sky when it initiates the year.
>
> May Anubis unite for you your head to your bones.
>
> May you emerge from the hidden region without being destroyed.
>
> May you observe the sun's glow in the netherworld when it passes you by.
>
> May the primordial waters overflow your domain, immerse your path and irrigate to a depth of seven cubits near your tomb.
>
> May you sit down at the river's edge at your moment of rest and wash your face and hands.
>
> May you receive offerings.
>
> May your nose inhale the breezes and your throat breathe freely.
>
> May Tayet clothe [you].
>
> May Neper give you bread and Hathor give you beer.
>
> May you suck from the udder of Sekhayet-Hor.
>
> May fine-quality unguents be opened for you.
>
> . . .
>
> May your *shabti*-figure be accepted when it comes over carrying sand from east to west.
>
> May you grasp . . . of your sycamore goddess and she lubricate your throat.
>
> May you drive [your opponents] away.
>
> . . .
>
> May you be triumphant in the sky, a shining one.
>
> May you descend to the slaughterhouse(?) without being annihilated.
>
> May you transform yourself into whatever you wish, like the phoenix, with each of your forms being that of a god, just as you desire.
>
> (Translation based on that of Wente 1990: 100–1)

The Tomb as Temple: Samut and Djehutyemheb

Samut and Mut

A good example of the way in which a Ramesside tomb became a place where the tomb-owner could worship the gods is the tomb of Samut (also known as Kyky), the 'Counter of the Cattle of Amen' at Thebes during the reign of Ramesses II. His tomb (TT409; Abdel-Qader 1966; Frood 2007, 84–91; Negm 1997) is located in the Asasif cemeteries, which were used during the reign of Amenhotep III and later. The entrance to the tomb is flanked by two round-topped stelae, cut into the rock, with a scene and hymn of Samut worshipping the solar deity Ra-Horakhty and his daughter the goddess Maat. The interior of the tomb consists of two small chambers which, at first sight, seem to be loosely modelled on the 'transverse hall' and 'long hall' format (Figure 15.1). However, the broader, shallower outer room does not contain scenes of Samut engaged in his quotidian duties, apart from a rather damaged scene which seems to show him receiving a report concerning agricultural produce. Rather, it is filled with scenes which in Dynasty 18 had featured in the long hall: elements of the funeral, the opening of the mouth and the weighing of the heart, designed to gain admission to the Osirian afterlife. The second chamber is in a poor condition, but the scenes here seem to show Samut in the presence of

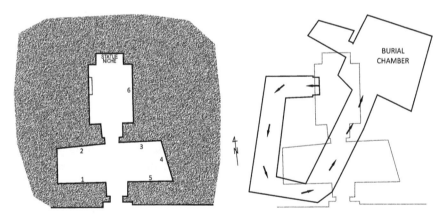

Figure 15.1 Plan of the superstructure and of the winding passage to the Burial Chamber in the tomb of Samut at Thebes. Surviving scenes/texts in the (damaged) superstructure refer to Samut: 1– Adoring Mut; 2 – Adoring Amen-Re and Ptah-Sokar; 3 – Funeral and Judgement; 4 – Adoring Hathor and Funeral; 5 – Adoring Anubis and Hathor; 6 – Adoring Ra-Horakhty (no scale on the original plan in Abdel-Qader 1966)

various deities: solar, Osirian and Theban. The most striking element of the tomb is a pair of long texts in the first chamber detailing Samut's personal devotion to the goddess Mut. The text is remarkable, beginning as a third-person biography and morphing into a first-person autobiography through the device of being a speech of the third person, seeing the life of Samut solely in terms of his relationship with the goddess:

> There was a man of Southern Heliopolis (i.e. Thebes), a real scribe in Thebes; Samut was his name by his mother, called Kyky, justified.
>
> He sought within himself in order to find a protector for himself. He found Mut at the head of the gods . . . a lifetime of life and breath under her control, and all that happens at her command. So he said: Look, I now give to her all my property and all that I have brought into being, because I know she is effective on my behalf, and she is uniquely excellent.
>
> I entered into her power in relation to my property, in exchange for the breath of life. No-one of my family shall divide it, because it belongs to her *ka* as offerings.
>
> I do not make a protector for myself among men. I [do not attach] myself to the powerful, nor even my son, since I found that she [will provide for the] funeral. Burial is in your hand, unique one . . . that I may be assembled as an effective mummy (*s3ḫ*), after life has proceeded.
>
> . . . As for the one who makes Mut as a protector, evil cannot assail him. He will be protected every day until he unites with the necropolis. (Translations based on Frood 2007: 85–7; Negm 1997: 40–2)

Part of Samut's devotion to the goddess – and particularly his apparent bequeathing of his property to her – may have something to do with the fact that he seems to be childless, but, in any case, the tomb itself has become part of her domain.

Djehutyemheb and Hathor

This reliance on a specific deity both for individual identification in one's lifetime, and as a intermediary for the afterlife, so evident in the tomb of Samut, can also be seen in the tomb of Djehutyemheb, 'Overseer of Fieldworkers of the Domain of Amen'. This tomb (TT194; Frood 2007: 91–4; Seyfried 1995), which, like that of Samut, dates to the reign of Ramesses II, is in the Asasif, and is cut into the courtyard of an earlier Dynasty 18 tomb, in this case the large and important tomb of the Royal Steward Kheruef. The best-preserved part of this small tomb is a transverse hall, which has scenes showing the tomb-owner and his family offering to Amen-Ra-Horakhty, Ra-Horakhty, Sokar and Nefertem, but also, more unusually, a series of rock-cut stelae. These take the form of contemporary two-register stelae: the upper register showing a deity to whom the stela is dedicated; the lower register with a short prayer/hymn and a kneeling figure of the worshipping dedicator of the stela, who is, in the case of those from the tomb of Djehutyemheb, the tomb-owner himself. The deities honoured here are specifically Theban and/or funerary: Amenhotep I, Ahmose-Nefertari, the Theban triad (Amen-Re, Mut, Khonsu), the Abydene triad (Osiris, Isis, Horus) or Hathor (an important local funerary goddess at Thebes). It is the latter goddess who is given particular prominence since the less well-preserved inner hall carries an extensive hymn to Hathor on the entrance to the Burial Chamber. Texts from the tomb (Frood 2007: 91–4; Seyfried 1995: 69–73) include a speech by Djehutyemheb to Hathor, noting that she had decreed the location of his tomb, seemingly in a dream:

> I have come before you, O lady of the Two Lands, Hathor great of love . . . I kiss the ground for your *ka*.
>
> I was your true servant, loyal to your command. I did not spurn the words of your mouth, I was not ignorant of your teaching. I was upon the path which you yourself set, upon the road which you made.
>
> You are the one who foretold my tomb in the beginning, as it was ordained to be. That which you said happened, your plan is [established, sanctified] is the place for my body.

Hathor's reply, which is also given in the tomb, indicates that she intends to intercede on Djehutyemheb's behalf with the gods of the afterlife, in the process giving an indication of the varied expectations of an afterlife among the gods which were expected by a Ramesside official:

> I have made a shrine for your mummy, and I have sanctified a place for your body. I will announce you to the great god (i.e. Osiris) and he will say to you 'Welcome'.
>
> I will commend you to Horakhty that he may place you among his adorers. I will hand you over to the lord of Heliopolis (i.e. Ra) that he may cause your offerings to endure.
>
> I will hand you over to Sokar and his *henu*-barque that you may enter the *shetayt*-shrine.
>
> I will hand you over to Nefertem that you may go around Memphis with him. I will commend you to the one perfect of face (i.e. Ptah).

Offerings and Offering-Systems in the New Kingdom

The text in the tomb of Samut for the benefit of the goddess Mut, although a remarkable example, is by no means the only example of a private endowment to a temple in the New Kingdom. Throughout the New Kingdom, wealthy private individuals found it useful to make such endowments, particularly to royal 'Mansions of Millions of Years' memorial temples, because it was a means of ensuring benefits for their own mortuary establishment (Haring 1997: 142–55). In this respect Senenmut of Dynasty 18 seems to have been especially well provided for, as described on a stela erected at Karnak describing a series of endowments (Dorman 1988: 29–31; Haring 1997: 143–4), including gifts of land and slaves to both the Amen temple at Karnak and Hatshepsut's Deir el-Bahri temple, two buildings whose construction and embellishment were significant achievements by Senenmut for Hatshepsut. The income from these endowments, as agricultural production or productive capacity, was primarily used for offerings at the two major temples, but a proportion of those offerings would be directed for the benefit of Senenmut himself: the Karnak bequest would be offered to one or several of the statues for which Senenmut is famous, placed within the Karnak temple, while the Deir el-Bahri offerings would, presumably, be directed to his Sheikh abd el-Qurna tomb.

This is interesting for two major reasons. The first is that it represents the expansion of the appropriate agencies by which the deceased could receive offerings, not just at his/her tomb but also through his/her statues in locations other than the tomb. Although this possibility has been noted for earlier periods (especially the example of Djefai-Hapi at Asyut in the Middle Kingdom – see Chapter 10), it seems to have become much more commonplace in the Ramesside Period. The second reason is that this system provides an alternative to that involving private *ka*-priests and was, presumably, considered more reliable because it was linked to a cult established by the king, indeed one vital to the king – his/her own memorial temple and main temple for Amen. However, some level of reliance on family remains because the third endowment by Senenmut mentioned on the Karnak stela seems to be a bequest of gardens to his siblings in return for their offerings of bread, flowers and water at his tomb.

An equally well-known endowment text (Haring 1997: 142; Morkot 1990), from the reign of Amenhotep III, concerns the gifting of resources to the Ptah Temple at Memphis in return for the regular provision of offerings to a statue of the king, the reversion of which would be presented to the (unknown) Memphite tomb of the donor, the Chief Steward Amenhotep. The presentation at the tomb was to be carried out by a lector-priest and a *wab*-priest (presumably the ultimate beneficiaries of the offerings), and included farinaceous foodstuffs produced from 80 litres of grain per day. The donation which had secured this regular income was principally made up of 118 hectares of land, but also included slaves and 2,000 pigs.

Anhurmose at Mashayikh:
Ramesside Tombs in the Provinces

Although they tend to be less well preserved than their Theban counter-parts, the small number of examples of elite Ramesside tombs which have survived from other parts of Upper and Middle Egypt show similar ten-dencies in their decoration and textual content (Hofmann 2004: 110–15). Some of them were produced by remodelling Middle Kingdom tombs, including the main tomb associated with the 'Two Brothers' burial at Rifeh (see Chapter 10 above, p. 159; David 2007: 13; Petrie 1907: Pls 29–30). A particularly interesting group of comparative tombs of the Ramesside period has survived at the site of Mashayikh near Naga ed-Der in Upper Egypt (Ockinga and al-Masri 1988–90). The most important tomb of this group is the rock-cut tomb of Anhurmose, who had a varied career during the reigns of Ramesses II and Merenptah, as he tells us in the longest autobiographical text to survive in a Ramesside tomb (Frood 2007: 107–16), particularly stressing his relationship with the god Shu. Internally the tomb has two major chambers, the first a typical pillared hall, and although the wall-scenes within the tomb are not divided vertically into two thematic zones, as in classic Theban tombs, the themes of worshipping gods by the tomb-owner and the funeral predominate. The question of the external appearance of the Mashayikh tombs is an interesting one. Within the tomb of Anhurmose (Ockinga and al-Masri 1988–90 (Vol. I): Pl. 25) and the nearby tomb of Imiseba (Ockinga and al-Masri 1988–90 (Vol. II): Pl. 61) the scenes of funeral depict the exterior of each tomb in classic Theban style with a small pyramid as the upper level of the tomb. While there is enough space for this to have been possible in the case of Anhurmose (Ockinga and al-Masri 1988: 4), it is unlikely that the overlying slope would have allowed such an arrangement for the tomb of Imiseba (Ockinga and al-Masri 1988–90 (Vol. II): 33), calling into question the reliance which can be put in every case on the depictions of the tomb within the tomb actually looking like the tomb.

The Ramesside Coffin

Just as the New Kingdom saw important changes in the form and decora-tion of the tomb, so too did it see significant shifts in coffin design. In the New Kingdom the anthropoid form came to dominate coffin typology, and it is easy to see why. In the Middle Kingdom the box-and-anthropoid pair of coffins provided an overlapping set of containers, with the box coffins related to the tomb itself in decorative content and, in a basic way, shape, while the anthropoid form was obviously based on the body. It was a small step to think of the box coffin as the tomb and the anthropoid coffin as the body. In the Ramesside period the word which was most commonly used to refer to the anthropoid coffin, *wt*, probably meant something like 'embalmed/preserved/wrapped body', and so the anthropoid coffin 'was meant to function as the external embalmed body of the deceased' (Cooney 2007a: 19). This can be seen in the way in which the anthropoid coffins are shown in Books of the Dead, stood upright in front of the tomb.

This coffin–body identification appears in other contexts as well. In a letter on a limestone ostracon, now in the Louvre, the well-known Scribe of the Tomb from Deir el-Medina, Butehamen, addresses his dead wife, Ikhtay, or rather her coffin: 'O noble chest of the Osiris, the Chantress of Amen, Ikhtay, who rests under you. Listen to me and send the message and say to her – since you are close to her – "How are you doing? How are you?"' (Frandsen 1992: 33; Wente 1990: 217–19). This unusual variant of a 'letter to the dead' clearly views the coffin itself as an active intermediary to whom communications to its owner could be addressed.

CHAPTER 16

Sennedjem

Building and Buying at Deir el-Medina

ⵕⵕⵕⵕ

The Servants in the Place of Truth

Arguably – although in the opinion of the present author there is little real argument – the community of the ancient world about which we know the most is the village of Deir el-Medina (Bierbrier 1982; Černý 1973; Valbelle 1985). For almost all of the New Kingdom – a period of nearly 500 years – the village (Figure 16.1) existed to serve one purpose: to house the specialized workers who would bring into being the royal tomb in the Valley of the Kings. The (almost) complete continuity of the use of the physically restricted Valley of the Kings for royal burial in Dynasties 18–20 meant that the workers for each succeeding royal tomb did not need to live anywhere other than the same place as their predecessors and, since skilled craftsmen were needed rather than large gangs of unskilled muscle, a fairly limited labour force was required. It was convenient to pass on those skills in the conventional Egyptian fashion – from father to son – and so Deir el-Medina developed into a settlement like no other; one which was founded in an otherwise unattractive location in the Theban hills and which continued to exist only through royal patronage. The villagers of Deir el-Medina were unlike the majority of the population of Egypt in two other important respects. Firstly, and unlike any other group outside the ruling elite of New Kingdom Egypt, they could enjoy the benefit of well-constructed, well-equipped and well-decorated tombs because their work on the royal burial equipped them with the skills (and, one suspects, some of the raw materials) to create such tombs for themselves. Secondly, again

---

Ancient Egyptian Tombs: The Culture of Life and Death   By Steven Snape
© 2011 Steven Snape

Figure 16.1 The site of Deir el-Medina, with the hill of Qurnet Murai immediately behind it

because of the nature of their employment, the villagers possessed a very high level of literacy, something which was also unusual outside the ruling elite. The legacy of that literacy is an archive of documents produced by the villagers, mostly from the Ramesside Period and mostly written in ink on convenient flakes of white limestone – ostraca – which is unique in the ancient world. Among a kaleidoscope of daily concerns which populate these documents, the topic of tombs and provision for the afterlife makes an inevitable appearance, and through these ostraca it is possible to gain insights which are not available from any other sets of evidence.

Aping the Rich? Tombs at Deir el-Medina

Although we know much less about the village in Dynasty 18 than we do in the Ramesside Period, the location of the cemetery of this earlier period is well known, on the slopes of the Qurnet Murai hill, to the east of the village, and therefore referred to as the Eastern Cemetery (Valbelle 1985: 6–10). This cemetery is literally stratified by age, with the bodies of the very young on its lower slopes and adults higher up. If these tombs had superstructures, none has survived, but the undecorated underground Burial Chambers have preserved enough evidence to draw some broad conclusions regarding the nature of these burials. Apart from the coffins, the most striking aspect of the tombs' contents is the quantity of furniture buried with the deceased, most of which was found bearing the use and wear marks of objects employed in everyday life. Another aspect of the equipment from these burials is the lack of labelling indicating ownership, something which stands in marked contrast to Ramesside practice. Indeed the contents of the Dynasty 18 tombs, with their emphasis on objects from daily existence, reflect the concerns present on the tomb-scenes from elite tombs of the same period with their 'everyday life' scenes, which again contrast with those from the Ramesside Period. However, it must be admitted that, since the number of intact tombs from this period at Deir el-Medina is small, it is perhaps dangerous to draw too broad a set of conclusions from the surviving evidence.

A further level of social stratification in Dynasty 18 Deir el-Medina seems to be that community leaders of the period built their tombs in the Western Cemetery, which is effectively another slope of the Theban mountain leading towards the high peak of the Qurn. Here three intact or near-intact tombs have been excavated, the most famous being that of Kha, Chief of Works at the royal tomb during the reigns of Amenhotep II–Amenhotep III, who was buried with his wife Meryt. However, the most extensive use of the Western Cemetery took place during the Ramesside Period; the most important tomb of this period is that of Sennedjem, who was buried in a well-decorated (and unrobbed) tomb (TT1; Figure 16.2) along with his wife Iy-Nofret, his sons and daughter-in-law Khons and Tamaket, and Isis, the daughter-in-law of Khons.

A tomb of one's own?

Although the tombs at Deir el-Medina give the impression of being quite literally part of the landscape and the long-standing family tombs of generations of villagers, the reality is not quite so straightforward. Deir el-Medina was a 'real' village in the sense of being a community composed of multi-generational families, but the privilege of both work and residence was in the gift of the state, and those who did not contribute to the project of building the royal tomb – as workers, their immediate support or their potential trainee successors – were not welcome. It was also the case that expansions in royal ambition might be matched by necessary expansions in the workforce required to achieve that ambition; the village went through several episodes of an increase in the workforce which meant that new residents required both houses and tombs. Indeed, one of the benefits of becoming a workman at Deir el-Medina was the assignment of a standard set of buildings, including a house, a hut close to the Valley of the Kings,

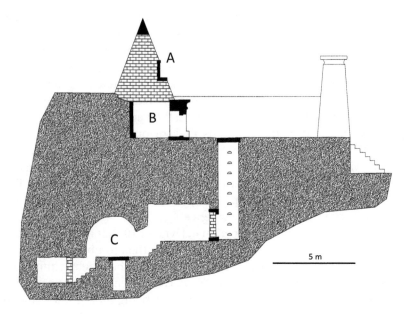

Figure 16.2   Cross-section of the tomb of Sennedjem at Deir el-Medina, Thebes (ignoring a number of important constructional features, for which see Bruyère 1959: Pl. 7; el-Naggar 1999: Pl. 315). Stone elements are shown in solid black and brick elements with rectangular fill. The pylon entrance is reconstructed. A – 'Upper Level' including mudbrick pyramid; B – 'Central Level' chapel and court; C – 'Lower Level' burial chamber(s)

a tomb (ꜥḥꜥt) and a structure called a ḫnw. This latter construction seems to have been primarily a place where the Living could gather, including the courtyard associated with the tomb (McDowell 1990: 123), but also with a wider range of roles (Bomann 1991: 119–21). The distribution of buildings at Deir el-Medina was official business, in the gift of the state, and, in order to accommodate new residents, included the re-use of tombs regarded as redundant. A number of texts reflect this re-commissioning of existing tombs for new owners (McDowell 1990: 125). For instance, an ostracon in Madrid, dated to Year 4 of an unnamed Ramesside king, records the 'inspection of the tomb (ꜥḥꜥt) of the guard Amenemope' by three captains – senior figures in the village. The purpose of this inspection was to facilitate it being handed over to the workman Menna. As part of this inspection an inventory was made of 'everything that was in it', but, frustratingly, the ostracon breaks off after the first item, a *wt*-coffin (McDowell 1999: 71–2; Zonhoven 1979: 98 n. 80).

The single most fascinating and informative set of documents about the way in which a tomb could change in its ownership comes from an ostracon dating to the reign of Ramesses III in the British Museum (BM 5624) and two related documents (Papyrus Berlin 10496 and Ostracon Florence 2621 – Blackman 1926; McDowell 1990: 130–2; 1999: 68–9). The author of this substantial text is Amenemope, who begins this complicated legal narrative by providing some background information in referring to the aftermath of the Amarna Period when the Deir el-Medina gang was expanded by Horemheb, an act which had profound implications for old and new residents of the village alike:

> Year 7 of King Djeserkheperre Horemheb (was) the date that Khay, my ancestor, was enrolled in the necropolis (gang). The mayor (?) of Thebes Djehutymose divided up the properties in the necropolis for the gang of Pharaoh. By an order he gave the tomb of Amen(mose) to Khay, my ancestor. Hel, my ancestress, was his lineal descendant. He had no male heirs and his property became abandoned.

Over 140 years later, Amenemope, in need of a tomb, and with no desire to build one from scratch, approached the oracle of King Amenhotep I. The oracle (a statue of the god which could communicate in some way its response to questions asked) gave Amenemope the answer which he had, presumably, been hoping for:

> Now, later, in Year 21, second month of summer, day 1, I stood before Amenhotep, saying to him, 'Direct (me) to a tomb among the ancestors.' By a writing he gave to me the tomb of Khay and I began to work in it.

Having had the ownership of the tomb of his ancestor Khay affirmed by the god's oracle, all seemed well for Amenemope, and he set about adapting the old tomb for his own use. But, a year later, a problem arose:

> Now, later, I was building and the workman Khaemnun was working in his tomb. In the first month of summer, day 6 he had a day off and found the opening in it, and descended into it with the w'rt-officer Neferhotep while I was not there.
>
> Now, later, in the first month of summer, day 7, the chief workman Khonsu was found sitting and drinking. Afterwards I was standing with Hori, son of Huynefer, and the workman Bakenwerel. I did not know where the opening of my tomb was. The scribe Amennakht found the opening (?) saying, 'Come down! See the place which opens into the tomb of Khaemnun!'

It seems as though Khaemnun, while working on his tomb, had broken through into the adjacent tomb of Amenemope.

Frustratingly, and as with so many of these documents, the narrative breaks off at the point when the reader has become tantalizingly engrossed with the subject matter and characters involved.

Tomb re-use and additions to the decoration

Tombs could be added to in a number of ways, including what might be thought of as the least likely change: adjustments to the decoration of the Burial Chamber. The interment of later 'residents' into family tombs might prompt a re-design, as was the case in the tomb of Khabekhnet, a son of Sennedjem, at Deir el-Medina, but one who owned his own tomb. Khabekhnet's tomb was designed and built during the reign of Ramesses II, although its Burial Chamber bears a text referring to later inhabitants of the tomb. Of this list the Foreman Nekhemmut and his father Khonsu were descendants of Khabekhnet; the names of a wider group of workmen also appear whose relationship to the Khabekhnet family is not known (Eyre 1984: 200–1).

A tomb inspection at Deir el-Medina

As one would expect, the villagers were sensitive to any unofficial disturbance of their tombs, and their inspection seems to have been the occasion for committees of village notables to be formed, not least because of the necessity of maintaining an appropriate degree of distance from the sometimes valuable tomb property involved. Such an inspection took place in Year 25 of Ramesses III when a commission composed of 'The chief workman Khonsu, the chief workman Khew, the police inspector Neferhotep, the police inspector Khaemope, the guard Penmennefer, Khaemnun, Userhat, Aanakht, Irsu, Huynefer, Neferher and the scribe Amennakht' carried out the inspection of a 'ruined tomb', described as being 'opposite the burial place of Amennakht (son of) Ipuy'. A report on the inspection was recorded on a large potsherd which is now in Vienna, and on a separately identified fragment from the beginning of the text (McDowell 1999: 69–71; Zonhoven 1979). It is curious that the name of the owner of the tomb is not mentioned in this report since one would guess that his or (less likely) her name would appear on at least some of the tomb's extensive contents, which are listed as:

One coffin (*wt*) of god's stone.
One sarcophagus (*krst*) with a linen pall (?).
One coffin (*wt*) with a linen pall (?).
One ebony folding stool with duck's heads – repaired.

Two couches.

One footstool of papyrus.

Three head-rests.

One *irks*-basket, filled with old rags.

Two pairs of sandals.

One palette.

One metal *gȝy*-bowl.

One leather water skin.

One wooden *dbw*-box containing one knife, one (hair?)-pin, one metal dish, one libation vessel, one razor-case, one rotating razor, and one scraping razor.

Granite vessels: five *mnt*-vessels.

One metal dish.

One *t̠(ȝ)b*-vessel.

One staff.

One food basket (with) bread.

One wooden *k̠rn*.

One alabaster *k(ȝ)b*-vessel.

Two wooden *nši*-containers for medicine.

One wooden *dbw*-box containing one faience amulet, one alabaster *k(ȝ)b*-vessel, one *hnw*-vessel for unguent, ten . . .

One wooden *dbw*-box containing one alabaster *k(ȝ)b*-vessel, one comb, one eye tweezer, one alabaster *nmst*-vessel, one *h̠ʿr*, and two pieces of scenting material.

The conclusion of the inspection seems to be contained in the first line of the text which might be (heavily) restored as '[It has been closed again and sealed] with a seal'.

An interesting point which is raised by this brief report is the quantity and range of objects buried with this unknown person, all of which, with the exception of the coffins/sarcophagi, appear to be everyday possessions taken to the tomb. Such an assemblage seems consistent with the range of goods found in the small number of undisturbed private burials of Dynasty 18 from Deir el-Medina, perhaps most strikingly that of Kha and Meryt, which, apart from the coffins, had a low number of specifically 'funerary' objects (specifically, two funerary papyri and two *shabti*s – see Meskell 1997; Valbelle 1985: 12–13). The inspection text does not contain any specifically funerary objects such as canopic jars, *shabti*s or copies of the Book of the Dead (McDowell 1999: 69–71, which also provides a translation of, and references to, this text; Valbelle 1985: 299). In this respect, as with the decoration of the tomb chapels, Ramesside tombs appear more 'funerary' in character than the Dynasty 18 'everyday life' emphasis. (For further discussion on the contents of New Kingdom tombs at Deir el-Medina, and how they might be used to pursue questions of a social anthropological nature, see Meskell 1999: esp. 148–215.)

Painting a tomb

Apart from royal tombs, there is usually little indication as to who carried out the skilled task of decorating the walls of tombs in Thebes during the New Kingdom. One rare exception comes from the tomb of Kynebu (TT 113; Kampp 1996: 394–5), who was '*Wab*-Priest over the Secrets of the Estate of Amen, and Priest in the Temple of Tuthmosis IV', and therefore a middle-ranking official who was connected to both the temple of Amen at Karnak and the cult of one of the kings of Dynasty 18. The tomb, located in the Lower Enclosure at el-Khokha, is singularly unimpressive in a manner typical of many Theban tombs of this period – all that is preserved is a small rectangular room with a standard set of scenes principally depicting banqueting, the deceased worshipping Amenhotep I and Ahmose-Nefertari, and an elaborate funeral procession. But a graffito from this tomb, written in Year 1 of the short-lived Ramesses VIII (Amer 1981), gives some indication regarding how long it took to carry out its decoration.

> First month of the Inundation season, Day 13: Beginning to inscribe in it.
> First month of the Winter season, Day 2: Finishing in it.

The period covered is 3 months and 19 days, just short of 100 days. There are obviously a number of unknown variables here – how many draughts-men and painters were involved, whether the activity described was consistent or sporadic – but the sense that a tomb could potentially be decorated in much less than a year gives some sense of the scale of work involved.

Plagiarism in tomb decoration

The source of most scenes within New Kingdom tombs is, unsurprisingly, other tombs. The issue of how scenes might be copied from one tomb to another is a complicated one, but one particularly interesting example might serve as an illustration of the process. TT65 belonged to Imiseba, 'Chief of Temple Archives' and 'Overseer of Works of all the Monuments (*mnw*) of Amen at Karnak', who was born under Ramesses III and died under Ramesses IX. His roles and responsibilities gave him particularly privileged access to, and interest in, the decoration of monuments at Thebes, and it would not be surprising if his tomb did not incorporate this interest in some way. This tomb (discussed by Bács 2001) was a re-used T-shaped Dynasty 18 tomb at Sheikh abd el-Qurna, which had been previously owned by Nebamun, an official of Hatshepsut. The re-decoration of the tomb involved painting the walls of the transverse hall, which had originally been decorated with conventional early Dynasty 18 scenes of Nubian and Asiatic tribute-bearers, with scenes of festival which would not have been out of place in a royal temple, including the Opet, New Year and Valley festivals, showing Ramesses IX offering to divine barques. The long hall was provided with excerpts from the Book of Gates, which could have come straight off the wall of a royal tomb, with a particular emphasis on the barque of the god Ra, perhaps as a deliberate counterpoint to the barques of divine procession in the broad hall. If this suggests that the distinction between what was appropriate in a royal context, and what in a private one, was being blurred in the late New Kingdom, a further remarkable piece of evidence might suggest in more precise detail the mechanics of how royal scenes were selected for Imiseba's tomb. A graffito in the tomb of Ramesses VI, from Year 9 of Ramesses IX, was left by the scribe Amenhotep and his son Amennakht – both from Deir el-Medina – who recorded their visit 'to look at the mountains' (and, presumably, the decoration of the then-open Ramesside royal tomb) after they had completing the decoration of Imiseba's tomb (McDowell 1999: 242).

But if the open, accessible nature of even relatively recent Ramesside royal tombs provided a source of inspiration for private tomb decoration at the end of the New Kingdom, the underlying insecurity in royal tombs that it represents was to have much more serious repercussions for the development of royal tombs in the post-Ramesside Period. The end of Dynasty 20 might well be regarded as the beginning of a seismic shift in the way tombs were regarded in ancient Egypt, and as marking the point when a broadly continuous line of development which can be traced from the Predynastic Period, particularly in terms of the tomb as a place of interaction, performance and self-presentation, had largely come to an end.

Evidence for New Kingdom tomb construction apart from Deir el-Medina

In spite of the evidence which allows us fascinating insights into tomb acquisition and usage within the Deir el-Medina community, the mechanisms of acquiring and decorating a tomb for the rest of New Kingdom Egypt are frustratingly obscure. As Eyre (1987b: 196–9) notes, the Deir el-Medina archive does not suggest that the workmen undertook private commissions to work on elite non-royal tombs at Thebes, and the elite tombs themselves do not offer up information which might suggest that they, like those of the

Old Kingdom, were, in theory at least, the gift of the king as a mark of royal favour. Relatively little evidence survives regarding the freelance decoration of New Kingdom tombs at Thebes – perhaps unlike coffins (tangible objects), service was not the subject of written contracts.

A tantalizing set of papyrus documents dating to Year 15 of the reign of Ramesses III, found near the enclosure wall of the Djoser Step-Pyramid at Saqqara, refers to preparations being made for the construction of a large private tomb for the General May (Posener-Kriéger 1981). Presumably this tomb in the New Kingdom Memphite necropolis was of the 'temple-tomb' type discussed in Chapter 14. The activities described in the papyri include work carried out by the scribe Bukenetef, who seems to have been in charge of the project, such as the acquisition of measuring ropes to lay out the area where the tomb was to be constructed (Posener-Kriéger 1981: 50), and the beginning of its construction using a workforce of undescribed size. This document seems to have been a report prepared for the state administration, suggesting that this tomb may have been a royal gift to the general.

Buying a coffin

The tombs of the Old Kingdom are relatively helpful in suggesting through the texts on them the means by which they were constructed. Tombs of the New Kingdom are less well documented. However, for the New Kingdom at Thebes, and especially for the Ramesside Period, in the Deir el-Medina archive we have a very helpful source of information as to the cost of individual items of burial equipment for private tombs. Alongside their employment as workers on the royal tomb in the Valley of the Kings and other royal tomb projects, notably the tombs of selected members of the royal family in the Valley of the Queens, Deir el-Medina workmen were able to use their skills for a little private enterprise, particularly in the production for sale of individual items of funerary equipment. The ostraca from Deir el-Medina provide an insight through the receipts and contracts associated with this trade. (The fundamental compendium of the prices of goods and services contained within the Deir el-Medina material is Janssen 1975 – with a discussion of the cost of items of burial equipment on pp. 209–48; see also Cooney 2007a).

The identification of particular items of funerary equipment through the names on the ostraca is sometime problematic and the descriptions are vague; thus the only price of *shabti*s is that of 1 *deben* (a unit of value equating to 91 g of copper) for 40 *shabti*s, which seems rather cheap, although we know nothing of their quality, while the price for a set of *ḳbw n wt*, canopic jars, at 5 *deben*, does not define the material of these jars, and the length of a *prt m hrw*, '(Chapters of) Coming Forth by Day' papyrus, costing 60 or 100 *deben*, is not known. More reliable data can be derived from the better-documented trade in coffins.

As Janssen notes, there are four words for coffin used in the ostraca, but, since the box-coffin fell out of use during Dynasty 19, and the ostraca referring to the sale of coffins are later than that date, none of the four words can refer to that type of coffin. The most commonly used word is *wt*, sometimes qualified as *wt ꜥꜣ* ('large coffin') and *wt šri* ('small coffin') – usually the outer and inner coffins in a nested pair. Other terms for coffin – *swḥt*, *mn-ꜥnḫ* and *ḏbꜣt* – also occur, although it is not altogether clear what they mean. Possibly some level of synonym is being employed – *swḥt* derives from the word for egg and may be related to a conceptualization of the coffin as a seemingly inert object containing the possibility of emerging life, while the term *mn-ꜥnḫ*, 'firm of life', clearly has this conceptualizing element to it. In addition, *mn-ꜥnḫ* appears to be specifically a synonym of the *wt ꜥꜣ*, that is to say the outer anthropoid coffin, while a *swḥt* seems to be the same as a *wt šri*, the inner anthropoid coffin. *ḏbꜣt* seems to refer to an outer sarcophagus, and only a few examples are known.

The price of a coffin (Cooney 2007a; Janssen 1975) is partly dependent on the quality of its decoration, and whether or not it is varnished, as much as the wood and labour involved in producing the coffin itself. The 'guide price' for a *wt*-coffin in the period from the reign of Ramesses II to the end of Dynasty 20 is between 20 and 40 *deben* (one example, described as 'decorated' and 'varnished', cost 33 *deben*), but with the possibility of paying much more. The most expensive recorded was a pair of inner and outer coffins, originally priced at 140 *deben* and 60 *deben*, respectively, but both undergoing further work which took the final price to 200 *deben* and 95 *deben*; it is notable that the inner coffin, presumably more elaborately decorated, was the more expensive of the pair. Where the wood for a *wt*-coffin is separately invoiced, 4–5 *deben* seems to be standard, while the work of decoration seems, typically, to cost 10 *deben*. Some ostraca list the prices paid for the work on the coffin exclusive of the price of the wood, ranging from 2 to 15 *deben*. For comparison, in the same period, a donkey typically cost 25–40 *deben*, a pig 3–5 *deben*, a bed 15–20 *deben* and a pair of sandals 1–3 *deben*.

A resident of Deir el-Medina, instead of decorating his own tomb, might employ a more skilled colleague. This situation is described in an ostracon which is self-described as 'What Aanakht gave Merysekhmet in exchange for the painting of his *shetay* (*štꜣy*)'. The word *shetay* refers to 'underground' or 'hidden' rooms, and in the context of this text 'Burial Chamber' seems likely (Cooney 2007a: 40). The value of the goods was 6½ *sniw*, made up of a collection of goods including clothing, sandals, vegetables and baskets of grain. A *sniw* is a measure of value based on an amount of silver, about 1/12 *deben* in weight, and with an equivalent value of about 1 *sniw* = 5 *deben*. Given that copper and silver themselves fluctuated in relative value during the Ramesside period, these equivalencies are only approximate (Janssen 1975). However, the total value of goods for the painting of Aanakht's burial chamber included 2½ *sniw* of pigment, presumably for use in the job itself, so the cost of the labour itself was therefore 4 *sniw* = 20 *deben*. Unfortunately the tomb of Aanakht has not been located, so we do not know how much wall-space could be painted, and the quality of that painting, for 20 *deben*.

Ancestors in the home

It is worth noting at this point that the Ramesside Period at Deir el-Medina has provided the most intriguing evidence for the possibility that, in addition to the tombs themselves, private houses of the Living were appropriate places within which to make offerings to/communicate with dead ancestors. Physical manifestations of this practice are suggested by so-called 'ancestor busts' (Friedman 1985) and stelae which show the Living offering to the Dead, especially the *ȝḫ iḳr n Rˁ* (*Akh iker n Ra*) stelae (Demarée 1983). Textual evidence to support this in-house communication with dead ancestors comes from Papyrus Sallier IV, the 'Calendar of Lucky and Unlucky Days', which urges the living to *iri prt-ḫrw n ȝḫw m pr.k*, 'Make voice-offering to the *akhu* in your house' (Posener 1981: 400).

CHAPTER 17

Petosiris

A Dying Tradition

rJrJrJrJ

Trends in Tomb Building in the Post-Imperial Age

It is all too easy to be dismissive of tomb building after the end of the New Kingdom. Whichever artificial point might be adopted to mark the end of dynastic Egyptian 'culture' – the arrival of Alexander the Great, the death of Cleopatra VII, the edict of the Christian Emperor Theodosius which officially closed the pagan temples, the Muslim invasion – almost the whole of the vast period from the death of Ramesses XI to any of those events is startlingly poor in high-quality tombs.

This view is not entirely the fault of those who find post-New Kingdom Egypt confusing and disappointing – an era typified by weak, fragmentary native Egyptian rule and foreign conquest – and easily dismissed. Rather, for burial practices at least, it is a view which is based on the nature of the archaeological evidence, which indicates that, with some impressive exceptions, there is an undeniable retreat from the concept of the private (and indeed royal) tomb as a visible locus of public display. Although the specific nature of that tomb-based display shifted in both emphasis and content in the two millennia from c.3000 to 1000 BC (the Early Dynastic Period to the end of the New Kingdom), the possession of a large, well-decorated and partially accessible tomb was a consistent ambition for elite Egyptians. This ambition was largely absent in the Third Intermediate Period (Dynasties 21–4), the Late Period (Dynasties 25–31) and the Graeco-Roman Period. This was not so much a question of the availability of resources with which to undertake tomb building – although this must have been a contributory factor in some instances – but was primarily due to a series of underlying

Ancient Egyptian Tombs: The Culture of Life and Death   By Steven Snape
© 2011 Steven Snape

reasons which were as much social, economic and political as they were religious. The millennium between the end of the Ramesside Period and the absorption of Egypt into the Roman Empire saw a series of developing situations, very few of which were to the advantage of Egypt as an independent nation. The internal divisions of the Third Intermediate Period, the unified but often foreign-dominated Late Period and the post-Alexander rule by kings (and queens) of Macedonian origin (the Ptolemaic Period) brought with them a number of cultural changes that would have a significant impact on attitudes to the afterlife, and with it the role of the tomb as a vehicle for these attitudes.

The Demise of the Valley of the Kings

The end of the New Kingdom saw the abandonment of the Valley of the Kings as a centralized location for royal burial. This happened for two main reasons. The first was the collapse of royal authority, which saw the end of Thebes as the royal religious capital linking the presence of the imperial deity Amen-Re at his temple at Karnak with the royal tombs in the Valley of the Kings and the mediating presence of the 'Mansions of Millions of Years' on the West Bank. By the end of Dynasty 20, kings had long since attempted to build these latter structures – Ramesses IV seems to have been the last king to have had (unrealized) ambitions in this regard, although, paradoxically, the tombs of Dynasty 20 kings were, on average, significantly larger than those of their more glorious Dynasty 18 predecessors. Royal authority, such as it existed at the end of Dynasty 20, seems to have shifted north. Ramesses XI's tomb at Thebes was unfinished, and the fact that he is referred to in his throne-name as 'Chosen of Ptah' rather than 'Chosen of Ra' or 'Beloved of Amen' – as was the case with almost every one of his predecessors since Ramesses II – might suggest that a search for his burial should take place in the domain of Ptah, i.e. the Memphite area. Indeed it may even be that he was the first to adopt the custom, prevalent in the Third Intermediate Period and Late Period, of burial within temple precincts. More generally, the power-bases of those individuals who, in the Third Intermediate Period and Late Period, claimed the title of king tended to be in the Delta, where topography necessarily precluded burial in a desert valley.

The second significant factor is best exemplified by the most famous class of documentary records from the Late New Kingdom, the so-called 'Tomb Robbery Papyri', whose title accurately describes their contents: records of the legal process of examining and trying those individuals involved in the robbery of royal tombs during the reigns of Ramesses IX and

Ramesses XI (Peet 1930). The essential vulnerability of those tombs at a time of political and economic crisis must have thrown into sharp relief their essential design flaw, especially as royal tombs of the Ramesside period were significantly more visible and vulnerable than Ineni's vision of a hidden royal burial. The partial isolation of royal tombs was now a weakness, not a strength, as their known but generally unfrequented location provided an ideal combination for nefarious activity, particularly for those involved in the royal funerary industry in the first place.

In addition, the type of tomb robbery which, if the papyri are to be believed, typified the late New Kingdom – opportunistic pilfering and rather more serious breaking-and-entering by small groups of individuals connected to the Theban West Bank tomb industry – became replaced by a more systematic process with official backing. This involved the superficially selfless activity of collecting the bodies from already-robbed royal tombs and reburying them in hidden 'caches'. The two most important of these to be discovered to date are those in the re-used tomb of Amenhotep II (KV35) and in the family tomb of the High Priest Pinudjem II (DB320). A beneficial side-effect, at least as far as those carrying out the reburying was concerned, was the opportunity to remove items of value from what survived of the royal burial equipment. It is therefore likely that this activity was carried out with the sanction of the effective state authorities of the time, including General Piankhy, who, during the reign of Ramesses XI, was waging an expensive civil war against the Viceroy of Kush (Nubia) Panehesy. A letter from this period (Wente 1990: 194–5) refers to Piankhy telling the necropolis scribe Butehamen to 'Uncover a tomb among the ancient tombs and preserve its seal until I return.' To this same period can be dated the *c.*4,000 graffiti (some in Butehamen's distinctive handwriting) identifying the specific locations of ancient tombs on the Theban West Bank, presumably as a prelude to their 'restoration' (Jansen-Winkeln 1995; Reeves and Wilkinson 1996: 205). Other evidence supports the idea that, once the quarry of king's bodies had been exhausted, the process moved on to other members of the royal family (including a cache of reburied royal princesses – Dodson and Janssen 1989) and private individuals (Dodson 1991).

Private Tombs in the Third Intermediate Period

After the Ramesside Period the most important general trend in private tombs was the move away from obvious, elaborately decorated superstructures which made a public statement about the tomb-owner, to more modest burials where the emphasis was focused inwards on the body and its immediate equipment. As one scholar of the mortuary culture of the period notes, 'there are not many tomb superstructures which can be dated to the Third Intermediate Period' (Aston 2009: 401). A good example of this general phenomenon, where a simple tomb or grave of this period might contain a relatively elaborately decorated coffin, but little else, was found at Amarna (Taylor and Boyce 1986). In a sense, the writing had been on the wall for decorated tombs from as early as Dynasty 19, when there seems to have been a general scaling-back of resources put into tombs and, post-Ramesses II, 'fewer and fewer families invested in stone sarcophagi and decorated tomb chapels for the nuclear family – not only at Deir el Medina, but throughout Thebes and Egypt as a whole' (Cooney 2007b: 288). This retreat from the decorated tomb had a corollary in the increased level of intricate detail found on anthropoid coffins of the Third Intermediate Period – the balance between coffin and tomb, which had been important from at least as early as the Middle Kingdom, had now shifted entirely towards the coffin, leaving the tomb as merely the receptacle for the coffin set and the body it contained. The determinants for this change may well include a generally depressed level of economic ability with regard to the tomb, but this itself is less likely to have been as important as the instability of the period, which resulted in a greater emphasis on the security of the tomb and (perhaps with the royal caches in mind) led to the potentially peripatetic nature of burial. A suitably decorated and inscribed coffin was, in some ways, a self-sufficient mobile tomb, if the idea of the tomb as a place of persona and performance were abandoned, which, for the most part, it was. None of this is surprising in an era when the officially sanctioned emptying of royal and private tombs is the best illustration of underlying economic and political instability.

This changed attitude can be seen at Thebes in the early part of the Third Intermediate Period, including tomb DB320 itself, which was presumably chosen as the destination for the most significant of the royal caches for the very reasons which led to its earlier use for the burial of the family of the High Priest Pinudjem II: it was an underground tomb in the cliffs above Deir el-Bahri, with a genuinely hidden character, and intended to be so. It is likely that DB320 began life as a modestly sized Ramesside tomb but was remodelled and extended to create a vertical shaft 15 m deep with a long horizontal corridor 120 m long at its base, and with no obvious superstructure. DB320 was to point the way forward for tomb design inasmuch as the High Priests of Amen-Re were the closest thing to royalty in Third Intermediate Period Thebes and could, presumably, have commanded enough resources to create reasonably impressive tombs but, perhaps with the example of the robbed Valley of the Kings tombs in mind, chose to be buried in hidden – or at least discreet – family vaults. It is therefore likely

Figure 17.1 Mourning woman on a wooden stela of the Third Intermediate Period. The background shows tomb superstructures which are more likely to be ancient New Kingdom, rather than contemporary, examples

that the contemporary view of Theban cemeteries in the Third Intermediate Period was one which regarded the visible landscape as populated by increasingly ancient tomb superstructures, rather than one replenished by new private monuments (Figure 17.1).

Royal Tombs of the Third Intermediate Period and Late Period

Although Egypt in the Third Intermediate Period lacked an overall centralized authority, it had no shortage of kings. Local rulers, especially those based in the Eastern Nile Delta, claimed royal titles in a way which ignored the reality of a royal power which was shared with other regionally dominant polities, especially the High Priests of Amen, who effectively ruled much of Upper Egypt. Although this was an era in which Delta cities came to prominence as royal seats, their very nature made them unsuitable to be regarded as potential monumental copies of Karnak + Valley of the Kings + 'Mansions of Millions of Years', even if the most significant East Delta city, Tanis, was styled as 'Thebes of the North'. Instead, a new arrangement for royal mortuary monuments needed to be settled, taking into account the specific geographical limitations of burial in the Nile Delta, the more limited resources available to Third Intermediate Period 'kings' in comparison with their New Kingdom predecessors, and considerations of the security of the burial, especially in the context of events at Thebes which began at the end of the New Kingdom and continued into the Third Intermediate Period. The solution was to bury these rulers within the precincts of the major temples of their capital cities.

This had a number of advantages. Firstly, in the Nile Delta the highest parts of naturally occurring or artificial mounds were obvious places for both burial and monumental architecture, where they would be safe from the annually rising waters of the inundation. Secondly, burials within temple precincts would come with a built-in oversight by caretakers in the form of temple priests. Thirdly, the temple precinct was an appropriate architectural setting – the superstructures of royal tombs could be a monumental good fit within an already impressive temple. Fourthly, the location of a royal tomb within the temple of a god, perhaps especially that of Amen at Tanis, may have provided a very suitable replacement for the missing 'Mansion of Millions of Years' – a place where the integration of king with god could take place. It might even be that the works of individual kings in serving the god could be shown on the walls of these temples, although this is difficult to assess given the poor state of Third Intermediate Period and Late Period temples in the Delta today.

Royal tombs of the Third Intermediate Period at Tanis (and elsewhere)

The royal tombs which belong to some, but far from all, of the known kings of Dynasties 21 and 22 at Tanis represent a significant departure from earlier attempts to provide suitable royal burial. Clustered in the south-west corner of the temple enclosure at Tanis – itself largely constructed from stone removed from the nearby Ramesside metropolis of Pi-Ramesse – these tombs consisted of underground chambers constructed of limestone blocks, sometimes lined with re-used slabs of granite, and sometimes with their walls decorated with scenes and texts taken from the canon of New Kingdom funerary literature (Montet 1947, 1951, 1960). As Myśliwiec (2000: 29) notes, 'How modest these small rooms are, with their unappealing relief decoration.' These chambers were accessed, sometimes via an antechamber, from a short vertical shaft – the tombs were only a few metres underground. Within these chambers, the burial equipment consisted of little more than a stone sarcophagus and its contents, and a few additional objects, but the quality of some of these objects, from the unrobbed parts of this mini-necropolis, and especially from the tomb of Pseusennes I, are some of the finest from any royal tomb in Egypt.

It has been argued that the low emphasis on elaborate burial in the Third Intermediate Period may be a result of an attitude to burial shared by the dominant Libyan elite and that the provision of 'an elaborate physical environment for the dead and a focus for mortuary cults was doubtless not a major feature of semi-nomadic societies such as theirs' (Taylor 2000: 364). However, the Tanis royal tombs may once have possessed superstructures in the form of small chapels, perhaps similar to those of those princes of Dynasty 22 who were buried in the temple precincts at Memphis, just as their fathers were at Tanis and in similar subterranean tombs (Kitchen 1979: 281), such as that of Prince Shoshenq, son of Osorkon II.

Extraordinarily, no private tombs are known from Tanis (although blocks from private tombs were re-used in the tomb of Shoshenq III – see Aston 2009: 408), but the presence of a hitherto undiscovered cemetery somewhere on the edges of the temple enclosure would not be surprising, nor would the tombs of missing Dynasty 21–2 kings at sites such as Bubastis, or perhaps Leontopolis (Tell Muqdam). In addition, it may be that temple enclosures were more widely used for the burial of members of local 'dynasties', as suggested by evidence from Balamun (Spencer 2003), Hermopolis Magna (Spencer 2007), Herakleopolis Magna, Abydos and Thebes (Aston 2009: 401).

Royal tombs of the Late Period at Sais (and elsewhere)

The practice of royal burial within temple enclosures was retained in the Late Period. Although no trace of them has been detected at the site itself, Herodotus refers to the tombs of the kings of Dynasty 26 in the 'temple of Athena (i.e. Neith)' at Sais in the following terms:

> The people of Sais buried all the kings who came from the province inside this precinct . . . in the temple-court, a great cloistered building of stone decorated with pillars carved in imitation of palm-trees and other costly ornaments. Within the cloister is a chamber with two doors, and behind the doors stands the sepulchre . . . great stone obelisks stand in the enclosure and there is a stone-bordered lake nearby . . . . (Herodotus II: 169–70)

The description seems to be of a standard temple-precinct containing the cult temple itself, a sacred lake and a group of royal tombs (Lloyd 1988: 203). Although this description is somewhat vague, it nevertheless fits with what we know of royal tombs of the Third Intermediate Period and Late Period. As far as the survival of this royal necropolis, it may be relevant to note that Herodotus goes on to inform us (Herodotus III: 16) that the Persian king Cambyses, after his successful conquest of the Nile Delta, ordered the destruction of the body of his enemy King Amasis, who had been buried at Sais. The other Delta cities which produced native Egyptian dynasties in the Late Period are Mendes (Dynasty 29) and Sebennytos/Samannud (Dynasty 30). At Mendes a sarcophagus set in a massive limestone block which formed the centrepiece of the burial of King Nepherites (Nefarud) I still remains in place, surrounded by the fragmentary traces of the brick-lined burial pit; nothing remains of the superstructure (Redford 2004). All that remains of the burials of the last Egyptian kings of Dynasty 30 are two sarcophagi belonging to Nektanebo I and Nektanebo II, and, as these sarcophagi came to light in modern times being re-used in Cairo and Alexandria, it is not known whether the tombs they were intended for were in Sebennytos or in a quite different part of Egypt.

Private Tombs of the Late Period

The archaizing revival at Thebes

Two major sets of tombs with elaborate superstructures are known from Late Period Thebes. These began in Dynasty 25, a dynasty of Nubian kings who had come to Egypt with (often disappointed) expectations of the perpetuation of traditional Egyptian culture, which they attempted to revive through a strong archaizing tendency. This tendency was exhibited in their own royal tombs, built not in Egypt but in their Nubian homeland, utilizing the general concept, if not the specific architectural detail, of the monumental pyramid, but, at Thebes, their highest-ranking 'servants' were buried in tombs which had both an archaizing and monumental flavour to them.

God's Wives at Medinet Habu
Within the enclosure of the now-ancient temple built for Ramesses III at Medinet Habu, the 'God's Wives of Amen' built a row of tombs with chapel superstructures. These important priestesses, effectively the predominant religious official at Thebes, were the daughters of kings, and they required mortuary provision appropriate to their status. The first mudbrick chapels were built for Shepenwepet I (Daughter of Osorkon III) and Amenirdis I (Daughter of the Nubian king Kashta), but the latter was later replaced in stone by Shepenwepet II, whose own chapel was remodelled to include shrines and vaults for God's Wife Nitocris, and her real mother (by Psammetichus I), Mehytenweskhet (Figure 17.2). These tombs therefore cross the span from the end of the Third Intermediate Period, through the Nubian Dynasty 25, to the Egyptian Dynasty 26, but with a consistency of both form and function.

Temple-tombs in the Asasif
Close to Deir el-Bahri, a series of extremely large and complex temple-tombs began during Dynasty 25. The tomb of Harwa (TT37) set the

Figure 17.2 The tomb-chapels of the God's Wives of Amen at Medinet Habu

standard for later tombs of this type, the most impressive of which belonged to Montuemhat (TT34; Figure 17.3) and Pabasa (TT279). The standard format of these tombs (Eigner 1984) consisted of a superstructure made up of a pylon-fronted mudbrick enclosure containing two courts, the second of which led to a complex of subterranean rooms, including a substantial pillared court and Burial Chamber. The decoration of these underground rooms represents the most extreme example of archaism, with motifs and specific scenes copied from tombs of all periods. It may be that the complexity of the underground rooms was an attempt to re-create the mythical 'Tomb of Osiris'.

Security of the tomb

The most striking burial of local elites following contemporary practice was the set of nine shafts, with no surviving superstructures, cut into the floor of Hatshepsut's temple at Deir el-Bahri, which led to chambers containing the family burials connected with the priests of Montu, a total of 60 individuals, which spanned the period *c.*700–650 BC (Aston 2003: 147). It is very striking that, between Dynasties 27 and 31 (525–332 BC), no new tombs seem to have been built at Thebes. The burial equipment for well-provisioned tombs in the long period from *c.*750 to *c.*300 BC consisted of objects, usually of wood, making up a regular burial set (Aston 2003: Figs 3,

Figure 17.3   The tomb of Montuemhat (TT34) in the Asasif cemetery at Thebes

7, 11, 16 and 18); standard items within this set included an anthropoid coffin/sarcophagus (sometimes with an elaborate *ḳrsw* outer coffin), accompanied by a painted stela and wooden figure of the composite funerary deity Ptah-Sokar-Osiris (Figure 17.4).

In the Memphite necropolis (Stammers 2009) the drive for security and archaism found expression in tombs based on a series of very deep shafts, at the bottom of which were small chambers filled with massive stone sarcophagi. These shafts were designed to be filled with sand after the interment in order to make the burial completely inaccessible. The best-known clusters of these tombs are close to the Old Kingdom pyramids of Unas and Userkaf at Saqqara, and at Abusir.

Figure 17.4   The Burial Chamber of a Third Intermediate/Late Period tomb
(© Garstang Museum of Archaeology, University of Liverpool)

Changing Traditions in Graeco-Roman Egypt

The fourth century BC in Egypt has been characterized as one of 'Egypto-hellenistic eclecticism' (Myśliwiec 2000), and the term eclecticism is one which is often used to describe elements of cultural production during the period, particularly in literature (Lichtheim 1980: 4–5). Two elements of this eclecticism are particularly important. One is the tendency towards archaism, which involved the seeking out of models from the golden age of Egyptian culture. The other is the way in which traditional Egyptian cultural mores were combined with new modes of expression, the most important of which was Hellenism. In the Ptolemaic Period the ruling elite, whatever their ethnic origins, were culturally Hellenistic – a Hellenism given a local flavour by the rich spice of Egyptian culture, but fundamentally Hellenistic nonetheless. This combination can be seen in a wide variety of places: the city of Alexandria, the syncretism of Greek and Egyptian deities, the mummy-cases of well-to-do provincials which depict Egyptian gods on the body but are provided with a Greek-style portrait mask.

The tomb of Petosiris

The most striking example of the Egyptohellenistic eclecticism is the tomb of Petosiris, the largest and most impressive of a series of tombs with temple-shaped superstructures built in a tightly grouped necropolis at the site of Tuna el-Gebel, part of the desert edge close to the important city of Hermopolis Magna in Middle Egypt (Lefebvre 1923–4). Petosiris and his family served as an effectively local dynasty of High Priests of the temple of Thoth at Hermopolis Magna in the turbulent period from the later part of Dynasty 30, through the Persian Dynasty 31, to the beginning of the Macedonian/Ptolemaic Period. It is likely that the superstructure of the tomb of Petosiris (Figure 17.5) was directly modelled on the additions to the temple of Thoth at nearby Hermopolis Magna, for which Petosiris was responsible (Snape and Bailey 1988). In word and image (on the tomb walls) and by its very architectural form, this tomb is the last one from ancient Egypt which offers us the memorialization of the life of the tomb-owner by reference to his actions.

Externally the tomb is composed of the same two core elements as a cult temple of the Ptolemaic Period. The entrance consists of a transverse hall, or *pronaos*, which has a façade composed of columns linked by half-height screen walls, allowing light to flood into this hall. This leads to the second element, a lower square room whose roof is supported by four pillars; in a temple this would be referred to as the *naos* and a shrine would contain the statue of the god. Instead, since this is a tomb not a temple, the floor of this chapel contains a shaft leading to the Burial Chambers of Petosiris and his family.

Figure 17.5 The Tomb of Petosiris at Tuna el-Gebel

The form of the tomb represents a rare example of post-Ramesside innovation within Egyptian culture which seems to be uninfluenced by foreign elements, as can be seen by the development of this temple form to late in the Roman Period. However, there are two other factors which need to be considered: the decoration on the walls of the tomb, and its texts, which can reveal the underlying religious beliefs which inform the contemporary view of the afterlife and the tomb itself.

The texts in the tomb include selections from well-established forms of funerary literature, including the Pyramid Texts and the Book of the Dead (Lichtheim 1980: 45). In addition they include a long autobiographical text composed by Petosiris which purports to honour his father Sishu, but expresses his own achievements. In fact this text has much in common with autobiographical texts of the First Intermediate Period, such as that of Ankhtify, in that it presents the tomb-owner as a man of action in a problematic era. It reflects on the unsettled conditions of the period:

> I spent seven years as controller for this god [i.e. Thoth], administering his endowment without any fault being found, while the Ruler of Foreign Lands [i.e. presumably one of the Persian kings of Dynasty 31] was Protector in Egypt, and nothing was in its former place . . . .
>
> When I became controller for Thoth, lord of Khmun (Hermopolis Magna) I put the temple of Thoth in its former condition . . . .
>
> I stretched the cord, released the line, to found the temple of Ra . . . .
>
> I built the house of the goddesses inside the house of Khmun having found their house was old. (Lichtheim 1980: 46–7)

It is remarkable that the work of founding temples is claimed by Petosiris and an obvious indicator that this is a time without kings because founding temples is what kings do.

The traditional purpose of the tomb as a place of interaction between the Living and the Dead is also referred to, but in a rather unusual way in a text within the tomb for the benefit of Petosiris' father, Sishu. This section of text begins with a conventional *hetep-di-nesu* formula asking for the regular set of offerings for the '*ka* of the owner of this tomb', but what follows is an address to the Living, not one which has the usual message of asking for offerings for the tomb-owner, but one which seeks to benefit the Living: 'O you who are alive on earth, and you who shall be born, who shall come to this desert, see this tomb and pass by it. Come, let me lead you to the way of life' (Lichtheim 1980: 50).

But the most commented-on aspect of this tomb is its figured decoration. Around the interior walls of the *pronaos* are depicted a series of offering-bearers, agricultural workers and all the range of 'everyday life' characters who would not be out of place in an elite tomb from almost any point in the pre-Ramesside dynastic period. However, these conventional scenes are depicted in a far from conventional manner, on a 'double-style' which combines Egyptian with Hellenistic modes of two-dimensional representation.

Alexandria and after

This double-style can also be seen in tombs in the Ptolemaic capital at Alexandria, but in ways which are increasingly detached from their Egyptian origins, and on the walls of tombs which are hardly recognizable as Egyptian. These are tombs which come from a Hellenistic cultural background but seem to be a specifically Alexandrian invention (Venit 2002: 14) adapted to the particular circumstances of the limestone ridges of the Mediterranean coast, most notably at Alexandria itself, but also on sites west of Alexandria at Marina el-Alamein and at Zawiyet Umm el-Rakham. These take the form of subterranean courtyards open to the sky, surrounded by series of rooms where the burial of the dead was carried out in long narrow compartments (*loculli*) closed by decorated slabs. Although these tombs were designed for the performance of ritual bringing together the Living and the Dead, this bears little relationship to the intention of dynastic Egyptian tombs as places of encounter.

The rarity of tomb building in Roman Egypt can be seen as the natural endpoint of an increasingly inward-looking tendency in burials after the New Kingdom: 'Although some personal tombs were built at this time, more usually bodies were either placed in small graves or entrusted to mortuary workers for burial in pits or re-used tombs, depending on the site ... the mummified body itself became the focus of the aesthetic attention once lavished on the decoration and equipage of tombs' (Riggs 2005: 1–2). An example of this is a document of AD 125, in which a man expresses the hope that 'my wife organize my funeral and burial and treatment of my body in the native fashion' (Montserrat 1997: 33), a sentiment which is a very long way from the often-expressed hope of the Old Kingdom Egyptian for a well-provisioned tomb.

Epilogue

As an observer of Egyptian peasant life in the 1920s, Winifred Blackman noted:

> One day a week – in some parts of Egypt on Thursday, in others on Friday – the villagers pay a visit to the graves of their relations and friends. The ceremony is

called eṭ-Ṭala', meaning the coming forth or the going up . . . . On the day of eṭ-Ṭala' the souls of the dead are believed to return to their graves, and they expect their relatives to meet them there. (Blackman 1927: 117)

The provision accorded a sheikh, a local saint or holy man, was even greater:

> Among the Muslims it is the custom to erect over the grave of such a person a small whitewashed building, crowned with a dome, the outer and inner walls being usually decorated with line-drawings in colours and with inscriptions consisting of passages from the *Korān*. In many cases it is customary to provide a 'servant', or sometimes a number of 'servants', whose salary is paid out of an endowment of land or money, augmented by the donations of those who visit the tomb. (Blackman 1927: 240)

A set of examples of modern 'letters to the dead' is discussed by el-Leithy (2003). And so, although from a quite different religious background to the tombs of the Dynastic Period discussed in this book, tombs in the landscape of modern Egypt can continue to be architecturally striking buildings which express personal and local identity, and are places of encounter between the Living and the Dead.

References

৷৲৷৲

For bibliographic references to Egyptian elite tombs, whether discussed in this book or not, the reader is referred to the Porter and Moss 'Topographical Bibliography' series.

Abdel-Qader, M. (1966) 'Two Theban Tombs, Kyky and Bak-en-Amun', *Annales du Service des Antiquités de l'Égypte* 59: 157–84.

Adams, B. (1987) *The Fort Cemetery at Hierakonpolis.* London.

Aldred, C. (1970) 'The Foreign Gifts Offered to Pharaoh', *Journal of Egyptian Archaeology* 56: 105–16.

Alexanian, N. (2006) 'Tomb and Social Status: The Textual Evidence' in M. Bàrta (ed.) *The Old Kingdom Art and Archaeology: Proceedings of the Conference Held in Prague, May 31–June 4, 2004.* Prague, 1–8.

Allen, J. P. (1994) 'Reading a Pyramid' in C. Berger, G. Clerc and N. Grimal (eds) *Hommages à Jean Leclant*, 1. Cairo, 5–28.

Allen, J. P. (2003) 'The High Officials of the Early Middle Kingdom' in N. Strudwick and J. Taylor (eds) *The Theban Necropolis: Past, Present and Future.* London, 14–29.

Allen, J. P. (2005) *The Ancient Egyptian Pyramid Texts.* Atlanta.

Allen, J. P. (2006) 'Some Aspects of the Non-Royal Afterlife in the Old Kingdom' in M. Bárta (ed.) *The Old Kingdom Art and Archaeology: Proceedings of the Conference Held in Prague, May 31–June 4, 2004.* Prague, 9–17.

Altenmüller, H. (1974) 'Zur vergöttlichung des Unas im Alten Reich', *Studien zur Altägyptischen Kultur* 1: 1–18.

Amer, A. M. A. (1981) 'A Unique Theban Tomb Inscription under Ramesses VIII', *Göttinger Miszellen* 49: 9–12.

Arnold, D. (1974–81) *Der Tempel des Königs Mentuhotep von Deir el-Bahari* (3 vols). Mainz am Rhein.

Arnold, D. (1976) *Gräber des Alten und Mittleren Reiches in El-Tarif.* Mainz am Rhein.

Ancient Egyptian Tombs: The Culture of Life and Death   By Steven Snape
© 2011 Steven Snape

Arnold, D. (1999) 'Old Kingdom Statues in Their Architectural Setting' in *Egyptian Art in the Age of the Pyramids*. New York, 41–9.

Arnold, D. (2008) *Middle Kingdom Tomb Architecture at Lisht*. New York.

Arnold, D. and E. Pischikova (1999) 'Stone Vessels: Luxury Items with Manifold Implications' in *Egyptian Art in the Age of the Pyramids*. New York, 121–131.

Arnold, F. (1998) 'Die Priesterhäuser der Chentkaues in Giza. Staatlicher Wohnungsbau als Interpretation der Wohnvorstellungen für einen "Idealmenschen"', *Mitteilungen des Deutschen Archäologischen Instituts Abteilung Kairo* 54: 1–18.

Assmann, J. (1991) *Das Grab des Amenemope TT 41*. Mainz am Rhein.

Assmann, J. (1996) 'Preservation and Presentation of Self in Ancient Egyptian Portraiture' in P. Der Manuelian (ed.) *Studies in Honor of William Kelly Simpson*, I. Boston, 55–81.

Assmann, J. (2003) 'The Ramesside Tomb and the Construction of Sacred Space' in N. Strudwick and J. H. Taylor (eds) *The Theban Necropolis: Past, Present and Future*. London, 46–52.

Assmann, J. (2005) *Death and Salvation in Ancient Egypt* (trans. D. Lorton). Ithaca, NY.

Aston, D. A. (2003) 'The Theban West Bank from theTwenty-fifth Dynasty to the Ptolemaic Period' in N. Strudwick and J. H. Taylor (eds) *The Theban Necropolis: Past, Present and Future*. London, 138–66.

Aston, D. A. (2009) *Burial Assemblages of Dynasty 21-25*. Vienna.

Ayrton, E. R. and W. L. S. Loat (1909) 'Untitled Report' in F. Ll. Griffith (ed.) *Egypt Exploration Fund Annual Report 1908-1909*. London, 2–5.

Ayrton, E. R., C. T. Currelly and A. E. P. Weigall (1904) *Abydos III*. London.

Bács, T. A. (2001) 'Art as Material for Later Art: The Case of Theban Tomb 65' in W. V. Davies (ed.) *Colour and Painting in Ancient Egypt*. London, 94–100.

Baines, J. (1987) 'The Stela of Khusobek: Private and Royal Military Narrative and Values' in J. Osing, and G. Dreyer (eds) *Form und Mass: Beiträge zur Literatur, Sprache und Kunst des alten Ägypten (Fs. G. Fecht)*. Wiesbaden, 43–61.

Baines, J. (1998) 'The Dawn of the Amarna Age' in D. O'Connor and E. H. Cline (eds) *Amenhotep III: Perspectives on His Reign*. Ann Arbor, 271–312.

Bakr, M. I. (1992) *Tell Basta I: Tombs and Burial Customs at Bubastis*. Cairo.

Bárta, M. (2005) 'Architectural Innovations in the Development of the Non-Royal Tomb during the Reign of Nyuserra' in P. Jánosi (ed.) *Structure and Significance: Thoughts on Ancient Egyptian Architecture*. Vienna, 105–30.

Barthelmess, P. (1992) *Der Übergang ins Jenseits in den thebanischen Beamtengräbern der Ramessidenzeit*. Heidelberg.

Bell, L. D. (1985) 'Luxor Temple and the Cult of the Royal Ka', *Journal of Near Eastern Studies* 44: 251–94.

Bestock, L. D. (2007) 'Finding the First Dynasty Royal Family' in Z. A. Hawass and J. Richards (eds) *The Archaeology and Art of Ancient Egypt. Essays in Honor of David B. O'Connor*. Cairo, 99–108.

Bierbrier, M. L. (1982) *The Tomb-Builders of Pharaoh*. London.

Bietak, M. (1996) *Avaris: The Capital of the Hyksos*. London.

Blackman, A. M. (1926) 'Oracles in Ancient Egypt II', *Journal of Egyptian Archaeology* 12: 176–85.

Blackman, A. M. (1935) 'The Stela of Nebipusenwosret: British Museum No. 101', *Journal of Egyptian Archaeology* 21: 1–9.

Blackman, A. M. and M. R. Apted (1914–1953) *The Rock Tombs of Meir (6 vols).* London.

Blackman, W. S. (1927) *The Fellāḥīn of Upper Egypt.* London.

Boeser, P. A. (1909) *Riksmuseum van Oudheden: Beschreibung der Aegyptischen Sammlung II.* Leiden.

Bolshakov, A. O. (1991) 'The Old Kingdom Representations of Funeral Procession', *Göttinger Miszellen* 121: 31–54.

Bolshakov, A. O. (1992) 'Princess *Ḥm.t-rᶜ(w)*: The First Record of Osiris?' *Chronique d'Égypte* 67: 203–10.

Bolshakov, A. O. (1997) *Man and His Double in Egyptian Ideology of the Old Kingdom.* Wiesbaden.

Bomann, A. H. (1991) *The Private Chapel in Ancient Egypt.* London.

Borchardt, L., O. Königsberger and H. Ricke (1934) 'Friesziegel in Grabbauten', *Zeitschrift für Ägyptische Sprache und Altertumskunde* 70: 25–35.

Breasted, J. H. (1906) *Ancient Records of Egypt I.* Chicago.

Brinks, J. (1979) *Die Entwicklung der königlichen Grabanlagen des Alten Reiches: eine strukturelle und historische Analyse altägyptischer Architektur.* Hildesheim.

Brovarski, E. (1981) 'Ahanakht of Bersheh and the Hare Nome in the First Intermediate Period and Middle Kingdom' in W. K. Simpson (ed.) *Studies in Ancient Egypt, the Aegean, and the Sudan: Essays in Honor of Dows Dunham.* Boston, 14–30.

Brovarski, E. (1994a) 'Abydos in the Old Kingdom and First Intermediate Period: Part 1' in C. Berger, G. Clerc and N Grimal (eds) *Hommages à Jean Leclant 1.* Cairo, 99–121.

Brovarski, E. (1994b) 'Abydos in the Old Kingdom and First Intermediate Period: Part 2' in D. P. Silverman (ed.) *For His Ka: Essays Offered in Memory of Klaus Baer.* Chicago, 15–44.

Brunton, G. (1920) *Lahun I: The Treasure.* London.

Brunton, G. (1927–30) *Qau and Badari I–III.* London.

Bruyère, B. (1926) *Rapport sur les fouilles de Deir el-Médineh 1924–25.* Cairo.

Bruyère, B. (1937) *Tell Edfou 1937.* Cairo.

Bruyère, B. (1959) *La Tombe No.1 de Sen-nedjem à Deir el Médineh.* Cairo.

Castel, G. (2005) 'Le mastaba de Khentika dans l'oasis de Dakhla (fin de VIe dynastie): Étude architecturale' in P. Jánosi (ed.) *Structure and Significance: Thoughts on Ancient Egyptian Architecture.* Vienna, 209–45.

Castillos, J. J. (1982) 'Analyses of Egyptian Predynastic and Early Dynastic Cemeteries: Final Conclusions', *Journal of the Society for the Study of Egyptian Antiquities* 12: 29–53.

Černý, J. (1961) 'The Stela of Merer in Cracow', *Journal of Egyptian Archaeology* 47: 5–9.

Černý, J. (1973) *A Community of Workmen at Thebes in the Ramessid Period.* Cairo.

Chassinat, E. and C. Palanque (1911) *Une campagne des fouilles dans la nécropole d'Assiout.* Cairo.

Chauvet, V. (2004) The Conception of Private Tombs in the Late Old Kingdom (unpublished Ph.D. thesis, Johns Hopkins University).

Chauvet, V. (2007) 'Royal Involvement in the Construction of Private Tombs in the Late Old Kingdom' in J.-C. Goyon (ed.) *Proceedings of the Ninth International Congress of Egyptologists Grenoble, 6–12 September 2004.* Leuven, 313–21.

Collier, M. and B. Manley (1998) *How to Read Egyptian Hieroglyphs.* London.

Cooke, A. E. (2005) The construction and architecture of *mastaba* tombs in the Unas Cemetery (unpublished Ph.D. thesis, University of Liverpool).

Cooney, K. M. (2007a) *The Cost of Death. The Social and Economic Value of Ancient Egyptian Funerary Art in the Ramesside Period.* Leiden.

Cooney, K. M. (2007b) 'The Functional Materialism of Death in Ancient Egypt: A Case Study of Funerary Materials from the Ramesside Period' in M. Fitzenreiter (ed.) *Das Heilige und die Ware: Eigentum, Austausch und Kapitalisierung im Spannungsfeld von Ökonomie und Religion.* London, 273–99.

Dakin, A. N. (1938) 'The Stela of the Sculptor Sirē at Oxford', *Journal of Egyptian Archaeology* 24: 190–7.

Daressy, M. (1902) *Fouilles de la Vallée de Rois (1898–1899)* Cairo.

David, A. R. (2007) *The Two Brothers: Death and the Afterlife in Middle Kingdom Egypt.* Bolton.

Davies, N. de G. (1901) *The Rock Tombs of Sheikh Saïd.* London.

Davies, N. de G. (1902) *The Rock Tombs of Deir el-Gebrâwi* (2 vols). London.

Davies, N. de G. (1903-8) *The Rock Tombs of El Amarna* (6 vols). London.

Davies, N. de G. (1923) 'Akhenaten at Thebes', *Journal of Egyptian Archaeology* 9: 132–52.

Davies, N. de G. (1926) *The Tomb of Huy, Viceroy of Nubia in the Reign of Tutankhamun.* London.

Davies, N. de G. (1932) ' Tehuti: Owner of Tomb 110 at Thebes' in S. R. K. Glanville (ed.) *Studies Presented to F. Ll. Griffith.* London, 279–290.

Davies, N. de G. (1941) *The Tomb of the Vizier Ramose.* London.

Davies, N. de G. (1943) *The Tomb of Rekh-mi-Re* (2 vols). New York.

Davies, N. de G. and M. F. L. Macadam (1957) *A Corpus of Inscribed Egyptian Funerary Cones.* Oxford.

Davies, N. M. (1938) 'Some Representations of Tombs from the Theban Necropolis', *Journal of Egyptian Archaeology* 24: 25–40.

Demarée, R. J. (1983) *The ꜣḫ iḳr n Rꜥ Stelae - On Ancestor Worship in Ancient Egypt.* Leiden.

De Meyer, M. (2005) 'Restoring the Tombs of His Ancestors? Djehutinakht, Son of Teti, at Deir al-Barsha and Sheikh Said' in M. Fitzenleiter (ed.) *Genealogie: Realität und Fiktion von Identität.* London, 125–35.

Der Manuelian, P. (1998) 'A Case of Prefabrication at Giza? The False Door of "Inti"', *Journal of the American Research Center in Egypt* 35: 115–27.

Devauchelle, D. (1996) 'Les contrats de Djéfaihâpy' in B. Menu (ed.) *Égypte pharaonique: pouvoir, société.* Paris, 159–95.

Dodson, A. (1991) 'A Twenty-First Dynasty Private Reburial at Thebes', *Journal of Egyptian Archaeology* 77: 180–2.

Dodson, A. and J. J. Janssen (1989) 'A Theban Tomb and Its Tenants', *Journal of Egyptian Archaeology* 75: 125–38.

Dorman, P. F. (1988) *The Monuments of Senenmut: Problems in Historical Methodology*. London.

Dorman, P. F. (1991) *The Tombs of Senenmut: The Architecture and Decoration of Tombs 71 and 353*. New York.

Dorman, P. F. (1995) 'Two Tombs and One Owner' in J. Assmann, E. Dziobel, H. Guksch and F. Kampp (eds) *Thebanische Beamtennekropolen*. Heidelberg, 141–54.

Dorman, P. F. (2003) 'Family Burial and Commemoration in the Theban Necropolis' in N. Strudwick and J. Taylor (eds) *The Theban Necropolis: Past, Present and Future*. London, 30–45.

Dziobek, E. (1987) 'The Architectural Development of Theban Tombs in the Early Eighteenth Dynasty' in J. Assmann, G. Burkard and V. Davies (eds) *Problems and Priorities in Egyptian Archaeology*. London, 69–79.

Dziobek, E. (1992) *Das Grab des Ineni: Theben Nr. 81*. Mainz am Rhein.

Dziobek, E. (1994) *Das Gräber des Vezirs User-Amun Theben Nr. 61 und 131*. Mainz am Rhein.

Dziobek, E. (1995) 'Theban Tombs as a Source for Historical and Biographical Evaluation: The Case of User-Amun' in J. Assmann, E. Dziobel, H. Guksch and F. Kampp (eds) *Thebanische Beamtennekropolen*. Heidelberg, 129–40.

Edel, E. (1984) *Die Inschriften der Grabfronten der Siut-Gräber in Mittelägypten aus der Herakleopolitenzeit*. Opladen.

Edel, E. (2008) *Die Felsgräbernekropole der Qubbet el Hawa bei Assuan 1: Architektur, Darstellungen, Texte, archäologischer Befund und Funde der Gräber*. Paderborn.

Edgar, C. C. (1907) 'Middle Empire Tombs in the Delta' in G. Maspero (ed.) *Le Musée Égyptien II*. Cairo, 109–18.

Eigner, D. (1984) *Die Monumentalen Grabbauten der Spätzeit in der Thebanischen Nekropole*. Vienna.

el-Leithy, H. (2003) 'Letters to the Dead in Ancient and Modern Egypt' in Z. Hawass (ed.) *Egyptology at the Dawn of the Twenty-First Century: Proceedings of the Eighth International Congress of Egyptologists, Cairo 2000. I: Archaeology*. Cairo, 304–13.

el-Naggar, S. (1999) *Les voûtes dans l'architecture de l'Égypte ancienne*. Cairo.

Emery, W. B. (1938) *The Tomb of Hemaka*. Cairo.

Emery, W. B. (1949) *Great Tombs of the First Dynasty I*. Cairo.

Emery, W. B. (1954) *Great Tombs of the First Dynasty II*. London.

Emery, W. B. (1958) *Great Tombs of the First Dynasty III*. London.

Englund, G. (1978) *Akh – une notion religieuse dans L'Égypte pharaonique*. Uppsala.

Enmarch, R. (2008) *A World Upturned: Commentary on and Analysis of 'The Dialogue of Ipuwer and the Lord of All'*. Oxford.

Epigraphic Survey (1980) *The Tomb of Kheruef: Theban Tomb 192*. Chicago.

Eyre, C. J. (1984) 'A Draughtsman's Letter from Thebes', *Studien zur Altägyptischen Kultur* 11: 195–207.

Eyre, C. J. (1987a) 'Work and the Organization of Work in the Old Kingdom' in M. A. Powell (ed.) *Labor in the Ancient Near East*. New Haven, 5–47.

Eyre, C. J. (1987b) 'Work and the Organization of Work in the New Kingdom' in M. A. Powell (ed.) *Labor in the Ancient Near East*. New Haven, 167–221.

Eyre, C. J. (1994) 'Weni's Career and Old Kingdom Historiography' in C. J. Eyre, A. Leahy and L. M. Leahy (eds) *The Unbroken Reed: Studies in the Culture and Heritage of Egypt in Honour of A. F. Shore*. London, 107–24.

Eyre, C. J. (2002) *The Cannibal Hymn: A Cultural and Literary Study*. Liverpool.

Eyre, C. J. (2009) 'Belief and the Dead in Pharaonic Egypt' in M. Poo (ed.) *Rethinking Ghosts in World Religions*. Leiden, 33–46.

Farid, S. (1964) 'Preliminary Report on the Excavations of the Antiquities Department at Tell Basta (Season 1961)', *Annales du Service des Antiquités de l'Égypte* 58: 85–98.

Faulkner, R. O. (1952) 'The Stela of the Master-Sculptor Shen', *Journal of Egyptian Archaeology* 38: 3–5.

Faulkner, R. O. (1969) *The Ancient Egyptian Pyramid Texts*. Oxford.

Faulkner, R. O. (1973–8) *The Ancient Egyptian Coffin Texts* (3 vols). Warminster.

Faulkner, R. O. and C. Andrews (ed.) (1989) *The Ancient Egyptian Book of the Dead*. London.

Fischer, H. G. (1965) '*Biȝ* and the Deified Vizier *Mḥw*', *Journal of the American Research Center in Egypt* 4: 49–53.

Fischer, H. G. (1968) *Dendera in the Third Millennium B.C. down to the Theban Domination of Upper Egypt*. New York.

Fischer, H. G. (1976) 'Some Early Monuments from Busiris, in the Egyptian Delta', *Metropolitan Museum Journal* 11: 5–24.

Fischer, H. G. (1996) *The Tomb of 'Ip at el-Saff*. New York.

Fischer-Elfert, H.-W. (1998) *Die Vision von der Statue im Stein. Studien zum altägyptischen Mundöffnungsritual*. Heidelberg.

Frandsen, P. J. (1992) 'The Letter to Ikhtay's Coffin: O. Louvre Inv. No. 698' in R. J. Demarée and A. Egberts (eds) *Village Voices: Proceeding of the Symposium 'Texts from Deir el-Medina and their Interpretation', Leiden, May 31 – June 1 1991*. Leiden, 31–49.

Franke, D. (1984) *Personendaten aus dem Mittleren Reich (20.–16. Jahrhundert v. Chr.)*. Wiesbaden.

Franke, D. (1991) 'The Career of Khnumhotep III of Beni Hasan and the so-called "Decline of the Nomarchs"' in S. Quirke (ed.) *Middle Kingdom Studies*. New Malden, 51–68.

Frankfort, H. (1930) 'The Cemeteries of Abydos: Work of the Season 1925–26', *Journal of Egyptian Archaeology* 16: 213–19.

Fraser, G. W. (1902) 'The Early Tombs at Tehneh', *Annales du Service des Antiquités de l'Égypte* 3: 67–76 & 122–130.

Frazer, J. G. (1930) *The Golden Bough: A Study in Magic and Religion*. London.

Freed, R. (1996) 'Stela Workshops of Early Dynasty 12' in P. Der Manuelian (ed.) *Studies in Honor of William Kelly Simpson*, I. Boston, 297–336.

Friedman, F. M. D. (1985) 'On the Meaning of Some Anthropoid Busts from Deir el-Medina', *Journal of Egyptian Archaeology* 71: 82–97.

Frood, E. (2007) *Biographical Texts from Ramessid Egypt*. Atlanta.

Gaballa, G. A. (1977) *The Memphite Tomb-Chapel of Mose*. Warminster.

Gardiner, A. H. (1913) 'An Unusual Sketch of a Theban Funeral', *Proceedings of the Society of Biblical Archaeology* 35: 229.

Gardiner, A. H. (1955) 'A Unique Funerary Liturgy', *Journal of Egyptian Archaeology* 41: 9–17.

Gardiner, A. H. and T. E. Peet (1952–5) *The Inscriptions of Sinai* (2 vols). London.

Gardiner, A. H. and K. Sethe (1928) *Egyptian Letters to the Dead*. London.

Garnot, J. (1938) *L'Appel aux Vivants dans les Texts Funéraires Égyptiens des Origines à la Fin de l'Ancien Empire*. Cairo.

Garstang, J. (1901) *El Arábah*. London.

Garstang, J. (1904) *Tombs of the Third Egyptian Dynasty at Reqaqna and Bêt Khallaf*. London.

Garstang, J. (1909) 'Excavations at Abydos 1909: Preliminary Description of the Principal Finds', *Liverpool Annals of Archaeology and Anthropology* 2: 125–9.

Godenho, G. (2007) Manifestations of Elite Culture in Egypt's First Intermediate Period (unpublished Ph.D. thesis, University of Liverpool).

Goedicke, H. (1971) *Re-used Blocks from the Pyramid of Amenemhet I at Lisht*. New York.

Grajetzki, W. (2006) *The Middle Kingdom of Ancient Egypt*. London.

Grébaut, E. (1890-1900) *Le Musée Égyptien. Recueil de monuments et de notices sur les fouilles d'Égypte. Tome Premier*. Cairo.

Griffith, F. Ll. (1889) *The Inscriptions of Siût and Dêr Rîfeh*. London.

Griffith, F. Ll. and P. Newberry (1894–5) *El Bersheh* (2 vols). London.

Griffith, F. Ll. (1903) 'The Inscriptions' in W. M. F. Petrie, *Abydos II*. London, 41–6.

Griffiths, J. G. (1970) *Plutarch's De Iside et Osiride*. Swansea.

Griffiths, J. G. (1982) 'Osiris' in W. Helck and W. Westendorf (eds) *Lexikon der Ägyptologie*, IV. Wiesbaden, 623–33.

Habachi, L. (1985) *Elephantine IV: The Sanctuary of Heqaib*. Mainz am Rhein.

Haeny, G. (1997) 'New Kingdom "Mortuary Temples" and "Mansions of Millions of Years"' in B. E. Schafer (ed.) *Temples of Ancient Egypt*. New York, 86–126.

Haring, B. J. J. (1997) *Divine Households: Administrative and Economic Aspects of the New Kingdom Royal Memorial Temples in Western Thebes*. Leiden.

Harpur, Y. (1987) *Decoration in Egyptian Tombs of the Old Kingdom: Studies in Orientation and Scene Content*. London.

Harpur, Y. M. (2001). *The Tombs of Nefermaat and Rahotep at Maidum*. Oxford.

Harvey, S. (1998) The Cults of King Ahmose at Abydos (unpublished Ph.D. thesis, University of Pennsylvania).

Harvey, S. (2004) 'New Evidence at Abydos for Ahmose's Funerary Cult', *Egyptian Archaeology* 24: 3–6.

Hassan, S. (1932–1960) *Excavations at Gîza* (10 vols). Cairo.

Hassan, S. (1975a) *Excavations at Saqqara 1937–38, I: The Mastaba of Neb-Kaw-Her*. Cairo.

Hassan, S. (1975b) *Excavations at Saqqara 1937–38 III: Mastabas of Princess Hemet-R' and Others*. Cairo.

Hayes, W. C. (1935) 'The Tomb of Neferkhewet and His Family', *Bulletin of the Metropolitan Museum of Art* 30: 17–36.

Hayes, W. C. (1953) *The Scepter of Egypt: A Background for the Study of the Egyptian Antiquities in The Metropolitan Museum of Art*, I. New York.

Hofmann, E. (2004) *Bilder im Wandel. Die Kunst der Ramessidischen Privatgräber* Mainz am Rhein.

Hornung, E. (1983) *Conceptions of God in Ancient Egypt: The One and the Many* (trans. J. Baines). London.

Hornung, E. (1999) *The Ancient Egyptian Books of the Afterlife* (trans. D. Lorton). New York.

Ikram, S. (1995) *Choice Cuts: Meat Production in Ancient Egypt*. Leuven.

James, T. G. H. (1953) *The Mastaba of Khentika Called Ikhekhi*. London

Janośi, P. (1999) 'The Tombs of Officials: Houses of Eternity' in *Egyptian Art in the Age of the Pyramids*. New York, 27–39.

Jansen-Winkeln, K. (1995) 'Die Plünderung der Königsgräber des Neuen Reiches', *Zeitschrift für Ägyptische Sprache und Altertumskunde* 122: 62–78.

Janssen, J. J. (1975) *Commodity Prices from the Ramessid Period*. Leiden.

Jeffreys, D. G. (1985) *The Survey of Memphis*. London.

Junker, H. (1929–1955) *Gîza: Grabungen auf dem Friedhof des Alten Reiches bei den Pyramiden von Gîza* (12 vols). Vienna.

Kahl, J. (1999) *Siut-Theben: zur Wertschätzung von Traditionen im alten Ägypten*. Leiden.

Kahl, J. (2006) 'Ein Zeugnis altägyptischer Schulausflüge', *Göttinger Miszellen* 211: 25–9.

Kahl, J. (2007) *Ancient Asyut: The First Synthesis after 300 Years of Research*. Wiesbaden.

Kampp, F. (1996) *Die Thebanische Nekropole: Zum Wandel des Grabgedankens von der XVIII. bis zur XX. Dynastie*. Mainz am Rhein.

Kampp-Seyfried, F. (2003) 'The Theban Necropolis: An Overview of Topography and Tomb Development from the Middle Kingdom to the Ramesside Period' in N. Strudwick and J. Taylor (eds) *The Theban Necropolis: Past, Present and Future*. London, 2–10.

Kamrin, J. (1999) *The Cosmos of Khnumhotep II at Beni Hasan*. London.

Kanawati, N. (2003) *Conspiracies in the Egyptian Palace: Unis to Pepi I*. London.

Kanawati, N. (2005) 'Decoration of Burial Chambers, Sarcophagi and Coffins in the Old Kingdom' in K. Daoud, S. Bedier and S. Abd el-Fatah (eds). *Studies in Honor of Ali Radwan*. Cairo, 55–71.

Kemp, B. J. (1967) 'The Egyptian 1st Dynasty Royal Cemetery', *Antiquity* 41: 22–32.

Kemp, B. J. (1976) 'Abydos' in W. Helck and W. Westendorf (eds) *Lexikon der Ägyptologie*, I. Wiesbaden, 28–41.

Kemp, B. J. (2006) 'Tell el-Amarna 2005–06', *Journal of Egyptian Archaeology* 92: 21–56.

Kemp, B. J. (2007) *How to Read the Egyptian Book of the Dead*. London.

Kemp, B. J. and R. Merrillees (1980) *Minoan Pottery in Second Millennium Egypt.* Mainz.

Kitchen, K. A. (1979) 'Memphite Tomb-Chapels in the New Kingdom and Later' in M. Görg and E. Pusch (eds) *Festschrift Elmar Edel.* Bamberg, 272–84.

Kloth, N. (2002) *Die (auto-)biographischen Inschriften des ägyptischen Alten Reiches: Untersuchungen zu Phraseologie und Entwicklung.* Hamburg.

Lansing, A. and W. C. Hayes (1937) 'The Museum's Excavations at Thebes', *Bulletin of the Metropolitan Museum of Art* 32: 4–39.

Leahy, A. (1977) 'The Osiris "Bed" Reconsidered', *Orientalia* 46: 424–34.

Leahy, A. (1989) 'A Protective Measure at Abydos in the Thirteenth Dynasty', *Journal of Egyptian Archaeology* 75: 41–60.

Lefebvre, G. (1923–4) *Le tombeau de Petosiris* (3 vols). Cairo.

Leprohon, R. J. (1978) 'The Personnel of the Middle Kingdom Funerary Stelae', *Journal of the American Research Center in Egypt* 15: 33–8.

Lichtheim, M. (1973) *Ancient Egyptian Literature: A Book of Readings, I: The Old and Middle Kingdoms.* Berkeley.

Lichtheim, M. (1976) *Ancient Egyptian Literature: A Book of Readings, II: The New Kingdom.* Berkeley.

Lichtheim, M. (1980) *Ancient Egyptian Literature: A Book of Readings, III: The Late Period.* Berkeley.

Lichtheim, M. (1988) *Ancient Egyptian Autobiographies Chiefly of the Middle Kingdom.* Göttingen.

Lloyd, A. B. (1988) *Herodotus. Book II (Commentary 99–182).* Leiden.

Loat, W. L. S. (1923) 'A Sixth Dynasty Cemetery at Abydos', *Journal of Egyptian Archaeology* 9: 161–3.

McDowell, A. G. (1990) *Jurisdiction in the Workmen's Community of Deir el-Medina.* Leiden.

McDowell, A. G. (1999) *Village Life in Ancient Egypt: Laundry Lists and Love Songs.* Oxford.

Mace, A. C. and H. E. Winlock (1916) *The Tomb of Senebtisi at Lisht.* New York.

Malek, J. (1981) 'Two Problems Connected with New Kingdom Tombs in the Memphite Area', *Journal of Egyptian Archaeology* 67: 156–65.

Malek, J. (1985) 'The Tomb-Chapel of Hekamaetre-neheh at Northern Saqqara', *Studien zur Altägyptischen Kultur* 12: 43–60.

Malek, J. (1989) 'An Early Eighteenth Dynasty Monument of Sipair from Saqqâra', *Journal of Egyptian Archaeology* 75: 61–76.

Malek, J. (1990) 'New-Kingdom Pyramidia', *Journal of Egyptian Archaeology* 76: 180–4.

Malek, J. (1994) 'King Merykare and His Pyramid' in C. Berger, G. Clerc and N. Grimal (eds) *Hommages à Jean Leclant*, 4. Cairo, 203–14.

Malek, J. (2000a) 'The Old Kingdom' in I. Shaw (ed.) *The Oxford History of Ancient Egypt.* Oxford, 89–117.

Malek, J. (2000b) 'Old Kingdom Rulers as "Local Saints" in the Memphite Area during the Middle Kingdom' in M. Bárta and J. Krejci (eds) *Abusir and Saqqara in the Year 2000.* Prague, 241–58.

Manniche, L. (2003) 'The So-Called Scenes of Daily Life in the Private Tombs of the Eighteenth Dynasty: An Overview' in N. Strudwick and J. Taylor (eds) *The Theban Necropolis: Past, Present and Future*. London, 42–5.

Martin, G. T. (1974–89) *The Royal Tomb at El-Amarna* (2 vols). London.

Martin, G. T. (1985) *The Tomb-Chapels of Paser and Ra'ia at Saqqara*. London.

Martin, G. T. (1986) 'Shabtis of Private Persons in the Amarna Period', *Mitteilungen des Deutschen Archäologischen Instituts Abteilung Kairo* 42: 109–29.

Martin, G. T. (1989) *The Memphite Tomb of Horemheb Commander-in-Chief of Tutankhamun I: The Reliefs, Inscriptions and Commentary*. London.

Martin, G. T., with contributions by J. van Dijk, D. A. Aston, M. J. Raven and K. J. Frazer (1997) *The Tomb of Tia and Tia: A Royal Monument of the Ramesside Period in the Memphite Necropolis*. London.

Meskell, L. (1997) 'Intimate Archaeologies: The Case of Kha and Merit', *World Archaeology* 29(3): 363–79.

Meskell, L. (1999) *Archaeologies of Social Life*. Oxford.

Midant-Reynes, B. (2000) *The Prehistory of Egypt* (trans. I. Shaw). Oxford.

Minault-Gout, A. (1992) *Le mastaba d'Ima-Pepi (Mastaba II)*. Cairo.

Montet, P. (1947) *La nécropole royale de Tanis I: Les constructions et le tombeau de Osorkon II à Tanis*. Paris.

Montet, P. (1951) *La nécropole royale de Tanis II: Les constructions et le tombeau de Psousennes à Tanis*. Paris.

Montet, P. (1960) *La nécropole royale de Tanis III: Les constructions et le tombeau de Chéchanq III à Tanis*. Paris.

Montserrat, D. (1997) 'Death and Funerals in the Roman Fayum' in M. L. Bierbrier (ed.) *Portraits and Masks: Burial Customs in Roman Egypt*. London, 33–43.

Moreno Garcia, J. C. (1998) 'De L'Ancien Empire à la Première Période Intermédiaire: l'autobiographie de Qar d'Edfou, entre tradition et innovation', *Revue d'Egyptologie* 49: 151–60.

Morkot, R. G. (1990) '*Nb-Maat-Ra*-United-with-Ptah', *Journal of Near Eastern Studies* 49: 323–37.

Morris, E. F. (2007a) 'Sacrifice for the State' in N. Laneri (ed.) *Performing Death: Social Analyses of Funerary Traditions in the Ancient Near East and Mediterranean*. Chicago, 15–37.

Morris, E. F. (2007b) 'On the Ownership of the Saqqara Mastabas and the Allotment of Political and Ideological Power at the Dawn of the State' in Z. A. Hawass and J. Richards (eds) *The Archaeology and Art of Ancient Egypt: Essays in Honor of David B. O'Connor*. Cairo, 171–90.

Morschauser, S. (1991) *Threat-Formulae in Ancient Egypt: A Study of the History, Structure and Use of Threats and Curses in Ancient Egypt*. Baltimore.

Moussa, A. M. and H. Altenmüller (1971) *The Tomb of Nefer and Ka-hay*. Mainz am Rhein.

Moussa, A. M. and H. Altenmüller (1977) *Das Grab des Nianchchnum und Chnumhotep* Mainz am Rhein.

Munro, P. (1993) *Der Unas-Friedhof Nord-West I. Topographische, historische Einleitung, das Doppelgrab der Königinnen Nebet und Khenut*. Mainz am Rhein.

Murnane, W. J. (1995) *Texts from the Amarna Period in Ancient Egypt*. Atlanta.

Murnane, W. J. and C. C. Van Siclen III (1993) *The Boundary Stelae of Akhenaten*. London.

Myśliwiec, K. (2000) *The Twilight of Ancient Egypt*. Ithaca, NY.

Naville, E. (1886) *Das Ägyptische Todtenbuch der XVIII. bis XX. Dynastie*. Berlin.

Negm, M. (1997) *The Tomb of Simut Called Kyky: Theban Tomb 409 at Qurnah*. Warminster.

Newberry, P. (1893–1900) *Beni Hasan* (4 vols). London.

Niwinski, A. (1984) 'Seelenhaus' in W. Helck and E. Otto (eds) *Lexikon der Ägyptologie*, V. Wiesbaden, 806–13.

Ockinga, B. (1997) *A Tomb from the Reign of Tutankhamun at Akhmim*. London.

Ockinga, B. and Y. al-Masri (1988-90) *Two Ramesside Tombs at El Mashayikh* (2 vols). Sydney.

O'Connor, D. (1975) 'Political Systems and Archaeological Data in Egypt: 2600–1780 BC', *World Archaeology* 6: 15–38.

O'Connor, D. (1979) 'Abydos: The University Museum–Yale University Expedition', *Expedition* 21: 46–9.

O'Connor, D. (1985) 'The "Cenotaphs" of the Middle Kingdom at Abydos' in P. Posener-Kriéger (ed.) *Mélanges Gamal eddin Mokhtar*. Cairo, 161–77.

O'Connor, D. (2009) *Abydos: Egypt's First Pharaohs and the Cult of Osiris*. London.

Orel, S. E. (1994) 'A Stela of Khnumhotep in the British Museum (BM625)' in C. J. Eyre, A. Leahy and L. M. Leahy (eds) *The Unbroken Reed: Studies in the Culture and Heritage of Egypt in Honour of A. F. Shore*. London, 227–41.

Otto, E. (1960) *Das ägyptische Mundöffnungsritual*. Wiesbaden.

Otto, E. (1968) *Osiris and Amon*. London.

Owen, G. and B. Kemp (1994) 'Craftsmen's Work Patterns in Unfinished Tombs at Amarna', *Cambridge Archaeological Journal* 4(1): 121–9.

Parkinson, R. B. (1991) *Voices from Ancient Egypt: An Anthology of Middle Kingdom Writings*. London.

Parkinson, R. B. (2008) *The Painted Tomb-Chapel of Nebamun*. London.

Peet, T. E. (1914a) *The Stela of Sebek-khu*. Manchester.

Peet, T. E. (1914b) *The Cemeteries of Abydos*, II. London.

Peet, T. E. (1930) *The Great Tomb-Robberies of the Twentieth Egyptian Dynasty*. Oxford.

Peet, T. E. and W. L. S. Loat (1914) *The Cemeteries of Abydos*, III. London.

Pérez Die, M. C. (1990) 'La necrópolis del Primer Período Intermedio de Heracleópolis Magna: Estado de la cuestión' *Hathor* 2,94–100.

Pérez-Die, M. C. (2005) 'La nécropole de la Première Période Intermédiaire – début du Moyen Empire à Héracléopolis Magna: nouvelles découvertes et résultats récents (campagne 2001)' in L. Pantalacci (ed.) *Des Néferkarê aux Montouhotep: Travaux archéologiques en cours sur la fin de VIe dynastie et la Première Période Intermédiaire. Actes du Colloque CNRS, Université Lumière-Lyon 2, tenu le 5–7 juillet 2001*. Lyon.

Petrie, W. M. F. (1888) *Tanis II. Nebesheh and Defenneh*. London.

Petrie, W. M. F. (1900) *Dendereh, 1898*. London.

Petrie, W. M. F. (1901) *Diospolis Parva*. London.

Petrie, W. M. F. (1907) *Gizeh and Rifeh*. London.

Petrie, W. M. F. (1909) *Qurneh*. London.

Petrie, W. M. F. (1914) *Tarkhan II*. London.

Pflüger, K. (1947) 'The Private Funerary Stelae of the Middle Kingdom and their Importance for the Study of Ancient Egyptian History', *Journal of the American Oriental Society* 67: 127–35.

Plater, C. (2001) Aspects of the Interaction between the Living and the Dead in Ancient Egypt (unpublished Ph.D. thesis, University of Liverpool).

Podvin, J.-L. (2000) 'Position du mobilier funéraire dans les tombes égyptiennes privées du Moyen Empire', *Mitteilungen des Deutschen Archäologischen Instituts Abteilung Kairo* 56: 278–334.

Polz, D. (2007) *Der Beginn des Neuen Reiches: Zur Vorgeschichte einer Zeitenwende*. Berlin.

Posener, G. (1981) 'Les 'afārt dans l'ancienne Égypte', *Mitteilungen des Deutschen Archäologischen Instituts Abteilung Kairo* 37: 393–401.

Posener-Kriéger, P. (1968) 'Remarques sur l'ensemble funéraire de Neferirkare Kakai à Abu Sir' in W. Helck (ed.) *Festschrift für Siegfried Schott*. Wiesbaden, 112–20.

Posener-Kriéger, P. (1976) *Les archives du temple funéraire de Néferirkarê-Kakaï (Les Papyrus d'Abousir). Traduction et Commentaire* (2 vols). Cairo.

Posener-Kriéger, P. (1981) 'Construire une tombe à l'ouest de Mn-nfr (P Caire 52002)', *Revue d'Égyptologie* 33: 47–58.

Quibell, J. E. (1898) *El Kab*. London.

Quibell, J. E. (1908) *The Tomb of Yuaa and Thuiu*. Cairo.

Quibell, J. E. (1923) *Excavations at Saqqara, 1912–1914: Archaic Mastabas*. Cairo.

Quibell, J. E. and A. G. K. Hayter (1927) *Excavations at Saqqara. Teti Pyramid, North Side*. Cairo.

Rammant-Peeters, A. (1983) *Les pyramidions égyptiens du Nouvel Empire*. Leuven.

Ramond, P. (1977) *Les stèles égyptiennes du Musée G. Labit à Toulouse*. Cairo.

Randall-MacIver, D. and A. C. Mace (1902) *El Amrah and Abydos*. London.

Raven, M. J. (1991) *The Tomb of Iurudef: A Memphite Official in the Reign of Ramesses. II*. London.

Redford, D. (2001) 'Mendes' in D. Redford (ed.) *Oxford Encyclopedia of Ancient Egypt*, 2. Oxford, 376–7.

Redford, D. B. (2004) *Excavations at Mendes 1: The Royal Necropolis*. Leiden.

Reeves, C. N. (1990) *Valley of the Kings: The Decline of a Royal Necropolis*. London.

Reeves, C. N. (2001) *Akhenaten: Egypt's False Prophet*. London.

Reeves, C. N. and R. H. Wilkinson (1996) *The Complete Valley of the Kings*. London.

Reisner, G. A. (1918) 'The Tomb of Hepzefa, Nomarch of Siût', *Journal of Egyptian Archaeology* 5: 79–98.

Reisner, G. A. (1923) *Excavations at Kerma*, V. Cambridge, MA.

Reisner, G. A. (1931) 'Inscribed Monuments from Gebel Barkal', *Zeitschrift für Ägyptische Sprache und Altertumskunde* 66: 89–100.

Reisner, G. A. (1932) *Naga ed-Dêr III: A Provincial Cemetery of the Pyramid Age.* Berkeley.

Richards, J. (2000) 'Time and Memory in Ancient Egyptian Cemeteries', *Expedition* 44(3): 16–24.

Richards, J. (2002) 'Text and Context in Late Old Kingdom Egypt: The Archaeology and Historiography of Weni the Elder', *Journal of the American Research Center in Egypt* 39: 75–102.

Richards, J. (2003) 'The Abydos Cemeteries in the Late Old Kingdom' in Z. Hawass (ed.), *Egyptology at the Dawn of the Twenty-First Century: Proceedings of the Eighth International Congress of Egyptologists, Cairo 2000. I: Archaeology.* Cairo, 400–7.

Richards, J. (2005) *Society and Death in Ancient Egypt: Mortuary Landscapes of the Middle Kingdom.* Cambridge.

Riggs, C. (2005) *The Beautiful Burial in Roman Egypt: Art, Identity and Funerary Religion.* Oxford.

Roehrig, C. (1999) 'Reserve Heads: An Enigma of Old Kingdom Sculpture' in *Egyptian Art in the Age of the Pyramids.* New York, 73–81.

Romer, J. (1974) 'Tuthmosis I and the Bibân el-Molûk: Some Problems of Attribution', *Journal of Egyptian Archaeology* 60: 119–33.

Romer, J. (1976) 'Royal Tombs of the Early Eighteenth Dynasty', *Mitteilungen des Deutschen Archäologischen Instituts Abteilung Kairo* 32: 191–206.

Roth, A. M. (1991) *Egyptian Phyles in the Old Kingdom: The Evolution of a System of Social Organization.* Chicago.

Roth, A. M. (1988) 'The Organization of Royal Cemeteries at Saqqara in the Old Kingdom', *Journal of the American Research Center in Egypt* 25: 201–14.

Roth, A. M. (1992) 'The Pesesch-Kef and the "Opening of the Mouth" Ceremony: A Ritual of Birth and Rebirth', *Journal of Egyptian Archaeology* 78: 113–47.

Roth, A. M. (2002) 'The Meaning of Menial Labour. "Servant Statues" in Old Kingdom Serdabs', *Journal of the American Research Center in Egypt* 39: 103–21.

Ryholt, K. (1997) *The Political Situation in Egypt during the Second Intermediate Period (c.1800–1550 BC).* Copenhagen.

Schäfer, H. (1908) *Priestergräber und andere Grabfunde vom Ende des Alten Reiches bis zur griechischenzeit vom Totentempel des Ne-User-Rê.* Leipzig.

Scharff, A. (1947) *Grab als Wohnhaus in der ägyptischen Frühzeit.* Munich.

Schiaparelli, E. (1927) *Tomba Intatta dell'Architetto Cha.* Turin.

Seidlmayer, S. J. (1990) *Gräberfelder aus dem Übergang vom Alten zum Mittleren Reich: Studien zur Archäologie der Ersten Zwischenzeit.* Heidelberg.

Seidlmayer, S. J. (2000) 'The First Intermediate Period' in I. Shaw (ed.) *The Oxford History of Ancient Egypt.* Oxford, 118–47.

Seyfried, K. J. (1987) 'Entwicklung in der Grabarchitektur des Neuen Reiches al seine weitere Quelle für theologische Konzeptionen des Ramessidenzeit' in J. Assmann, G. Burkard and V. Davies (eds) *Problems and Priorities in Egyptian Archaeology.* London, 219–53.

Seyfried, K. J. (1995) *Das Grab des Djehutiemhab (TT 194).* Mainz am Rhein.

Silverman, D. P. (1988) *The Tomb Chamber of Ḥsw the Elder: The Inscribed Material at Kom El-Ḥisn*. Winona Lake.

Silverman, D. P. (2009) 'Non-Royal Burials in the Teti Pyramid Cemetery and the Early Twelfth Dynasty' in D. P. Silverman, W. K. Simpson and J. Wegner (eds) *Archaism and Innovation: Studies in the Culture of Middle Kingdom Egypt*. New Haven and Philadelphia, 47–101.

Silverman, D. P., M. Robinson, E. Brovarski, R. van Walsem, H. Willems, O. Kaper, R. Freed and J.-L. Lachevre (1992) *Bersheh Reports*, I. Boston.

Simpson, W. K. (1963) *Heka-Nefer and the Dynastic Material from Toshka and Arminna*. New Haven.

Simpson, W. K. (1974) *The Terrace of the Great God at Abydos: The Offering Chapels of Dynasties 12 and 13*. New Haven.

Simpson, W. K. (1976) *The Mastabas of Qar and Idu*. Boston.

Simpson, W. K., R. K. Ritner, V. A. Tobin and E. F. Wente (2003) *The Literature of Ancient Egypt* (3rd edn). New Haven.

Smith, M. (2009) 'Democratization of the Afterlife' in J. Dieleman and W. Wendrich (eds) *UCLA Encyclopedia of Egyptology*. Los Angeles.

Smith, S. T. (1992) 'Intact Tombs of the Seventeenth and Eighteenth Dynasties from Thebes and the New Kingdom Burial System', *Mitteilungen des Deutschen Archäologischen Instituts Abteilung Kairo* 48: 193–231.

Smith, S. T. (2003) *Wretched Kush: Ethnic Identities and Boundaries in Egypt's Nubian Empire*. London.

Smither, P. C. and A. N. Dakin (1939) 'Stelae in the Queen's College, Oxford', *Journal of Egyptian Archaeology* 25: 157–65.

Snape, S. (1986) Mortuary Assemblages from Abydos (unpublished Ph.D. thesis, University of Liverpool).

Snape, S. (1994) 'Statues and Soldiers at Abydos in the Second Intermediate Period' in C. J. Eyre, A. Leahy and L. M. Leahy (eds) *The Unbroken Reed: Studies in the Culture and Heritage of Egypt in Honour of A. F. Shore*. London, 304–14.

Snape, S. and D. Bailey (1988) *The Great Portico at Hermopolis Magna: Present State and Past Prospects*. London.

Spanel, D. (2001) 'Herakleopolis' in D. Redford (ed.) *Oxford Encyclopedia of Ancient Egypt*, 2. Oxford, 91–3.

Spencer, A. J. (1982) 'First and Second Owners of a Memphite Tomb Chapel', *Journal of Egyptian Archaeology* 68: 20–6.

Spencer, A. J. (2003) *Excavations at Tell Balamun 1999–2001*. London.

Spencer, A. J. (2007) 'The Possible Existence of Third Intermediate Period Elite Tombs at el-Ashmunein', *British Museum Studies in Ancient Egypt and Sudan* 8: 49–51.

Spiegelberg, W. (1896) *Die Ägyptische Sammlung des Museums Meermanno-Westreenianum im Haag*. Strassburg.

Stadelmann, R. (1997) 'The Development of the Pyramid Temple in the Fourth Dynasty' in S. Quirke (ed.) *The Temple in Ancient Egypt: New Discoveries and Recent Research*. London, 1–16.

Stammers, M. (2009) *The Elite Late Period Egyptian Tombs of Memphis*. Oxford.

Steckeweh, H. (1936) *Die Fürstengräber von Qaw*. Leipzig.

Stevens, A. (2006) *Private Religion at Amarna: The Material Evidence*. Oxford.

Strudwick, N. (1985) *The Administration of Egypt in the Old Kingdom*. London.

Strudwick, N. (1994) 'Change and Continuity at Thebes: The Private Tomb after Akhenaten' in C. J. Eyre, A. Leahy and L. Montagno Leahy (eds) *The Unbroken Reed: Studies in the Culture and Heritage of Ancient Egypt in Honour of A. F. Shore*. London, 321–36.

Strudwick, N. (2005) *Texts from the Pyramid Age*. Atlanta.

Taylor, J. H. and A. Boyce (1986) 'The Late New Kingdom Burial from beside the Main Chapel' in B. J. Kemp (ed.) *Amarna Reports*, III. London, 118–46.

Taylor, J. H. (1989) *Egyptian Coffins*. Princes Risborough.

Taylor, J. H. (2000) 'The Third Intermediate Period' in I. Shaw (ed.) *The Oxford History of Ancient Egypt*. Oxford, 330–68.

Tooley, A. M. J. (1995) *Egyptian Models and Scenes*. Princes Risborough.

Ucko, P. J. (1969) 'Ethnography and Archaeological Interpretation of Funerary Remains', *World Archaeology* 1/2: 262–80.

Valbelle, D. (1985) *'Les Ouvriers de la Tombe': Deir el-Médineh à l'époque Ramesside*. Cairo.

Valloggia, M. (1986) *Le Mastaba de Medou-Nefer*. Cairo.

Vandier, J. (1950) *Mo'alla: la tombe d'Ankhtyfy et la tombe de Sebekhotep*. Cairo.

van Dijk, J. (1988) 'The Development of the Memphite Necropolis in the Post-Amarna Period' in A. P. Zivie (ed.) *Memphis et ses nécropoles au Nouvel Empire: nouvelles données, nouvelles questions*. Paris, 37–46.

Venit, M. J. (2002) *Monumental Tombs of Ancient Alexandria*. Cambridge.

Verner, M. (1986) 'A Slaughterhouse from the Old Kingdom', *Mitteilungen des Deutschen Archäologischen Instituts Abteilung Kairo* 42: 181–9.

von Bissing, F. W. (1905–11) *Die Mastaba von Gem-ni-kai* (2 vols). Berlin.

von der Way, T. (1996) 'Überlegungen zur Jenseitsvorstellung in der Amarnazeit', *Zeitschrift für Ägyptische Sprache und Altertumskunde* 123: 157–64.

Ward, W. A. (1980) 'The Middle Egyptian Title *Ṯꜣw*, "Journeyman, Trainee"', *Zeitschrift für Ägyptische Sprache und Altertumskunde* 107: 170–4.

Ward, W. A. (1982) *Index of Egyptian Administrative and Religious Titles of the Middle Kingdom*. Beirut.

Wegner, J. (2007) *The Mortuary Temple of Senwosret III at Abydos*. Philadelphia.

Wegner, J. (2009) 'The Tomb of Senwosret III at Abydos: Considerations on the Origins and Development of the Royal Amduat-Tomb' in D. P. Silverman, W. K. Simpson and J. Wegner (eds.) *Archaism and Innovation: Studies in the Culture of Middle Kingdom Egypt*. New Haven and Philadelphia, 103–68.

Weill, R. (1958) *Dara: Campagnes de 1946–58*. Cairo.

Wengrow, D. (2006) *The Archaeology of Early Egypt: Social Transformations in North-East Africa, 10, 000 to 2650 BC*. Cambridge.

Wente, E. (1990) *Letters from Ancient Egypt*. Atlanta.

Wiebach, S. (1981) *Die ägyptische Scheintür. Morphologische Studien zur Entwicklung und Bedeutung der Hauptkultstelle in den Privat-Gräbern des Alten Reiches.* Hamburg.

Wildung, D. (1977) *Egyptian Saints: Deification in Pharaonic Egypt.* New York.

Wilkinson, T. A. H. (1999) *Early Dynastic Egypt.* London.

Willems, H. (1988) *Chests of Life: A Study of the Typological and Conceptual Development of Middle Kingdom Standard Class Coffins.* Leiden.

Wilson, J. A. (1944) 'Funeral Services of the Egyptian Old Kingdom', *Journal of Near Eastern Studies* 3: 201–18.

Wilson, J. A. (1947) 'The Artist of the Egyptian Old Kingdom', *Journal of Near Eastern Studies* 6: 231–49.

Winlock, H. E. (1920) 'Excavations at Thebes 1919-20', *Bulletin of the Metropolitan Museum of Art* 15: 12–31.

Winlock, H. E. (1923) 'The Museum's Excavations at Thebes', *Bulletin of the Metropolitan Museum of Art* 18: 11–39.

Winlock, H. E. (1955) *Models of Daily Life in Ancient Egypt from the Tomb of Meket-Re at Thebes.* New York.

Yoyotte, J. (1960) 'Les pèlerinages dans l'Égypte ancienne' in J. Yoyotte (ed.) *Les Pèlerinages.* Paris, 19–74.

Žabkar, L. (1968) *A Study of the Ba Concept in Ancient Egyptian Texts.* Chicago.

Zivie, A. P. (1984) 'Un chancelier nommé Nehesy' in F. Daumas (ed.) *Mélanges Adolphe Gutbub.* Montpellier, 245–52.

Zivie, A. P. (1988) 'Aper-El et ses voisins: considérations sur les tombes rupestres de la XVIIIème dynastie à Saqqarah' in A. P. Zivie (ed.) *Memphis et ses nécropoles au Nouvel Empire: nouvelles données, nouvelles questions.* Paris, 103–12.

Zivie, A. P. (1990) *Découverte à Saqqarah: le vizir oublié.* Paris.

Zonhoven, L. M. J. (1979) 'The Inspection of a Tomb at Deir el-Medina (O. Wien Aeg. 1)', *Journal of Egyptian Archaeology* 65: 89–98.

Further Reading

Allen, J. P. (2008) 'The Biographical Inscription from the Mastaba of Intef(?)' in D. Arnold, *Middle Kingdom Tomb Architecture at Lisht*. New York, 89–93.

Altenmüller, H. (1998) *Die Wanddarstellungen im Grab des Mehu in Saqqara*. Mainz am Rhein.

Arnold, D. (2003) *The Encyclopedia of Ancient Egyptian Architecture* (trans. S. H. and H. Gardiner). London.

Assmann, J. (1995) *Egyptian Solar Religion in the New Kingdom: Re, Amun and the Crisis of Polytheism*. London.

Assmann, J. (1996) 'Der literarische Aspekt des ägyptischen Grabes und seine Funktion im Rahmen des "monumentalen Diskurses"' in A. Loprieno (ed.) *Ancient Egyptian Literature: History and Forms*. Leiden, 97–104.

Ayrton, E. R. and W. L. S. Loat (1911) *Pre-Dynastic Cemetery at El Mahasna*. London.

Badawy, A. (1978) *The Tomb of Nyhetep-Ptah at Giza and the Tomb of Ankhmahor at Saqqara*. Berkeley.

Baer, K. (1960) *Rank and Title in the Old Kingdom: The Structure of the Egyptian Administration in the Fifth and Sixth Dynasties*. Chicago.

Baines, J. (1986) 'The Stela of Emhab: Innovation, Tradition, Hierarchy', *Journal of Egyptian Archaeology* 72: 41–53.

Baines, J. (1999) 'Forerunners of Narrative Biographies' in A. Leahy and J. Tait (eds) *Studies on Ancient Egypt in Honour of H. S. Smith*. London, 23–37.

Baines, J. and P. Lacovara (2002) 'Burial and the Dead in Ancient Egyptian Society: Respect, Formalism, Neglect', *Journal of Social Archaeology* 2: 5–36.

Baines, J. and N. Yoffee (1998) 'Order, Legitimacy and Wealth in Ancient Egypt and Mesopotamia' in G. Feinman and J. Marcus (eds) *Archaic States*. Santa Fe, 199–260.

Bietak, M. and E. Reiser-Haslauer (1978–82) *Das Grab des Anch-Hor Obersthofmeister der Gottesgemahlin Nitokris I–II*. Vienna.

Bourriau, J. (1988) *Pharaohs and Mortals: Egyptian Art in the Middle Kingdom.* Cambridge.

Bourriau, J. (1991) 'Patterns of Change in Burial Customs during the Middle Kingdom' in S. Quirke (ed.) *Middle Kingdom Studies.* New Malden, 3–20.

Brack, A. and A. Brack (1977) *Das Grab des Tjanuni: Theben Nr. 74.* Mainz am Rhein.

Brunner, H. (1936) *Die Anlagen der ägyptischen Felsgräben bis zum mittleren Reich.* Glückstadt.

Brunner-Traut, E. (1977) *Die altägyptische Grabkamer Seschemnofers III aus Giza.* Mainz am Rhein.

Bruyère, B. (1948) *Rapport sur les fouilles de Deir el-Médineh 1935–40.* Cairo.

Capart, J. (1907) *Une rue de tombeaux à Saqqarah.* Brussels.

Chauvet, V. (2007) 'Decoration and Architecture: The Definition of a Private Tomb Environment' in S. D'Auria (ed.) *Servant of Mut: Studies in Honor of Richard A. Fazzini.* Leiden, 44–52.

Cherpion, N. (1989) *Mastabas et hypogées d'Ancien Empire: le problème de la datation.* Brussels.

Corbelli, J. A. (2006) *The Art of Death in Graeco-Roman Egypt.* Princes Risborough.

Curto, S. and M. Mancini (1968) 'News of Kha and Merit', *Journal of Egyptian Archaeology* 54: 77–81.

Daoud, K. A. (2005) *Corpus of Inscriptions of the Herakleopolitan period from the Memphite Necropolis.* Oxford.

D'Auria, S. H. (1999) 'Preparing for Eternity' in R. E. Freed, Y. J. Markowitz and S. H. d'Auria *Pharaohs of the Sun: Akhenaten-Nefertiti-Tutankhamen* London, 162–175.

D'Auria, S., P. Lacovara and C. Roehrig (1988) *Mummies and Magic.* Boston.

Davies, N. de G. (1915) *The Tomb of Amenemhet (No. 82).* London.

Davies, N. de G. (1922) *The Tomb of Puyemre at Thebes.* London.

Dodson, A. and S. Ikram (2008) *The Tomb in Ancient Egypt.* London.

Downes, D. (1974) *The Excavations at Esna.* Warminster.

Duell, P. (1938) *The Mastaba of Mereruka* (2 vols). Chicago.

Dziobek, E. and M. Abdel Raziq (1990) *Das Grab des Sobekhotep: Theben Nr. 63.* Mainz am Rhein.

Eaton-Krauss, M. (1984) *The Representations of Statues in Private Tombs of the Old Kingdom.* Wiesbaden.

Edwards, I. E. S. (1975) 'Bill of Sale for a Set of Shabtis', *Journal of Egyptian Archaeology* 57: 120–4.

Firth, C. M. and B. Gunn (1926) *Teti Pyramid Cemeteries* (2 vols). Cairo.

Forman, W. and S. Quirke (1996) *Hieroglyphs and the Afterlife in Ancient Egypt.* London.

Franke, D. (1994) *Das Heiligtum des Heqaib auf Elephantine. Geschichte eines Provinzheiligtums im Mittleren Reich.* Heidelberg.

Fraser, P. M. (1972) *Ptolemaic Alexandria* (3 vols). Oxford.

Gardiner, A. H. (1913) 'In Praise of Death: A Song from a Theban Tomb', *Proceedings of the Society of Biblical Archaeology* 35: 165–70.

Garstang, J. (1907) *The Burial Customs of Ancient Egypt.* London.

Grajetzki, W. (2003) *Burial Customs in Ancient Egypt: Life in Death for Rich and Poor*. London.

Grajetzki, W. (2008) 'The Emptiness of Old Kingdom Tombs', *The Heritage of Egypt* 1: 17–20.

Griffiths, J. G. (1966) *The Origins of Osiris*. Berlin.

Griffiths, J. G. (1980) *The Origins of Osiris and His Cult*. Leiden.

Guksch, H., E. Hofmann and M. Bommas (eds) (2003) *Grab und Totenkult im Alten Ägypten*. Munich.

Hartwig, M. (2004) *Tomb Painting and Identity in Ancient Thebes, 1419-1372 BCE*. Brussels.

Hodel-Hoenes, S. (1991), *Leben und Tod im Alten Ägypten. Thebanische Privatgräber des Neuen Reiches*. Darmstadt.

Hölscher, U. and P. Munro (1975) 'Der Unas-Freidhof in Saqqara', *Studien zur Altägyptischen Kultur* 3: 113–25.

Janssen, J. J. and P. W. Pestman (1968) 'Burial and Inheritance in the Community of the Necropolis Workmen at Thebes', *Journal of the Economic and Social History of the Orient* 11: 137–70.

Jaroš-Deckert, B. (1984) *Grabung im Asasif 1964–1970, V: Das Grab des Ini-iti. f.* Mainz am Rhein.

Kanawati, N. (1980–92). *The Rock Tombs of el-Hawawish: The Cemetery of Akhmim* (10 vols). Sydney.

Kanawati, N. (2001) *The Tomb and Beyond: Burial Customs of Egyptian Officials*. Warminster.

Kemp, B. J. (1966) 'Abydos and the Royal Tombs of the First Dynasty', *Journal of Egyptian Archaeology* 52: 13–22.

Kemp, B. J. (2005) *Ancient Egypt: Anatomy of a Civilisation* (2nd ed.). London.

Kuhlmann, K. and W. Schenkel (1983) *Das Grab des Ibi, Obergutsverwalters der Gottesgemahlin des Amun: (Thebanisches Grab Nr. 36)/1: Beschreibung der unterirdischen Kult- und Bestattungsanlage*. Mainz am Rhein.

Labrousse, A. (1996) *L'architecture des Pyramides à Textes*. Cairo.

Lange, H. O. and H. Schäfer (1902) *Grab- und Denksteine des Mittleren Reiches im Museum von Kairo (CCG 20001–20780)*. Berlin.

Lapp, G. (1993) *Typologie der Särge und Sargkammern von der 6. bis 13 Dynastie*. Heidelberg.

Lehner, M. (1997) *The Complete Pyramids*. London.

Lilyquist, C. (1979) *Ancient Egyptian Mirrors*. Munich.

Lull, J. (2002) *Las tumbas reales egipcias del Tercer Período Intermedio (dinastías XXI – XXV): Tradición y cambios*. Oxford.

McFarlane, A. (2000) *Unis Cemetery at Saqqara I: The Tomb of Irukaptah*. Warminster.

Mackay, E. (1921) 'The Cutting and Preparation of Tomb-Chapels in the Theban Necropolis', *Journal of Egyptian Archaeology* 7: 154–68.

Malek, J. (1988) 'The Royal Butler Hori at Northern Saqqara', *Journal of Egyptian Archaeology* 74: 125–36.

Manniche, L. (1988) *Lost Tombs: Study of Certain Eighteenth Dynasty Monuments in the Theban Necropolis*. London.

Martin, G. T. (1991) *The Hidden Tombs of Memphis: New Discoveries from the Time of Tutankhamun and Ramesses the Great.* London.

Miller, P. (1937) 'A Family Stela in the University Museum, Philadelphia', *Journal of Egyptian Archaeology* 23: 1–6.

Montet, P. (1928–36) 'Les tombeaux de Siout et de Deir Rifeh', *Kêmi* 1 (1928): 53–68; *Kêmi* 3 (1930): 45–111; *Kêmi* 6 (1936): 131–63.

Müller, H. W. (1940) *Die Felsengräber von Elephantine aus der Zeit des Mittleren Reiches.* Glückstadt.

Munro, P. (1977) *Die Spätägyptischen Totenstelen.* Glückstadt.

O'Connor, D. (1995) 'The Earliest Royal Boat Graves' *Egyptian Archaeology* 6, 3–7.

O'Connor, D. (1996) 'Sexuality, Statuary and the Afterlife: Scenes in the Tomb-chapel of Pepyankh (Heny the Black). An Interpretive Essay' in P. Der Manuelian (ed.) *Studies in Honor of William Kelly Simpson, I.* Boston, 621–33.

Petrie, W. M. F. (1900) *Royal Tombs of the First Dynasty 1900 Part I.* London.

Petrie, W. M. F. (1901) *Royal Tombs of the First Dynasty 1900 Part II.* London.

Petrie, W. M. F. (1925) *Tombs of the Courtiers and Oxyrhynkhos.* London.

Quirke, S. (2001) 'Judgment of the Dead' in D. B. Redford (ed.) *The Oxford Encyclopedia of Ancient Egypt,* 2. Oxford, 211–14.

Raven, M. J. (2005) 'Egyptian Concepts on the Orientation of the Human Body', *Journal of Egyptian Archaeology* 91: 37–53.

Reisner, G. A. (1936) *The Development of the Egyptan Tomb down to the Accession of Cheops.* Cambridge, MA.

Reisner, G. A. (1942) *A History of the Giza Necropolis, I.* Cambridge, MA.

Roehrig, C. (2003) 'The Middle Kingdom Tomb of Wah at Thebes' in N. Strudwick and J. Taylor (eds) *The Theban Necropolis: Past, Present and Future.* London, 11–13.

Roth, A. M. (1993) 'Social Change in the Fourth Dynasty: The Spatial Organization of Pyramids, Tombs, and Cemeteries', *Journal of the American Research Center in Egypt* 30: 33–55.

Spencer, A. J. (1982) *Death in Ancient Egypt.* Harmondsworth.

Steindorff, G. (1913) *Das Grab des Ti.* Leipzig.

Strudwick, N. (1996) *The Tombs of Amenhotep, Khnummose and Amenmose at Thebes.* Oxford.

Taylor, J. H. (2001) *Death and the Afterlife in Ancient Egypt.* London.

Toda, E. (1920) 'La découverte et l'inventaire du tombeau de Sen-nezem', *Annales du Service des Antiquités de l'Égypte* 20: 145–60.

Tooley, A. M. J. (1989) Middle Kingdom Burial Customs: A Study of Wooden Models and Related Material (unpublished Ph.D. thesis, University of Liverpool).

Trigger, B. G., B. J. Kemp, D. O'Connor and A. B. Lloyd (1983) *Ancient Egypt: A Social History.* Cambridge.

Tylor, J. J. (1895) *The Tomb of Paheri.* London.

Tylor, J. J. (1896) *The Tomb of Sebeknekht.* London.

Verner, M. (2002) *Abusir: Realm of Osiris.* New York.

Vischak, D. (2003) 'Common Ground between Pyramid texts and Old Kingdom Tomb Design: The Case of Ankhmahor', *Journal of the American Research Center in Egypt* 40: 133–57.

Willems, H. (2004) 'Recent Investigations at Deir el-Barsha', *Egyptian Archaeology* 25: 10–12.

Winlock, H. E. (1942) *Excavations at Deir el Bahri 1911–1931*. New York.

Zandee, J. (1960) *Death as an Enemy: According to Ancient Egyptian Conceptions*. Leiden.

Index

꒿꒿꒿꒿

Aanakht   238, 243–4
Abu Ghurob   55, 207
Abu Roash   51, 52
Abusir   33, 51–2, 55, 58–9, 68, 107, 120, 160, 254
Abusir el-Bana   120
Abydos   6, 13–14, 24–8, 47, 62, 82, 97–104, 114, 117, 119, 120–35, 139, 148, 154, 163–4, 166, 171, 173, 176, 215, 219, 226, 251
'Admonitions of Ipuwer'   105
Ahmose   122, 131, 177, 202–4, 229, 240
Ahmose son of Ibana   131, 202, 203
akh/3ḫ   54, 69, 70, 74, 81, 83, 95, 244
Akhenaten   207–9, 211–12, 214
Akhet   54
Akhetaten   207, 209, 211, 213
Akhethotep   58
Akhetmehu   88
'akhifier'   70, 129
Akhmim   143, 144
Alexandria   14, 252, 255, 258
Amada   130
Amarna   6, 178, 182, 191, 207–9, 211–16, 222, 223–4, 237, 248
Amasis   251
Amduat   54, 182, 189
Amen   20, 171, 178, 180, 183–5, 205, 207–8, 227–30, 232, 237, 240, 246, 248–50, 252–3

Amen-Re   20, 178, 180, 184, 185, 227–9, 246, 248
Amenemhat   114, 126, 129–3, 143, 154–5, 158, 168–9, 172, 174, 179, 205
Amenemhat-Itj-Tawy   133
Amenemhat I   114, 143, 155, 168–9, 172
Amenemhat II   126, 129, 131–2, 155, 158, 172
Amenemhat III   130–2, 174, 179
Amenemope   222, 236, 237
Amenhotep-Huy   186, 192
Amenhotep I   177, 181, 229, 237, 240
Amenhotep II   190, 235, 247
Amenhotep III   121, 177, 190, 199, 204, 207, 212, 219, 222, 224, 227, 230, 235
Amenirdis I   252
Amenmose   118
Amennakht   237–8, 241
Ammit   198
Anedjib   30
Anhurmose   231
Ani   197
Ankhesenpepi II   53
Ankhi   81
Ankhka   17, 20
Ankhmahor   72, 82, 83
Ankhmeryremeryptah   82
Ankhreni   128
Ankhtify   105, 108–15, 131, 149, 157–9, 257

Ankhty 93
Antefoker *see* Intefiker
Anubis 48–9, 69, 73, 119, 126, 150, 196, 198, 212, 221, 226–7
Any 214
Apa Jeremias 216
Aper-El 216
Apophis 182, 183
Apuia 57, 217–18, 220–1
Asasif 227–8, 252, 254
Asenkai 82, 89
Aswan 25, 90–1, 100, 107, 148, 166, 183
Asyut 97, 106, 143–4, 148, 150–1, 155–8, 193, 230
Aten 207–9, 211–15
Atet 36
Atum 147
Ayn Asil 95

ba 54, 70, 198, 202, 213–14
Badari 103
Badarian 7, 8
Bak-Amen 205
Bakenwerel 237
Baket III 154, 155
Balamun 251
Balat 44, 95, 96
Barnugi 148
Benben 214
Beni Hasan 6, 92, 115, 142–4, 146–9, 151–6, 158, 160–3, 169, 171, 200
Berlin 126, 128, 237
Bia 41, 48, 107
boats 32, 74, 160, 162–3, 169
Bolton 126–8
'Book of Caverns' 182
'Book of Gates' 182, 241
'Book of the Dead' 188, 196–9, 225, 237, 239, 257
'Book of the Two Ways' 144, 198
'Book of What is in the Underworld' 182
British Museum 132, 191, 197, 237
Bubastis 108, 148, 251

Bukenetef 242
Busiris 48, 120, 226
Butehamen 232, 247
Byblos 105

Cairo 8, 13, 28, 85, 99, 128, 169, 252
Cairo Bowl 85
Cambyses 251
'Cannibal Hymn' 53
canopic equipment 37, 62, 159–60, 171, 206, 218, 239, 242
'Chapters of Coming Forth by Day' 188, 196
Cleopatra VII 245
Coffin Texts 53, 70, 119, 136, 143–4, 196, 198, 225
Coptos 114, 115, 193
Cusae 97, 149

Dahshur 14, 31, 42, 51, 122, 156, 172–4
Dakhleh 44, 95–6
DB320 247–8
Debehen 47, 71–2, 75, 77, 87
Ded-Iku 132
Dedi 85
Deir el-Bahri 166–8, 176, 183, 185, 188, 230, 248, 252–3
Deir el-Gebrawi 71, 89
Deir el-Medina 131, 194, 204, 221, 232–44
Den 15, 17, 26–7, 29
Dendera 91
Deshasheh 81
'Dialogue of Ipuwer' 105
Djau 71, 89, 97, 120
Djau-Shemai 120
Djedkare 56
Djedu 120
Djefai-Hapi 150–1, 158, 230
Djehuty 72, 192
Djehutyemheb 227–9
Djehutymose 237
Djehutynakht 115, 151
Djer 15, 62, 120–1

djeryt 73–5, 80, 201
Djoser 17, 26–31, 52, 59–60, 66, 139, 242
Dra Abu el-Naga 177
Drei-Ebenen-Grab 224
Duamutef 147
Duat 53–4, 119, 202

Edfu 107, 108, 150
el-Amrah 219
el-Bersheh 115, 143–4, 148, 151, 156
el-Kab 131, 199–203, 209, 215
el-Qasr wa es-Sayed 82
el-Tarif 166–7
Elephantine 91–4, 98, 112, 132, 166
Ennead 147

Faiyum 106, 133
false door 37, 39–40, 44, 47, 58, 61, 66, 70, 73, 75, 81, 83, 87, 98–9, 111, 126, 141, 143, 154, 174
Field of Offerings 197–8
Field of Reeds/Iaru 119, 220
'Foremost of the Westerners' 119, 121

Garstang 5, 23, 101–2, 123–9, 133–5, 142, 146, 160–4, 255
Geb 147
Gebel Asyut el-Gharbi, 156
Gebel Barkal 150
Gebel Durunka 157–8, 163
Gebel es-Silsila 183
Gebelein 143, 144
Giza 31, 35–9, 45, 47–8, 51–2, 55–6, 65, 68, 71–2, 75–7, 80, 82–3, 88–9, 114, 142, 216
God's Wives of Amen 252–3
Great God 48–9, 67, 69, 81–3, 124–5, 129, 132, 149, 229

Hapy 147
Harkhuf 92–3, 100
Harwa 252
Hathor 97, 149, 173, 226–9

Hatnefer and Ramose 204
Hatnofer 183
Hatnub 99
Hatshepsut 177, 181–5, 188, 191–2, 204, 216, 230, 241, 253
Hawara 174, 179
heb-sed 28
Hekaib 92–3, 107
Heliopolis 55, 172, 228–9
Hellenism 255
Hemaka 15, 17, 20
Hemen 109, 111, 149
Her-neith 17
Herakleopolis Magna 106, 251
Hermopolis Magna 115, 251, 256–7
Herodotus 72, 251
Hetep 174
hetep-di-nesu/htp-di-nsw 49–50, 124, 129, 141, 143–4, 194, 214, 257
Hetepdief 28
Hetepherakhet 48
Hetepheres 62
Hetepsekhemwy 28
Hezi 81
Hierakonpolis 8, 24–5, 199
ḥm-nṯr priest 41
Horemheb 207, 217–20, 237
Horus 20, 49, 109, 111, 118–19, 121, 147, 149, 194, 198, 229
Huni 31
Huy 186, 191, 192, 218
Huya 207, 211, 213–15, 219, 222
Huynefer 237–8
Hyksos 177, 202

Iah 131
Iarti 89
Ibi 53, 132
Ibu 113
ibw-tent 75
Idi 99, 114
Idu 68, 70, 72, 74–5, 89
Idu Seneni 82, 89
Ihy 89, 174
Ikhernofret 126–9

Ikhtay 232
imakhu 48–9, 69, 75, 82, 89, 95, 101, 131, 143, 197
Imet 112
Imhotep 30, 107, 172
Imiseba 231, 240–1
Imiu 85
Imset 147
Ineni 176, 178, 180–1, 183, 185–7, 190–1, 200, 203, 209, 247
Inikaf 88
Inpy 173
'Instruction for Merikare' 99, 113
Intef 85, 167
Intefiker 171–2, 176
Inti 81
Ipuky 187
Iput I 57
Iput II 53
Ipuwer 105, 114
Ipuy 238
Ipy 215
Irsu 238
Isis 73, 118–19, 121, 146–7, 198, 229, 235
Iti-ibi 157
Iti-ibi-iker 157
Itiweret 172
Itj-Tawy 133, 171, 187
Iurudef 221, 222
Iww 99–100, 120
Iwy 218
Iy 124, 126–7, 235

K93.11 177
K94.1 177
ka-priest 33, 41, 43, 73, 82, 89, 107, 150, 230
Ka'a 17
Kaaper 93
Kadesh 185
Kagemni 56, 58–9, 61
Kahun 173
Kaikherptah 48
Kaimen 200

Kamose 177
Karnak 171, 178, 180, 183–4, 230, 240, 246, 249
Karoy 177
Kashta 252
Keminub 172
Kerma 150
Kha 235
Kha and Meryt 204, 239
Khabekhnet 238
Khaefre 31, 33–4, 88, 140
Khaemnun 237–8
Khaemope 238
Khasekhemwy 26, 28
Khay 237
Khendjer 121
Khenemti 89
Khentika 44–5, 58–9, 95–6
Khentika-called-Ikhekhi 77
Khentikaupepi 95–6
Khentkawes I 38
Khentyamentiu 119–20
Khenu 43, 52
Kheruef 209, 212, 219, 228
Khety 106, 154–5, 157, 168, 176
Khety II 157
Khew 238
Khmun 257
Khnemet 172
Khnum 145, 149, 160
Khnum-Nakht 145, 159–60
Khnumhotep 38, 43, 59, 67, 77, 174
Khnumhotep II 155–6
Khnumhotep III 156
Khnumhotep IV 156
Khokha 204, 240
Khons 235
Khonsu 184–5, 229, 237–8
Khufu 28, 31–7, 51–3, 56, 62, 68, 114, 140, 179
Khui 108
Khuit 57
Khuu 108
Kom Dara 108–9

Kom el-Hisn 108, 148
Koran 259
Kush 178, 247
KV20 181, 188
KV34 181
KV35 247
KV36 204
KV38 181
KV39 177
KV46 204
Kyky 227–8
Kynebu 240

Lake of Fire 198
lector-priest 69, 73–5, 80, 89, 94,
  128, 132, 194–5, 230
Leontopolis 251
Lepsius 99
Lisht 114, 133, 168
Lisht North 171–2
Lisht South 172
'Litany of Ra' 189
Liverpool 5, 102, 112, 123–4, 127,
  135, 142, 146, 161–4, 255
Louvre 118, 232
Luxor 20, 194

maat 20–1, 69, 97, 198, 227
mahat 123–34, 176
Maherperi 204
Manchester 126, 129, 194
'Mansion of Millions of Years'
  183–5, 188, 230, 246, 249–50
Marina el-Alamein 258
Mashayikh 231
May 69, 83, 194, 213, 226, 242
Maya 217
Medinet Habu 185, 252–3
Mehu 48, 107
Mehytenweskhet 252
Meidum 14, 31–2, 36, 51, 64
Meir 59, 71, 78–9, 96–7, 143–4,
  148–9, 156
Meketre 168–70
Mekhu 92, 93, 94

Memphis 13–14, 25, 46, 71–2, 74,
  90–1, 94–5, 108, 111, 172, 178,
  180, 192, 215–16, 218–22, 229–30,
  251
Mendes 108, 114, 251
Meni 83
Menkaure 47, 52, 75, 87
Menna 236
Merefnebef 80, 82
Merenptah 231
Merenre 52–3, 92, 95, 98–9, 107,
  120
Merer 108
Mereruka 56, 58–9, 61, 66, 72–5
Meresankh III 71–2
Merika 17, 20
Merikare 99, 106–8, 114, 157
Merirtifi 84
Meryre I 209, 211
Meryrenefer Qar 107
Merysekhmet 243
Meryt 204, 235, 239
Mesehti 157
Metropolitan Museum 169
Mitanni 190
Mnevis 208
Moalla 97, 108, 110, 112, 143–4, 148,
  155, 159
Montu 253
Montuemhat 253–4
Montuhotep II 166–9, 176–7
Mose 220
mummification 8, 37, 138, 170
Mut 184–5, 227–9
muu-dancers 175, 195, 201
mysteries of Osiris 122, 128–9

Naga ed-Der 103, 231
Nakht 145, 172
Nakht-Ankh 159–60
Nakhtamen 221
Nakhti 158
Naqada 8, 24–5
Narmer 24
Nebamun 191, 241

Nebamun and Ipuky 187
Nebemakhet 88
Nebipusenwosret 132
Nebit 174
Nebitef 84
Nebkauhor 57–60
Nebqed 198–9
Nebra 28
Neby 132
Nectanebo II 199
Nefarud 251
Nefer 59–63, 89
Neferefre 33, 59
Neferher 238
Neferhotep 133, 237–8
Neferhotep I 133
Neferirkare 33, 52, 56, 59–60, 86, 120
Neferkare 95, 111
Neferkauhor 115
Neferkhewet 204–5
Nefermaat 36
Neferseshem 200
Nefertari 218, 229, 240
Nefertem 228–9
Nefertiti 207, 211–14, 218
Neferure 183
Nehesy 216
Neith 53, 147, 251
Nekhbet 199
Nekheb 199
Nekhebkau 112
Nekhemmut 238
Nekhty 99
Nektanebo I 252
Nektanebo II 252
Nenki 81
Neper 226
Nepherites 251
Nephthys 73, 118–19, 146–7
Neshmet barque 226
Niankhba 58
Niankhkhnum 38, 43, 59, 67, 77
Niankhsekhmet 87
Ninetjer 28
Nitocris 252

Niuserre 56, 58, 60, 71, 107
Nofret 36, 64, 235
nomarch 97, 149, 151
Nubia 91–4, 100, 129–30, 150, 178, 190, 222, 247
Nut 54, 111, 146, 147
Nykaiankh 91

obelisks 55, 96, 178, 183, 251
Onuris 226
'Opening of the Mouth' 78, 142, 198
Opet festival 20
oracle 237
Osireion 122
Osiris 5, 48–9, 53–4, 69, 97, 116–36, 145–8, 176, 182, 184, 196–8, 212, 216, 218, 221, 229, 232, 253–4
Osiris Bed 121
Osorkon II 251
Osorkon III 252
ostracon/ostraca 194, 232, 234, 236–7, 242–3

Pabasa 253
Pahery 200–4
Panehesy 209, 214, 247
Papyrus Anastasi I 226
Papyrus Sallier IV 244
Paser 221
Peet 101, 129, 133–5, 247
Pehenwikai 81
Penmennefer 238
Pentu 209, 214
Pepiankh 59
Pepiankh Heny 'the Black' 78–80
Pepiankhheryib 97
Pepi I 52–3, 68, 97–8, 107
Pepi II 52–3, 58, 73, 92–3, 95, 97, 111, 120, 168
Pepinakht 92–3, 95, 100
Peqer 129, 226
Per-shenay 82
Peribsen 28
personal piety 223

Peteti   83
Petosiris   245, 253, 255–7
Petrie   6, 8, 9, 11–13, 91, 131, 151,
    158–9, 163–4, 204, 231
phoenix   202, 226
Pi-Ramesse   216, 222, 250
Piankhy   247
Pinudjem II   247–8
Plutarch   118
prt-ḥrw   44, 50, 143, 244
Psammetichus I   252
Pseusennes I   250
Ptah   131, 172, 221, 229–30, 246
Ptah-Sokar   48–9, 227
Ptah-Sokar-Osiris   216, 254
Ptahhotep   74
Punt   93, 185, 193, 216
Pyramid Texts   53–5, 70–1, 111,
    117–19, 140, 144–5, 172, 182, 196,
    257

Qar   43, 68, 72, 74, 76, 80, 107, 150
Qau (el-Kebir)   84, 103, 113, 128, 156
Qebhsenuef   147
Qila el-Dabba   95, 96
Qubbet el-Hawa   90–4, 148
Qurnet Murai   234

Ra   54, 55, 70, 86, 172, 182, 189, 218,
    227, 229, 241, 244, 246, 257
Ra-Horakhty   218, 227–9
Rahotep   36
Rai   187
Raia   221
Ramesses II   120, 134, 185, 216, 220–1,
    226–8, 231, 238, 243, 246, 248
Ramesses III   185, 237–8, 240, 242,
    252
Ramesses VI   241
Ramesses VIII   240
Ramesses IX   240–1, 246
Ramesses XI   245–7
Ramesseum   155, 185
Ramose   183, 204, 209, 211–12, 219
Rawer   56

Reisner   68, 103, 150
Rekhmire   186, 190–5, 200, 209
Rennefer   205
Reserve Heads   64
Reversion of Offerings   42
Rifeh   145, 147, 149, 151, 156–9, 163–4,
    231
rn   21, 66, 70
Royal Scottish Museum   204
Ruyu   205

Sabni   92–5, 100
saff-tombs   167
Sahure   33–4, 52, 87
saint   93, 98, 107, 113, 217, 259
Sais   251
Samannud   251
Samut   223, 227, 228, 229
Sankhenptah   84
Saqqara   7, 13–18, 20, 22, 23, 25–6,
    28–30, 35, 38–41, 43, 48, 51–2, 56–60,
    67–8, 72, 74, 77, 80–1, 84, 86–7, 89–90,
    95, 106–7, 126, 138, 142, 168, 174,
    215–22, 242, 254
Sasobek   132
Sat-Hathor-Iunet   173
Satmerhut   172
s3ḥw   54, 70, 194
Sebennytos   251–2
Sehetebibreseneb   131
Sekhayet-Hor   226
Selket   147
Semerka   88
Semna   130
Semty   132
Seneb   131
Senebsumai   132
Senebtisi   172–3
Senenmut   176, 183, 185, 188–91,
    200–4, 230
Sennedjem   233–43
Sennui   150
Senwosretankh   172
Senwosret I   126, 132–3, 155, 171–2
Senwosret II   155, 173

Senwosret III   121–2, 128–9, 132, 156, 173–4
serdab   26, 56, 59, 60, 66–7, 74, 99, 169
Seth   118, 147, 182
Seti I   120, 122, 188, 222
shabti   197, 206, 214–16, 239, 242
Shashotep   149, 151, 158
Sheikh abd el-Qurna   185–9, 204, 209, 230, 241
Sheikh Said   115, 154
Shemai   114, 115, 120
Shen   133
Shepenwepet I   252
Shepseskaf   51
Shepsi   84
Shoshenq   251
Shu   147, 226, 231
Shunet es-Zebib   26–9
Siamen   222
Siese   172
Sinai   128
Sinuhe   175
sm-priest   194
'smashing of the red pots'   220
Snefru   28, 31, 36, 42, 51–3
Sobek-khu   126, 129–30, 220
Sobekemhat   174
Sobekhotep   84, 132
Sobekhotep II   132
Sobeknakht   171, 200
Sohag   222
Sokar   41, 48–9, 69, 216, 226–9, 254
sons of Horus   147
soul-house   164
sun-temples   55, 207

Tamaket   235
Tanis   249–51
Tarkhan   7–15, 19, 32, 39, 138
Tayet   226
Tefnut   147
Tell Muqdam   251
'Terrace of the Great God'   125, 129, 132

Teti   51–3, 56–8, 61, 72, 77, 80, 82, 90, 98, 106–7, 115, 120, 174, 216–17, 220–1
Teti Pyramid Cemetery   56–8, 72, 77, 82, 107, 174, 220, 221
Thebes   72, 97, 109, 143, 155, 160, 166–7, 171–2, 176–87, 190–2, 194, 199–200, 204–6, 208–9, 211–12, 215–16, 219–25, 227–9, 236–7, 240–2, 246, 248–54
Theodosius   245
Thoth   41, 69, 198, 256–7
Thuyu   204
Tia and Tia   220–1
Tihna   91
Tiy   211, 212, 213
Tomb of Osiris   253
Tomb of the Two Brothers   159
Tomb Robbery Papyri   246
Tombos   222
Toulouse   131
tribute   178, 189, 192–33, 211, 241
TT1   235
TT8   204
TT34   253–4
TT37   252
TT40   191
TT41   222
TT55   211, 240
TT60   171
TT61   189
TT65   240
TT71   188
TT81   185, 187
TT100   191
TT110   192
TT113   240
TT131   188
TT159   187
TT181   187
TT188   212
TT192   212
TT194   228
TT279   253
TT280   169

TT311   168, 188
TT353   183, 188
TT409   227
Tuna el-Gebel   256
Tura   47, 58, 87, 98, 114, 140
Turin Canon   106
Tutankhamen   4, 191, 216–17, 220, 222
Tuthmosis I   177, 180–1, 205
Tuthmosis II   177, 181
Tuthmosis III   181–2, 188–92, 204–5
Tuthmosis IV   190, 204, 240

Udjebten   53
Umm el-Qa'ab   13, 26–9, 114, 120–3,
   129, 133
Unas   40, 43, 48, 51–3, 56–9, 60, 73,
   90, 107, 140, 172, 216–17, 254
Unas Causeway Cemetery   40, 43,
   58, 60
User-Amun   176, 185, 188–90
Userhat   238
Userhet   142, 146
Userkaf   254

Valley of the Kings   122, 167, 177,
   179–85, 188–9, 204, 233, 235, 242, 246,
   248–9
Vienna   238

wab-priest   128, 230, 240
wabet   71–80, 94, 192
Wadi Hillal   199
Wadjkawes   40, 52
Wadjmose   201, 203
Wagaf   133
Wah   170
Wahka I   113
Wahka II   113
Washptah   86, 87
Weni   47, 97–101, 114, 119–20
Wepwawet   119, 126, 150
Weren   222
Winlock   168–9, 172, 173
wt-priest   69, 74–7, 80

Yuya and Thuyu   204

Zawiyet Umm el-Rakham   258

Lightning Source UK Ltd.
Milton Keynes UK
UKHW010630061218
333512UK00002B/18/P